# Making Micronesia

# Making Micronesia

*A Political Biography of Tosiwo Nakayama*

**David Hanlon**

University of Hawai'i Press
Honolulu

Printed in the United States of America

22  21  20  19  18  17      6  5  4  3  2  1


**Library of Congress Cataloging-in-Publication Data**

Hanlon, David L., author.
Making Micronesia : a political biography of Tosiwo Nakayama /
David Hanlon.
    pages cm
Includes bibliographical references and index.
ISBN 978-0-8248-3846-1 (cloth : alk. paper)
1. Nakayama, Tosiwo, 1931–2007.   2. Presidents—Micronesia
(Federated States)—Biography.   3. Micronesia (Federated States)—
Politics and government.   I. Title.
DU567.H36 2014
996.6—dc23
[B]
                    2013040335

ISBN 978-0-8248-7516-9 (pbk.)

Maps by Manoa Mapworks, Inc.

Designed by Wanda China

*For the people of*
*the Federated States of Micronesia*

# Contents

# List of Illustrations

# Acknowledgments

This project began with an exchange of letters between Prof. Robert Kiste, then director of the Center for Pacific Islands Studies at the University of Hawai'i, Mānoa, and Mr. James Naich, the deputy head of mission for the Federated States of Micronesia's embassy in Washington, D.C., Naich sought a biographer for Tosiwo Nakayama, the first president of the FSM. When Kiste asked for my suggestions in a subsequent phone call, I volunteered myself. Several months later, on 7 August 2000, there followed an introductory meeting at the Best Western near the Honolulu International Airport. Present were Tosiwo Nakayama, his daughter Sydnina, Kasio Mida, the FSM consul general for Honolulu, Danny Rescue, a staff member of the consulate, Bob, and myself. We chatted over lunch about a possible biography. Nakayama shared some of his stories, and voiced his concern over the current generation's failure to appreciate the history of the FSM's founding. Though a quiet, reserved man, Nakayama expressed a willingness to use his public life as a vehicle for the telling of that history. I later drafted a proposal for his review and approval, and agreed to visit him later that year at his home on Weno in Chuuk State where we spent a week together revisiting his life, times, and public career.

I feel extremely fortunate for the opportunity and freedom that was given me. Nakayama did not ask for a court history or hagiography. He was willing to let me tell his story as I saw fit and for an audience that extended well beyond the nation he helped bring into existence. My deepest regret is that he did not live to see the completion of this biography. A host of unexpected professional and administrative obligations extended the length of this project far longer than I anticipated. My first task in this acknowledgments section, then, is to apologize to the late president and his family for the delay, and to thank them for the hospitality they showed me in late December of 2000 and early January of 2001. I need to cite as well the invaluable assistance of Asterio Takesy, a family member, trusted associate of Tosiwo Nakayama, and currently the FSM ambassador to the United States. He facilitated my time and travels in the region, suggested interview subjects, and followed up with letters of introduction to key figures in Nakayama's past.

The numerous meetings with former colleagues and associates of Tosiwo Nakayama over the summers of 2001, 2002, and 2003, and in early 2010 proved invaluable to this project. I wish to thank the following for their time, patience, and insights. In Chuuk, I benefited from my conversations with Susumu Aizawa, Erhart Aten, Soukichy Fritz, and Shigeto Hashiguchi, all of whom have since passed away, and Masachiro Chrislib. I thank as well Jojo Peter and Marilyn Bisalen of the College of Micronesia's Chuuk campus for their gracious assistance during my time there. On Kosrae, there was Singkitchy George, the late Hiroshi Ismael, former FSM president Jacob Nena, Claude Philip, and Thurston Shiba. While in the Marshalls, I had the opportunity to speak at length with Ataji Balos, Carmen Bigler, Tony deBrum, Chuji Chutaro, Charles Dominik, the late Carl Heine, and Wilfred Kendall. Polycarp Basilius, Barrie Michelsen, Daiziro Nakamura, former president Kuniwo Nakamura, Rev. Billy Quartei, Carlos Salii, the late Peter Sugiyama, former president Johnson Toribiong, and Victorio Uherbelau all made time for me. I would be remiss if I didn't mention Arthur Ngiraklsong, the chief justice of the Republic of Palau's Supreme Court. He facilitated my visit to Palau in numerous ways, and is, along with Kuwahara Sueo of Kagoshima University, one of the kindest, most considerate men I have ever met. My time on Pohnpei was filled by interviews and conversations with the late Andon Amaraich, former FSM president John Haglelgam, Bethwel Henry, Fr. Francis X. Hezel, S.J., Ieseke Iehsi, Kohsak Keller, former FSM vice president Redley Killion, Quirino Mendiola, the late Resio Moses, Fred Ramp, former FSM president Joseph Urusemal, and Kario Welleby. On Yap, I spoke with Isaac Figir, Edmund Gilmar, James Mangefel, and Aloysius Tuuth. In Honolulu, I was fortunate to meet with a vacationing Willard Muller and his wife Carol, and also Hans Williander from Chuuk who was living in Hawai'i at the time. My research also took me to Washington, D.C., where I interviewed Ed and Joan King, and James Stovall.

My formal investigation into the life of Tosiwo Nakayama began with an initial award from the University of Hawai'i's University Research Council. A generous grant from the Bank of Guam made possible my travels through the region. I wish to thank in particular the late Anthony A. Leon Guerrero, chairman of the bank's board of directors, Bridget Stiverson, and Jackie Marati. No research project can succeed without the support of archivists and librarians. I received wonderful assistance and support from Rufino Mauricio, the then director of the FSM's National Archives and Cultural and Historic Preservation Office; Bruce Robert and his staff at the College of Micronesia's national campus library; and Nick Goetzfridt of the University of Guam's library. I benefited as well from the expertise and cheerful ways of University of Hawai'i librarians Jane Barnwell, Stu Dawrs, Lynette Furuhashi, Eleanor Kleiber, Dore Minatodani, and the late Karen Peacock.

A visiting professorship at the Kagoshima University's Research Center for the Pacific Islands allowed me to refocus on this project after six good but demanding years as director of the Center for Pacific Islands Studies at Mānoa. I thank the many fine people who made my stay in Japan such a productive and enjoyable time. They include Yoshida Hiroki, president of Kagoshima University, Tominaga Shigeto, director of the center, and Professors Noda Shinichi, Nagashima Shunsuke, Hidaka Tetsushi and his wife Kimiko, Kawai Kei, Kuwahara Sueo, Nishimura Akira, Nishimura Satoru, Torii Takashi, Iitaka Shingo, now of Kochi Prefectural University, and Kusumoto Hiroko, the center's administator. I also benefited tremendously from a month's stay in Canberra with the Australian National University's School of Culture, History, and Language as a visiting fellow. While there, I had the opportunity to give a talk on the life of Tosiwo Nakayama. I am indebted to Brij Lal, Vicki Luker, Margaret Jolly, Katerina Teaiwa, Chris Ballard, the late Hank Nelson, Jack Corbett, and Valerie Bichard for their warm hospitality and professional encouragement. Closer to home, the UHM Department of History's monthly forum, ably directed by Suzanna Reiss and Matt Romaniello, provided a public venue for a summary presentation of my work in December of 2010. I'm also appreciative of the opportunity that Greg Dvorak of Hitotsubashi University gave me to speak on Tosiwo Nakayama's ties to Japan at the Transoceania Conference that he so ably organized in July of 2012 in Tokyo.

The list of those who guided me in one way or another goes on to include Craig Howes and Peter Hempenstall; both men taught me much about the many and varied approaches to the practice of biography. Masako Ikeda of the University of Hawai'i Press was nothing but encouraging and professional in helping to bring this manuscript to publication; Wendy Bolton proved to be a very patient and effective copy editor; and Jane Eckelman of Manoa Mapworks worked her usual magic with the maps for this volume. The comments of the two anonymous readers contracted by the University of Hawai'i Press to review an earlier draft of this manuscript proved extremely helpful. I wish to thank as well Ned Shultz, the former dean of the School of Pacific and Asian

Studies at the University of Hawai'i at Mānoa, and Tisha Hickson, Jan Rensel, and Terence Wesley-Smith of the Center for Pacific Islands Studies; Fr. Rich McAuliffe, S.J., and Melba Veloroso of the Micronesian Seminar on Chuuk; Patrick Blank of the FSM's Public Information Office on Pohnpei; and Bill Acker, Margie Falanruw, Mike McCoy, Sue Moses, Glenn Petersen, Manuel Rauchholz, Ken Rehg, and Justina Takesy whose ties to the different FSM states run deep and true. I'm grateful for the love and support of Maikel O'Hanlon, Lauren Ferry, Emma, Theo, and Katherine Ludwick, and Alyna O'Hanlon, all of whom live on the eastern and far eastern edges of Tosiwo Nakayama's world. Finally, there is Katherine Swiger Hanlon whose love and patience are limitless; she put up with the absences, doubts, distractions, frustrations, long hours, and anxieties that were all a part of this investigation into the life of an incredible man. Thank you one and all.

# Introduction:

*Writing a Biography of Tosiwo Nakayama*

Tosiwo Nakayama, the first president of the Federated States of Micronesia, spent his last two years in Waipahu, a former plantation town on the island of Oʻahu flattened, paved over, and built upon with shopping malls and tract houses. Japanese and later Filipino immigrants once worked the sugarcane fields of Waipahu. More recently, the town has become home to an increasing number of people from the islands called "Micronesia," most notably those from Chuuk and the Marshall Islands. Their presence is the result of provisions within the Compacts of Free Association between the United States and the governments of the Federated States of Micronesia (FSM) and the Republic of the Marshall Islands that allow for the visa-free movement of Micronesians into the United States and its territories. Tosiwo Nakayama played a long and crucial role in negotiating the compact for the FSM.

Proximity to quality health care brought Nakayama to Hawaiʻi as a weakened heart and a series of strokes had left him blind in one eye and unable to walk or talk. Tending to his needs in a two-story rented townhouse in Waipahu were some of his most immediate family members; they included his daughter Sydnina, his youngest son Masami, and other female members of his extended family who were resident on the island at the time. The United States government extended no recognition to this former head of state lying seriously ill within its borders, and members of the FSM consulate in Honolulu seemed perplexed about the protocol involved in his presence. The circumstances of his dying revealed something of the ambivalence with which the nation-state he helped to build is regarded. The restrained responses to his weakened condition remind us of how belittling the prefix "micro" can be; "micro" as in "Micronesian," meaning tiny or small, and not terribly important to those for whom size matters. That is the way the islands have been viewed historically; that is the way Micronesian immigrants are viewed today in Hawai'i.

Tosiwo Nakayama died on 29 March 2007, at the Hawaii Medical Center West in Waipahu. His contributions to the founding of the Federated States of Micronesia did not allow him to escape the dismissive, still colonizing gaze cast upon people from distant islands to the west of Hawai'i. His was a remarkable life, nonetheless, for the ways in which he sought to create a Micronesian nation and reconfigure the self-imaging of its people. The study of his life also invites a reconsideration of migration, transnational crossings, and the actual size of island worlds. Nakayama's efforts at forging a politically unified Micronesia notwithstanding, his story encourages a reconsideration of the Oceanic world in ways that challenge political boundaries and anthropological categories.

## A Man of Many Islands

An examination of the life and times of Tosiwo Nakayama certainly involves much more than a narrative of political events. There is a complex history here that defies easy categorization. Nakayama did not bring the Federated States of Micronesia into being by himself; he worked with many others including Andon Amaraich of Chuuk and Bethwel Henry of Pohnpei, both of whom deserve their own biographies. The prolonged negotiations and subsequent compromises that enabled the realization of the Federated States of Micronesia do not lend themselves to a simple, romanticized history of resistance and independence. There exist too the many-layered cultural contexts that informed Nakayama's life and career; these cannot be quickly or summarily rendered. His clan membership through his mother Rosania linked him with islands in Yap, a fact that contributed significantly to his success as a legislator in the Congress of Micronesia and later as the first president of the Federated States of Micronesia. Members of his clan, Pike, can be found residing on islands and atolls that stretch from Yap in the west to the Mortlocks in what is today southeastern Chuuk State. His marriage to Miter Haruo allowed him to transcend the strong prejudices of the Chuuk Lagoon people against outer islanders; Miter was a senior woman in the Lagoon area's most prominent clan, the Sópwunupi. It is perhaps an obvious and too simple statement, but one still worth making; the blood of women made possible Nakayama's political career.

Nakayama was a man who lived in a world of islands. Located some 246 kilometers to the northwest of the Chuuk Lagoon, Piserach in Namonuito

Atoll was the place of his birth—on 23 November 1931—and the first of many islands that figure prominently in his life history. Nakayama spent his earliest years on Onoun, another of Namonuito's islands, where his father Nakayama Masami worked as the resident trader for the Japanese trading firm, Nan'yō Bōeki Kaisha or Nambō as it was commonly known. While still a very young boy, Tosiwo Nakayama moved with his family to Lukunor, also called Luku-noch, one of the Mortlock Islands in the southeastern region of Chuuk State. Subsequently, he lived on Dublon or Toloas, the Japanese administrative and later military center for Chuuk. War forced the civilian residents of Toloas to seek shelter elsewhere; the Nakayamas moved to Tol where they lived with the family of Aizawa Shōtarō, another Nambō trader, and in close proximity to Mori Koben, an early arriving Japanese trader in the Chuuk region who had achieved considerable prominence for his commercial acumen, cultural knowledge, and his position as the head of a large local family. Following his father's forced repatriation to Japan in the postwar period, young Tosiwo Nakayama divided his time between Onoun and Weno in the Chuuk Lagoon where he alternated school with work.

As he became more publicly and politically prominent, his island horizons expanded even farther. His participation in the Inter-District Advisory Committee meetings on Guam in the 1950s and later the Congress of Micronesia on Saipan brought him into contact with island peoples from other areas of the Trust Territory. His membership on the Congress of Micronesia's Future Political Status Commission took him to numerous Pacific Island states, including Samoa, New Guinea, and the Cook Islands, as he and other members sought to identify a working governmental structure for the one-day independent Micronesian nation. Nakayama also traveled to the island of Manhattan within the confines of New York City to testify before the United Nations Trusteeship Council on matters involving the United States' administration of the Trust Territory of the Pacific Islands through which the Caroline, Mariana, and Marshall Islands were then governed. His two terms as president of the Federated States of Micronesia between 1979 and 1987 saw him travel to numerous island states and foreign countries in his efforts to secure international recognition and assistance for the government that he headed. The most important of these island states, both personally and politically, was Japan.

His father Masami came from the Tsurumi section of Yokohama where he learned to speak English and was influenced by the international character of that major port city. The younger Nakayama first visited Japan in 1961 in search of his father who had been repatriated after the war without his family. Tosiwo Nakayama returned to Japan on numerous occasions for both diplomatic and personal reasons. In 1984, for example, he received an invitation to have tea with Crown Prince Akihito at the Imperial Palace in Tokyo. Two years later, in 1986, he again met Akihito, this time at the Green Summit in Kumamoto on the island of Kyushu. Nakayama also visited Japan in 1989 for Akihito's coronation as emperor. From 1991 until 2003, Nakayama headed the Japan-FSM Parliamentarian Friendship Society, an organization that seeks to maintain the historical connections between Japan and its former Mandate Islands. While he acknowledged the advantages his paternal ancestry provided him, Nakayama understood its limits. In the early 1980s, he consistently opposed Japan's plans to dump nuclear waste in the Western Pacific. In his later years, he told the story of Japanese visitors—dignitaries, government officials, businessmen, and tourists—who came to his office looking for "Nakayama Tosiwo" and with a very definite set of expectations as to what "President Nakayama" would look like. They were surprised, even startled, to find a "black Nakayama."

In many ways, Nakayama's travels reflected a long-standing historical pattern in the region called Micronesia, and foreshadowed the renewal or intensification of that pattern following the implementation of the Compact of Free Association between the United States and the Federated States of Micronesia. Voyaging had enabled the settlement of the islands, and allowed for communication and exchange thereafter. The *sawei* exchange system, with its center on Yap, had stretched to islands as far east as Namonuito. The Ralik and Ratak chains had served as the loci of exchange, travel, and political organization in what is now the Marshalls. There was too the ocean traffic that moved between the Central Carolines and the Mariana Islands that proved pivotal in the repopulation of the Northern Marianas in the nineteenth century. Later colonial regimes, including those established by Germany and Japan, prohibited unauthorized interisland travel.

For island people, the ocean has always presented not an obstacle but a necessary avenue of travel and opportunity that is intimately linked to their well-being and survival.[1] Islands and atolls may be physically limited, but when seen as a part of a larger integrated Oceanic environment, they become quite large. The total area of the old American-administered Trust Territory, stretching from the Marshalls in the east to Palau in the west, approximated that of the continental United States. As part of a grander Oceanic environment, islands and atolls should be understood as large not small; the view from their shores to the horizon should be regarded as potentially more inspiring than intimidating, more motivating than discouraging. Survival for island peoples necessitated at times exploratory voyaging, interisland travel, and migrations to new places; this movement carried risk but also offered an expanded range of contacts, linkages, possibilities, opportunities, material goods, effective technologies, and new ideas. We might better understand Namonuito Atoll, Nakayama's birthplace, in this more enlarged way—as part of a vast, surprisingly connected Oceanic region to which the word "Micronesia" does no justice.

## Making Micronesia

What Nakayama himself actually understood as Micronesia remains in some doubt. I believe it is more accurate to say that he believed deeply in the possibility of a Micronesia. The title of this book, *Making Micronesia,* rests on this interpretation. Nakayama's more localized efforts at making or creating a Micronesia stand in stark contrast to earlier colonial efforts to define, control, and refashion the islands to serve decidedly metropolitan purposes.[2] Early on in his career, Nakayama freely acknowledged the diversity and differences that separated the islands and their people, and that kept them from speaking together on the question of a future government. His work as a translator for Chuukese representatives to the Trust Territory's Inter-District Advisory Committee in the early 1950s and later his membership in the Council of Micronesia, the precursor of the Congress of Micronesia, brought him into contact with other islanders who had experienced the horror and hardship of wars fought between foreign combatants on Micronesian territory. The physical distance from which the islands were administered in the first decades of the American administration, the slow and uncertain pace of postwar reconstruction, and the incompetency and indifference of some administrators led Nakayama to conclude early on that island people should govern themselves. Nakayama spoke of a common lifestyle and the shared experiences of war and colonial rule as a basis for unity despite differences. In none of his writings, speeches, or interviews did he ever emphasize the adjectives "tiny" or "small" to refer to the islands. He dismissed belittling, politically self-serving criticisms from beyond that characterized the islands as such, and advocated unrelentingly for the right of Micronesian peoples to represent and govern themselves. One observer characterized Nakayama as developing a deep, quiet radicalism born of persistence, toughness, and patience.[3]

After only three years of formal schooling in postwar Chuuk, combined with several years of on-the-job training with the district administration, Nakayama received a Trust Territory government scholarship to the University of Hawai'i, Mānoa. He studied there from 1955 to 1958, and, with East-West Center support, again from 1967 to 1969. More important than the education he received were the friendships and acquaintances he made. In Hawai'i he met other Trust Territory students being educated for positions of leadership in the government. These students formed strong bonds of friendship that later came into play when many of them were involved in negotiations over the creation of future governments for the islands. The plight of Native Hawaiians impressed itself on the minds of these students. Many, including Tosiwo Nakayama, would later say that witnessing the dispossession of Native Hawaiians in their home islands convinced them of the need for self-government.

Nakayama was a quiet man who appeared distant and aloof to outsiders. An expatriate friend and associate from his Congress of Micronesia days wrote, "Warm and charming as he could sometimes be, you sensed that he'd just as soon be left alone, in his house, on his island, thank you very much."[4] Others closer to Nakayama understood his reserve and quiet demeanor differently. While he spoke Chuukese and had limited fluency in Japanese, Nakayama used English to help legislate and negotiate the Federated States of Micronesia into existence. He spoke softly, and in simple declarative sentences. He would sometimes drop an article, a possessive, or a preposition, and on occasion employ an awkward phrase or word. Nonetheless, his proficiency in English was quite remarkable, and enabled him to engage with the most sophisticated or complicated of ideas. He was a modernist; he believed in the promise of modernity. He used words like "democracy," "development," "nation," and "sovereignty," in ways that seemed quite literal, practical, and uncritical. While many within and beyond Micronesia worried about the growing dependency caused by the infusion of large amounts of American aid in the late 1960s and early 1970s, Nakayama argued that it was not nearly enough. When asked what would be the economic foundations for an autonomous, self-governing Micronesian nation, he pointed to the sea, the sun, and the wind. Referring to outside development specialists, Nakayama said, "They tell us we have nothing to gain from the land, and practically nothing to gain from the sea. These people are a bunch of liars. They lie; they fool us.... In Japan, they bottle and sell Fujiyama air. Things will change. Air will become very precious. Sunshine might become like medicine."[5]

Nakayama did not write or articulate in detail his worldview or political philosophy. His views are to be ferreted from the many speeches and interviews he gave as well as a modest body of correspondence from his congressional and presidential years. He was quite aware of what was going on in the world, and took strong positions for indigenous rights and a nuclear free Pacific, but he made no reference to literary, philosophical, or political writers. In this feature, he was unlike Jean-Marie Tjibaou, Bernard Narikobi, and Haunani-Kay Trask who wrote extensively about their visions for their respective peoples.

One of the paradoxes of his career was his view on traditional or chiefly leadership. In his early adult years, he benefited from the support and patronage of the powerful and revered chief Petrus Mailo of Weno in Chuuk. Nakayama was solicitous of chiefly input and encouraged the active participation of chiefs at the 1975 Micronesian Constitutional Convention. The role of chiefs in the government of the Federated States of Micronesia proved a divisive, highly contentious, potentially subversive issue during the convention. A last-minute resolution affirming a future but unspecified role for chiefs allowed the convention to reach a consensus of sorts on this sensitive issue and move on to approval of a draft constitution. Nakayama and the pro-constitution forces relied on chiefly delegations to tour the different island groups and help win popular support for the constitution and later the Compact of Free Association. He received strong backing throughout his career from the paramount chiefs of Yap and developed very close relationships with several Pohnpeian chiefs both before and during the establishment of the FSM national government's capital on that island. He nonetheless saw their time as leaders as having passed, passing, or soon to pass in the different island groups.

It is not fashionable to speak of nation building in these times when the emphasis falls on border crossings, the blurring of boundaries, and the global migration of people, ideas, technologies, and goods that challenge the relevance and viability of the nation-state. Nonetheless, Tosiwo Nakayama, as a disciple of modernity, was very much committed to nation building. There might be those who would cast a critical or suspicious eye on Nakayama's early political career, seeing him as a tool, puppet, or self-serving careerist. Gramscian analysis might understand Nakayama and others like him as local elites or tools of a hegemonic order who wittingly or unwittingly collaborated in their own subjugation and in the victimization or subordination of their people.[6] Nakayama's early administrative employment in Chuuk and his work in the Congress of Micronesia could easily be construed as a mimetic effort to use the principles and procedures of democratic government to serve the American agenda of domination over the islands.[7] But we are well advised to keep in mind the ways in which the ideological tools and constructs of domination can be used by subordinate or subaltern peoples to counter or at least mitigate subjugation and domination.[8]

There were many who doubted the possibility of a unified, self-governing Micronesia. It sounded like such a preposterous, impractical, outrageous, and unworkable idea. Tosiwo Nakayama countered that doubt and skepticism with stories that spoke of his hopes and aspirations. He dismissed criticisms of the region as too diverse and divided. He believed differences among Micronesians were exaggerated by outsiders whose own interests, prejudices, and worldviews were served by the presumption of divisiveness. He did not share

understandings of Micronesia as a colonial construct. He saw links, connections, and commonalities that the name "Micronesia" spoke well enough to. He
articulated his belief on numerous occasions during the ratification campaign
for the FSM constitution that the resources of the surrounding seas could easily provide the revenues to sustain a unified government. During his trips to
various islands during the ratification campaign, he often told the story of a
previously dismembered ocean deity made whole again by those who redis-
covered their belief in him. Tosiwo Nakayama was very much a storyteller. For
those who wondered what leverage Micronesia's representatives had in their
negotiations with a country as large, rich, and powerful as the United States,
Nakayama cited another tale about a young boy who, alone among a crowd,
showed that the way to make a large elephant move was to squeeze its balls.

Stories aside, we should not underestimate the enormous complexities
of establishing a nation-state anywhere in the world, especially in the Micronesian area. A study of Tosiwo Nakayama's life also offers the opportunity to
glimpse local engagements with the American colonial presence, and the creation of a nation-state against a formidable array of local and external forces,
not the least of which were the divisions among Micronesians themselves.
For the FSM, there were thirteen years of negotiations with the United States
government; negotiations that included eight formal negotiating sessions held
in different locations ranging from Washington, D.C., to Hilo, Honolulu, and
Guam. These formal sessions were separated by extended periods of delay,
confusion, uncertainty, frustration, and, at times, strained relations.

Over the life of the negotiations, the Micronesian team, of which
Nakayama was a pivotal member until 1979, had to deal with four presidential
administrations, CIA surveillance, and the complicated, conflicting requirements of the different American military branches and civilian bureaucracies.
There were also the decisions of the Marianas, Marshalls, and Palau to pursue
their own separate negotiations with the United States; proposed cuts by the
American side in already agreed upon levels of funding; and American reluctance to follow through on capital improvement projects deemed a necessary
prerequisite to any compact of free association. With negotiations completed
in 1982, there followed a four-year period that included a local education program and countrywide referendum on the draft compact, and reviews by the
four remaining island state legislatures (Chuuk, Kosrae, Pohnpei, and Yap),
the FSM and U.S. congresses, and the United Nations. Formal dissolution of
the Trust Territory government's administering authority over the Federated
States of Micronesia did not come until 1986, Nakayama's next-to-last year as
president.

Paralleling the complex negotiations over the Compact of Free Association were the sometimes confusing talks with the Trust Territory government over separation and transition; the physical and political difficulties of establishing a capital for the new government on a reserved, not always appreciative Pohnpei; and the intense debates over states' rights, powers, and revenue entitlements. Within the FSM, there was concern over the possible domination of Chuuk at the expense of the smaller states, most notably Kosrae and Yap. Nakayama was at the center of all this, and his mediation skills were sometimes required in the settlement of more immediate, personal, and ethnic crises such as the stabbing of a Chuukese young man by a Yapese youth in 1986 on Pohnpei.

Nakayama had been a strong advocate of independence during his time in the Congress of Micronesia. He said during the course of a weeklong series of interviews at his home on Weno in early January of 2001 that his early work for the Trust Territory government in Chuuk, then called Truk, had convinced him that Americans could not administer the islands effectively or prepare them for self-government. He thought Micronesians needed to govern their own islands. There is more than a little irony in Nakayama's call for unity and independence. To be sure, it was the Chuukese or Trukese delegation in the Congress of Micronesia that was most critical of the American administration in the late 1960s and early 1970s. Members of the Chuukese delegation in this period were also quite adamant in their insistence on independence for the future Micronesian state. Nonetheless, Chuuk is considered the most divided and contentious of the Micronesian island groups. It is a description with a historical pedigree that goes back almost to first contact between the islands and the larger world. "Dreaded Hogoleu" is the term used by one early nineteenth-century visitor to describe the factionalism and rivalry that seemed to characterize the Lagoon group then.[9] Members of Chuuk's congressional delegation were among the most determined and outspoken critics of Nakayama during his time as president.

Nakayama was a facilitator, a consensus seeker not given to confrontations or public posturing. He showed little emotion and was a quiet man who preferred private conversations and small social gatherings. As president of the Congress of Micronesia's Senate from 1965 to 1967 and again from 1973 to 1978, he rarely spoke for the congressional record on key matters affecting policy or legislation; he confined himself instead to procedural matters, and left the more public speeches to others. Nakayama was truly a self-effacing leader; he voted for his opponent, Amata Kabua of the Marshalls, in the 1965 election that brought him the presidency of the Congress of Micronesia's Senate for the first time. His most-famous congressional utterance was only seven words long and came on the closing day of a Senate session in 1970: "Mr. President and Honorable Members of the Senate," he said, "Micronesia ought to be an independent state."[10] To some, his eventual endorsement of free association with the United States seemed a startling reversal and contradiction of his earlier advocacy of independence. Nakayama himself did not see it that way. The constitution of the FSM was the foundation of an autonomous, self-governing, and sovereign nation, a fact to which American negotiators had begrudgingly acquiesced after initial opposition and considerable delay. The FSM Constitution took precedence over any and all other agreements. To Nakayama's way of thinking, the entry into a compact of free association was itself a demonstration of sovereignty—the act of a sovereign nation. When considering the dangers of continuing to associate with the United States, Nakayama thought like Andon Amaraich. There were many sharks in the ocean; it was to the FSM's ultimate advantage to be allied with the biggest, ugliest, and meanest of them.[11]

The word in Chuukese for someone like Tosiwo Nakayama is "mósónósón," meaning humble, attentive, dutiful, and responsible.[12] These traits, considered essential for an effective Chuukese chief, help explain his success as a constitution maker and nation builder. His mild-mannered demeanor also allowed him to bear numerous insults and affronts with quiet dignity throughout his career. This was particularly true on Pohnpei, which became the capital of the FSM in 1979. In Nakayama's first years as president, Leo Falcam, the governor of Pohnpei, always insisted on protocol in any ceremonial or state occasion that recognized Pohnpei and its governor first, and the FSM and its president second. Nakayama ignored the slights with patience and dignity with an eye to maintaining good relations between his national government and its host state. In yet another humbling moment at that 1979 inauguration, the United States High Commissioner for the Trust Territory of the Pacific Islands, Adrian Winkel, was accorded greater recognition and deference than the president of the sovereign nation whose inauguration he had come to observe.

Nakayama encountered considerable political opposition during his life. Representatives of the U.S. government allegedly conspired, though unsuccessfully, to defeat him in his 1979 race for an at-large seat from Chuuk in the FSM congressional elections.[13] A defeat in that race would have precluded any possibility of his becoming president as the FSM Constitution stipulates that only the holders of four-year, at-large seats are eligible for election to the presidency by their fellow congressmen. There were also threats of violence to his person in that election as well as two death threats during his presidency.

A more difficult problem for Nakayama was Faichuk, a group of four main islands in the west of the Chuuk Lagoon that sought recognition as a separate state within the FSM. Kosrae, Pohnpei, and Yap opposed Faichuk statehood on the grounds that it would create in effect a second Chuukese state. Distrust of Chuuk ran strong throughout the rest of the FSM because of the corruption, mismanagement, and free spending that made the state a serious drain on the financial health and political stability of the fledgling nation. At a special session of the FSM Congress on Chuuk in 1981, however, members were bullied and intimidated into passing a Faichuk statehood bill. The decision on whether to sign, veto, or let the bill stand fell to Nakayama. General consensus was that the future of the nation rested with his decision. Several members of the Congress admitted that they had passed the problem to Nakayama. They hoped that he would do what they could not—namely, say "no" to Faichuk.

Consummate politician that he was, Nakayama flew to Chuuk to meet with Faichuk leaders. In those meetings, Nakayama pointed out the technical problems with the bill as well as the lack of infrastructure and services in Faichuk that would render statehood meaningless. He indicated his intention to veto the bill for these reasons, but with the promise of increased funding for Faichuk that would allow the area to prepare itself for a changed political relationship with Chuuk and the FSM. It was shrewd, effective bargaining that won over, for the time being, many of the statehood movement's leaders. More important, it preserved the union.

## "You Did What, Mr. President?!?"

I first met Tosiwo Nakayama on Pohnpei in 1973. My wife Kathy and I were Peace Corps volunteers preparing to leave the island after three years of teaching English and social studies at a Catholic mission school in the south of the island. We were in Kolonia at the time, the aptly named capital of the island. The Congress of Micronesia was holding a session on the island, one in a series of visits designed to better connect this still fledgling representative body with its widely dispersed constituency of atoll and island dwellers spread across an area about the size of the continental United States. Negotiations with the United States over a new political status had already begun, and members of the Congress' Joint Committee on Future Status, formerly known as the Future Political Status Commission, were also seeking the input of elected and traditional leaders in the different island districts. There was a reception for the Congress near the Catholic Mission in Kolonia to which Kathy and I were invited. I remember sitting in one of the chairs that lined the walls of the long, rectangular meeting room with tiled floor, thinly paneled walls, and a corrugated tin roof. Nakayama, then president of the Congress of Micronesia's Senate, came up to us, extended his hand, and said simply "Tos Nakayama." I remember being struck by his modesty and good looks. Twenty-seven years later, I met him again, this time in the restaurant of the Honolulu Airport's Best Western Hotel where I agreed to work with him on the story of his life.

Living for almost eight years on the island of Pohnpei had taught us to look beyond labels such as "underdeveloped." I learned something of how rich life could be amidst communities bound together by a strong sense of kin, clan, family, and church relationships. I remember marveling at how in control people seemed to be of their lives despite a succession of colonial regimes in the region. In more academic environments of the early 1980s, the word "agency" spoke to the belated realization of Pacific peoples' roles in the making of their own worlds and in their encounters with others. I wrote a general history of the island of Pohnpei that sought above all else to portray a rich and dynamic island world that persevered against an array of external threats, not the least of which was epidemic disease. Later, I authored another book that took a larger regional view of the way people engaged with the externally imposed discourses and forces of development. While the balance of power in this engagement was decidedly asymmetrical, I saw agency too in different people's efforts to make a better world that would still be their world. I saw agency in the person of Tosiwo Nakayama in 1973.

The issues surrounding and even confounding a biography of Tosiwo Nakayama are many and considerable. This is a project that I was initially asked to do by those close to Nakayama, personally and professionally. They perhaps sought a life history that celebrates a man and his many accomplishments. It would be easy enough to make this biography a hagiography. Among the more than fifty formal interviews I recorded with Nakayama's colleagues and associates, only one individual ventured comments that were substantively critical of Nakayama on grounds that he was far more a politician than a leader. The vast majority of individuals I interviewed across the former Trust Territory of the Pacific Islands spoke glowingly of Nakayama, including those in the Marshalls and Palau who had opposed him in his efforts to promote Micronesian unity. It would be naïve, perhaps, to expect that I as a stranger to most of these individuals could elicit within a single meeting comments that were other than positive. Still, I found their observations and reflections extremely helpful in trying to reconstruct the life of a quiet man.

The limitations of formal interviews are but a part of the larger problem of doing a life history of Tosiwo Nakayama. Biography can certainly be an alien intrusion into lives whose parameters are defined, even subsumed by a complex, interlocking network of kin, clan, and family. In writing about Tosiwo Nakayama, I in no way mean to elide or deny the complexities that surround the practice of cross-cultural biographies. Mark Peattie has argued that biography is a problematic project in Japan where people see themselves not as individuals so much as members of a group or larger society; their life histories are not just about themselves but are rather linked to these broader entities and the histories of those entities.[14] If that caution is pertinent to an area such as Japan, it is at least as relevant for an area such as Micronesia where individual identity is subsumed under a host of relational identities and obligations, and where the efforts of outside interrogators to separate out individual life histories can be seen as a practice that reflects foreign interests, values, and assessments of who and what are important. We might expect, then, that Tosiwo Nakayama, born of a Japanese father and an island woman, would have been doubly averse to any writing of his life story. But he wasn't. One of the principal reasons behind Nakayama's cooperation in this biography project was his belief that the early history of self-government in the FSM is being forgotten and that current leaders have lost a sense of vision and commitment to the nation in favor of more immediate parochial and personal interests.

As with any major writing project, I experienced times of anxiety and doubt. Soon after agreeing to take on this project, I asked Tosiwo Nakayama if I could have access to his personal papers. He replied that had he any, he would most certainly make them available to me. Unfortunately, he continued, he had thrown them all away shortly after leaving the presidency in 1987. I was dismayed. My inner voice cried out, "You did what, Mr. President?!?" The lack of personal papers aside, Nakayama's life is certainly not without documentation. There are the microfilmed records of the Trust Territory administration housed at the University of Hawai'i, Mānoa, and other select sites throughout the region. This rather extensive collection is made up of 2,169 reels of microfilmed reports, correspondence, minutes of meetings, and government publications, much of it concerned with matters of governance and future political status. I also made use of the microfilmed records of the FSM's early years that are housed at the FSM capital in Palikir and the *National Union,* the official newsletter of the FSM government. There are also the journals of both the Congress of Micronesia and the Congress of the Federated States of Micronesia as well as the annual reports on the administration of the Trust Territory of the Pacific Islands by the United States Department of State and the Trust Territory High Commissioner's office. *Highlights,* the Trust Territory government's monthly news summary, proved helpful as did several newspapers published at different times in Chuuk from the 1950s through the early 1970s.

The secondary and periodical literature is considerable; Nakayama's name figures prominently in studies of politics, governance, constitutionalism, and the Compact of Free Association. Official American records from Nakayama's time, however, proved more difficult to access; many are still classified. Those that are available can be accessed only though a time-consuming application process as specified in the U.S. Congress' Freedom of Information Act (FOIA). I did secure information from the Department of Justice on an alleged threat against Nakayama's life in 1985. The Central Intelligence Agency, however, declined to provide relevant documentation on the grounds that it jeopardized national security interests. The Department of State failed to follow through on my requests, while the representatives charged with handling FOIA requests at the Department of Interior simply denied the existence of an entity called the Trust Territory of the Pacific Islands. The Pacific Collection on the fifth floor of the University of Hawai'i at Mānoa's Hamilton Library holds the university's international student records on Micronesians from the 1950s; these include quite detailed reports typed on 3 × 5 inch index cards about the many future political leaders of Micronesia who studied in Hawai'i during this period. As indicated earlier, I spent considerable time with Nakayama himself in late December of 2000 and early January of 2001 at his home on Weno where I conducted thirteen hours of recorded interviews with him. Though slowed by the years and poor health, he was gracious, patient, and generous with his time. I enjoyed his hospitality, laughed at his sense of humor, and found his recollections invaluable. There were very few observations and comments from those interviews that I was not able to document elsewhere. His insights and explanations added importantly to the archival record.

While trained to think laterally, critically, and with the aid of theory, I have opted to organize this biography chronologically. I do so for two reasons. First, Nakayama's life was deeply affected and directed by the interaction of global events and local experiences that included competing colonial regimes, world war, reconstruction, development, and the quest for autonomy and self-government. In so many ways, Nakayama's story parallels and reflects the more general political history of the islands from the 1930s through the turn of the century. I also seek to represent his story in ways that those whose lives have been so profoundly affected by his efforts will recognize and find accessible. I hope this will not be the only biography of Tosiwo Nakayama; his achievements and those of his generation deserve multiple studies. I have opted here to focus on his political and public life that is reasonably well documented. In so doing, I am acutely aware of those parts of his story that need further investigation, not the least of which is the intensity of political and clan rivalries within the Chuuk Lagoon area that had a major impact upon the quest for autonomy and self-government in the larger region.

Throughout I have identified citizens of Japan by listing their family names first followed by their given names as in Mori Koben or Nakayama

Masami. For Micronesians of Japanese ancestry, I give the first name followed by the family name as in Tosiwo Nakayama or Susumu Aizawa. On a more orthographic note, I have employed the more recent spellings and local names for the various islands that make up the area called "Micronesia." Except when quoting directly from sources or referring to older accounts, I use "Chuuk" instead of Truk, "Pohnpei" rather than Ponape, "Kosrae" in place of Kusaie, "Weno" over Moen, and "Toloas" for Dublon. To avoid confusion with the more general literature on this time period, I have opted to use more current and common spellings of Chuukese place names; for example "Weno" rather than Wénéé, "Tol" for Ton, and "Toloas" over Tonowas. I have also endeavored to indicate where appropriate older or alternative names for islands mentioned in this study. I have found it more difficult to avoid using the words "Micronesia," "Micronesian," and "Micronesians." I have written elsewhere about the artificial nature of these designations. Rather than constantly qualify their usage throughout this work or employ alternative phrasing that would prove awkward and distracting, I have compromised in favor of clarity and common usage. I strongly believe, however, that the Micronesia Tosiwo Nakayama sought to make differed substantially from the belittling, inaccurate, and colonially constructed term that remains so prevalent in the writing about this sea of islands.

# A World of Islands

TOSIWO NAKAYAMA'S LIFE is most closely associated with islands that make up the geographical region called "Micronesia." These islands lie spread across a vast expanse of ocean in the Western Pacific.[1] Geographers locate the overwhelming majority of these islands and atolls as being north of the equator and west of the international date line. Considered by some to be among the most peripheral of peripheries, these bodies nonetheless have been at the center of several of the more historically prominent events of the twentieth century. Tarawa, the Chuuk Lagoon, Guam, Saipan, Angaur, and Peleliu served as sites for some of the most vicious, destructive battles fought between Japanese and American forces during World War II. Tinian, Bikini, and Kwajalein are important in the earliest chapters of the planet's nuclear history. The islands also figure prominently in a myriad of twenty-first-century issues involving the Law of the Sea, global warming, and environmental conservation. World war and nuclear testing are but parts of a much deeper colonial history that goes back to the 1521 landing of Magellan on Guam, includes six separate colonial administrations, and is encapsulated in the very word "Micronesia." Understanding Tosiwo Nakayama and what he accomplished requires a consideration of this colonial history and the deeper, more localized past that preceded it.

Drawing from the descriptions of the French voyager Jules Dumont d'Urville and other early explorers of the area, the geographer Gregoire Louis Domeny de Rienzi in 1831 asked for and received official approval from

La Société de Géographie in Paris to call the islands Micronesia. The term, derived from the Greek and meaning "tiny islands" marked in the minds of Domeny de Rienzi and others the most essential, distinguishing feature of the islands.[2] Being more metaphorically blunt, a later European observer likened them to a "handful of chickpeas flung over the sea."[3] The names of particular island groups within the Micronesian geographical area—the Carolines, Marianas, Gilberts, and Marshalls—represent markers of earlier, more localized European activities that commemorated the names of Spanish royalty or British sea captains.

Having been named Micronesia, these islands would be further distinguished by proper adjectives that reflected more than three centuries of varied and changing colonial rule. Between 1668 and 1986, the islands, at different times, would be described as Spanish, German, Japanese, and American. British annexation in 1902 gave a different colonial history to the Gilberts or Kiribati, while Nauru, also classified as Micronesian, passed from German to Australian colonial control in 1914. Beginning in 1899, successive waves of German, Japanese, and American colonialism provided the Caroline, Marshall, and Mariana Islands with a shared or bound-together experience. Underneath these island names and the adjectives that modified them lay more local histories for which imperial travelers had little time, interest, or need. Calling on this shared history as well as linkages and connections that extended back much further in time, Tosiwo Nakayama sought to help fashion an independent, self-governing island nation.

The area within the Micronesian geographical region that most immediately concerns us in this study is the Federated States of Micronesia (FSM). The FSM is one of the four political entities to emerge from the former Trust Territory of the Pacific Islands that was administered by the United States as a United Nations–designated strategic trusteeship; the other three entities are the Republic of the Marshall Islands, the Republic of Palau, and the Commonwealth of the Northern Mariana Islands. Greg Dening wrote in a 1978 review that the Pacific as a whole is an underdeveloped region historically.[4] His statement remains true today and particularly for the islands called Micronesia. This study seeks to contribute to the ongoing development of the practice of history in the area through the biography of Tosiwo Nakayama, the first president of the FSM and the individual most responsible for its emergence as a self-governing entity. His story, like that of Micronesia, has been largely blanketed under the term "Americanization," for some, a one-word history of everything that has transpired in the Caroline, Mariana, and Marshall Islands since 1944 when U.S. military forces seized control of the islands from Japan.

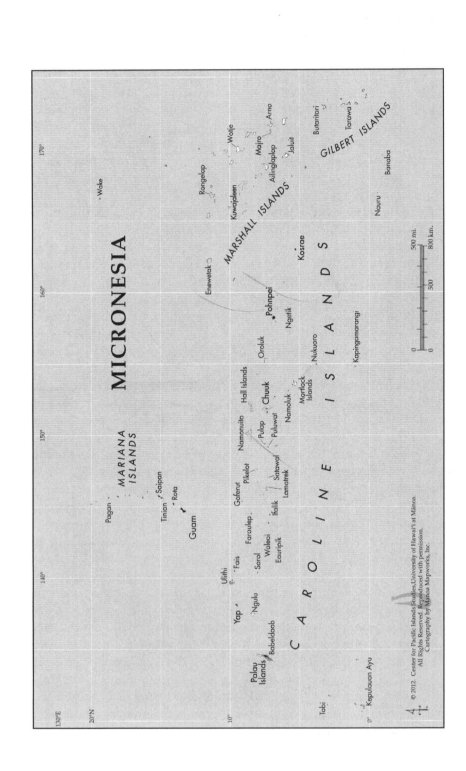

## Namonuito Is a Big Place

Tosiwo Nakayama lived, worked, and traveled in a world of islands that was actually larger than the area called Micronesia. He was born on the island of Piserach, which is a part of Namonuito Atoll in the Central Caroline Islands. Lying 246 kilometers northwest of the Chuuk Lagoon, Namonuito is the largest atoll in the Carolines, second only to Kwajalein in the larger Micronesian region.[5] The atoll is triangular in shape and consists of seven major islands and several smaller ones; the atoll's total land area is 4.5 square kilometers. Onoun, also known as Ulul, is the largest and most densely populated island; it occupies the southwestern corner of the atoll. Piserach Island rests in the southeast corner with a third major island, Magur, to the north. Epeli Hau'ofa cautions against understanding an atoll such as Namonuito as small; he wrote of the ways in which the ocean links and binds people in a larger configuration that joins land and sky into a contiguous environment.[6] Indeed, land comprises but a part of Namonuito's environment. The total area of the atoll, including the waters within its lagoon, is 2,267 square kilometers, extending over three and a half degrees of latitude. For atoll dwellers such as those on Namonuito, the ocean is rich in marine resources and has always presented an avenue of travel intimately linked to their well-being and survival. We might then better understand Namonuito Atoll, Nakayama's birthplace, in this more enlarged way—as part of a vast, surprisingly connected Oceanic region. Indeed, Namonuito once existed as the eastern end of the *sawei*, a confederation of atolls and islands in precolonial times that centered on Yap to the west. Given this expanse, it should not be surprising that Tosiwo Nakayama and others of his generation thought grandly, expansively, and inclusively in their efforts to help fashion a modern independent government for islands previously linked and autonomous in the more distant past.

We don't have a written description of Namonuito from the 1930s when young Tosiwo Nakayama lived there. Later visitors provided accounts of its physical features that the intervening years probably did not alter too much. Willard Muller, the district administrator for Chuuk, visited Onoun in the mid-1950s and remarked on its lushness and spaciousness, describing it as one of the largest and prettiest of the islands west of the Chuuk Lagoon area.[7] Underneath a canopy of breadfruit trees, coconut palms, and tall banana plants lay a profusion of color made of green palm fronds, flaming red and bright yellow hibiscus, oleander, frangipani, and ginger flowers. In the cut and cleared spaces near small dispersed settlements grew a wide variety of cultivated tree and plant crops that provided coconuts, bananas, papayas, breadfruit, taro, and tobacco. While animal life was limited, the immediately

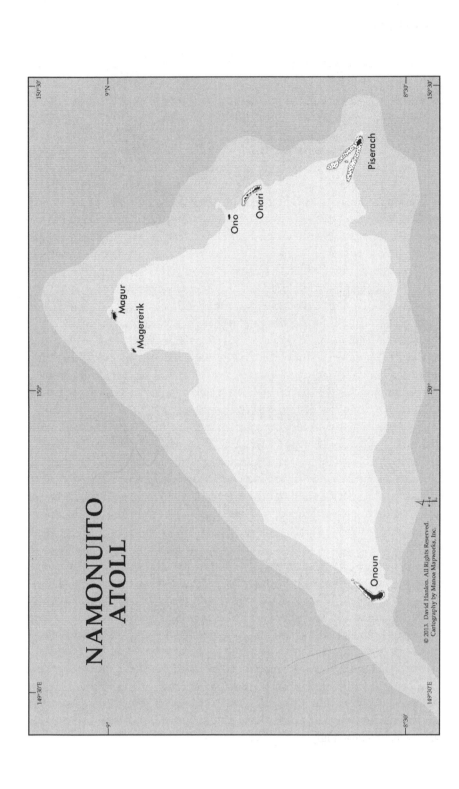

NAMONUITO
ATOLL

Magur

Magererik

Ono

Onari

Piserach

Onoun

© 2013 David Hanlon. All Rights Reserved.
Cartography by Manoa Mapworks, Inc.

surrounding sea offered an abundance of marine riches. Ninety-six kilometers to the east of Namonuito lay Fayu, an uninhabited island still visited on occasion by the residents of Namonuito and other islands for its rich fish and sea turtle populations.

The people of Namonuito were never really alone or isolated. Their skills as navigators and voyagers put them in touch with other islands. The Russian explorer Fedor Lütke admired the seafaring abilities of Namonuito's residents.[8] Thomas Gladwin, an anthropologist who worked for the Trust Territory government and proved a prominent figure in Tosiwo Nakayama's early life, wrote of the importance of voyaging to the people of Polowat. His assessment applied equally to the atolls and islands located near Polowat, including Namonuito. Gladwin wrote:

> Historically, it was essential that Puluwat be a part of this larger island world. It would never have developed as it has if it stood alone.... Dozens of islands stretched over a thousand miles of ocean from Yap on the west to Truk and the islands beyond in the east have been linked by their seafaring men and their sailing canoes in a network of social, economic, and often political ties without which they probably could not have survived, much less enjoyed the complex and secure way of life they now enjoy. The opportunity to exchange people, goods, and information permits these tiny communities to survive disasters, most notably typhoons, to draw from a pool of ideas and innovations larger than just their own, to integrate when useful into larger political groupings, and to extend the choice in marriage beyond the limited numbers of unrelated partners available on one's own island.[9]

A number of the clans resident on Namonuito trace their origins and early histories through the village of Mechitiw on the island of Weno in the Chuuk Lagoon as do clans in the Mortlocks.[10] These claims to relationships that link Namonuito and the Mortlocks with the Lagoon area find linguistic substantiation in the mutual intelligibility between speakers of Lagoon Chuukese and the related dialects in the islands to the northwest and southeast. As a young boy, Nakayama lived on Namonuito, in the Mortlocks, and on the islands of Tol and Toloas in the Lagoon area. The relationships he formed on these island places, coupled with the histories that linked them, provided him an advantage later in his public and political life that helped to overcome the prejudice of Lagoon people against outer islanders whom they regarded somewhat disparagingly as *Re Faan* or "people from below."[11]

## The *Sawei* and Other Voyaging Routes

Namonuito's history also bound it to islands to the west. The atoll marked the eastern boundary of an exchange system, centered on Yap, called the *sawei* that stretched over more than 1,600 kilometers.[12] There were other atoll exchange systems in the Central Carolines that centered on Woleai and Lamotrek; the *sawei,* however, was the most extensive and far-reaching. In precolonial times, the *sawei* involved the presentation of tribute and exchange goods to Yap from the islands and atolls to the east. Every two or three years, lengthy canoe voyages would begin from Namonuito, picking up representatives and offerings from each island on the way west. By the time the voyaging party reached Ulithi near Yap, it numbered at least ten canoes. Those islands closer to Yap enjoyed higher status, and assumed responsibility for leading the voyaging party to Yap. At Gachpar village in the Gagil district of Yap, three forms of tribute were made—religious tribute to the god Yongelap, canoe tribute to the chiefs of Gachpar, and finally land tribute offered by outer island lineages to their Yapese clan mates. The tribute offered at Gachpar included woven banana fiber loincloths, sennit, twine, turtle and coconut shell, and mother-of-pearl and spondylus shell. At the same time, Yapese hosts assumed responsibility for the care of their guests and provided gifts in return. These gifts consisted of natural products that were scarce in the lands from which the voyagers came. Among the more valued and desired were turmeric, red earth pigment, tridacna shell, whetstones, Polynesian chestnuts, and orange wood used in construction of ancestral altars. Wood for the building of canoes and foreign goods secured later from Western traders could also be used as return gifts to the voyagers.

The *sawei* exchange system allowed Gachpar to establish an alliance that provided it with leverage and resources in its struggles for power with the rival districts of Tomil and Rull. In response, Tomil and Rull established links with Palau where high-quality aragonite rock, chiseled into stone money or *fei* and transported back to Yap, became a valuable cultural good used to cement alliances and enhance status and prestige. The voyaging network that sustained the *sawei* endured into the nineteenth century as did Yap's trade with Palau for stone money. The close proximity of the atolls in the *sawei* exchange system, and the wealth of shoals and reefs between them, served as navigational markers and allowed for relatively secure and easy passages.

While the *sawei* system brought all of its members into contact at tribute time, most interaction was more locally focused. Linguists divide the *sawei* islands and atolls into three distinct groups that reflect the cultural contact that their geographical proximity encouraged. The eastern group consisted of

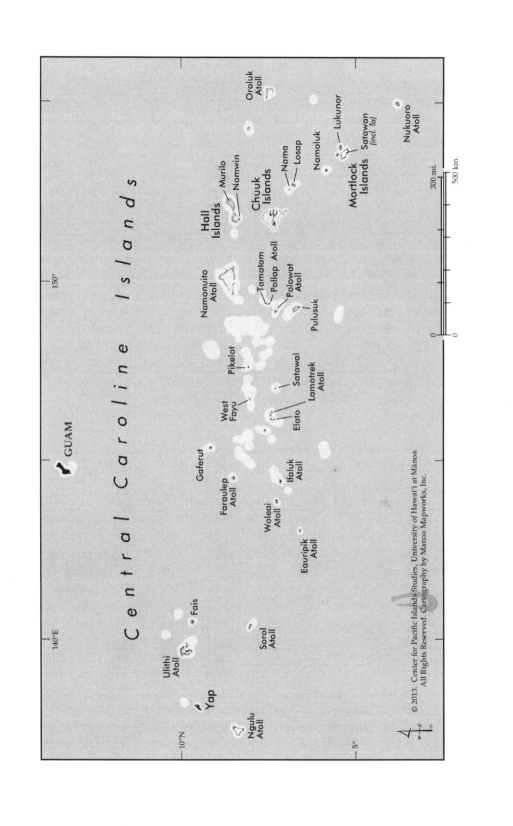

Central Caroline Islands

GUAM

Ulithi Atoll
Fais
Yap
Ngulu Atoll
Sorol Atoll
Eauripik Atoll
Woleai Atoll
Faraulep Atoll
Gaferut
Ifaluk Atoll
West Fayu
Elato
Lamotrek Atoll
Satawal
Pikelot
Namonuito Atoll
Tamatam
Pollap Atoll
Polowat Atoll
Pulusuk
Hall Islands
Murilo
Nomwin
Chuuk Islands
Nama
Losap
Namoluk
Mortlock Islands
Lukunor
Satawan (incl. Ta)
Oroluk Atoll
Nukuoro Atoll

140°E
150°
10°N
5°

0    300 mi.
0    500 km.

© 2013. Center for Pacific Islands Studies, University of Hawai'i at Mānoa.
All Rights Reserved. Cartography by Mānoa Mapworks, Inc.

*sawei* members Pulusuk, Polowat, Pollap, and Namonuito as well as the more easterly, non-*sawei* islands of Murilo, Losap, Nama, and the Mortlocks.[13] This more regular contact made possible the establishment of kinship and clan links among islands; it also allowed for the assertion of dominance within a regional grouping. Survival was always an issue, and often entailed rivalries and wars between neighboring islands. Polowat, for example, warred against Namonuito in the early nineteenth century.[14] As a result of its victory, Polowat received tribute from Namonuito until 1910. Pulusuk and Pollap also acknowledged Polowat's dominance. That dominance did not prevent war with or among Polowat's tributaries. Namonuito warred with nearby Pulap. In retaliation for earlier attacks on Magur, warriors from Onoun raided Pollap sometime before 1880 and reportedly killed a large percentage of the population.[15] Word of Polowat's plans to attack Namonuito for the slaughter of people under its dominion caused the residents of Onoun to permanently flee their island on a foreign ship.[16] Two groups later resettled the island, one from Piserach in the atoll and another from nearby Tamatam Island in Pollap Atoll.[17]

The Central Carolines also established early voyaging links with the Mariana Islands to the north.[18] Carolinian voyagers had found their way to the Marianas before the Spanish suppression of the Chamorros there. With Spain's conquest and colonization of Guam and the rest of the Mariana Islands, voyaging contact ceased for a time. Islanders' desire for trade, coupled with Spain's need to repopulate the Northern Marianas with Carolinians, rekindled travel, contact, and exchange between the two areas in 1787. This pattern continued into the nineteenth century. Saipan became a place of refuge when natural disasters struck. Residents of Satawal and Lamotrek sought the relative safety of the Marianas when a series of typhoons devastated their islands between 1847 and 1849. The need for plantation labor also led to an increased Carolinian presence in Saipan. Carolinian oral traditions and archival evidence from the Marianas indicate that 265 people were taken from Pulusuk for plantation work on Rota in 1865. Over the next four years, an individual by the name of J. H. G. Johnston recruited a large number of islanders from Namonuito for plantation work on Saipan and Tinian.[19] Johnston had the benefit of threat and coercion from Polowat in his recruiting efforts. Polowatans profited from this role; guns and other goods earned as a "recruiting" commission allowed the atoll to further assert its dominance over nearby atolls and to war successfully against the Chuuk Lagoon.

The Carolinians who settled in the Marianas came to be known as the *Re Falawasch*. By 1869, the number of *Re Falawasch* living more or less permanently on Saipan reached 331. Their principal settlement was at Arabwal on Saipan's eastern lagoon, a site first settled around 1818 by voyagers from Elato and Lamotrek. The year 1889 witnessed the establishment of a second settlement of Carolinians on Saipan. These settlers came from Onoun and had been working on the plantations of Tinian before moving to Saipan. They created the village of Tanapag, eight kilometers north of Garapan. Many converted to Catholicism and married Chamorro women. Residence on Saipan weakened their ties to Namonuito, and contact with their home atoll ceased as a result of Japan's interdiction against interisland voyaging soon after its seizure of the Caroline, Mariana, and Marshall Islands from Germany in 1914. Nonetheless, these Carolinians from Onoun and elsewhere remained *Re Falawasch* and among them were relatives of Tosiwo Nakayama such as Joe Lafoifoi who would be there to support him on Saipan during the Micronesian Constitutional Convention in 1975.

## Clan Histories and Connections

Clan histories and connections figured prominently in Tosiwo Nakayama's life. By the principle of matrilineal descent, Nakayama, through his mother Rosania, belonged to a clan called Pike or Piik that took its name from the island of Pikelot.[20] The clan was not large; its membership, however, was dispersed across the Central Carolines, and went by various names on different islands. On Ifaluk, for example, Kaúfanúa was the clan's name.[21] In 1982, Nakayama as president of the FSM traveled by field trip ship to Yap. The ship stopped at a number of islands and atolls on the way to Yap Proper. At Ifaluk, Nakayama encountered a woman who identified herself as the chiefess of the island. The woman, a member of the Pike or Kaúfanúa clan, reminded him of his clan roots on Ifaluk and his association with the island.[22]

The importance of clan membership, with its emphasis on reciprocity and obligation, is difficult to overstate. Clans offered identity, security, belonging, and connection that could extend over vast distances of open ocean. As Glenn Petersen has written, "by virtue of their unchallengeable membership in a lineage within a clan, individuals are free to move elsewhere... and claim as their birthright access to the land and labor of their fellow clan mates there."[23] Sharing, corporate holding, and use rights determined the governance of natural resources. Clan affiliation also offered support, solace, and refuge in time of danger or natural disaster. Nakayama thought that his clan connection was little known and did not really explain the strong support that he received from Yap throughout his public career. Others, including the fifth president of the FSM Joseph Urusemal from Ulithi in Yap State, claimed, on the other hand, that Nakayama's clan affiliation was generally known and was one of the reasons the people of greater Yap State were so comfortable with him.[24]

Nakayama's mother Rosania also connected him to the voyaging world of the Central Carolines. Her brothers, Nakayama's uncles, included Raatior, an accomplished navigator whose own uncle Opich was skilled in ways of navigation taught on Namonuito and known as *weriyeng*.[25] Opich had sailed frequently between Namonuito and Saipan in the years before interisland sailing was interdicted by the Japanese colonial administration. Nakayama wanted very much to be part of this seafaring tradition. In 1951, he left his employment with the Truk District administration on Weno to return to Namonuito in hopes of studying navigation from his uncle Raatior. He reached Onoun only to find out that Raatior had passed away.

The ocean was a comfortable and familiar environment for Tosiwo Nakayama throughout his life. Despite his separation from the navigational tradition of his ancestors, Nakayama was at home on the water. There are several stories that speak directly to his comfort and skills on the ocean. Willard Muller, the then district administrator for Truk, recounted an event that occurred at Polowat during a tour of the western islands of the district by field trip ship in the mid-1950s.[26] Among the party of officials accompanying Muller was Tosiwo Nakayama who was working as a clerk in the Truk District's Island Affairs office. Upon concluding their business at Polowat, the official party got into a motorized whaleboat that was to take them back to the ship at anchor just outside of the reef. Several hundred yards from shore, the boat was hit by a large wave that lifted the stern and then dropped it sharply. The impact dislodged the two copper pintles that connected the heavy wooden rudder to the boat, thus allowing it to steer. Without a steering mechanism, the boat engine was of no use; the strong current now carried the boat away from the waiting ship toward the reef. The only way to stop the drift and restore steering was to slip the displaced rudder pintles back into the empty, tube-like copper sleeves that attached the rudder to the stern. That could only be done by going over the side and working underwater in what Muller described as rough, shark-infested seas. While Muller and others hesitated, the boat continued to drift away from the ship at anchor and toward the reef with its pounding waves and crashing surf. From his seat near the bow, Tosiwo Nakayama surveyed the problem and responded. He quickly removed his shoes, slid over the side, slipped beneath the surface of the water, and began to work the pintles back into place. Nakayama had to make several prolonged dives. Resurfacing after each of his dives, he gave instructions to those in the boat on the alignment and positioning of the rudder. It took several minutes but Nakayama managed to reattach the rudder to the stern; soon after, the whaleboat was again headed toward the ship. The district administrator confessed to feeling like a miserable coward for hesitating "while this young islander took the risk."[27] Muller made amends by asserting himself during a similar incident that occurred within the Chuuk Lagoon a year later.

Polycarp Basilius, a member of the Congress of Micronesia and an ardent advocate of Palauan separation who opposed Nakayama's effort to establish a unified government for the larger region, spoke of a 1970 investigative trip that he and Nakayama were to make to Kosrae as members of the Micronesian Shipping Commission.[28] Nakayama at this time was a member of the Congress of Micronesia's Senate. Somewhat ironically, Basilius was given to seasickness and developed second thoughts about sailing to Kosrae. He asked Nakayama to stand in for the both of them, make the visit, and hold the planned meetings and hearings. Nakayama agreed. On the return trip, the ship's radio broke and the directional signal from Pohnpei was lost. Nakayama stepped forward to suggest that the captain use a battery-powered, commercial radio to pick up broadcasts from Pohnpei and then sail the ship in the direction of the strongest radio signal. The makeshift navigational arrangement worked. The ship lost a day and a half on its return trip from Kosrae, but reached Pohnpei safely.

In March of 1983, Nakayama, at the end of his first term as president of the Federated States of Micronesia, traveled to Chuuk to lend national assistance to the effort to deal with an outbreak of cholera. During a lull in the relief efforts, the governor of Chuuk State Erhart Aten arranged for a fishing trip to Namonuito aboard a sixty-foot Japanese fishing boat.[29] The party left Weno in the evening and expected to reach Piserach at nine the next morning; it soon became apparent, however, that the captain had lost his way. Failing to factor in the strength of the current, the boat had accidentally sailed sixty miles east past Piserach. The captain had lost radio contact with the main Lagoon island of Weno and was unsure how to correct his course. Nakayama, who knew the area, asked the Japanese boat captain if he could be of any assistance. A conversation between the two men resulted in the captain readily agreeing to step aside in favor of Nakayama. Taking charge, Nakayama remembered what he had learned about a distinctive wave pattern that occurred near the southeastern end of the atoll during that time of year. With the help of his nephew and political aide Asterio Takesy, Nakayama, to the relief of everyone, managed to locate the wave pattern and eventually sighted Magur, one of the islands of Namonuito Atoll.

## The Chuuk Lagoon and Its Histories

The Chuuk Lagoon was another island world in which Tosiwo Nakayama lived; his time spent there was not without historical precedent. The archaeological record suggests that two thousand years ago, migrant voyagers sailed north from the Northern Vanuatu and Southern Solomons region and then spread out through what has today come to be called the Central and Eastern Carolines.[30] Linguists group the languages spoken in the Lagoon area, along with those in nearby islands, into the proto-Chuukic category of the nuclear Micronesian family.[31] This linguistic evidence suggests that Namonuito and surrounding islands were settled from or through the Chuuk Lagoon, which itself had contact with high volcanic islands to the east.

There is one oral tradition that speaks of the establishment of a political order based at Mt. Tonachaw on the island of Weno and headed by the holder of the title Soukachaw that linked Pohnpei and Kosrae with Chuuk and its immediately surrounding islands.[32] Moreover, the clan that eventually rose to dominance on Weno, the Sópwunupi, is thought to have left or perhaps fled Pohnpei for Chuuk.[33] Establishing themselves on Weno, they took the name Sópwunupi that translates from Chuukese as those from the "District of the Sacred Structure" and refers to the megalithic site of Nan Madol on Pohnpei. Tosiwo Nakayama, who married into the Sópwunupi clan, believed in this history, and cited it during his travels to promote Micronesian unity and the constitution of the Federated States of Micronesia. The designation of Pohnpei as the capital for the new government can be seen, then, as the reaffirmation of these earlier, precolonial clan ties between Chuuk and Pohnpei.

Enclosed by a reef that has a circumference of 225 kilometers, the Chuuk Lagoon encompasses an area of 2,125 square kilometers.[34] The Lagoon area includes more than a dozen inhabited islands that are actually the peaks of an extinct, mostly submerged volcano. Together, the landmass of the Lagoon islands measures 127 square kilometers and supports a current population of roughly 40,000. The volcanic soil of the Lagoon islands is considerably more fertile than that of the outer islands and atolls, and nourishes a broad variety of plant and animal life. The richness and diversity of the Lagoon islands' natural environment explains the migratory traffic that flowed through it in earlier times. The phrase *liwinin Weno, safenen Weno* alludes to this movement in its description of the main Lagoon island of Weno as a land of departures and returns.[35]

The Lagoon islands are distinguished historically and culturally into the Faichuk, Namonsafo, Northern Namoneas, and Southern Namoneas areas. Tol, Wonei, Pata, and Polle make up the Faichuk area. Romanum and Udot comprise Namonsafo. Weno, Fono, and Pis Mwar are referred to as Namoneas; and Toloas, Fefan, Uman, and Tsis join to form the Southern Namoneas area. Each of the islands further divides into political units headed by clan or *einang* leaders. The people of the Lagoon came to understand the outer islands, smaller in both size and population as Pattiw, Weito, Paafeng, Lukeisel,

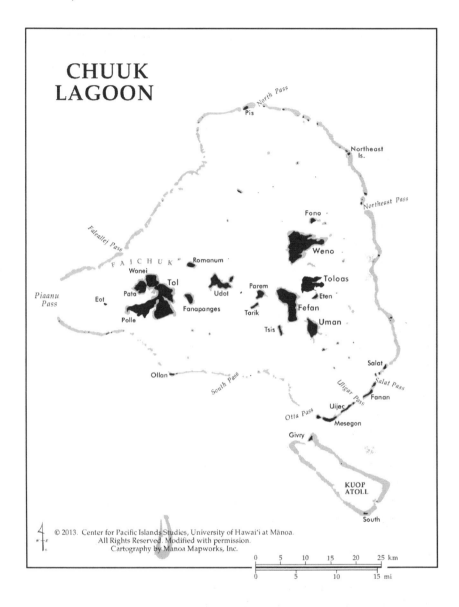

CHUUK
LAGOON

*North Pass*
Pis

Northeast
Is.

*Northeast Pass*

*Fatcallei Pass*

Fono ·

Weno

F A I C H U K    Romanum

Wonei

Tol                                   Toloas
Pata                Udot    Parem
Piaanu              Eot                        Eten
Pass                          Fanapanges    Tarik    Fefan
Polle                                Uman

Tsis

Salat

*Salat Pass*

Fanan

*Uligar Pass*

Ollan                   *South Pass*          Uijec

*Otta Pass*                Mesegon

Givry

KUOP
ATOLL

South

0        5        10        15        20        25 km

0            5                10            15 mi

and the Mortlocks. Pattiw was made up of Pulusuk, Polowat, and Pollap; Weito referred to the islands that comprised Namonuito Atoll to the northwest of the Chuuk Lagoon; Paafeng was the name for the Murilo and Nomwin Atolls. To the southeast of the Lagoon were Nama and Losap, called Lukeisel, while Namoluk, Etal, Lukunor, and Satawan comprised what came to be called the middle and lower Mortlocks.

Accounts of the Chuuk Lagoon's deeper past underscore the establishment of the aforementioned polity, the Soukachaw dynasty at Mt. Tonachaw on Weno that linked or connected Kosrae and Pohnpei to the Lagoon area. Historically, then, Weno existed as a site of power. Weno's three most populous villages—Mechitiw, Iras, and Lepukos—figure prominently in the island's histories, with Mechitiw being particularly important as a place of departures and returns. Over time, Weno and the other Lagoon islands emerged as a divided, contentious area marked by incessant conflicts among clans, villages, and islands. It was into this complex and conflicted environment that people from more distant lands and continents sailed.

## Continental Intrusions

The Spanish voyager Alonso de Arellano first sighted the Chuuk Lagoon in 1565; violence marked the encounter with canoes from Toloas, forcing Arellano to flee.[36] The passage of time and the lapse in contacts and encounters with the foreign world did not change things much. The French explorer Jules Dumont d'Urville wrote after a violent encounter with the people of Fefan in 1839: "The reputation of the Carolines has been tarnished for we have found here treacherous and wicked people, however engaging their appearance."[37] Traders such as Andrew Cheyne and Alfred Tetens encountered resistance to their commercial efforts. In 1844, Cheyne lost six of his crew while attempting to collect bêche-de-mer at Tsis. Cheyne's experiences led him to write in his influential hydrographic survey of the Pacific, that "no vessel should visit this group…unless well-manned and armed, as the natives…will be certain to attack any vessel which they may find in a defenseless state."[38] Chuuk came to be known as "dreaded Hogoleu."[39] Less visited than other islands and isolated from Western contact for long intervals, the Chuuk Lagoon area remained a place to avoid for most. The Lagoon area's reputation for violence did not deter missionaries, however.

In 1852, Protestant Congregational missionaries sponsored by the American Board of Commissioners for Foreign Missions in Boston, Massachusetts, began establishing mission stations on Pohnpei and throughout the Marshalls. The missionary initiative in Chuuk began later and through the Mortlocks where trained Pohnpeian missionaries were sent as advance agents. Success there and in nearby Nama led to the landing of the Pohnpeian missionary Moses at Uman in 1879. When the first white missionary, Robert W. Logan, arrived five years later, there were fifteen churches on four islands whose congregations numbered more than a thousand. Despite these successes, missionaries added to the negative image. They described Chuuk as dark. One termed it the "terror of the Carolines," a place known for "notorious inhospitality toward strangers." Another wrote, "Living in Ruk is like living over a volcano."[40]

Formal colonial rule came to Chuuk in 1886. Threatened by Germany's plans to annex the islands in support of its naval and growing commercial interests, Spain, dominant in the Marianas, asserted its centuries-old claim to the Caroline Islands based on the right of initial discovery. Pope Leo XII mediated the dispute between the two nations. The 1885 Protocol of Rome recognized Spain's claim to rule, while granting Germany commercial and naval access rights. Spain established two administrative centers for the Caroline Islands; officials on Pohnpei oversaw the Eastern Carolines, including Chuuk, while the Western Carolines were managed from Yap. Badly overextended abroad and domestically troubled, Spain presided over a declining empire in the late nineteenth century.

On Pohnpei, Spanish authorities gave little thought to Chuuk where no formal administrative presence was established; rather, the Spanish colonial administration depended on the periodic visits of its warships to effect an administrative presence in the Lagoon area. There was little to no Spanish administrative contact with islands beyond the Lagoon. Perhaps, one of the more significant developments during Spain's largely absentee rule over the greater Chuuk area was the increasing number of foreign traders—men like Jack Ehlers (later Hallers), Pierre Nedlic, and Charles Irons—who established themselves, married local women, and had families whose descendants would later come to figure prominently in the islands' affairs. None, however, proved more prominent or significant than the Japanese trader Mori Koben, a man to whom Tosiwo Nakayama was related. Rosania's father was the brother of Mori's Chuukese wife Isa. Through marriage, then, Nakayama was the grand nephew of Mori Koben and Isa.[41]

## Mori Koben

The Meiji Restoration of 1868 and the subsequent modernization of Japan disenfranchised the *bushi* or warrior class whose members were now forced to seek new avenues of support and distinction. Some turned to careers in overseas business ventures and commercial opportunities. A mix of romanticism, tenacity, persistence, drive, national mission, and a willingness to endure hardship and danger drove Japan's early presence in the Carolines. Mori Koben personified these traits.[42] Mori was born in Kochi City on the island of Shikoku to a *bushi* or samurai family. In his youth, Mori espoused a political idealism that was highly romantic, partisan, and zealous. In his teens, he became associated with a group that sought the expansion of Japanese interests in Korea through the overthrow of the Korean government. His support for the group resulted in his arrest and imprisonment.

The historian Mark Peattie speculates that Mori's exposure to Japanese travel writing on the Pacific, to the romanticized novels of Komiyama Tenko, Hisamitsu Yoshinori, and Yano Ryūkei, and to accounts of government-sponsored voyages of exploration and reconnaissance sparked Mori's interest in the islands. In late 1891, Mori sailed from Yokohama aboard the *Tenyū Maru* to become a resident representative of the Ichiya Company in the Caroline Islands. The trip proved an eventful one for Mori as it brought him to the Pacific. Several weeks later, the ship reached the Chuuk Lagoon and anchored off Weno. There, twenty-two years old, friendless, and with few possessions to his name, Mori disembarked to start a new life. He sought to establish himself on an island where Spanish colonial authority was almost nonexistent and among a people with a reputation for violence toward foreigners.

Reading the political landscape of the Lagoon area well, Mori allied himself with Manuppis, the most prominent chief on Weno. Manuppis resided at Iras village, near the site of what is now the Chuuk International Airport named in honor of Tosiwo Nakayama. Mori resorted to an established practice among new arrivals to Pacific Islands as a way to secure himself a place and a future; he served a chief. Armed with only a spear, Mori led a successful fight against a rival clan. The victory garnered for Mori a lifelong alliance with Manuppis. According to Peattie, Mori formed what in effect proved to be a small, private army equipped with Murata repeating rifles supplied by the Ichiya Company's schooner. Mori also found allies and friends among other Japanese traders who made their way to Chuuk and who were much like him in outlook and ambition; their ranks included Shirai Magohira and Akayama Shirosaburō. There would be others, but the three—Mori, Shirai, and Akayama—formed the core of a small group of kindred spirits who sought the expansion of their commercial interests in the Chuuk Lagoon area with the hope for a more formal and extensive Japanese presence in the islands.

Mori's relationship with Manuppis did not protect him and his compatriots from the hostilities of others in the Lagoon area. Indeed, the identification of Mori with Manuppis meant inevitable resentment and suspicion from those who opposed the Weno chief. Violent confrontations with other islanders in the Lagoon area were not uncommon for Mori in his first years. In 1896, Mori's friend and colleague Akayama Shirosaburō was ambushed and murdered on Tol by a man upset and jealous by the Japanese trader's interest in a local woman. Reports of the murder brought the Spanish vessel *Quiros* to the Chuuk Lagoon to conduct an investigation that went nowhere.

**Fig. 1.1.** Mori Koben, his wife Isa, and children (*Kochi Shimbun*).

   Preparations for fighting could sometimes prove as dangerous as the fighting itself. In the same year that Akayama was killed, Mori came close to dying in an accident. A mixture of gunpowder that Mori was preparing suddenly blew up, severing all the fingers of his right hand. With no medical personnel or facilities on Weno, Mori had to be his own doctor. The stopgap treatment held until he was able several weeks later to board a small trading schooner bound for Japan. Arriving in Yokohama, Mori proceeded to Tokyo where he had his wound treated. Remaining in Japan, however, held no allure for Mori. After several weeks of convalescence, including a visit to his home in Koichi City, he opted to return to Chuuk. In 1898, Mori married the twelve-year-old daughter of Manuppis, and gave her the name of Isa. She bore him twelve children, and helped him to develop an appreciation and sensitivity to life in Chuuk. With her guidance, Mori became fluent in Chuukese, adopted local ways, and established a network of relationships throughout the nearby islands.
   Mori continued to represent the Ichiya Company on Weno until it

folded. Before his 1898 accident, Mori had become the resident agent for the Nan'yō Bōeki Hiki Gōshigaisha or Hiki South Seas Trading Company soon after it opened a store on Weno. Spain's lack of an administrative presence in Chuuk prevented the policing of Japanese commercial activities, especially the selling of guns, dynamite, and alcohol. More Japanese traders now found their way to the Lagoon area. Mori became an independent trader for a time, and then accepted a position as a resident agent with the Jaluit Company in 1899. The hiring of Mori was notable given German traders' dislike of their Japanese competitors on the island. Mori would survive Germany's early attempts to rid the Caroline Islands of Japanese traders as he had Spain's absentee rule.

Spain's defeat in the Spanish-American War of 1898 left the overextended and financially drained imperial nation willing to sell its colonial possessions in the Caroline and Mariana Islands to Germany for 25 million pesetas or $4.2 millon.[43] As a consequence of the war, Germany replaced Spain as colonial overlord of the Caroline and Northern Mariana Islands. The Marshall Islands were already under German control as Germany had claimed Jaluit and its satellite islands in 1878. A formal claim to the rest of the Marshalls came in 1885 and was enforced by the presence of the German warship *Nautilus*. Indeed, it had been this German activity that had led Spain to reassert its claim to the Carolines in 1886. Germany placed its newly acquired colonies in the Carolines and Marianas under the German Protectorate of New Guinea.

The German cruiser *Kondor* reached Chuuk on New Year's Eve of 1900 to effect the change in colonial administrations. The new German governor, accompanied by a detachment of Papuan police, marched up the beach and arrested all of the Japanese traders in Chuuk with the exception of Mori whose employment with the Jaluit Company exempted him from the deportation that was the ultimate fate of his compatriots. There followed eight years of German governmental suspicion about his true loyalties and purpose. To escape the surveillance, Mori moved his family from Weno to nearby Tol, the largest, highest, and most fertile of the Lagoon islands. His spirits were most likely lifted in 1907 when the German administration relented and permitted the return of Japanese traders to the area. A ship belonging to the Nan'yō Bōeki Murayama Gomeigaisha or Murayama South Seas Trading Company arrived to open a trading store, and was soon followed by a number of other traders from Japan. A year later, the firm merged with the Hiki South Seas Trading Company to form the Nan'yō Bōeki Kaisha or Nambō, a business that would come to dominate commerce throughout the Caroline, Mariana, and Marshall Islands over the next three decades and during the course of Japanese colonial rule.

Germany would show itself to be a far more forceful and focused a presence than had Spain. As had Spain, the German government designated Yap and Pohnpei as the respective western and eastern administrative centers for the Carolines. The Jaluit Company, relieved of its administrative burden in the Marshalls, was granted exemptions and privileges as a way to revive commerce in Germany's larger Micronesian colony. Licensing fees were waived, monopolies granted, exclusive lease rights awarded, and private planting agreements with local chiefs honored, all as a way to return commercial vitality to the area. In return, the German colonial government required the Jaluit Company to assist with the collection of taxes, provide transportation for colonial officials, and allowed them to pay a reduced export tax. The stimulus did lead to enhanced production and the construction of new trading facilities at Eten in the Chuuk Lagoon and on Lukunor in the Mortlocks.

German colonial administrations made decided efforts to develop local island economies, effect land reform, enlist the power and prestige of chiefs, and recruit a steady and reliable labor force to serve the mining of phosphate on Angaur and Fais in the Western Carolines. Reponses varied from outright rebellion on Pohnpei to general acquiescence in the Marshalls and Yap where certain chiefly lineages found advantages to cooperating with the Germans. In Palau, the Germans found both allies and opponents in a more layered, complex environment of political rivalries and entrenched resistant cultural practices. The German administration's initial efforts in Chuuk focused heavily on pacification. Later, the Germans concerned themselves with labor recruiting, the promotion of certain cultural practices and the suppression of others, and relief efforts in response to typhoons that caused considerable damage in the Mortlocks and in the islands to the north and west of the Chuuk Lagoon.

The effort to pacify Chuuk, at least in German eyes, seemed to be working. German administrators found the Chuukese more compliant and cooperative with each official visit. Lands were cleared and planted with coconut trees and other fruit plants per German colonial orders. The German census enjoyed widespread cooperation as local chiefs reported the count of the people in their villages. No murders had occurred since the 1901 arrest of the three prominent Lagoon chiefs, and Tol, once considered particularly dangerous by the Germans, seemed safer. To solidify these gains, Victor Berg, who had replaced Albert Hahl as governor of the Eastern Carolines in 1901, divided the Chuuk Lagoon into six areas and appointed regional chiefs over each. Berg gave each of the chiefs a flag as a symbol of their new authority that now derived from the German colonial presence.

With Chuuk quiet and German efforts to end the illegal trade in guns appearing successful, there remained the problem of those weapons already in the possession of the Chuukese. Berg addressed the issue during a December

1904 visit to the islands. He collected 436 guns and more than 2,500 cartridges; as compensation for the surrender of these weapons and this ammunition, the administration paid out a total of 9,000 marks. With the Lagoon area now quiet, the administration turned its attention to what they regarded as social turbulence in the outer islands. A fleet of thirty war canoes from Polowat sailed into the Chuuk Lagoon during the district officer's visit, and the chief in charge was promptly arrested. The Germans had placed a limit on the number of canoes that could sail together on a single voyage as a way to limit the likelihood of war and ensure that the outer or remote islands had resident an adequate number of adult males to feed their populations. The administration also suppressed a revivalist movement in the Mortlocks that included the re-emergence of spirit mediums. In the Lagoon area, the administration sought to limit dance gatherings it felt were too long, exhausting, wasteful, and kept people from more productive activities and important social responsibilities.

In April of 1905, a typhoon devastated much of the Eastern Carolines. The island of Pohnpei was more or less leveled, with all food-bearing trees uprooted or stripped of all foliage and fruit. Namonuito Atoll experienced severe damage as well. The whole population of Piserach had to be temporarily relocated; another sixty people from Onoun moved to Saipan.[44] Most of them returned to their home atoll within a year or two when vegetation once again covered the islands. A particularly severe typhoon ravaged the Mortlocks in 1907 and took the lives of 227 persons on the island of Ta. Despite the opposition of island chiefs who saw their powers drastically affected by the movement of population away, 1,482 Mortlockese were temporarily resettled on Saipan. The majority of these were placed on underdeveloped tracts of land in the Garapan section. Those sent to Saipan were later moved to Pohnpei or the Chuuk Lagoon. The resettlement on Pohnpei took place on lands vacated by the people of Sokehs who were exiled to Palau in 1911 for their part in the revolt against German authority. Those who ended up in the Chuuk Lagoon area found temporary shelter on Eten Island where the local operations of the Jaluit Company were located.

Commercial activity was slow to recover. The typhoons destroyed coconut trees and disrupted copra production to such a degree that Governor Berg set mandatory quotas for Chuuk and Pohnpei on the number of coconut seedlings to be planted, and then set up a monitoring system to ensure that those quotas were met. Foreign landowners such as Dominique Etscheit, who had large holdings in the north of Pohnpei and claimed title to half of Onoun in Namonuito Atoll, were encouraged to start coconut plantations and plant other crops. Etscheit had struck a deal with the group from Piserach that had resettled Onoun sometime before 1880. The earlier residents of Onoun had fled under threat of retaliation from Polowat for their aforementioned attack on Pollap. In return for assisting with the expulsion of the other competing settler group from Tamatam, the Belgian was given usufruct to the north half of the island where he cleared land for a copra plantation.[45]

In the latter years of their administration on Chuuk, the Germans became the arbiter of local disputes, especially those involving land, and provided a final court of appeals for the entire population. The government finally set up an administrative center on Toloas with the people of that island providing free labor for the construction of the new office, residence, storehouse, and prison. Unlike Pohnpei where a labor tax was one of the causes of the 1910–1911 rebellion, people on Chuuk showed themselves more willing to work on government projects as a way to meet their tax obligations. Movement and migration continued among the islands, though under more direct colonial supervision and to satisfy the need for labor. The development of phosphate mining on Angaur and Nauru depended increasingly on Carolinian labor. By the end of German rule, more than thirteen hundred laborers on Angaur and Nauru were Micronesian. Over time, however, Chuukese enthusiasm for mine labor dwindled with the accounts of suffering and hardship from those who returned. Economic development continued to lag in Chuuk as it did in most other places throughout the German colony.

War would mark the end of German rule in the islands called Micronesia as it had some fifteen years earlier with the Spanish colonial presence. Using its alliance with Great Britain as a pretext, the government of Japan seized the Caroline, Mariana, and Marshall Islands from Germany. The League of Nations later legitimated this takeover with the award of a Class C Mandate to Japan for the administration of the islands.[46] Germany's agenda for economic development and modernization had not taken hold as planned. With Japan, it would be a very different story, one that would bear directly and intimately on the life of Tosiwo Nakayama. The most immediately important consequence of Japan's seizure of Germany's Micronesian colony was the arrival in Chuuk of Nakayama Masami, Tosiwo's father.

## Nakayama Masami

We don't know a great deal about Nakayama Masami prior to his arrival in Chuuk. An article in the *Truk Chronicle* gives his birth date as 29 October 1898.[47] He grew up in Tsurumi, one of the major divisions or wards of the port city of Yokohama. He had at least three younger brothers and a sister: Tosiwo and Hiroyoshi were the names of two of the younger brothers.[48] Hiroyoshi, the youngest, was actually a half brother as Masami's father had married the younger sister of his first wife after the latter's passing. Hiroyoshi was the child of that second marriage. There is no record of any strong political interests, commercial ambitions, or literary influences. We can assume, however, that growing up in Yokohama made its impression on the young Masami. With its shipping traffic and relatively large international population, Yokohama served as the major port through which almost all Japanese commercial traffic with the Pacific passed.

Growing up in Yokohama introduced Nakayama Masami to the larger world. A Japanese commercial firm hired him to work for its operations on Guam, and provided him with English language training as part of his preparations for work in that American colony; his English language instructor was an unnamed American of Japanese ancestry from California then living in Japan.[49] Tosiwo Nakayama remembered his father's fluency in English. According to Tosiwo, Masami stressed the importance of learning English to his children and later, during the war, expressed reservations about Japan's ability to effectively combat a larger, wealthier, and more technologically advanced United States. In addition to English, Masami spoke fluent Chuukese, and communicated quite effectively in the dialectical variations of Chuukese spoken elsewhere in the islands and atolls that surrounded the Lagoon. According to his son, Nakayama Masami was charged at one time with overseeing a group of stevedores on the dock at Toloas. Because he usually addressed them in Japanese, the workers assumed that he spoke no Chuukese and began making derogatory comments about him. To their embarrassment, Nakayama interrupted their conversations by speaking to them in very good Chuukese.

Nakayama Masami reached Chuuk in 1915 at the age of seventeen on a ship bound for Guam and the job that awaited him there.[50] For reasons that are not altogether clear, Nakayama decided to leave the ship. He disembarked at Toloas or Dublon as it was then known. There, he found Mori Koben, a small community of Japanese traders, and the opportunity to work as a local trader for the Nan'yō Bōeki Kabushiki Kaisha or Nambō, the trading company created by the previously cited merger of the Murayama and Hiki trading companies in 1908.

Some time after his arrival, Mori Koben arranged a marriage for Masami Nakayama with a woman of Namonuito descent who had been born on the small island of Fono, also known as Falo, off Weno and had grown up in the village of Iras on Weno. The young woman's name was Rosania, the daughter of Esoni (Lipis) of Namonuito and sister to Raatior, Aliwis, Raymond, Riali, and Dimas. Rosania had been adopted by her mother's sister, a woman named Sabrina married to the navigator Opich. Though resident elsewhere, Sabrina was the senior woman of the Pike clan on Onoun; as such and by the principle of matrilineal descent, Onoun's present and future ruling chiefs were drawn from her bloodline. The arranged marriage, more a reflection of Japanese than Chuukese cultural practice, ultimately facilitated Masami's assignment to Namonuito Atoll as the resident trader for Nambō. Using a sloop provided him by the company for use on Onoun, Nakayama collected copra from the Namonuito islands in return for trade goods, and then transported the copra to Toloas for further processing and shipment to Japan. Masami and Rosania had six children: sons Tadashi, Minoru (also known as Solomon), Tosiwo, Masao, and Matsuo, and a daughter, Yoshie who was later called Lucia. Tosiwo, the third son, was born on the island of Piserach on 23 November 1931. As the children of a foreign man, Tosiwo and his siblings had no paternal clan affiliations. Their Japanese ancestry, however, provided them with a very different and significant set of relationships, privileges, and advantages on islands that were now a Japanese colony.

In 1937, when Tosiwo was about six years old, his father was transferred to Lukunor in the Mortlock Islands where he served in a similar capacity as resident trader for Nambō.[51] The relationships the Nakayama family developed on Lukunor and in the larger Mortlocks proved enduring and politically significant. Rosania had particularly close ties with several Mortlockese families. Among them were the DeFangs. She and Kila DeFang became promised sisters during the Nakayamas' stay on Lukunor; later, Kila's son, Napoleon, recruited Tosiwo for school and later employment with the district government. The opportunities that arose from this recruitment constituted critical developments in the early public career of Tosiwo Nakayama. On Lukunor, Tosiwo Nakayama met Raymond Setik who became a good friend and later a strong political supporter in the Congress of Micronesia. Andon Amaraich, Nakayama's most trusted ally throughout his political career, was born on nearby Ta in 1932. The two would not meet until later, however.

The beaches and lagoon area of Lukunor presented a somewhat gentler environment; Nakayama remembered the lagoon in particular as narrower than that in Namonuito, but calmer and more beautiful. Life on Lukunor was comfortable and food plentiful. A large taro patch occupied the center of the island. With rice, sardines, and other canned goods in stock, the Nambō store on Lukunor supplemented the considerable food resources of the island. An Okinawan fishing boat operating in the area supplied smoked fish for export as well as local sale; the ship's operations also offered a modest source of income for island residents.

Having a Japanese father made Tosiwo and his siblings Japanese citizens with privileges and opportunities not available to island people. A two-tiered school system emerged in the Mandate Islands; a full, regular, eight-year elementary school or *Shōgakkō* for Japanese children, and a more basic, limited, three-year school system for Island children that focused on *jissai kyōiku* or practical education.[52] His two older brothers attended school on nearby Oneap in the Mortlocks; age and circumstance, however, combined to preclude young Tosiwo from any formal schooling during Japanese times. He did, however, learn to speak elementary Japanese from his father and playmates. He retained some of his Japanese language ability and used it in later life in varied circumstances that included the search for his father during a 1961 visit to Japan and during private discussions in public places with political colleagues like John Mangefel of Yap who also grew up learning Japanese as a child.

Lukunor was the center for all Japanese trade in the Mortlocks. There, the Nakayama family lived in a large company house with a tin roof and surrounded by a veranda; the grounds also included a second structure that served as both a store and a warehouse.[53] Nakayama Masami was the store manager and had others working under him. Following storms, he worked quickly and effectively to make the necessary repairs to his home and workplace. He was as hardworking as he was skilled. He dug a well on Lukunor that was still intact some fifty years later when his son Tosiwo, then president of the Federated States of Micronesia, visited the island in late July of 1981.[54] He could also fashion tools and household goods out of whatever might be available. This turned out to be a useful talent during the scarcity of the war period.

Nakayama Masami usually took his meals alone or with his two older sons.[55] The rest of the family would eat separately in another room. One of young Tosiwo's happiest times on Lukunor included those few occasions when he was allowed to eat with his father. Nakayama Masami was by all accounts a quiet, gentle man who rarely scolded or physically punished his children. Tosiwo remembered only one beating from his father, the result of putting sugar on his rice after he was told not to.

Rosania was Roman Catholic and raised her children in that religion. Lukunor was the first island in the greater Chuuk area to support a Catholic mission.[56] The choice of Lukunor resulted from the contact and rapport between Capuchins on Pohnpei and Saipan, and those Mortlockese who were evacuated to the two islands as a result of the devastating typhoon of 1907. The first missionaries reached Lukunor in 1911. Their efforts resulted in a large number of converts and the building of a church and school. In 1917, Japan expelled all German missionaries but in 1920 allowed Spanish Jesuits to enter Chuuk. Fr. Martin Espinal and Br. Aniceto Arizaela reopened the Lukunor mission in April of 1921 and served there for the next twenty-two years. They supervised the revival of church activities and the building of a larger church and accompanying school.

Tosiwo Nakayama attended the mission school but only for a few days; he found the appearance of the large, bearded Spanish brother frightening, and refused to attend the school any longer.[57] His parents expressed disappointment with him, but did not force his return. Attendance at the Japanese school on Oneap with his brothers was not possible as he was considered too young. He was left, in his own words, "to do nothing."[58] Among other things, "doing nothing" involved a field day sponsored by his father's company for the children of Lukunor. Young Tosiwo won one of the day's races, but learned that as a member of the sponsoring family, none of the prizes were for him. "Doing nothing" also meant showing off. Tosiwo was showing off his diving skills to some girls when the rowboat he was about to dive from moved slightly. The movement threw off his dive, and he ended up hitting his head on a rock underneath the water. His parents' scolding compounded the embarrassment. More serious was an illness that left him dizzy, vomiting, feverish, and unable to walk. His mother tended to him; she stayed long hours by his side while his father worked and was sometimes gone on trips to Toloas. The illness lasted roughly six months. Tosiwo spent much of that time in bed, on his back, and with little to do. He did learn songs by listening to the singing in the nearby mission school. He attributed his recovery to his mother's use of local medicine, and her patience in helping him to learn how to walk again.

Living on Lukunor, then, for young Tosiwo Nakayama was in his words a happy time. He felt quite comfortable, more so there than among the atolls of Namonuito. In fact, he thought of himself as from Lukunor. Upon returning to Onoun for a short visit with his mother on board a Nambō pompom or small, motorized watercraft, he pointed to a soursop tree and referred to the hanging fruit by the Mortlock word, *momiyap*.[59] People who heard him laughed, and corrected him saying on Onoun the fruit was called *lipeipau;* they also laughed at him for wearing a loincloth like people in the Mortlocks. Many years later, Tosiwo Nakayama returned to the Mortlocks on several different occasions to campaign, to promote a constitution, to advocate a compact of free association with the United States, and to visit the islands as the president of the Federated States of Micronesia. In this later capacity, the people of the Mortlocks greeted him with chants that recalled his deep personal connections to the islands.[60] This then was the world of islands into which Tosiwo Nakayama was born. It would grow larger as he grew older. He moved comfortably within this world and over the ocean spaces that joined its islands. His lived experiences on these islands created personal and familial relationships that linked him with earlier historical events, including ancestral clan movement and migration. In short, he was very much a child of this world.

## CHAPTER 2

# Japanese Times

JAPAN'S ACQUISITION of the Caroline, Mariana, and Marshall Islands prefaced and made possible Nakayama Masami's arrival in Chuuk. This chapter begins with a history of that acquisition and the subsequent establishment of Japan's administrative presence in the islands. A very young Tosiwo Nakayama was largely oblivious to the international developments and negotiations that placed the islands under Japanese control. The consequences of that colonization and the war that eventually followed, however, affected his life in profound and lasting ways, both personally and politically. In 1944, the privileges provided by his Japanese paternity dissolved under repeated American bombing that left significant areas of the Chuuk Lagoon in ruins. Hardship, want, confusion, and uncertainty followed in the war's wake. A familiar colonial order had collapsed in favor of one that would prove more foreign, aloof, and neglectful, if no less self-serving.

## Mandating Colonialism

In 1914, Japan, insisting on the responsibilities and prerogatives of its alliance with Great Britain, forcefully took possession of the Caroline, Mariana, and Marshall Islands from Germany.[1] British officials thought Japanese assistance in the Pacific unnecessary and worried about the use of the alliance as a cover for Japanese imperial expansion in the region. Informed by the troubled history of Japanese immigration on its West Coast and Japan's success in the 1905 war with Russia, the United States government also viewed Japan's Pacific acquisitions with suspicion. The American distrust of Japan had already led to the 1911 drafting of Plan Orange, a document that spelled out the American response to war with Japan some thirty years in advance of the actual outbreak of hostilities.[2] The American president Woodrow Wilson went to the Paris peace talks opposed to the annexation of Micronesia or any other German colonies. Committed to the creation of a clearer, more legally grounded international order, Wilson fretted that Japan's sanctioned acquisition of Micronesia would prove the first stepping-stone in a larger campaign that included the Philippines, Papua New Guinea, the East Indies, and Borneo.

At Paris, the debate came to focus on whether Japan would be allowed to annex the islands or hold them in guardianship.[3] Japanese representatives argued for the former. Wilson held to his principles, but found support lagging as Great Britain and its Commonwealth affiliates insisted on the right to take the spoils of war, an argument Japan found eminently compatible with its own position and interests. In 1919, Japan accepted as a compromise from the newly created League of Nations the award of a Class C Mandate over the islands, which allowed it to administer the islands under its own laws as if they were an integral territory but without the right of fortification. In effect, the Mandate compromise was little more than a fig leaf for annexation.

The granting of the Class C Mandate to Japan only deepened American suspicions about Japan's true intentions. The largely artificial controversy that began in 1920 over Japan's repeated refusal to allow the extension of a transpacific cable to Yap mirrored more the United States' concern over spreading Japanese influence in the region. The increasing size of Japan's navy and its advocacy of a southward expansionist program or *nanshin* that dated back to the Meiji period also worried American government officials and military planners. Japan eventually conceded on the issue, and accepted the limitations placed on the expansion of its fleet by the Washington Naval Treaty of 1922 as a way to minimize growing international scrutiny of its administration in the islands. While affirming an open door for commerce in East Asia, the treaty failed to extend the requirement to the Pacific Islands, thus allowing Japan the free hand it sought for the administration of the islands.

## The Japanese Administration of Its Mandate Islands

In general, the transition from German to Japanese rule came off seamlessly, at least from the colonizers' perspective. The German administration offered no resistance to the 1914 takeover of the different island districts by Japanese landing parties. The Japanese Navy held initial responsibility for the administration of the islands, and established a central office in Chuuk known as the Provisional South Seas Defense Force or Rinji Nan'yō Guntō Bōbitai.[4] The navy sponsored scientific and ethnographic surveys of the islands by scholarly teams as preface to the formulation of a region-wide administrative policy. In the interim, Japanese naval commanders relied on the procedures of the previous German administration, including the continuation of an adult poll tax and use of chiefs as local representatives. Using all available resources, the navy undertook public works projects, built hospitals and dispensaries, devised a system for health care provision, and created a rudimentary school system. The navy also engaged in economic development and assumed direct control of the phosphate mine at Angaur to ensure its effective functioning. A government-subsidized steamship line linked the islands to Japan, and provided both passenger and cargo support services. The navy's tenure, though brief, indicated that Japan was intent on establishing a lasting presence in the islands. The formal approval of the Class C Mandate for Micronesia required a civilian administration for the islands. As a result, the Japanese Navy's administrative tenure ended in late 1921. The following year saw the inauguration of the Nan'yō chō or South Seas government.

A lesser colony when compared to Taiwan and Korea, the Nan'yō chō was headquartered at Koror in Palau; the governor there held sole responsibility for the day-to-day administration of the entire colony.[5] He supervised all legislation, issued ordinances and proclamations, and held ultimate oversight over the court system. The administrative staff was drawn from the nation's imperial universities, and proved competent and effective. In each of the six districts a police force was created, headed by a superintendent under whom served inspectors, assistant inspectors, and patrolmen. The police force functioned as the backbone of the colonial administration and was supported by a native constabulary. The Japanese administration employed traditional chiefs as their representatives at the local village level and gave them the title of *sosoncho;* a *sonchō* or village headman worked in support of the *sosoncho* and could himself be a chief or someone in whom the Japanese had confidence.

The Japanese colonial administration initially endeavored to honor existing landholdings. The increasing number of Japanese immigrants did place pressure on local land, however. The government regarded vacant or unused land as unclaimed and thus the property of the colonial administration, a view that conflicted with local ownership and usage rights. Government surveys of land also tended to overlook or disregard local land tenure principles, thus resulting in the alienation of land from island peoples. The government's supervision of all land transactions confused rather than clarified ownership and use rights.

The terms of the Mandate agreement also committed Japan to the economic development of the islands.[6] Nambō, the Nan'yō Kōhatusu Kaisha (Nankō) or South Seas Development Company, and the Nan'yō Takushoku (Nantaku) or South Seas Colonization Company were the three engines of economic development during the Japanese colonial administration. Based in Koror, Nambō had branch offices in Chuuk, Pohnpei, and Saipan. The company focused on the copra trade; village producers throughout the islands received payment in Japanese trade goods at company stores such as the ones Nakayama Masami managed on Onoun, Lukunor, and later Toloas. Nambō also profited from a host of subsidiary businesses in the areas of marine and land transportation, refrigeration, and the canning and processing of marine products. Government subsidies allowed Nambō to grow, prosper, and diversify. With its shipping lines, plantations, wharves, and canneries, Nambō dominated trade in the islands.

Nankō resulted from the collaboration between government and industry in the islands. Under the direction of Matsue Hiroji, the company's most visible and ultimately successful venture was the sugar plantations on Saipan that, along with the phosphate mining on Angaur and Fais, provided the underpinning for the Mandate economy. In return for government support, Nankō was required to cooperate in the development of the Mandate. By the mid-1930s, Nankō stood as a substantial investor in the industrial enterprises of the colonial government. The third member of the economic triumvirate, Nantaku, existed as a state-run enterprise based in Palau and charged with the management of the phosphate mines on Angaur and Fais, and a host of subsidiary companies in various industries.

As it did in other areas of the Mandate Islands, Japanese commercial activity in Chuuk promoted the development of local infrastructure, including roads, wharves, harbors, and airfields. The expansion of shipping and airline service linked the islands to the rest of the empire. The shipping company Nippon Yūsen Kaisha sponsored two major lines of service, one being an eastern line that ran from Kobe, Japan to Jaluit in the Marshalls via Palau, Woleai, Chuuk, Pohnpei, and Kosrae. Nambō, under a contractual agreement with Nippon Yūsen Kaisha, managed Chuuk's two internal shipping lines—one that connected the Lagoon and the Mortlocks, and a second that ran two trips a year between Chuuk and Rabaul. The Mandate soon showed a favorable balance of trade. By 1932, local revenues precluded the need for grants from the government of Japan. In 1937, the Nan'yō government recorded a reserve of almost 3 million yen. Keeping things in perspective, the economic contribution of the Mandate to the larger empire showed itself to be quite small. The islands accounted for only 1 percent of total revenues generated by Japan's colonial empire.

Japanese immigration intensified dramatically in the 1920s and 1930s.[7] In 1925, there was a total of seven thousand Japanese nationals in the islands, five thousand of whom resided in the Marianas and worked on the Nankō sugar plantations. In 1930, the number of Japanese nationals residing in the Marianas reached twenty thousand. Okinawans, by 1925, constituted the majority of Japanese immigrants to the islands. In addition to work on the plantations, these immigrants found success as shopkeepers, artisans, dealers, and vendors of various goods and services. The earliest waves were predominantly male; they arrived with the hope of one day returning to their homeland with some degree of wealth. More immigrant families followed this first wave, so by 1935, the fifty thousand Japanese living and working in the islands outnumbered the indigenous population.

While the economic development of the islands served Japanese interests and needs, there existed employment opportunities for islanders that brought them a relative material prosperity not available under either the Spanish or German administrations. Nonetheless, Japanese held assumptions about Micronesians' limited capacity for work that reflected the lens of racial hierarchy through which many administrators and immigrants viewed the world.[8] Japanese regarded themselves as a unique and superior race whose goal was the assimilation of the islands' people. This was to be achieved through a host of initiatives that included productive labor, education, the exultation of the emperor, the organization of Micronesian young people into supervised youth groups, and observation tours for island leaders. Assimilation, of course, contravened the terms of the Mandate, and it did not include the rights of citizenship. Overall, the Japanese regarded Micronesians as a lesser or third-class people and referred to them by the term *santō kokumin*. In the racial ranking of the Japanese empire, Micronesians followed Koreans and Taiwanese. Among Micronesians, the Japanese regarded the Chamorro as more developed because of their longer history of colonization; the Carolinians and Marshallese followed in this ranking with the Yapese being considered the most primitive.

## Conditions in Chuuk

Chuuk, more specifically the Lagoon area, received significantly less attention than Palau, which hosted the Nan'yō's administrative headquarters, or Saipan where the development of the sugar industry caused a radical transformation in the social demographics and physical infrastructure of the island. Along with Yap and Pohnpei, Chuuk was one of the lesser developed district centers, though not as lightly touched as the more remote Marshalls district to the east. In Chuuk, civilian administrators chose as their local representatives at the village level individuals who were capable in the Japanese language; this meant the displacement of traditional leaders or chiefs who had served as "flag chiefs" under the German and Japanese naval administrations. As elsewhere in the Mandate, separate school systems were created—one for Japanese children and another for island children.[9] While Japanese children enjoyed the benefits of a full elementary-level education, young Micronesians were limited to a mandatory, three-year program that emphasized basic competency in Japanese. There was an additional two-year course for those who showed promise in the estimation of Japanese educators. As *santō kokumin* or third-class citizens, Micronesian students received training that allowed them to function in support of a society now directed and dominated by Japanese interests. For the very brightest, there was the opportunity to study at a three-year trade school in Palau that taught carpentry and woodworking, and later blacksmithing, automotive mechanics, and electronics. Enrollment in the three-year primary schools or *kōgakkō* was mandatory, and enforced. On Namonuito, the place of Tosiwo Nakayama's birth, Japanese officials forcefully removed five crying boys from the clutches of their fearful mothers for enrollment at the nearest school on Tol.[10]

By the end of the 1920s, half a dozen elementary schools and an equal number of Nambō branch stores operated in Chuuk.[11] The local Japanese population numbered about two hundred, with most employed by the Nan'yō government. The arrival of seven hundred Okinawan fishermen in Chuuk in the 1930s expanded these numbers considerably. Their presence meant large fishing fleets supported by drying and refrigeration plants and other maritime enterprises, including the cultivation of trochus beds. Okinawans manned a fifty-boat fishing fleet that caught tuna for the production of *Katsuoboshi*, the preserved tuna flakes that were then such a popular condiment in the Japanese diet. The Okinawans swelled the foreign population in Chuuk to 3,600 by 1937; a number that paled against the much larger Japanese, Okinawan, and Korean populations in Palau and Saipan. Chuukese worked in the *Katsuoboshi* factories and for other Japanese-owned shops and services that opened in Chuuk. By administrative intent, they were but minor players in the economic life of the area. Still, this economic activity generated what for island people was a considerable amount of newfound wealth. In 1937, the average annual income of Chuukese workers amounted to about US$50.

Most of the Okinawan fishermen settled on Toloas or Tol. As it had during German times, Toloas served as the administrative center for the new colonial presence in Chuuk. It had a branch government building, a post office, hospital, and a few other government buildings located along its southern side.

The arrival of fishermen and traders led to the construction of piers, sheds, shops, and canneries around the harbor. The colonial government's administrative offices sat amidst lush greenery atop a hill that overlooked the harbor. The anthropologist Umesao Tadao, described the town at Toloas as rustic and mean-looking, where only the main street was paved.[12] Side roads ran through a bedraggled row of stores near the shoreline. Heavy rains turned these unpaved side streets into bright, glue-like mud. While the main town at Toloas may have appeared less than attractive to visitors from Japan, it had novel attractions that evoked for its residents the Japanese homeland. Shops housed dentists, professional photographers, and mechanics. There was also a barbershop with full-length mirrors. Kimono-clad women walked about the streets, some from the geisha houses or flower quarters where men could eat, drink, and enjoy the company of women.

## The Nakayamas on Toloas

In 1940, Masami Nakayama took his family to Toloas where he assumed management of the Nambō store there.[13] Tosiwo was about eight years old at the time of the family's move from Lukunor. Toloas was a markedly different place from Lukunor and every other island in the Chuuk Lagoon area. Tosiwo found the island strange and intimidating at first, and missed his friends on Lukunor.[14] The discovery and repair of a broken bicycle proved a project that attracted other young boys and brought him new friends. He played with sticks, and later fashioned a slingshot that he used to fling stones at a Japanese workers' dormitory. He also aimed his slingshot at the house of a Japanese man married to a local woman. He could not remember why he disliked the man. "Just crazy kids' stuff" was the explanation a much older Tosiwo Nakayama gave for his behavior.[15]

The Nakayamas lived in one half of a duplex or split house on Toloas. While living in that house, Tosiwo became friends with a boy named Minoru whose family shared the duplex with the Nakayamas. Minoru's most distinctive physical features were his ears; one was smaller than the other. The two would meet four decades later when President Nakayama was on an official trip to Japan. Minoru subsequently visited Chuuk as an old man and prayed at the site of the house that the two families had shared. The family had another friend on Toloas, a woman named Kesia.[16] Rosania and her children had often stayed with this woman during stopovers on travels between Onoun and Lukunor. The women were good friends. Their friendship reflected earlier historical ties between Onoun and Toloas that were commemorated in part by the giving of the name Onoun to a piece of land on Toloas. This friendship, like so many others established in these years, linked the extended families of the two women long after their deaths. Later in life, Tosiwo Nakayama, remembering Kesia's kindness and friendship with his mother, brought her to live with his family on Weno.

## Fortification and the Coming of War

While research points to the period between 1939 and 1941 as the time that Japan began the deliberate fortification of the islands for purposes of war, there had been considerable building and infrastructure development in Chuuk and other islands beginning in the mid-1930s.[17] In the first four years of the decade, the Nan'yō chō sponsored the construction of communication and commercial facilities for general development purposes. Saipan and Palau, the two major centers of Japanese population, were the focus of this activity. The period from 1934 to 1939 brought the construction of airfields and communication facilities in the Caroline and Marshall Islands.

This Japanese construction activity, along with restrictions placed on foreign commercial shipping and the limited number of ports open to vessels from other countries, heightened American suspicions. Japan reacted with anger when the United States used its naval vessels to transport American scholars, scientists, and travelers on approved visits to the islands. To limit the intrusion and prevent any further information gathering by these ships, the Japanese government prohibited future visits on the grounds that the islands' harbors were too dangerous, and that the visits confused and unsettled the indigenous population. These tensions also reflected concerns over larger regional events. Japan's invasion of Manchuria in 1932 and its dramatic 1933 walkout from the League of Nations over the issue, its refusal to renegotiate the Washington Naval Treaty, its later announced abrogation of any and all treaties placing limits on the size of its navy, and the 1937 construction of three large battleships added to an international atmosphere already rife with suspicion, fear, and rumors.

The arrival of the Japanese Fourth Fleet in February 1941 transformed life in much of the Lagoon area.[18] With Chuuk designated as the central command area for the Mandate Islands and with the navy for all intents and purposes assuming the responsibility for government, the landscapes and seascapes of Chuuk changed. Planes arrived from Rabaul, and the Lagoon itself was filled with ships. The Japanese Navy stationed its two most powerful and modern battleships, the *Yamato* and the *Musashi,* at Chuuk.[19] The arrival of the fleet brought four thousand naval personnel to Chuuk; each passing month thereafter brought more sailors and soldiers. The increased military presence did mean employment for many Chuukese men; there were jobs as watchmen, stewards, attendants at clubs and bathhouses, carpenters' assistants, and spotters for merchant marine and naval vessels on their transit in and out of the Lagoon.

As war preparations quickened, the face of labor took on a more coercive character. The construction of airfields at Eten, Parem, and Weno utilized Korean conscripted labor under Japan's Military Manpower Mobilization Act. Japanese convicts from the Yokohama Central Prison, including five hundred members of the "Green Battalion," were also brought to Chuuk under this law and worked to exhaustion almost every day on the airfield at Weno. Laborers from the Lagoon area as well as conscripted workers from the Mortlocks and other islands in greater Chuuk worked on Eten. The arrival of the Fifty-Second Army Division from Kanazawa in late 1943 added even greater intensity to the already frenetic construction of caves, tunnels, concrete bunkers, ammunition dumps, and gun emplacements. The hauling of large naval guns to the top of Mt. Tonachau on Weno required a particularly prodigious effort.

The fortification of the Chuuk Lagoon area and the actual coming of the war drastically affected all areas of life. Prices in stores increased as the demand created by the new arrivals put pressure on store inventories. Missionaries, whose presence was once regarded as complementary to Japan's civilizing mission under its League of Nations Mandate, now found their travel restricted and the holding of church services prohibited. Those stationed in outlying islands were brought to the Lagoon area. On Lukunor, the Catholic church where Rosania and her children had worshiped was destroyed and replaced by a barracks for soldiers.[20]

Prior to the intensified preparations for war, most of the Japanese population in Chuuk had concentrated on Toloas. With the arrival of the soldiers, the military now took over Toloas and established themselves throughout much of the Lagoon area. By April 1944, there were 14,293 troops in Chuuk.[21] Beyond Toloas, the major loci of military activity included the airstrip and seaplane base on Weno. Work on the airfields at Eten and Parem had been completed by January 1944. The Japanese required that all able-bodied men on Weno contribute to the construction of the airstrip at Iras. This labor proved to be hard, demanding, dangerous, and seemingly endless with the constant repair work necessitated by the American air raids that began in February 1944. The increased military presence and activity also brought the confiscation of land. The military takeover of land in Chuuk surpassed that in the Marshalls and elsewhere in the Carolines. The Japanese military bulldozed Mechitiw, the village on Weno where many from the outlying islands such as Namonuito had established themselves. The villages of Sapwuk, Iras, and Tunnuk were also negatively impacted, and portions of their populations relocated. Restrictions compounded the difficulties. Sections of Eten, Parem, and Toloas were declared off-limits to Chuukese. People in parts of Fefan, Udot, and Uman also found themselves forced to relocate.

Land usage was often reorganized for maximum efficiency in meeting the food requirements of the military.[22] This was the case on Tol where the church at Fou and its surrounding grounds were turned into gardens. Sweet potatoes comprised an important part of the soldiers' diet. Chuukese men and women spent endless hours cultivating these gardens, including shoveling the human waste used to fertilize them. Women also grated copra for oil, cooked for the soldiers, and did their laundry. All of this work in support of the military came at the expense of family, clan, and village needs. Discipline proved harsh for those who refused to work or did not work hard enough. Once the American bombing commenced, the service required of Chuukese men could also prove dangerous, even deadly. The youth groups or *seinendan* that had been established earlier for general training and community service purposes took on military support roles. Members were trained to carry messages and to put out fires. Chuukese men served as lookouts on sea patrols and helped service the ships at anchor in the Lagoon. A considerable number of workers lost their lives when an American bomb hit a munitions ship docked at Toloas.

With preparations for war intensifying, the military came to dominate life on Toloas. Most Japanese civilians, including Nakayama Masami and his family, were relocated to Tol. Largely rural, much less populated, and with only a circumferential dirt road, Tol differed dramatically from Toloas. The Nakayamas lived close to the family of Aizawa Shōtarō on Tol.[23] The two men both worked as traders for Nambō. The residence of Mori Koben was also close by. Deep personal ties that extended back to Yokohama bound the Nakayama and Aizawa families. The marriage of Tadashi, the oldest of the Nakayama sons, to one of the Aizawa daughters further cemented the bonds. Tosiwo was befriended by Susumu Aizawa, the oldest of the Aizawa children. The two mixed-race boys moved easily about Tol, and had both Chuukese and Japanese friends. Tosiwo spoke better Japanese than Susumu, but was sometimes the object of teasing from Japanese playmates because of his darker skin. This was not an uncommon experience for children born of Japanese men and local women.

American military planners regarded the Chuuk Lagoon, the home base for the Japanese Pacific fleet, as a near impregnable fortress that posed a major threat to the central and southwest Pacific campaigns. In actuality, Japanese military capabilities in Chuuk were much less foreboding.[24] Japan's two largest battleships, the *Yamato* and the *Musashi,* had left the Lagoon in Novem-

ber 1943 for the safety of Palau. There were only forty anti-aircraft guns in
the entire Lagoon area, and most of the trained pilots barracked on Toloas
while their planes were kept on Eten and Weno. Ammunition, fuel, and general supplies were all scarce because of the disruption to Japanese shipping by
American submarines. Nonetheless, the American perception of Chuuk as a
near-impregnable fortress persisted. For this reason, the Americans carried
out an extraordinary aerial attack that centered on the fleet at anchor in the
Lagoon.

## The Bombings and Terror on the Ground

Operation Hailstone began on February 16, 1944, when seventy-two American Hellcat fighter planes set out from nine aircraft carriers one hundred miles
northeast of the Chuuk Lagoon.[25] The assault continued with repeated and
regular bombing raids during March and April from American airfields on
Kwajalein and Enewetak in the Marshalls. At the end of April, yet another
carrier-based attack on Chuuk was launched. When the bombing finally
stopped, forty-one ships had been sunk, including ten naval warships; two
hundred planes had been destroyed and another one hundred disabled. The
destruction also encompassed military barracks, airplane hangars, two thousand tons of food, and three large tanks holding seventeen thousand tons of
fuel. The fatalities amounted to six hundred military and naval personnel, not
including those who perished with their ships. Toloas, Weno, and Eten were in
ruins, and Chuuk was effectively neutralized as a military base. Nonetheless,
the bombing resumed. Following the last twice-daily raids in late April, B-24
bombers pounded Chuuk several times a week for the next two months. Oral
testimonies and photographs from the time reinforce the assessment of historian Mark Peattie: "wreck and ruin" were everywhere.[26] There was terror on
the seas as well, both before and after Operation Hailstone. American bombs
and torpedoes sank Japanese freighters, transports, and tankers. Lost were the
troops, planes, tanks, ammunition, fuel, and food that they carried. Merchant
marine ships carrying civilian passengers to and from the islands were targeted as well. After a visit with family on Chuuk, a close relative of Nakayama
Masami died on his return to Japan when an American naval vessel sank the
ship he was traveling on.[27]

Young Tosiwo Nakayama, twelve years old at the time, witnessed the initial attack from the top of a hill on Tol.[28] Under cover of a large tree that offered
no real protection, Nakayama saw U.S. planes bomb the ships at anchor in
the Lagoon. He saw the bombs drop, heard the deafening explosions, and was
awed and frightened by the large plumes of smoke emitted from the many

**Fig. 2.1.** The bombing of Toloas, April 1944 (Micronesian Seminar).

damaged ships. He marveled at these planes as they flew down, strafed Japanese planes, airfields, and other land targets, and then pulled up, turned, and circled back to repeat the maneuver. He could see the outlines of some of the pilots in their cockpits as they flew close to where he stood. The whiz of nearby bullets soon led the young Nakayama to abandon the hilltop from which he had been observing the first hours of the bombing.

The bombing of Chuuk caused immense hardship and suffering.[29] The continuous raids created levels of public terror, fear, and anxiety never before experienced in the Lagoon area as people needed to be constantly alert, aware of the planes, and quick to find shelter. At times, Japanese soldiers would commandeer caves and other natural shelters, forcing the Chuukese to look elsewhere. A conservative estimate puts the number of Chuukese killed in the raids at sixty-three with sixty wounded; these figures do not include those lost when the ships they were working on sank.[30] Almost as horrific was how many Chuukese were witness to the massive death. Wangko Wasan of Udot stated:

> In the beginning, it was fascinating to watch the soldiers pouring in by the hundreds, but as time went by it became unbearable to see dead bodies being unloaded from the ships like stacks of copra. There were endless loads of corpses ferried ashore for eventual cremation. We had

the feeling of the waste of human lives. There were all kinds of people; civilians, businessmen, and others, who just a while ago had been in their various destinations in the lagoon. It was heartbreaking to hear life and death stories from survivors.[31]

Fear caused many to ignore the wounded. Even the strongest of familial ties proved fragile when one's safety was threatened. People in fearful flight left the wounded behind: "We didn't even care if they were our family," said one.[32]

Food shortages developed quickly and were exacerbated by the disruption that American air and naval forces wreaked on Japanese shipping.[33] Some came to rely for food on what little the soldiers threw away or didn't eat. A simple maxim of the times stipulated that if you worked for the soldiers you ate; if not, you suffered. The threat of starvation was real throughout a good part of the Lagoon and worsened as thirty-eight thousand Japanese soldiers and civilians, as well as fifteen thousand Chuukese needed to be fed. Starvation conditions existed on Weno, Toloas, and Uman. Sweet potatoes were planted on every available piece of land; soldiers now worked their own gardens while laying claim to breadfruit and coconut trees. Local landowners risked beatings when they protested the seizure of their trees. Despite the dangers of Japanese reprisal, many Chuukese resorted to theft to support themselves and their families. It was common for people to pick and eat unripe breadfruit for fear that it would be taken later by others. In desperation, people searched mangrove swamps for fallen, even spoiled coconuts. Famine foods included grass shoots, leaves, young coconut tree trunks and fronds, and morning glory and wild yam vines that remained bitter even after extensive boiling. Still others ventured out onto the Lagoon's waters and harvested the fish that were killed or stunned by the explosion of bombs hitting the water. By the end of the war, people found themselves forced to eat lizards and rats and other vermin. One elderly Chuukese became so weak and emaciated from malnutrition and disease that his family was in the process of burying him alive when a neighbor intervened with the offer of a potato and some water.[34]

Tensions and fears developed within families as a result of the stress, and rumors spread about the execution and cannibalization of a man named Nekiroch by the Japanese.[35] In some areas, strong chiefs working in cooperation with Japanese officials were able to mitigate or at least ameliorate the food shortage and its consequences. In certain instances, this mitigation led to a resurgence of power and prestige for traditional leaders.[36] Petrus Mailo and Pwenni, chiefs on Weno and Penia respectively, enhanced their status with their effective and diplomatic intercessions in behalf of their people.[37] People, however, were prevented from finding solace in religion. The military discouraged people from attending church services, and sometimes harassed or beat those who did. Whereas the presence of missionaries had once been regarded as a complement to the uplifting and civilization of native peoples, the Japanese military now took a hard stand toward foreign missionaries and religious activity. They expelled missionaries, confiscated church buildings and other property, derided Christianity as a powerless religion that honored a false god, and told people to focus on their work.

The varying conditions on the different islands went a long way to determining the nature of the relationship between Chuukese and Japanese in the post-bombing, soon to be postwar period. On Tol, where a large number of Japanese and Chuukese took refuge, relations were relatively good, although Chuukese had to be careful to hide any negative emotions or feelings. Being a Mori, for example, had its advantages. The sons of Japanese men born to Chuukese women were considered Japanese citizens and, if old enough, could enlist in the Japanese Army as did several sons of Mori Koben's extended family.[38] The Nakayamas were spared much of the wartime suffering visited on other Chuukese. Having a Japanese father shielded the family from the harshness that most Chuukese experienced.[39] Tosiwo remembered his family on Tol as always having more than enough to eat.[40] Rosania often returned home from Japanese functions with extra food, part of which she sent to the nearby mission station where provisions were scarce. Amidst the horror of conditions elsewhere in the Lagoon, the mix of Japanese and Chuukese on Tol resulted in cross-cultural fraternization and socialization that included parties, sumo wrestling matches, and performances of traditional Chuukese chants and dances.[41]

While burdened with their own suffering and hardships, Chuukese expressed sympathy for the plight of soldiers, especially the sickly, emaciated, and starving battalion that was evacuated from Polowat to the Lagoon area.[42] The sight of suffering Japanese soldiers did not lessen or minimize the people's sense of their own plight, however. Many likened their treatment at the hands of the Japanese to that of slaves, animals, or, in a more biblical vein, the Israelites.[43] At times, Chuukese resisted forcefully. The Japanese had to quickly put down a strike by airfield workers. A woman, Biloris Samor, fought back when beaten by the Japanese; and a man, Kiman Phymon, took a machete and went looking to avenge the execution of a close family member for stealing tobacco.[44] Fear, however, proved the more dominant reaction. Anger and insult found expression in the composition of local songs whose language and metaphors were not intelligible to most Japanese.[45] As the end neared, rumors spread that the Japanese planned to kill and perhaps consume Chuukese as a way to address the severe food shortages.[46] Worries abounded too about brutal treatment at the hands of the approaching Americans. There was little sympathy for those few American airmen whose planes were shot down during the bombing raids. On Tol, Tosiwo Nakayama remembered a blonde-haired American aviator sitting in a boat, bound, and head down.[47] The airman then began to converse with his Japanese captors while they searched his papers. The conversation sounded relaxed, almost casual, even friendly. The soldiers had to intervene with a group of Chuukese men who wanted to stone the pilot. Later, the soldiers led the pilot away; Nakayama assumed the man was being taken to his execution.

## Surrender, Repatriation, and the Immediate Postwar Period

Mori Koben had not welcomed the coming of the war.[48] He remained on Chuuk and shunned the hypernationalism that shrouded the war effort. No one could raise questions as to his loyalty, however. He assisted with preparations, and called upon his Chuukese contacts and family to provide labor in support of Chuuk's fortification. A stroke left him unable to walk and a convalescent in his home on Tol. By the summer of 1943, he was reported to be having hallucinations that foresaw Japan's defeat. By the time the American bombing had begun, his family moved a now senile Mori to his eldest son's home on Polle where he spent his last months. He died on 23 August 1945, eight days after the surrender of Japan.

The end to hostilities on Chuuk took place in late August 1945.[49] The American presence consisted of a destroyer and destroyer escort. Arrangements for the Japanese military's capitulation were negotiated on 30 August 1945 on board the destroyer USS *Stack* at anchor off the Chuuk Lagoon's southern reef. Formal surrender came on the USS *Portland* three days later on 2 September. Confident that Chuuk and its surrounding islands had been effectively neutralized, the American ships left that same day after the conclusion of the surrender ceremony. The first American inspection of Chuuk did not take place until early October with formal occupation commencing on 24 November.

Chuukese wondered about the times to come and expressed puzzlement at the way elder Japanese cried upon hearing the emperor's surrender announcement while the younger soldiers simply withdrew, relieved that the war had ended with their lives spared.[50] All surviving military and civilian personnel, including Okinawans and Koreans, were gathered on Toloas. There were roughly thirty-eight thousand in all. During the balance of 1945, American occupying forces had Japanese troops clear war debris, store supplies, and rebuild as best they could the roads and airfields. The Americans

conducted interviews and interrogations in an effort to identify the perpe-
trators of wartime atrocities against captured American forces. Evacuations
and repatriation took longer than expected because of the lack of ships and
because of other, more pressing postwar priorities elsewhere. The repatriation
of Japanese soldiers began that October and concluded the day after Christ-
mas. Civilian repatriations continued much longer and were not completed
until 27 December 1946.[51] Nakayama Masami had wanted to remain in Chuuk
and for a time that seemed possible. On 15 January 1946, however, American
naval officials decided that Japanese civilian men married to island women
also had to leave.[52]

While Chuukese felt little loss at the soldiers' departure, civilian repatriation was a very different matter.[53] The departure of husbands, relatives,
friends, employers, and neighbors constituted an intensely personal and emotional experience for many. Sometimes the sudden unexpected announcement of departures compounded the shock and sadness. Some Chuukese
had developed especially strong ties with the Okinawan civilian population.[54]
Many Okinawans reciprocated those feelings. For a time, it looked as though a
compromise had been reached; all Okinawans who had resided in Chuuk for
more than ten years were given the option of staying. In the end, however, the
American military decide to repatriate all Okinawans as well as all Japanese
and Korean nationals.[55] Similarly, strong ties had developed with islanders
brought to Chuuk from elsewhere. Eight hundred of the 1,200 Nauruans sent
to Chuuk to supplement the wartime labor force returned home; here again,
there were bonds, friendships, and shared experiences that abruptly and sadly
ended with the Nauruans' departure.

Whatever ill feelings may have existed between the principal combatants of war did not show themselves in Nakayama Masami's interaction with
American troops. The elder Nakayama's ability to speak English permitted
him a more casual and relaxed relationship with the occupation forces. Tosiwo
Nakayama remembered his father's easy banter with American soldiers on
several occasions.[56] On the day of his repatriation, Rosania and the two older
Nakayama sons saw Masami off. Tosiwo stayed behind on Tol, sick and heart-
broken he said.[57] It would be fifteen years before Tosiwo would see his father
again. That meeting would take place in Japan and be the result of Tosiwo's
personal search for his father during a trip that took him around the world
and allowed him to evade the severe restrictions on travel in and out of the
American Trust Territory at that time.

The postwar occupation brought little relief to the Lagoon area, which
had suffered more than other Caroline Islands.[58] The logistics of reconstruction on Chuuk proved the most daunting of any Micronesian islands. Toloas

lay in near total ruin as a result of the bombing. The aerial attacks destroyed breadfruit trees and taro gardens on the affected islands, though Chuukese quickly took over the sweet potato, cassava, papaya, and banana gardens abandoned by the Japanese. The bombing of the Lagoon area had adversely affected marine resources as well. Many of the mines laid by the American Navy had yet to be cleared; as a result, there was only one pass into and out of the Lagoon. Given the small size of the American occupying force, there existed far fewer opportunities for employment than during Japanese times. The shelves of surviving stores, once fully stocked with a range of goods, were now bare.

As had been the case with the Spanish and German administrations, Chuuk's newest colonizers regarded the islands as less strategically and administratively important than other parts of the Micronesian geographical area. While American largesse diminished the immediate threat of starvation, Chuuk now suffered from neglect. Language and communication problems immediately surfaced as Americans and Chuukese struggled to understand each other. There existed an acute need for interpreters that went largely unfilled. The use of Chamorros from Guam to assist in the postwar administration of the islands did not really solve the problem as they did not speak Chuukese, only English and Japanese.[59]

The occupying American forces showed themselves unable to address the problems now facing Chuuk. Land use presented itself as an immediate and critical concern for the American administration. The navy established a Land Claim Commission, and incorporated the input of local chiefs and magistrates but had little success in resolving conflicting claims, some of which predated the war and Japanese colonization.[60] The people of Chuuk had hopes and expectations that went unfulfilled. The poverty and destitution observed by the Americans resulted from war, and in no way reflected the material situation of the islands prior to war. The Chuukese looked for a return of the local economy that had existed under the Japanese, one they had not controlled but still managed to derive benefit from.[61]

The United States Commercial Company, charged with overseeing the economic recovery of the islands, urged the revival of interisland boat travel, the salvage and use of equipment left behind by the Japanese, the expansion of the postal service to include Chuukese, a drop in prices, and an increase in the availability of consumer goods.[62] Despite these recommendations, reconstruction lagged and frustration grew. Americans showed themselves unable or unwilling to assist Chuukese in the recovery of their lost postal savings and in the pursuit of war claims for lost lives and property damage. If the reconstruction of the islands called Micronesia proceeded at a generally slow pace, the rebuilding and restoration of Chuuk proved especially so.

Racial bias also evidenced itself.[63] Many military personnel regarded Chuukese as inferior and referred to them as "Negroes" or "gooks," and expressed open amazement when Chuukese showed themselves adept at learning English or operating sophisticated equipment. While Chuukese had suffered at the hands of the Japanese military during the war, American administrators were cautioned against assuming a pro-American or anti-Japanese sentiment among the population, especially on those islands left relatively undisturbed by the hostilities. There were too many prominent Chuukese families with strong familial ties to Japan whose privilege would be sorely tested if not undermined altogether by a new regime whose language was English and whose currency was the dollar.

Anthropologists working for the naval administration that replaced the occupation forces worried about the long-term effects of such racial bias on American–Micronesian relations.[64] They had good reason to worry. The Japanese presented Chuukese with very clear and exact policies on what was expected of them. They were citizens of the empire, subjects of the emperor, and were expected to conduct themselves as much like Japanese as possible. At the same time, the Japanese were themselves an island people whose values, attitudes, respect behaviors, and ways of life were not totally alien or incomprehensible to people in Chuuk. The marriages, extended familial ties, and other social relationships that developed over Japan's more than thirty years in the islands reinforced these already existing affinities. Americans, on the other hand, came across as friendly and generous but ultimately somewhat remote and with a benevolence that masked different concerns, other priorities, and a sense of superiority. Their ideas about democracy, freedom, and the rights of the individual did not resonate well with a more communal people who placed their trust in chiefs and heads of families, and who thought first of their obligations to kin and clan. When asked what his reaction would have been to Japan's victory in World War II, Tosiwo Nakayama replied that he would have had no difficulty accepting that outcome.[65]

Having a Japanese father had spared Tosiwo Nakayama the more immediate hardships of wartime Chuuk. There was, however, much less of a buffer from the conditions of postwar Chuuk. After Masami's repatriation, the family moved to Netutu on Tol where life without a husband, father, and head of household became much more difficult.[66] Clothing was scarce as Tosiwo and his siblings wore tattered shirts, torn shorts, and old flip-flops or zoris. While still on Tol, Rosania gave birth to Matsuo, the youngest of the five Nakayama brothers. There was also throughout the Chuuk Lagoon area increasing resentment and suspicion of anyone who was half Japanese. Later in 1947, with the assistance of the chief of Tol, a half brother of Susumu Aizawa's mother who owned a motorized boat or pompom, the family returned to Onoun. Tosiwo was sixteen years old at the time and to this point in his life had received no formal schooling. Life on Onoun looked to be his future; yet war and its aftermath provided a common experience for a generation not only in Chuuk, but throughout the Caroline, Mariana, and Marshall Islands. Being caught in the crossfire of war ultimately taught Nakayama and others the importance of autonomy and self-government. A woman in Palau later said it best. Unimpressed by the distinction between the United States and the United Nations, she told a member of a UN Visiting Mission team sent to evaluate the American administration of the Trust Territory: "The next time you have a war, please don't have it here."[67]

The arrival of the United States did not bring liberation or more freedom, but simply another, even more alien colonizing regime. Life was not better under the first years of American rule. For the Nakayamas and others, it lacked the structure, order, focus, and relative material comfort of the prewar years. Later in life, Nakayama was asked to comment on the presence of the U.S. Navy Seabee team that arrived in Chuuk in the 1960s with an impressive collection of heavy equipment for civic construction projects. To promote community relations, the team also brought with them a projector that they used to show old films to two or three hundred Chuukese an evening. Nakayama took the opportunity at one of these screenings to reflect publicly and critically on the past. He said:

> You know some of the older people talk about the time when the Japanese came [after World War I]. They say there was a sort of Japanese Peace Corps that came first, then military civic action teams, and finally troops. Now, they wonder about the Americans.[68]

Tosiwo Nakayama's experiences with Americans during the first two decades of their administration of the islands certainly made him wonder. He conceded that there were some competent, capable, and well-intentioned people among them. Many of these first American administrators, however, lived apart in comfortable, well-provisioned communities and had, what he called, "the wrong attitude." "If you ask me what motivated me to stay as far away from the U.S., it was people's attitude. That and the fear of the loss of land. These islands are god-given. Who are we to give them away?"[69] The overall ineptitude, indifference, and aloofness of American administrators convinced Nakayama that only Micronesians could effectively and appropriately govern their islands.[70]

# CHAPTER 3

# An Education

THE WAR AND THE YEARS IMMEDIATELY FOLLOWING had severely disrupted the lives of many. Death, destruction, displacement, and the arrival of a new colonial order took a significant toll on the generation coming of age in the 1940s. With the outbreak of war, Tosiwo Nakayama's family had lost their relatively comfortable situation amidst the largely Japanese population on Toloas. They endured the war on Tol and later returned to Rosania's home island of Onoun after Masami's repatriation to Japan. Tosiwo Nakayama now faced a future bound tightly to the immediate confines of land, sea, and family. Circumstance and personal ambition, however, combined to offer him opportunities with a new colonial administration that held very decidedly different ideas about education, government, and development. In a postwar world marked by uncertainty, anxiety, and doubt, Tosiwo seized these opportunities and eventually emerged as an arbiter and intermediary between local island worlds and the forces of modernity. Tosiwo Nakayama's education occurred in Quonset hut classrooms and as an employee of the Trust Territory government. He made the best of a limited, fledgling colonial school system that consistently struggled to reconcile American educational practices with local realities and resources. As important as anything learned in a classroom, however, was the experience, knowledge, skill set, and personal contact that he derived from his work with the district administration. His employment with the local administration in Chuuk allowed him to move about the larger district where he participated in the promotion of representative government while earning the trust and confidence of those island communities with which he came in contact.

## Elementary and Intermediate Beginnings

In 1945, President Harry S. Truman awarded the U.S. Navy administrative responsibility for the islands.[1] The United Nations provided international recognition of that fact two years later by granting the United States a strategic trusteeship over the islands. The Trusteeship Agreement charged the United States with the political, economic, educational, and social advancement of the islands while acknowledging its strategic interests. The agreement was colonialism with a slightly different face, but colonialism nonetheless. In American officials' estimation, self-government in the newly created Trust Territory of the Pacific Islands was certainly to be desired and worked for, but at a gradual pace. The greatest threat to the establishment of a new order was the premature introduction of more representative forms of government. The perceived backwardness of the people added further justification to the need for a careful, deliberate approach.

In making its case for a formal structure of military government to replace the departing occupation forces, the navy had characterized social traditions and indigenous forms of political government as primitive, feudalistic, and revolving around family, clan, and village. Island peoples were said to seldom comprehend or respond rationally to Western-style government. "All in all," wrote one naval official, "the interests of the inhabitants (and incidentally the interests of the United States) would be best served by establishing in most of these islands, a strong but benevolent government—a government paternalistic in character, but one which ruled as indirectly as possible (i.e., one which made minimum interference with local family and organization and custom)."[2] This was "government from a distance" in both a real and metaphoric sense. Vast cultural differences and thousands of miles separated the islands from those who now administered them.

From its headquarters in Honolulu, the Commander-in-Charge of the Pacific Operations Area (CINCPOA) now held responsibility for the administration of the region. Local military governments were established for each of the major islands and were headed by a commanding officer; an executive officer and a group of civilian administrators completed the administrative staff. These civilian administrators were actually junior naval officers fresh from their training in military government at Stanford University's School of Naval Administration (SONA); they headed smaller individual offices or departments responsible for personnel matters, public health, public safety, legal affairs, field operations, economics, public works, and education. The title of these men as civil administrators, along with their civilian style of dress, was intended to blunt the more martial features of military government in the islands and thus deflect some of the criticism of naval government emanating from the Department of State and other government agencies in Washington, D.C. The navy concentrated its limited resources on governance, the reconstruction of islands' infrastructure, and the restoration of local economies. Education was less of a priority, though it proved the area that affected most immediately the life of Tosiwo Nakayama.

Soon after the end of hostilities, the navy established military day schools to help local laborers master the rudimentary English they needed to function effectively on different construction and clearing projects. Micronesians had found utility and worth in the Japanese school system, limited and discriminating though it was. According to Hezel, the navy did accede to the request of island communities for schools, but on the condition that local communities build, staff, and cover the salaries of teachers.[3] The idea as articulated by Deputy High Commissioner Rear Admiral Carleton Wright was to promote schools staffed by native teachers that offered education not in an alien culture, but through a curriculum that was locally appropriate and useful. Distance dictated the parameters of the education effort.[4] The navy donated construction supplies for the building of schools in the district centers, and left the outlying villages and outer islands to make do as best they could. In short, the responsibility for establishing a school system fell largely to the people.

Local teachers were recruited and their salaries paid by the communities in which they taught. A tax on copra sales provided modest and inconsistent compensation for island teachers; often, however, salaries went unpaid for long periods of time because of fluctuation in the international price of copra and the difficulty of sustaining the hard, regular physical labor required for its production. The quality of these earliest local schools left much to be desired as there were few trained teachers and little in the way of teaching materials. The navy's commitment to instruction in local island languages ignored the fact that the limited number of textbooks being supplied were in English, and referenced distinctly American history, geography, music, and cultural practices and values. Snow, sleigh rides, Thanksgiving, and John Phillip Sousa marches contributed to the core of a curriculum that had little relevance to Pacific Island settings. It all made for some very strange and peculiar classroom sessions. The ultimate purpose behind this educational approach was not at all subtle. The American naval administration hoped that this imposition of odd assorted texts and the values they embodied would provide a basic

education, while inculcating in island peoples a respect and loyalty for the
United States. By 1947, 152 elementary schools had been opened throughout
the Caroline, Mariana, and Marshall Islands. Avowals of importance and commitment aside, the shortcomings of such an education system showed themselves almost immediately.[5] Makeshift buildings, irrelevant, hand-me-down
texts, inexperienced teachers, unchallenged assumptions about the nature of
education, inadequate funding, and the failure to truly engage local communities in the development of an educational system all conspired to leave Micronesian schools in a disappointing state.

The problems with the schools became quickly and painfully obvious.
Administrators turned to teacher training programs as a way to bring about
change. These programs also offered intensive instruction in English. By 1948,
the teacher training programs formed the core curriculum for intermediate
schools located in the district centers and staffed by American expatriates.
Promising students from the elementary schools were chosen for an additional
two years of schooling at these intermediate schools with the expectation that
they would return to their home communities to teach. The very best students
from these intermediate schools were often sent to Guam where they attended
a teacher training facility established in early 1947 and known as the Marianas
Area Teacher Training School. Despite the hurried efforts to produce local
teachers with a basic proficiency in English, the training programs struggled
to supply capable instructors. These then were the general contours of the educational environment that Tosiwo Nakayama encountered. He would have to
make the best of a very uneven situation.

The end of the war and the repatriation of their father to Japan led the
Nakayamas back to Namonuito by 1947. Later in that same year, a field trip
ship stopped at the atoll. On board were naval administrators, education officers, and district leaders including Hachi Moses, the atoll chief for Chuuk
District. One of the purposes of the visit was to recruit students for the intermediate school on Weno. The situation was a far cry from an earlier Japanese
recruitment visit to Namonuito where students were forcibly removed from
their mothers' arms for school on Weno.[6] Tosiwo Nakayama was about sixteen years old at the time. With no formal schooling to this point in his life
and unable by his own admission to even write his name, he volunteered to
go.[7] He stood up at a community gathering on Onoun with the visiting officials and announced that he wanted very much to attend school on Weno. His
public declaration surprised the visitors who, after some deliberation among
themselves, agreed to accept him. His selection was not all that surprising; the
young Nakayama was clearly bright and eager, and was the nephew of Raatior,
the senior chief and designated magistrate for Onoun. Nakayama took a pig

with him to Weno as his "money" and sold it to cover his living expenses. His life was about to change in profound ways.

Truk Intermediate School enrolled roughly sixty students at the time.[8] It was situated on a hill overlooking the Lagoon in the Nantaku section of Weno where the main Japanese administration building had once stood. Students were generally grouped in dormitories by gender and according to their home islands. With few students enrolled from the northern and western islands, Nakayama lived in a dormitory with male students from the Mortlocks, an arrangement with which he was quite comfortable given his earlier time and familiarity with the area. Raymond Setik, a friend from Nakayama's Mortlock days and later a key congressional colleague and political ally, attended the intermediate school and resided in the same dormitory. The two renewed their acquaintance and became strong friends. Nakayama remembered the food as being terrible; the gardens left over from Japanese times provided the beans that, with bananas, were a staple of the students' diet. Sometimes, supplies ran out and there was no food at all. As a result, Nakayama and the other students welcomed the later introduction of canned food and other rationed goods provided by the naval administration.

Nakayama showed himself to be diligent, frugal, and adaptable. In an effort to save money, he collected spilled oil from the nearby power plant in a cut-off soda can and burned it as his nightlight. While other students were asleep, Nakayama studied past the school's curfew amidst the light and smoke of his makeshift lamp. The other students left him alone and did not bother him because, by his own account, he was so serious. Rivalries existed among students from the different islands. Nakayama recalled one fight between students from Uman and the western islands. The students fought with sticks and threw rocks at each other's dormitories. People got hurt. Nakayama had no interest in fighting and avoided it as much as possible. As required, Nakayama confined himself to the school's campus during weekdays. On Sundays, he visited Mechitiw, where people from Namonuito lived on Weno.

Nakayama spent a year at the intermediate school where he took basic courses in English conversation, reading and writing, as well as mathematics, geography, and social studies. He was among the youngest students at the school, as recruitment and admission operated on the assumption that older students could better handle the demands of school and being away from home. The American teachers at the intermediate school found it difficult at times to control the older students, however. Nakayama remembered his teachers as being somewhat intimidated, even fearful of the older, physically larger students. Despite this challenging classroom environment, he learned quickly and did especially well in English. Bored with his basic English language conversation class, he and a friend asked to be moved to a more advanced group. His teacher lent a sympathetic ear to Nakayama's request and sent him to the instructor of the more advanced class who gave him an impromptu placement examination. He was asked to follow the verbal directions provided and answer the questions asked. The test started off easily enough with commands and queries that were familiar. "Please stand up." "What are you doing?" "I'm standing up." "Please sit down." "What are you doing?" "I'm sitting down." "Please walk to the door." "What are you doing?" "I'm walking to the door." Then, the teacher asked Nakayama to turn around. He didn't understand the words, could not respond to the direction, and was thus unable to answer the follow-up question. In his own words, he failed "turning around," and was returned to the basic level English conversation class with his friend who had also failed the placement test.

The incident amounted to a very minor setback and evidenced more the determination with which the young Nakayama approached his studies. He asked questions of teachers and fellow students, and soon made up the initial skills gap that had separated him from the other students. His older classmates taught him how to do basic mathematical functions like addition, subtraction, division, and multiplication; he was soon better at mathematics than his student teachers. There were some in his classes who had received teacher training on Guam. Nakayama surpassed these students as well. He was also good at spelling, and recalled that he was the only student in his class able to spell the word "straight" when asked. Nakayama described himself as on a mission to learn so that he could return to Onoun, teach his people, and thus fulfill the promise he had made to Raatior in securing the chief's endorsement to study at Truk Intermediate School. Reflecting back on his early years, Nakayama endorsed an educational system that he himself had not experienced.[9] He underscored the intrinsic link between education and environment, and stressed the importance of an island-centered curriculum, community support, the employment of well-trained Micronesian teachers, and the exclusive use of the vernacular at the early elementary level. It had not been this way for him, but he wished it had.

Nakayama's performance at intermediate school caught the attention of Napoleon DeFang, a close family friend from the Mortlocks who now worked in the district education office, and Thomas Gladwin, an anthropologist with the naval administration.[10] Gladwin had arrived in Chuuk earlier in 1948 to work as a researcher with the Coordinated Investigation of Micronesian Anthropology (CIMA) project and later became the political affairs and economic officer for the district administration.[11] In all likelihood, it was DeFang who recommended Nakayama to Gladwin. The two went to Truk Intermediate School to recruit Nakayama to work in the Island Affairs office of the district administration under Gladwin's immediate supervision. Nakayama was called out of class to meet with the two. During their brief conversation, the anthropologist apparently recognized in the intermediate school student a great deal of promise. Nakayama was invited to leave school and work in the Island Affairs office for a monthly salary of $30.00. For some reason, Nakayama was more intrigued by the prospect of learning how to type. He thought that typing was a very useful skill and admired those who had proficiency with the typewriter. Nakayama informed the two that he could not accept their offer without the permission of his chief. DeFang told Nakayama that he and Gladwin had already communicated with Raatior and secured his permission. So in 1948 Nakayama decided to leave Truk Intermediate School after one year to work for Gladwin. However difficult he found adjustment to his new job, Nakayama did not lack for friends. With him in the Island Affairs section was Soukichy Fritz from the Mortlocks who would rise to be a future chief justice of the Chuuk State Supreme Court. Raymond Setik held a similar position in the nearby Finance section of the district government.

Nakayama's responsibilities required him at times to travel with Gladwin to the outer islands of the district.[12] On one occasion, he accompanied Gladwin on a field trip ship to the western islands that stopped en route at Namonuito. There, Gladwin ordered Nakayama to remain on ship while he went ashore and sought permission to resettle people from Tamatam in Pollap Atoll. Tamatam had been severely damaged by a series of natural disasters and was no longer able to sustain its population. The people of Namonuito balked at the proposition given their troubled history with Tamatam that included an unwanted group of settlers removed earlier in the century by the Belgian trader Dominique Etscheit in return for land and planting rights. Gladwin countered by reminding them that he had hired one of their own as an assistant; they needed, he argued, to reciprocate in good faith. Given the invocation of his nephew's name, Aluis, another of Nakayama's uncles and now the chief magistrate for the atoll, consented. The whole affair, however, left Nakayama feeling quite manipulated. His relationship with Gladwin became strained and remained so over the next two decades. Gladwin later showed himself to be an outspoken critic of the American administration and a strong advocate of independence for Chuuk and the rest of the Trust Territory. These were positions that Nakayama would come to share. Despite the affinity of their politics and the working relationship that helped inform it, Nakayama disliked the anthropologist's loud, aggressive, confrontational style. He was not alone in his feelings; Gladwin's fellow anthropologists also found him difficult. Unhappy with Gladwin, Nakayama resigned his job in 1951 to study navigation with

Raatior. He reached Onoun only to learn that his uncle had recently passed away. There would be no training in the art of navigation; there would, however, be two more years of formal schooling, this time at the Pacific Islands Central School on Weno.

## PICS

The Pacific Islands Central School (PICS) on Weno evolved from the U.S. Navy's earlier focus on teacher training.[13] The Pacific Islands Teacher Training School (PITTS), the successor to the Marianas Teacher Training School on Guam, moved to Chuuk in 1948 and soon expanded to a three-year program. In 1951, PITTS became a two-year high school with a new name—the Pacific Islands Central School. With its enrollment drawn from the entire Trust Territory, PICS' main purpose remained teacher training for the elementary schools. In 1956, PICS was transformed once again, this time into a three-year senior high school. Three years later, it was relocated to Pohnpei. Its graduates often received scholarships to study at the University of Hawai'i at Mānoa or the new Guam Territorial College that later became the University of Guam. While problems plagued the development of quality education in the Trust Territory, PICS did produce a group of graduates, mostly men, who assumed positions of leadership in the Trust Territory government, and later among the four separate governmental entities to emerge from that territorial grouping. Tosiwo Nakayama was one of them. A reporter for the *New York Times* wrote in 1959 of the importance of PICS: "If Micronesia ever becomes one nation, the cradle of it will have been a group of old U.S. Navy Quonsets, now falling apart, in a green valley on Moen [Weno] island in Truk."[14]

In 1951, the same year that administrative authority for the islands passed from the navy to the U.S. Department of the Interior, Nakayama returned to Weno, this time to attend PICS.[15] He did so at Napoleon DeFang's urging. DeFang was now the superintendent for elementary schools in Chuuk, and his support carried considerable weight. There were also the strong familial ties between Nakayama and DeFang that resulted from the fact that their mothers were promised sisters; this meant that they, in turn, were like brothers. Nakayama began attending classes immediately but soon discovered that his name did not appear on any of the class lists or the school register. Nakayama asked Cy Pickerill, the principal of the school, why his name had been omitted. Her investigation showed that only one slot had been allotted in the school to a student from Namonuito and that student was Kisao Bob. She recommended that Nakayama speak to the other student and work out the situation. He did just that. Perhaps feeling lonely, uncomfortable with his new environment,

**Fig. 3.1.** The Pacific Islands Central School (PICS), Weno, Chuuk, 1955 (Trust Territory Photo Archives, Pacific Collection, Hamilton Library, University of Hawaiʻi, Mānoa).

and unsure of his abilities, Kisao Bob quickly agreed to vacate his assigned place in favor of Nakayama.

To support himself, Nakayama took a number of on-campus jobs. One of his first regular jobs was to clean the girls' lavatory.[16] The assignment initially confused him as his still developing grasp of English led him to believe that he had been assigned to the girls' laboratory. He was quite startled when people at the school clarified his task as it put him in a very culturally and socially embarrassing situation given the norms that governed gender roles and the interaction between males and females in Chuuk. Nakayama, however, did not complain or avoid the work; though teased by other male students, he simply replied that he was doing his job. Later one of his jobs at PICS involved clerking at the student store where he sold school supplies, small food items, and personal goods to students from behind the store's main counter. Nakayama didn't understand at first what the female students meant by Kotex. He soon learned and was comfortable enough filling their requests from the store shelves. They wrapped or otherwise hid their purchase from others before returning to their dormitory, but did not seem at all awkward or uncomfortable with Nakayama as their sales clerk, at least as he remembered it.

Nakayama would also prove to be a loyal friend.[17] He befriended a
Saipanese girl whose boyfriend at PICS hailed from the Marshall Islands.
The constant companionship and public displays of affection between the
Chamorro girl and the Marshallese boy bothered school officials. The PICS
principal, Cy Pickerill, asked Nakayama if he were aware of the relationship.
He replied that he had seen them together and knew of their feelings for one
another but expressed no disapproval or condemnation. Pickerill used the
conversation with Nakayama to confront the couple and reprimand the two
for their behavior. When he learned of Pickerill's action, Nakayama felt his
confidence betrayed and refused to confirm his understanding or knowledge
of the relationship at a disciplinary meeting with all parties concerned. He
felt that Pickerill had abused the privilege of their private conversation. As a
result of his personal protest, sanctions against the couple were cancelled and
an apology issued.

By all accounts, Nakayama flourished at PICS. Despite his limited educational background, he excelled in his classes and earned the praise of his teachers, many of whom regarded Nakayama as their favorite student.[18] His favorite
subject was social studies. His teachers often singled out his schoolwork for
praise in the hope that it might inspire others. While at PICS, he made a con-
scious decision not to room with other Chuukese students but to live in the
Pohnpeian dormitory.[19] He thought the Chuukese were not as committed to
their studies as they should be. He called them "rough" in the way they handled
things. He also disliked their penchant for getting into fights, especially with
students from Palau. It was rarely a fair fight as the Chuukese combatants often
received reinforcement from their juniors at the nearby intermediate school.

Nakayama later took other jobs that required more responsibility and
skills than those he had needed in his initial student employment cleaning
lavatories and clerking at the student store. At one point, he filled in for the
dean of students who was delayed in his return to Weno from a trip to the
Mortlocks. Nakayama graduated at or near the top of his teacher training class
of thirty-three students in 1953.[20] His completion of the two-year program of
study at PICS had prepared him for a career as an elementary schoolteacher
that never eventuated. Recruitment and retention proved key issues in the
staffing of local schools. It quickly became obvious that many graduates of the
intermediate schools were not interested in becoming teachers. The pay was
comparatively poor, and government jobs were more attractive in terms of the
nature of the work and the prospects for future advancement. Like many other
early graduates of PICS, Nakayama, despite the training he received, never
took up a career in the classroom because of the alternatives open to him.

After completing study at PICS, Nakayama returned in 1953 to the

**Fig. 3.2.** A young Tosiwo Nakayama, 1951 (Micronesian Seminar).

Island Affairs office where he now worked under another anthropologist, Frank Mahoney. He was hired to be more than just a clerk. As district tax collector, Nakayama had responsibility for the collection of over $25,000 in import and other taxes. He supervised the distribution of these funds as salaries to elementary schoolteachers and for other community purposes.[21] He did so responsibly and, in the process, earned a reputation for honesty. Nakayama's ability to navigate effectively the cultural differences that he encountered in his job was no mean feat. Americans and Chuukese had very different understandings of work. The success of any undertaking in the islands necessitated careful attention to social relationships. An individual needed to understand his or her place and show proper respect and deference to one's elders. Hierarchies among the different clans and islands of what was now Chuuk District necessitated recognition and accommodation. All of this required patience, forbearance, and time, an approach very much at odds with Americans' emphasis on efficiency, productivity, and getting any job done as quickly and as cost-effectively as possible. Nakayama carried out his assignments in ways that certainly impressed his supervisors. Russ Curtis, the head of the Truk District Island Affairs office, gave him high marks for his punctuality, dependability, initiative, quality of work, supervisory ability, and care of equipment.[22]

Nakayama's responsibilities also included assisting in the establishment of municipal governments and courts throughout the district, and in translating documents considered critical to these projects from English into Chuukese. Nakayama and other staff members of the Island Affairs office were assigned the task of translating the newly compiled Trust Territory Law Code into Chuukese. It proved an extremely arduous and tedious task that none of the staff enjoyed. The result of their efforts was a collection of loose, single-spaced, mimeographed sheets of legal-sized paper that must have seemed overwhelming to municipal judges and other officials struggling to grasp the complexities of a foreign legal system.[23] Still, there was now a *puken annuk* or judge's manual. The patience and persistence that Nakayama displayed in the completion of this assignment were part of the repertoire of skills that impressed people on both sides of the cultural divide.

Nakayama ended his second term with the Island Affairs section in 1955 when he left to attend the University of Hawai'i at Mānoa. Beginning in 1948, the Trust Territory government had provided a limited number of annual scholarships for study in Hawai'i and Guam.[24] Recipients were selected through a competitive process at the district level. A college degree was not the main objective as funding support was usually limited to two years. The purpose of the scholarships was to provide advanced education and training for exceptionally promising students who were then expected to use their skills for the betterment of their islands, often through employment with the Trust Territory government. Scholarships were awarded to young men and women but with a decided preference for the former, a fact that reflected the gender privileging of both American and Micronesian societies. The colonially reinforcing features of these scholarships notwithstanding, students and their families saw them first and foremost as an opportunity.

## Hawai'i

The Truk District government had only one scholarship to award for study abroad in 1955. A five-member selection committee was charged with deciding among the pool of applicants that included Napoleon DeFang, Susumu Aizawa, and Sasauo Haruo, Tosiwo Nakayama's future brother-in-law. Nakayama was not the first choice of the committee.[25] In the end, however, he received the committee's endorsement and the scholarship to study at the University of Hawai'i at Mānoa. Nakayama was but one of many Micronesians studying at the university in this period. The roster of names reads like a "Who's Who" of future Micronesian leaders. Their ranks included Alfonso Oiterong, Thomas Remengesau, David Ramarui, Roman Tmetuchl, Daiziro and Kuniwo Nakamura, and Lazarus Salii of Palau; Petrus Tun and John Mangefel from

Yap; Carmen Bigler, John and Dwight Heine, Oscar DeBrum, Ekpap Silk, and Amata Kabua of the Marshalls; Olympia Borja from the Marianas; Nick Bossy, Gideon Doone, and Soukichy Fritz from Chuuk; and Kumiko Alonzo, Leo Falcam, Bethwel Henry, and Bailey Olter from Pohnpei.

Daiziro Nakamura, who in the mid- to late 1970s headed the Trust Territory government's Education for Self-Government Program and later served as the administration's archivist before returning to Palau from Saipan in 1981, saw the students' experiences at the University of Hawai'i as being absolutely pivotal to the future of the islands and the governments that eventually emerged from the Trust Territory umbrella.[26] Had there been no Hawai'i experience, things would have turned out much differently for this generation of leaders and the island nations they helped create. Hawai'i provided another link, a more constructive one, to a generation that shared the experience of war. The plight of Native Hawaiians struck the students, and also heavily informed their future aspirations for their home islands. The opulence of Waikīkī contrasted sharply for these students with the way most Native Hawaiians and local people lived. While they were still young and their political ideas were just beginning to take shape, many recognized the necessity of avoiding the dispossession that had become so clearly a fact of life for the Hawaiians they encountered. Whether or not they recognized themselves as Micronesians remains an open question; they were, however, very much aware of their shared experiences and common interests.

In his letter of application, Nakayama had expressed a strong desire to study in Hawai'i rather than Guam.[27] Moreover, he preferred a program of general courses based at the Mānoa campus of the university rather than enrollment in the agricultural training program at Lahainaluna School on Maui. His preferences were honored as his leadership abilities, social skills, and keen intelligence suggested a career in administration rather than agriculture. Nakayama found the transition to life in Hawai'i quite difficult at first. To this point in his life, he had three years of formal schooling—one at the Truk Intermediate School and two at PICS. His six years of work experience with the Chuuk District government had certainly developed skills, but study at an American university was a formidable, intimidating, even unsettling academic challenge for someone who had never before left his home islands. Recognizing his limited educational background and his generally poor performance on the California Achievement Tests he took soon after arriving, educational officials in Hawai'i assigned Nakayama to classes at the nearby and affiliated University High School.

Nakayama did take an early morning speech class on the university campus, but spent the rest of the day at the high school taking courses in general education, creative writing, and journalism. He found the different kinds of writing required by these courses confusing, and comprehended by his own estimate about 50 to 60 percent of what was said in his classes. For his creative writing class, Nakayama wrote a short essay dated 27 September 1955:

> My name is Tosiwo Nakayama, born 23 November 1931. At the age of twenty, I attended Pacific Islands Central School of the Caroline Islands. Graduated in 1952, I got a job as an office clerk. At the same time, I forced myself to translate for people who cannot speak English whenever they wish to talk to American officers. Now that I am in Honolulu to go to school on a scholarship I would like to devote much time learning to speak good English along with other things. I am taking most of my classes at University High School and this one course in the U. of Hawaii. I am three weeks old on this island. (I have been in Hawaii three weeks).[28]

Nakayama struggled with his courses. He had little interest in reading because of the pain and discomfort it caused his eyes; fifteen minutes at a time were all he could manage. He disliked subjects that were too abstract, and preferred courses that were of more immediate practical value. Memorization was also difficult for him. He felt generally lost, and had a hard time being prompt for his first University High School course because of the tight scheduling and the time it took him to walk between campuses. He diagnosed his early academic difficulties as resulting from his not knowing how to study. A pair of glasses and the willingness of his creative writing teacher Ms. Sue Oda to tutor him helped, but his academic difficulties continued into the new year. His inability to keep up with the reading requirements of a world history course led his advisors to fear he would develop a reading block. He persevered, however. The quality of his writing improved and he found it easier to compose longer assignments. He received Cs and Bs in most of his courses. By the end of the 1955–1956 academic year, he was able to express interesting ideas in compelling stories; one of his supervisors wrote that given all of the difficulties he had encountered his first year, his ability to do acceptable work was quite an achievement.

University officials charged with the supervision of Micronesian students thought that adjustment to Hawai'i would be facilitated by placement with local families. Nakayama lived his first year with Albert Tester, his wife, and their two children on nearby McKinley Street.[29] A zoologist by training, Tester had taken leave of his job at the University of Hawai'i to head the fisheries section of the Trust Territory's Department of Resources and Development.[30] The Testers' experience in the islands and their university affiliation made them an ideal host family. By 1955, Tester had returned to the university where he was in the process of compiling an impressive research record on tuna and on shark sensory systems. Nakayama had his own room, and usually took morning and evening meals with the Testers. He found the family environment supportive and comfortable, though lonely. He left the Tester home at the end of his first year and took up residence with other Micronesian students at the Atherton YMCA on University Avenue directly across from the Mānoa campus; the building came to be known unofficially in those days as "Micronesian House."

Once past his first year difficulties, Nakayama engaged more actively with his surroundings. He took all of his courses on the university campus now. His instructors noted a marked increase in his self-confidence and his verbal communication skills. School records describe Nakayama in his second year as a "very mature, quiet boy" who demonstrated an extraordinary capacity for leadership that was evident to all.[31] This leadership ability was all the more remarkable given Nakayama's age as most Chuukese males in their early twenties were still considered adolescents by their elders. A. R. King, the educational administrator in Chuuk, had written an earlier letter of support in which Nakayama was "giving every evidence of being well-adjusted and happy. His progress is excellent in every sphere."[32] King characterized Nakayama as reliable and possessed of a fine intellectual curiosity and honesty. "He is very well liked by everyone and his group work, whether he is a leader or follower, is always of the highest caliber. He has many friends from all districts."

Nakayama joined Ka Hui Kokua, the university youth chapter of the American Red Cross, and took a more active role in the Micronesian club, serving as its vice president for the 1956–1957 academic year. His dry sense of humor showed itself in these college organizations. At one club meeting, Thomas Remengesau, a future president of the Republic of Palau, complained at length about the failure of some members to pay their club dues. Nakayama became somewhat irritated at Remengesau's persistence and the long discussion that ensued. Remengesau then asked, "Why have dues, if you don't pay? What does the treasurer do when some don't pay?" Nakayama replied, "She weeps."[33] The response evoked a great deal of laughter that ended the discussion and defused the tension that was developing within the group. Like so many others, Remengesau would later express admiration for Nakayama's social skills and his ability to function effectively within a group.

Nakayama interceded a second time when the issue of an increase in club dues arose again. Marion Saunders, the advisor to the club who worked in the university's international student office, announced that the club would need to increase its dues to cover the costs of baseball equipment for its team. Nakayama was not present at the meeting during which Saunders made her suggestion; he later recommended the club schedule games with military teams who could be expected to bring the necessary bats, balls, gloves, and catcher's equipment.[34] Nakayama also suggested that Saunders contact local military personnel who had lived, worked, or fought in what was now the Trust Territory of the Pacific Islands. Saunders followed up on Nakayama's advice and ended up securing donations of old or surplus sports equipment for the Micronesian students club. This would by no means be the last time that Nakayama would ask for and receive assistance from a United States governmental or military agency.

Nakayama was able to continue for a third year as extra funds became available when Napoleon DeFang, the recipient of a Chuuk District scholarship for the years 1956–1958, decided to return to Chuuk from Guam early rather than complete his second year of study.[35] Nakayama, along with other Micronesian students, continued to take English language courses with instructors such as the noted linguist Samuel Elbert. They also took classes in political science from Profs. Richard Kosaki and Norman Meller, and in anthropology from Leonard Mason.[36] All four of these educators had direct personal and professional connections to the islands. Leonard Mason, for example, had carried out applied research in the Marshalls through the CIMA project in the late 1940s and early 1950s; he had also played a pivotal role in the resettlement of the Bikini islanders following their displacement as a result of American nuclear testing in 1952. Meller had worked as a naval field officer on Saipan in the immediate postwar period and would go on to serve as a legal consultant in the establishment of the Congress of Micronesia in 1965 and the convening of the Micronesian Constitutional Convention a decade later; these were events and institutions with which Nakayama would be intimately involved.

Taking courses from faculty who had experience in the region made a difference. Nakayama found Kosaki to be a firm, but effective and compassionate teacher. He appreciated the extra time that Kosaki allowed his Micronesian students to complete their in-class examinations. Mason struck Nakayama and others as particularly demanding and tough, but also fair and, when necessary, compassionate. He had been out drinking the night before one of Mason's exams, and was quite hungover when he took the test. Nakayama believed Mason was aware of his hangover because he allowed him to leave the examination room several times to drink water from a nearby fountain.

Nakayama found these higher-level courses to be of limited practical value. He took them more to satisfy academic requirements than for their relevance to Micronesia. He had little interest in accounting courses and found himself constantly behind in his readings for a government course. One of his supervisors found it amazing that Nakayama still got a grade of D for that latter course despite being so far behind in his reading.[37] He did, however, enjoy the company and camaraderie of his fellow students. Nakayama found Lazarus Salii to be particularly impressive in the classroom. For Mason's anthropology class, Salii sometimes borrowed Nakayama's textbook the night before an examination, read the assigned chapters for the first time, and scored higher than anybody else on the next day's examination. On one occasion, Nakayama felt sure that he had outperformed Salii on an exam because the Palauan had finished so quickly and turned in his paper to the instructor without double-checking his answers. When the exams were returned and the two compared results, Salii had again bested Nakayama. All Nakayama could say to Salii was "Oh, you're very good."[38]

Tosiwo Nakayama and Lazarus Salii became good friends. They and other Trust Territory students in Hawai'i frequented places like the Kuhio Grill and Charley's Tavern in Mō'ili'ili where they drank beers, conversed about a host of topics, played pool, and sometimes ate. The strong friendship that developed between the two would be tested during the 1975 Micronesian Constitutional Convention on Saipan. Salii's strong opinions, his impatience, and his changing views on Micronesian unity sorely tested Nakayama's efforts to see to completion a draft constitution for a united Micronesia. Still, the two remained friends. Years later, Nakayama refused to believe that his friend, the first president of the Republic of Palau, had taken his own life; he thought Salii was assassinated by individuals acting in behalf of the United States government.[39]

The University of Hawai'i was much more of an intimate, private college than the larger, research-driven, and politically compromised university it would later become.[40] Its physical plant and student enrollment were considerably smaller then. Many faculty members lived on or near campus, and there was a closer bond between students and teachers. Nakayama was not married during his first period of study in Hawai'i and did not return home during his three years there. There were sometimes picnics in Nanakuli along the Leeward Coast of O'ahu with the family of a young Hawaiian woman who had befriended many of the Micronesian students and who was known to them as "Baby." Nonetheless, life was not easy for these island students living now on another Pacific island that had been radically transformed by its annexation to the United States. The pace of urban life was much faster; the physical environment much different, the food initially strange, and the demands of school heavy. Loneliness was a problem for Nakayama as was the unwanted attention and affection of a local private schoolteacher. Nakayama sometimes took refuge in beer and in long bus rides around the island of Oʻahu. He was arrested once in 1957 for public intoxication and given a suspended sentence.[41] Those students who took short visits to Oʻahu's neighbor islands found environments that were more comfortable and familiar. Students on Oʻahu had to adjust to a very different way of life and to develop study habits that allowed them to keep up with their academic requirements. Not all could or did. The stipend provided by their Trust Territory scholarships often proved inadequate; many students had to seek part-time employment to cover their living costs.[42] Nakayama, for a time, worked as a dishwasher at a restaurant near the university.

Nakayama did well enough in his second- and third-year classes, although by his own admission he did not work very hard. He did show himself to be conscientious and courteous. He made it a point to attend classes; notify his instructors of the reason for any absence; and make up missed assignments as promptly as he could. He never claimed to have mastered English; the high level of competency he did develop simply reflected his recognition of the need to learn the dominant language of power and administration in the Trust Territory at that time. Nakayama never received a degree from the University of Hawaiʻi, although he did return in 1967 for two years of additional study sponsored by the East-West Center, an institution for cross-cultural learning and exchange created by American president Lyndon Johnson located right across from the university campus on what became East-West Road. By this time, Nakayama was serving as a member of the Congress of Micronesia Senate and dealing with issues of governance and nation building in an environment far more contentious and complex than a university campus. The respite from his congressional duties was a welcome one. While busier and more burdened that he had ever been, Nakayama did not change his demeanor or his way of dealing with people. Victorio Uherbelau, a Palauan student majoring in English literature at Mānoa then, remembered Nakayama as being very relaxed, unassuming, kind, and anything but a politician consumed with his own status and importance.[43]

## Government 101

Government employment complemented Nakayama's limited formal education. He learned about government and administration through the doing of them. Nakayama was deeply involved in local government, first facilitating and then directing its development. Both before and after his time at PICS, Nakayama had worked in the Island Affairs office of the Chuuk District administration. These early work experiences, coupled with later and higher positions of responsibility in the district administration, provided him with an immediate, practical, and hands-on education in the affairs of government. He traveled widely throughout the district, meeting and dealing with a variety of people and their concerns. The district became another classroom; the day-to-day flow of administrative tasks and responsibilities constituted his course of study. Nakayama served as both translator and mediator. He stood between a dominant system of government seeking to remake the islands and their people, and a mix of local, diverse, and sometimes divided island and atoll populations. It was no easy task.

Americans brought their sense of government with them. Governing authority was centralized in the high commissioner's office, located first in Honolulu during navy times and later on Guam with the 1951 transfer of administrative authority from the navy to the United States Department of the Interior. Department heads acted with the high commissioner's cognizance in their respective fields of jurisdiction. The distance that separated headquarters on Guam from what ultimately became the six administrative districts of the Marshalls, Northern Marianas, Palau, Pohnpei, Chuuk, and Yap exacerbated the already formidable task of administering a world of islands spread over a vast expanse of ocean that approximated the continental United States in area. District administrators found most of their time taken up with local matters that included land issues, the development of infrastructure, and the general establishment of an orderly governmental presence. Poor communication and the absence of a regular and dependable transportation system that could link the islands with Trust Territory headquarters exacerbated the administrative problems.

Committed by the terms of the 1947 UN Trusteeship Agreement, American naval administrators sought to use what they understood as traditional government as a vehicle for the nurturing of more representative self-government.[44] Deputy High Commissioner Admiral Leon Fiske had cautioned during navy times that self-government did not necessarily mean democracy.[45] Americans simply assumed that government in the islands would gradually come to reflect the structure and principles of their own system. In their zeal, administrators accepted as traditional many of the political configurations they encountered upon entering the islands. The effects of three centuries of contact and colonial rule on island structures of government did not factor into the navy's assessment. Local realities tested colonial principles. Societies still governed or influenced by chiefs proved impediments to the development of more representative forms of government as the navy presented them. Officials at the district level encouraged islanders to speak their minds and later expressed frustration with what they understood to be indecision, silent acquiescence, or mindless deference. These administrators came to see distance, the lack of a shared language, the inability of different island people to recognize common interests, and the reluctance to modernize politically as severely limiting the possibilities for a more representative form of government.

There soon emerged the belief that self-government would have to develop incrementally and from a more fundamental level of social organization. The decision was made to create a uniform system of self-government beginning at the municipal level. Depending on variable factors that included size, population, and location, whole islands, atolls, or sections thereof were designated as individual municipalities. Traditional chiefly systems were to function along a parallel track for the time being. The selection of magistrates for the different municipalities could be through election, the assumption of the position by ruling chiefs, or by the navy's appointment of individuals in consultation with local chiefs and elders. With the exception of Palau and Kosrae, chiefs filled the newly created municipal posts in the first Territory-wide elections held in 1947. Municipalities then were seen as the first and necessary building blocks for a new form of self-government. Representatives of the United States indicated to the UN Trusteeship Council in 1949 that their plan was to develop self-government at the municipal level as preface to the development of more district-wide legislatures.

Self-government at the municipal level was based on two principles: that there be a minimal number of officials, and that the authority and duties of the municipalities be simply but precisely defined. To those ends, each municipality designated two officers: an executive head or chief magistrate, and a treasurer. A community court judge could be appointed, but frequently the chief magistrate filled that function as well. A council of elders often served as an advisory group to the chief magistrate. Once established, the municipalities had the responsibility of carrying out the enforcement of territorial and district laws; they were empowered to make local rules as well as levy, collect, and expend local taxes, compile vital statistics, and keep records on matters of municipal finance. That was the theory anyway.

In Chuuk, the district administration created the Truk Atoll Council, a body of chief magistrates from the Lagoon area.[46] An earlier attempt to create a separate council for the outlying islands and atolls had failed as magistrates from those areas could not agree upon an agenda, a set of common goals, or a presiding officer. The Truk Atoll Council met monthly with the district administrator for sessions that varied from a couple of hours to all day. Discussions were conducted in Chuukese with minutes kept in both Chuukese and English. The members of the council were the chief magistrates of the fifteen Lagoon islands. In October 1952, a gathering of all magistrates was held on Weno with the idea of organizing a District Council of Magistrates. By 1954, that body had become the Truk District Council of Magistrates and was composed of the chief magistrates from the twenty-two outlying islands and atolls as well as the Lagoon group.[47] From the District Council of Magistrates there emerged a five-member Permanent Advisory Council whose principal function was to liaise with the district administration on the establishment of a district-wide legislature. The meetings of the council soon became weeklong affairs. Their agendas expanded to include an array of local administrative issues ranging from taxes, elections, and the sale and consumption of alcohol, to committee reports on education, health, land, and agricultural and fisheries development.

As noted earlier, Tosiwo Nakayama had left Truk Intermediate School after one year to work for the district administration. From November 1949 to February 1951, he worked as a clerk in the district government's Island Affairs office under Thomas Gladwin.[48] His responsibilities involved municipal activities. He served in effect as the district treasurer and tax collector. He audited the district treasury's books; interpreted policies and regulations; acted as the district government's representative on field trip ships; and was responsible for the booking and collection of passenger fees. After completing his years at the Pacific Islands Central School, Nakayama returned to government employment as the principal clerk for the Island Affairs office under Russ Curtis from 22 May 1953 to 27 August 1955. He now worked more directly in municipal affairs. In addition to his former duties, Nakayama served as an official interpreter in community meetings; he gave presentations on the organization and rules of procedure for municipal governments, and reported on tax collections to the Truk District Council of Chief Magistrates. He also helped supervise the election of municipal judges.[49] In the more traditional outer islands of the district, people preferred to whisper their vote in his ear rather than make a mark on a piece of paper.[50] They left it to him to record their votes appropriately. It was a sign of their trust in him.

Beginning in April 1957, the Trust Territory administration embarked upon an aggressive program of chartering both new and already established municipalities. The UN Trusteeship Council supported the process as a move toward self-government. Chartering was seen as an opportunity to teach local officials parliamentary procedures necessary to conduct council meetings and to encourage greater local initiative. Upon returning from Hawai'i in 1958, Nakayama served for three years as an economic and political advisor under then district administrator Boyd Mackenzie. As specified in his job description, he worked closely with the district Congress and municipal councils in economic and political matters; assisted the district administrator in promoting the economic, political, and social development of the people of the district; coordinated the work of the district political development team; and assisted the district Congress and the municipal councils in drafting resolutions, ordinances, and budgets.[51] He also participated actively in the meetings and workshops that were a part of the chartering process in the different municipalities.

Municipal officials and district congressmen in this formative period found themselves confronted with the complexities of a very alien legislative process that required training in the structure, procedures, rules of order, role of committees, offering of motions, and the review and approval of a budget. The Trust Territory administration made a concerted effort in most districts to equip members of the new legislative bodies with an understanding of the rudiments of the parliamentary process. In Chuuk, the Education department was asked to translate *Robert's Rules of Order* on parliamentary procedures into Chuukese for distribution to chief magistrates, municipal officers, and schoolteachers. With help from Thorwold Esbensen of the Education department, Tosiwo Nakayama and Napoleon DeFang translated the book into Chuukese.[52] One hundred copies of the 6¾" × 4¼" book were produced. To inform the people of Chuuk about general news and the activities of government, members of the Department of Education were also charged with producing a weekly newspaper, the *Truk Review*.[53] The paper published its stories in both English and Chuukese. The members of its editorial board included Nakayama, DeFang, and Raymond Setik as well as several expatriate officials of the district government. Nick Bossy, a graduate of Xavier High School in Chuuk who had just returned from a year's study at the University of Hawai'i, was named editor of the year-old paper in 1959. Bossy of Weno would prove to be one of Nakayama's most strident opponents in the years to come.

The year 1957 also witnessed the inauguration of a district-wide legislature for Chuuk. As the Chuukese had been deemed "not prepared to cope with the complexities of self-government," a district-wide legislature was late in developing.[54] Convened before its charter was actually approved, the legislature had jurisdiction over all of Chuuk; membership in the unicameral body was limited to elected officials. The fear that the creation of a legislature and the elections of its members might alienate traditional leaders was less prominent in Chuuk because of the diffuse and declining state of chieftanship in the islands. As initially conceived, legislatures were intended to serve in an advisory capacity, and to help formulate and unify public opinion. Officials hoped that the legislatures would help close the widening divide between American administrators at headquarters and the people in the districts. Members of the legislature, however, sought considerably more than an advisory role; they

**Fig. 3.3.** Raymond Setik and Tosiwo Nakayama outside of the Truk District Administration building (Trust Territory Photo Archives, Pacific Collection, Hamilton Library, University of Hawai'i, Mānoa).

increased the reach of their powers by adding to the duties of local administrative agencies. They also responded to numerous petitions of grievance by insisting that the district administrator investigate and address the complaints.

The agenda for Congress meetings included the distribution of local tax revenues from the sale of cigarettes and beer to local schools, road repair and maintenance projects, and the salaries for teachers and local district officers.[55] Congressmen also concerned themselves with the screening and appointment of individuals to various district boards and the commissioning and later review of reports or studies on matters in the fields of health, education, economic development, and government operations. In these ways, the Congress extended its involvement in the government of the district. While the Truk District Congress did not conduct its business with the speed, order, efficiency, priorities, or productivity that Trust Territory government officials wanted, it functioned nonetheless and demonstrated in the process a strong desire and increasing ability on the part of its members to represent and govern Chuuk.

Nakayama's familiarity with the workings of this modern style of government facilitated his career in politics as he was voted to serve in the Truk District Congress at a time when elections were relaxed, informal, influenced by family, clan, and sectional loyalties, and more often the product of consensus or acclamation rather than competition. Between 1958 and 1960, Nakayama, replacing his older cousin Leon Episom, served as a representative from Onoun in the Second, Third, and Fourth Truk District Congress.[56] He was the parliamentarian for the Third Congress, after having lost an election for that position to Napoleon DeFang at the opening of the Second Congress.[57] His colleagues in that Third Congress included Andon Amaraich and Soukichy Fritz from the Mortlocks, and Petrus Mailo and Sasauo Haruo from Weno.[58] With Petrus Mailo ill, Nakayama chaired the Fourth Congress that opened on 7 November 1960. Nakayama left the Truk District Congress the next year to serve as one of Chuuk's representatives to the Trust Territory–wide Council of Micronesia.

## Storyteller

Nakayama had a dry, witty, understated, sometimes off-color sense of humor that sustained him throughout his public career. Two of his stories, both involving trips to the outer islands of Chuuk District, evidence this particular brand of humor while offering insight into cross-cultural encounters over issues of government and education. Nakayama's responsibilities as director of adult education for Chuuk District involved largely political education in the structures, functions, and procedures of municipal government. He did work closely with district Department of Education personnel and sometimes accompanied representatives of that department on tours to the outer islands of the district. On these trips, he held community meetings on municipal government matters while education personnel conducted their workshops or training sessions for teachers and parents.

On a trip to the island of Polowat in late 1958, Nakayama traveled with Cy Pickerill, who had been the principal of PICS during his time there. Pickerill was now a district-wide teacher trainer. She had come to Chuuk in 1951 from her position as a supervisor of intern teachers at the University of Hawai'i.[59] She was in her early sixties at the time. Before assuming her duties at PICS, she sought to acclimate herself to life in the islands by living with a local family on Tol and developing a basic competency in the language. She left PICS in 1955 to focus on teacher training at the elementary school level. Accompanied by local educational officials, Pickerill visited elementary schools throughout the district, meeting with skeptical parents and children in the cause of education. By all accounts, she was determined, fearless, energetic, and not at all deterred by the rigors of travel or what to her were the inconveniences of village life. She did insist upon and receive in the performance of her duties a small boat with a forward cabin where she stored her teaching materials to keep them dry. Aside from her teaching materials, her most precious possessions were a tent and portable bathtub. She took these wherever she traveled; a bath at the end of the day in the privacy of the tent was a luxury she insisted upon.

Tosiwo Nakayama remembered her as a not particularly happy person, a feature other observers also noted. She expressed frustration at having to confront classes of "noisy, squirming inattentive little ones without chalk, blackboard, paper, places to write, et al."[60] She was exasperated by teachers who failed to show up for school, were ill-trained and ill-prepared, and asked impossibly difficult questions of children who had a hard enough time answering "what's your name?" She lamented the lack of reading materials and other resources in such related areas as health and hygiene. Despite her strong efforts and persistent ways, she found it beyond her power to transform what she understood as the dismal face of education in Chuuk.

In 1958, Nakayama and Pickerill were on Polowat together.[61] The visiting party shared the same accommodations on the island. Pickerill complained that someone was missing the hole in the latrine floor and fouling the outhouse. She accused Nakayama of being the culprit. He denied the accusation but could do little more than that. He learned soon after, however, that it was Pickerill herself whose aim was amiss. The incident did not prevent the two from working together on the trip. Pickerill recruited her former pupil to help with an art class that she was demonstrating. She invited the students to draw a picture of daily life on the island. One young boy drafted a picture of a man with his penis protruding from one of the legs of his shorts. The picture offended the American educator's sensibilities. She called Nakayama over and told him that the drawing was interesting, even well done, but inappropriate. She asked Nakayama to have the boy redo the assignment or at least remove the protruding penis from the picture. Diplomat that he already was, Nakayama gently explained the white lady's criticism to the young boy and her request that he adjust his drawing. The young boy immediately began to cry at the rejection of his artwork. Nakayama offered what comfort he could; he supposed the boy was embarrassed by the rejection of his picture and by the stern demeanor of Miss Pickerill. He thought the whole incident amusing, and also informing of how strange and missionary Americans could be.

There was also a great deal of humorous misunderstanding that emanated from the land-side of the beach. Despite becoming assistant district administrator in 1961, Nakayama continued to assist in the development of municipal government. He had worked with the people of Nama to develop a charter for their newly recognized municipality. A series of community meetings and workshops ended with the promise that the new charter would be put into final form on Weno, sent to headquarters for review and approval, and then returned and formally presented to the people of Nama. Strik Yoma of Pohnpei, working in the political affairs office at headquarters, arrived in Chuuk as the Trust Territory government's official representative and boarded a ship to Nama for the presentation of the charter. Assuming that the foundation of their new municipal government would be etched or embedded in an object of significant size as befitted its importance, the people of Nama built a large wooden palanquin to transport the charter to shore. They waited just offshore in the shallows for the ship's longboat that was carrying the charter. Upon learning that the charter Yoma brought was written on paper and stored in his briefcase, the people of Nama simply put him and his briefcase on the palanquin and proceeded to shore for the scheduled ceremonies.[62] For Nakayama, the story underscored the local in local government.

## Petrus Mailo and Miter Haruo

Tosiwo Nakayama was not from the Chuuk Lagoon. He knew that and so did everyone else. Nakayama was initially reluctant to apply for the Chuuk District scholarship as he had been involved in its creation and funding; more important, however, he believed the scholarship was intended for the benefit of people from Chuuk, meaning the Lagoon islands.[63] He hailed from Namonuito and Japan. There were two people, however, whose strong support would connect him more closely and intimately with Weno and the Lagoon world, and thus help enable his later political career as an elected representative of the entire district. One individual was Petrus Mailo; the other was Miter Haruo.

As the most prominent and powerful leader of his generation in the Lagoon area, Petrus Mailo figured prominently in Nakayama's educational and early political career.[64] He had sat as a member of the scholarship board that selected Nakayama for study in Hawai'i. As the assistant district administrator from 1961 to 1965, Nakayama provided Petrus Mailo, the mayor of Weno, with regular briefings. The two had served together earlier in the Truk District Congress, and would do so again in the Council of Micronesia, and later still the Congress of Micronesia. Indeed, it was Petrus Mailo who, as one of the senior and most respected members of the first Congress of Micronesia, nominated Nakayama for the Senate presidency. Born in 1903, Petrus Mailo took his last name from his father, a local village chief who later became senior chief of Weno. During Japanese times, the elder Mailo had functioned as the senior chief for all of Weno. He died in 1944 and was succeeded by his oldest son Albert who quickly evidenced an inability to lead. Petrus replaced his brother shortly thereafter and worked to blunt the hardship and suffering that resulted from the escalating demands of the Japanese military for land, labor, and other resources during the final year of the war.

Among his most notable achievements was the founding of the Truk Trading Company in 1948. The company proved one of the very few bright spots in the otherwise flawed and dismal record of the Trust Territory government in the area of economic development. In 1947, using a $250,000 loan from a bank on Guam, the navy set up the Island Trading Company (ITC) to replace the earlier United States Commercial Company (USCC). The ITC bought copra from Micronesians for $80 per ton and sold it in San Francisco for $320. In six months, the Guam loan had been repaid and the company was in the black. Closing its books for 1947, the company had a surplus of $1,000,000. Seeing an opportunity to reduce appropriations, the U.S. cut the Trust Territory allotment by $500,000 the next year, and used half of the ITC surplus to make up the difference. The remaining $500,000 was put into a local start-up fund for Micronesian trading companies. Petrus Mailo used Chuuk's share of the fund to create the Truk Trading Company, a cooperative that secured the balance of its inaugural capital funding through the selling of shares. Shares were sold at all-day frolics or *löchap* during which sales pitches alternated with culturally themed songs and skits that exhorted different groups to compete with one another in the purchase of shares for the betterment of greater Chuuk.[65]

The TTC's complex along the Weno waterfront included a local handicraft store, barbershop, car repair business, restaurant, pool hall, shooting gallery, and a movie theater. After selling his copra or trochus shell to the TTC, an individual could buy tinned goods at the American commissary run by the TTC. All of the thirty-nine populated islands of the Truk District were represented among the TTC shareholders. Many shares were taken in family names, but only individuals could vote, and no person was allowed to own more than 10 percent of the total shares. Stock that cost $25 was soon paying dividends of $20 annually. The TTC also increased its revenue by serving as the exclusive agent for a number of popular American products, including cigarettes. There were other cooperatives established in this period, most notably the Truk Trading Cooperative, headed by Chief Ring of Lukunor, and the Nama Island Trading Company, but none approached the success of the TTC. In 1952, the company had sales of $1,200,000.

Petrus Mailo was by all accounts a very impressive man whose influ-

**Fig. 3.4.** Chief Petrus Mailo (Trust Territory Photo Archives, Pacific Collection, Hamilton Library, University of Hawaiʻi, Mānoa).

ence extended far beyond commercial enterprises. In a statement that betrayed his own prejudice, Thomas Gladwin called Mailo "a champion of his people" and a "statesman who but for the setting and character of his task, could take his place among the historic molders of our common destiny."[66] The basis of his power and influence was his mastery of *itang*—the knowledge, language, and value system of an earlier Chuuk. Mailo once told a group of listeners that their ancestors had learned, and they should too, that there was nothing more important in their lives than the land they lived on and their relationship to it.

> We take life from the soil of our land. Don't reach beyond your grasp for what you don't have. If you reach beyond your grasp for the white man's knowledge but let go of your own knowledge, you will fall.... In the government, a job assignment just hops from one person to another, but an assignment of soil cannot hop away. Hold onto the Trukese pattern of things, the Trukese customs, the Trukese ways, the Trukese orientation.[67]

Petrus Mailo was also critical of the Americans. On one occasion in 1961, he sat patiently while Juan Pepe Benitez, the deputy high commissioner, gave a speech brimming with unbridled enthusiasm for the future of economic development in the islands. Following Benitez' speech, Petrus Mailo gave one of his own in Chuukese that likened the previous speaker to a *kuning* or Pacific golden plover, a big, foolish, light-hued bird that "comes down to earth once a year and flaps his wings and makes a lot of noise and then flies away."[68]

Mailo was concerned about the direction of things in Chuuk. In February 1970, about a year and a half before his death, he made a plea, asking all concerned to deal with the then existing social problems on Weno that he viewed as stemming largely from a lack of leadership.[69] He urged leaders to reactivate the traditional system of family relationships. He insisted that matrilineal clans must meet their responsibilities toward their members; that clan chiefs must exercise their authority over the clans; that section leaders must do the same; that local legislators and members of Chuuk's Congress of Micronesia delegation must be responsible to their constituents; and that missionaries must expand their pastoral work to reach all of the people.

Petrus Mailo was distrustful of those he considered to be less than full-blooded Chuukese; these included people from islands beyond the Lagoon as well as those of Japanese or other foreign parentage. To his way of thinking, the latter groups had used their foreign connections to secure wealth and advantage, and often benefited from their role as intermediaries with an American administration that viewed them as less foreign and more capable than full-blooded Chuukese. Tosiwo Nakayama fit both categories, a fact that caused Petrus Mailo to be initially wary of him.[70] Gladwin mentions that Petrus Mailo "could not bring himself to entrust the Truk Trading Company to the power of men who set themselves at a distance from the culture to which they were born."[71] He actively worked to prevent the "half castes" from taking control of the company by using his own funds to buy stock such that he became the majority stockholder.

Gladwin described Mailo as a born leader.[72] He was aggressive, intelligent, and personally ambitious in a culture that was suspicious of those very traits. Nevertheless, Gladwin saw Petrus Mailo as passionately and wholeheartedly Chuukese. Never on any issue had he been accused of being a tool of the American administration. Mailo had to manipulate people to gain prestige and authority, but he did so skillfully and without abusing his position. He relished power but knew he had to use it for the benefit of others as well as himself. Gladwin's comments are instructive in that they underscore a difference between Petrus Mailo and Tosiwo Nakayama. Nakayama was neither manipulative nor totally Chuukese. His power stemmed from his developing expertise and visibility in the area of government, his humble demeanor, and his ability to bring people together. He was a consensus builder, not a chief. Still, having a Japanese father and a mother from Namonuito made him both a "half caste" and a *Re Faan* or atoll dweller from "down there." His marriage to Miter Haruo, a member of Weno's most prominent clan, the Sópwunupi, contributed significantly to the enhancement of his connections with the Lagoon islands by way of one of its most powerful clans.

Miter Haruo was born on 8 August 1938.[73] She began school at the age of ten, not a particularly late age in those postwar years when American-style schools were still new and female students were few. She moved on to Truk Intermediate School and then to PICS from which she graduated in 1955. Miter left Chuuk that same year to study at the Trust Territory Nursing School on Guam; she received a degree in nursing and returned to Chuuk in 1957 to work as a public health nurse at the district hospital. Her duties included promoting health education to village groups and organizations, and fostering community involvement in local health programs. One of her assignments took her to Polowat with Cy Pickerill in 1958. Tosiwo Nakayama was on that same trip, though the two had little personal interaction despite the visiting party's shared accommodations. Nakayama insisted that he had no interest in her at the time.[74] That would change later in the year when the two were together on Guam to attend separate conferences.[75] Susumu Aizawa claimed that Petrus Mailo initially opposed the marriage of a clanswoman to a Namonuito man with a Japanese father.[76] Nonetheless, the two got married in a civil ceremony on 5 May 1960. Their first child Rosemary was born a month later on 6 June 1960. A more formal wedding took place at the Immaculate Heart of Mary Roman Catholic Church in the Tunnuk section of Weno on 10 September 1963.

Miter Nakayama struggled with health issues most of her adult life. She was nonetheless a powerful and prominent woman in her own right as well as a supportive spouse. She was one of the founders of the Trukese-American Women's Association in 1959. In 1965, Miter, along with Denita Bossy, the wife of Nick Bossy, were the first two women ever elected to office in Chuuk; they each served a single term in the Truk District Congress. Miter was the mother of twelve children and a devout Roman Catholic who later in life traveled to Rome to meet the pope. As a senior clanswoman, she was an ardent defender of Sópwunupi's interests, and filed several lawsuits in the 1990s in behalf of the clan's land claims and offshore resource rights.[77]

## Trust Betrayed

Nearly thirteen years of exposure to the Trust Territory government through school and employment had convinced Tosiwo Nakayama that island peoples needed to govern themselves. Whatever American administrators meant by the phrase "self-government," Nakayama regarded it literally as a necessity and a right. He had learned quickly and worked hard. The years between 1948 and 1961 had seen him make the most of the educational opportunities given him in a new, struggling, underfunded, colonially directed educational system. He had risen from the position of clerk in the Islands Affairs section of the Chuuk District administration to assume major administrative responsibilities in the areas of taxation, municipal government, and adult political education. His American teachers in both Chuuk and Hawai'i regarded him highly. His superiors in Chuuk were equally enthusiastic about his abilities. Nakayama did not always return the compliments, however. He was grateful for the kindness and support that he received, but critical of those whom he saw as failing Chuuk. Nakayama could not overlook the mismanagement, indifference, lack of progress, and slighting of Chuukese skills. Willard Muller, Chuuk's first district administrator under the Department of the Interior, had high words of praise for Nakayama. Perhaps he read the young islander's quiet ways, respectful demeanor, and general competence as uncritical acceptance of the American presence. If so, he misread Nakayama badly. Discouraged by the labor unrest, personnel squabbles, and dysfunctional character of the American presence, Nakayama signed a petition to have Muller removed.[78] Nakayama thought no better of Muller's successor, Roy Gallamore, whose administration he criticized for being too cautious and doing nothing.[79]

Weno's landscape testified to the sorry state of affairs.[80] The only roads maintained were those that were used by the Americans. Their housing area sat atop a lush, green hill whose vegetation surrounded Quonset huts that were spacious, bright, well built, and nicely furnished. This contrasted sharply with the makeshift town developing quickly and haphazardly along Weno's northern shoreline. The administration buildings near this area had deteriorated significantly from navy times. The grass went uncut, paint peeled from the walls, and needed repairs were ignored. The area bore witness to a colonial presence that was itself neglectful, shoddy, and stagnant. John Griffin, an editorial page writer for the *Honolulu Advertiser,* offered a summary of the first ten years of civilian rule in American Micronesia. Griffin wrote of proposals for economic rehabilitation that gathered dust on forgotten shelves while the Trust Territory limped along with a caretaker budget of less than $7 million annually, and under the direction of a staff made up of aging holdovers from the navy government, tired veterans of the Department of Interior's Bureau of Indian Affairs, and dedicated young recruits who soon became jaded or left in frustration.[81] It all seemed much more like a rust territory than a trust territory.

CHAPTER 4

# Representing Micronesia, 1961–1975

TOSIWO NAKAYAMA'S CAREER in government closely paralleled the trajectory of political development during the Trust Territory period. What would become the Congress of Micronesia evolved from a series of earlier representative bodies that included municipal councils, district legislatures, the Trust Territory–wide Inter-District Advisory Committee, and the Council of Micronesia. Nakayama had been involved at each of these levels, having worked on the development of municipal government in his role with the Island Affairs office in Chuuk and later as advisor to the district administrator. A practical man, he utilized the tools of representative government to build consensus and common purpose among disparate groups of island peoples. Unity and self-determination were his ultimate goals. Nakayama looked beyond the contradictions of colonially introduced institutions of democratic government to find weapons of the weak among the arsenal of the strong. He came to believe in a Micronesia and articulated that vision with increasing emphasis and effect during the first ten years of the Congress of Micronesia. In many ways, he helped refashion the Trust Territory of the Pacific Islands into Micronesia and then represented that entity to its inhabitants, representatives of the United States government, and the larger world.

## Early Efforts at Territory-Wide Representative Government

The cause of representative government moved guardedly forward under the naval and later civilian administrations of the Trust Territory government.[1] The first direct participation by indigenous representatives in government

93

took place on Guam at the 1949 civilian administrators' conference. Each civilian administrator brought with him two local representatives from his assigned district. The transfer of administrative authority from the navy to the Department of the Interior slowed but did not derail local input into the administration of the Trust Territory. District administrators' conferences were held in 1953, 1954, and 1956, again with two representatives from each of the districts.

The 1956 gathering proved notable for its advocacy of a Territory-wide legislature. At the next annual conference, delegates voted to call themselves the Inter-District Advisory Committee to the High Commissioner. Usually convened on Guam, the committee consisted of Trust Territory officials, district administrators, and two local representatives from each of the districts. Petrus Mailo served as one of the two representatives from Chuuk for the first four advisory committee meetings. Members were encouraged to think "territorially," which meant an awareness of not just their home island or district but the larger territory. They showed themselves more than willing and able to do this, but not to the exclusion of local concerns. While administrative voices sought to shape and direct the discussion, the district representatives became increasingly vocal about the needs of their constituents back home. They asked for immediate assistance with infrastructure restoration and development, and addressed larger issues involving economic development, landownership, and foreign assistance.

As had been evidenced earlier in the district legislatures, members of the Inter-District Advisory Committee wanted more than an advisory role in the government of their islands. Members in attendance at the sixth conference that met in September 1961 voted to change the name of the committee to the Council of Micronesia.[2] In its concerns and general approach, the council foreshadowed what would become the Congress of Micronesia some four years later.[3] Taking themselves more seriously than the Trust Territory administration intended, the members of the Council of Micronesia envisioned a legislative body for the islands that would actually possess the power to govern. In the promotion of this goal, they considered drafting a bill of rights, queried the high commissioner about lifting the existing ban on foreign investment in the islands, and challenged the then two-tiered salary schedule in the Trust Territory that favored expatriate workers over Micronesian employees. The council as a whole made recommendations in the areas of economic development, emphasizing the need for more copra warehouses, increasing the number of ships to be operated in the territory, and expanding maritime service to the outlying islands. There was discussion of an economic development fund and a Territory-wide association of trading companies. The conference as a whole also endorsed a design for the Trust Territory flag that showed six stars, representing each of the six districts, in a sea of light blue. Tosiwo Nakayama, then senator in the Truk District Congress and a political and economic advisor to the district administration, attended the session as special participant and observer.[4]

Nakayama's presence at the September Council of Micronesia meeting was significant in that it foreshadowed his membership in the council the following year. Though only thirty years old, he had come out quite publicly and prominently in favor of self-government. Earlier in 1961, Nakayama had attended a meeting of the UN Trusteeship Council as a Micronesian representative with the American delegation reporting on the administration of the Trust Territory. The specifics surrounding the selection of Nakayama are not clear. Those who made the decision seriously misjudged his resolve. His quiet demeanor belied the intensity of his feelings about the failings of the administration. Despite being asked by members of the American delegation to tone down his criticism of the Trust Territory government, he still managed to deliver a strong statement in favor of accelerated self-government for the islands.[5] His call for more representative government encouraged the similar recommendations of the UN Visiting Mission to the Trust Territory later that year. One observer credited Nakayama's UN speech with moving the Council of Micronesia to take a more aggressive stand on representative government for the islands.[6] Upon returning from the trip to New York, Nakayama addressed the council on Guam and recommended the exploratory study of a full-fledged Trust Territory legislature. Nakayama and the council were not alone in their efforts to move a reluctant Trust Territory administration and a distant, indifferent U.S. Congress. The postwar world's recognition of the rights of all people to govern themselves, the emergence of nation-states from old colonial configurations, the increasing influence of communist-bloc nations in the developing world, and the UN Trusteeship Council's increasing criticism of the Trust Territory administration put the United States on the defensive.

The next convocation of the Council of Micronesia took place at the Palau Congress Building in Koror in 1962.[7] Tosiwo Nakayama was now one of the two elected delegates from Chuuk. The gathering marked the first time that a representative body of island leaders had met within the boundaries of the Trust Territory. The Palau Congress building where the council met was a curious structure that suggested a colonial presence seeking to acclimate itself and its way of government to local conditions. The building consisted of a tin roof and heavy cement block columns that braced walls with large screened windows and wooden louvers. In the central chamber, tables and chairs were

**Fig. 4.1.** Tosiwo Nakayama at the United Nations, 1961 (Micronesian Seminar).

arranged round a raised dais for Dwight Heine, the chair of the council. The building's offices and library were used for committee meetings. Messengers distributed materials, ran errands, relayed written communications among the members, and collected ballots during votes; translation services were provided for those members not proficient or comfortable in English. Many of the members knew each other from their student days in Hawai'i. In addition to Dwight Heine and Tosiwo Nakayama, there was David Ramarui of Palau, the vice chair of the council; Amata Kabua of the Marshalls; Joab Sigrah of Pohnpei; and Joseph Tamag of Yap.

The most notable development at the 1962 Palau meeting was a council resolution that created a Legislative Drafting Committee charged with making written recommendations on the organization, structure, functions, and procedures for a proposed Territory-wide legislature much like the one Nakayama had urged at the United Nations the year before.[8] Appointed to the drafting committee, Nakayama played a prominent role in its deliberations and in the drafting of its report to the full council. Before the meeting of the next council, members of the drafting committee divided themselves into two groups and toured the territory seeking input from traditional leaders, elected officials, government workers, and representatives of local communities. One group visited the eastern districts; Nakayama traveled with the group touring the west. The whole committee presented its report before a special session of the Council of Micronesia that met in March 1963 on Saipan.[9]

The actual structure of the territorial legislature was the subject of considerable debate. In the end, the Legislative Drafting Committee submitted two proposals for the full council's consideration; one in support of a unicameral legislature, the other in support of a bicameral division. Nakayama endorsed the unicameral option. In his presentation before the council, he prefaced his recommendation with a short speech that underscored the many problems confronting the Trust Territory and that bore directly on the issue of self-government and the choice of a structure for a Territory-wide legislature.

> If we look at the Territory, there are certain problems that face us. There is the factor of distance, the vast physical distance between districts. We have six districts in a large area of ocean. This in itself creates a problem. How to overcome the problem of distance [*sic*]. All of us know from experience that because of these distances we have another problem, that of communication. Also deriving from the problem of distance is another one, of transportation. Because of the distance, lack of communication, lack of transportation, there have developed different languages, different beliefs, different customs.[10]

He also cited the issue of costs and the fact that there were very few qualified candidates available to run for election. In light of these realities, Nakayama recommended the council endorse a unicameral body with two at-large candidates from each district and the balance of district representation to be determined proportionally by population.

Heinrich Iriarte of Pohnpei was the most vocal critic of the unicameral approach. The Pohnpeian articulated the fears of the majority of council members who worried that the more populous districts would dominate a unicameral Congress. The council thus voted in favor of a bicameral structure modeled on the U.S. Congress that consisted of a General Assembly and a smaller House of Delegates. Members did accept Nakayama's recommendations on two-year terms for assemblymen representing specific electoral districts and four-year terms for at-large delegates. With these amendments, the council formally adopted the committee's bicameral recommendation on 22 March 1963.

American representatives sought to impose their imprint on a locally driven, democratic process that was moving faster than expected. At the fourth regularly scheduled meeting of the Council of Micronesia in November 1963, U.S. Assistant Secretary of the Interior John Carver gave an opening address that reminded those present that the "decision to give legislative power to a Territory-wide legislature is with the United States; the decision to use these powers wisely is with you. That is why we have not hurried the process; that is why we think the time is now close."[11] High Commissioner M. Wilfred Gooding reminded those present of the required consultations between the council and the Trust Territory government before any convocation of the new legislature could take place.[12]

On 28 September 1964, U.S. Secretary of the Interior Stewart L. Udall issued Secretarial Order #2882 that effectively chartered the Congress of Micronesia.[13] Consistent with the recommendations of the report adopted by the Council of Micronesia, the Congress was modeled after the bicameral structure of the U.S. Congress with proportional representation based on population in the General Assembly and with each district electing two at-large members to a House of Delegates. The term of office for members of the House of Delegates was set at four years; members of the General Assembly sat for two-year terms. As initially constituted, the Congress was to serve as a body of advice and consent with only a small portion of the territory's funding to allocate and little or no governing power. Any legislation passed by the Congress of Micronesia was subject to final veto by the high commissioner. Council members objected to those sections of the secretarial order that prohibited the taxing of United States or Trust Territory property, that denied Congress the power to amend the Trust Territory Bill of Rights, and that restricted Congress' participation in the drafting of the annual budget for the territory. Limits on congressional powers were compounded by requirements to work under the 745-page law code of the Trust Territory and to abide by legislative regulations governing quorums, conferences, resolutions, votes, committee reports, protocols of address, the introduction of bills, the rules of debate, and budget authorizations and appropriations. Regular meetings were scheduled to run for thirty days on Saipan with provision for special sessions. Legislators received compensation and travel assistance while engaged in legislative activity. There were also provisions for a full-time legislative counsel and supporting staff. When the apportionment process for the General Assembly was complete, Chuuk had five seats, the Marshalls and Pohnpei four each, the Marianas and Palau three each, and Yap one.

## The Congress of Micronesia

Voting remained a strange and uncertain practice for many.[14] Twenty years of American rule had not yet changed that fact. To facilitate name recognition, election officials in Chuuk and Palau permitted candidates to place familiar symbols next to their names on the printed ballots. In Chuuk, drawings of breadfruit proved particularly popular but were later deemed too influential and thus prohibited.[15] The geography of the Trust Territory certainly did not prove conducive to elections. The distance separating outlying islands from the district centers, the less than reliable shipping service to those islands, and the lack of an effective communications system at the time often combined to cause delays in the collecting, accounting, and reporting of votes. In the more distant, less colonially affected atolls and islands of the Central Carolines, election boxes were taken from village to village or from house to house. As with earlier municipal elections, some voters whispered their preferences to election officials who then marked their ballots. By the first election for the Congress of Micronesia, however, the tradition of voters in the more remote islands of Yap and Truk crawling the last thirty feet on their hands and knees to election officials had pretty much ended.[16] All in all, the earliest political campaigns proved subdued affairs with candidates relying more on name recognition and family and clan connections than active campaigning. For the first Congress of Micronesia election in early 1965, the Truk District Congress put forth a list of recommended candidates. Tosiwo Nakayama's name was on that list.

Practically all candidates spoke English; most had a high school or equivalency degree, and about half had some college education.[17] Public service, experience in district legislatures, and membership in the Council of Micronesia all proved helpful to a candidate's chances of electoral success. Reflecting the gendered order of things in the islands, no women ran for Congress in this first election. Newly elected members to the General Assembly were slightly older than those elected to the House of Delegates and had less education. Seven of the twenty held chiefly or senior clan titles. Members of the House of Delegates also had more legislative experience and more knowledge of business conditions than their Assembly counterparts. The younger legislators were more highly educated and acculturated. Nakayama was thirty-four years of age at the time; he won election easily and closely fit the profile of those younger members who were more closely identified with change.

The First Regular Session of the Congress of Micronesia in 1965 was held at the Mariana Islands Community Club, also known as the Toppa Tappi Club. After that, the Congress met in a refurbished set of buildings that stood below Mount Tapochao and commanded an impressive view of half the island of Saipan. The site had been the residence of Japanese colonial officials and later that of the commander of American military forces on the island immediately after the war. The U.S. Central Intelligence Agency later constructed three buildings on the site in support of its East Asian training operations. The Congress inherited those structures and used them to house its meeting chambers, committee rooms, staff quarters, and support offices.[18]

**Fig. 4.2.** The Congress of Micronesia buildings on Saipan (Trust Territory Photo Archives, Pacific Collection, Hamilton Library, University of Hawai'i, Mānoa).

A two-week training workshop preceded the opening session of the Congress. The East-West Center's Institute for Technical Change sent a three-man team to lead the workshop. Norman Meller, one of Nakayama's teachers at the University of Hawai'i, was a member of the team.[19] The training included instruction in the organization of a legislature; members' qualifications, rights, and limitations; decision-making, parliamentary, and legislative procedures; and the role of legislative staff. With this basic orientation completed, members of the two houses met separately to receive instruction in the drafting of the rules for their respective houses. Tosiwo Nakayama was appointed to the drafting committee for the House of Delegates. The second week of the workshop provided instruction in the functioning of the Trust Territory government. When the drafting committees had completed their work, the respective houses met to review and approve them, and then caucus for the selection of officers and committee members as called for by the rules.[20]

John Ngiraked from Palau looked to have a lock on the presidency of the House of Delegates.[21] Prior to the formal convening of Congress, the House caucus had voted 5–4–2 in favor of Ngiraked with Bailey Olter of Pohnpei and Tosiwo Nakayama of Chuuk finishing second and third, respectively. The support for Olter and Nakayama appeared to come from the eastern districts. The vote seemed to eliminate the candidacy of Nakayama who then defeated Olympia Borja of the Marianas and Amata Kabua of the Marshalls for the vice presidency of the House of Delegates. With one Palauan delegate not present for the caucus vote, the assumption was that Ngiraked would easily win the formal election to be held on the opening day of the Congress. Things changed quickly, however. The eastern districts of the Trust Territory had fared poorly in the selection of officers and committee chairs. That development fed the already existing tensions among the different districts, including a cultural divide and rivalry that separated the Eastern and Central Carolines and the Marshalls from the Marianas and the Western Carolines. The seating of Marianas delegate Jose Cruz figured prominently in the selection of a president for the House of Delegates.

Cruz had been convicted of a felony some years earlier while resident in the United States. As a result, his credentials were being challenged on the grounds that the conviction, by House of Delegate rules, prevented his seating. Andon Amaraich, the other Chuukese member of the House of Delegates and chair of the credentials committee, argued that Cruz had not committed or been convicted of any crime in the Trust Territory. His endorsement followed a private conversation in which Amaraich agreed to support Cruz on condition that the Marianas delegate vote for Nakayama as president of the House.[22] Cruz agreed. At about the same time, Olter showed no interest in pursuing his candidacy, while Petrus Mailo is said to have lobbied heavily for Nakayama. The next day, after the official opening ceremony, the House voted 6–5 against a motion to name Ngiraked president and proceeded to accept the recommendation of the credentials committee that Cruz be seated. The House of Delegates then voted again on the office of president; this time, the result was 7–5 in favor of Nakayama. Cruz's vote, Olter's four, and Nakayama's original two made seven.

Those in attendance at the opening ceremony for the Congress described it as a deeply moving and inspiring moment. Not all shared in the euphoria, however. Some observers were less than confident about the effectiveness of the Congress in its initial year of existence.[23] Both houses were slow in making the difficult leadership decisions as formality, patronage, and cultural politics took precedence in those first days. The General Assembly debated a dress code while the House of Delegates concerned itself with hiring staff. Both houses seemed to spend more time deciding how to furnish their quarters than functioning as legislative bodies. The amount of time spent partying at the Trust Territory Headquarters Club and feasting with different islands communities on Saipan provoked criticism as well. The lack of trained personnel made it difficult to keep accurate records or chart the legislative process. The equipment that staffers used was old and included typewriters and mimeograph machines. Members showed themselves to be proficient in referring measures to committee, but confusion and uncertainty were more the order of the day when deciding how to handle a committee report. The attachment of amendments proved a particularly awkward and difficult process to master. Congressmen sometimes took shortcuts to move things along. The requirement that a bill be reprinted after being amended and before final consideration was often ignored. This caused more confusion and delay. A third of the Congress' inaugural session had passed before the General Assembly cleared its first bill. It took more than half of the session before any measure originating in the House of Delegates made it to the General Assembly.

All of this was to be expected, however, as delegates and assemblymen came to grips with a legislative process that was highly complex, conducted in a foreign language, and grounded in a system of law that was equally alien. Members of Congress also had to learn how to deal with an administration that was aloof, silent, defensive, and often late with its submissions. Meant to be little more than a consultative body, the Congress of Micronesia nonetheless found a way to assert itself. Promoting a sense of solidarity was the fact that many of the congressmen knew each other from the Pacific Islands Central School, the University of Hawai'i, and the Council of Micronesia. Despite its lack of true legislative power, the Congress strove to make itself an equal branch of government by criticizing the administration through the passage of joint resolutions, by refusing to act at times on legislation proposed by the Trust Territory government, and by deliberately taking actions on matters that were beyond its charter. The Congress, for example, passed legislation that sought to cancel the Trust Territory government's right of eminent domain only to have it vetoed by the high commissioner. The bill was seen as encroaching on the powers of the Trust Territory government and in conflict with both the UN Trusteeship Agreement and the secretarial order delineating the jurisdiction of the Congress.[24] A bill requiring the advice and consent of the Congress on all major executive appointments within the Trust Territory was also vetoed on the grounds that it exceeded the powers granted by Secretarial Order #2882.[25] Though unsuccessful, bills such as these evidenced Congress' desire to broaden its powers. Symbolic gestures also proved an effective part of Congress' legislative repertoire. In behalf of Micronesian unity, the Congress acted to restrict the entry of non-Micronesian businesses; establish a junior college; designate a Micronesia Day; and adopt a territorial flag. The Congress also renamed the House of Delegates and the General Assembly as the Senate and House of Representatives, respectively. When the Congress adjourned on 11 August 1965, 204 bills, joint resolutions, and single House resolutions had been considered, with the majority being resolutions. Sixty-nine items were passed, of which twenty-two were resolutions.[26] Resolutions proved a way for congressmen to express their views in areas where they had no legislative power or authority.

To skeptics, the creation of the Congress of Micronesia looked to be part of a larger agenda of a Micronesia being remade yet again by its latest colonial overlord. It is, perhaps, a more accurate assessment to view the Congress as a body attempting to co-opt the language and institutions of colonial domination for more local purposes and objectives. Mimicry there certainly was, but mimicry that Homi Bhabha describes as unsettling to colonial authorities in its "almost the same but not quite" features.[27] Although modeled closely after the U.S. Congress, the Congress of Micronesia could be deceptive, even subversive in its hybridity. The localized cultures and histories that informed its operation created critical distinctions and crucial differences that made it exasperating for those who expected an eminently manageable mock legislative body that would serve the dominant interests of the larger political system that had created it. To be sure, the members of the first Congress of Micronesia came to their elected positions privileged by varying circumstances that included chiefly rank or support; relatively high levels of education; competency in English; success in commercial endeavors; and previous work experience provided through positions of standing within the Trust Territory government. Although some might describe them, and correctly, as an emerging elite, their

efforts also need to be understood as affected by a host of personal relationships; kinship obligations; ethnic loyalties; private ambitions; and localized
politics and rivalries. They were not unaware of how far removed their work
was from the everyday concerns of those they represented. An able, committed cadre of American expatriate lawyers assisted the congressmen in their
work.[28]

In its early years, members of Congress sought to reach out to their constituents as a way to inform them about the business of the Congress, and to
bridge the cultural and class differences that separated members from those
they represented. In preparation for its regular session in July 1967, the Congress of Micronesia created two travel committees to tour the districts and to
consult with local residents on its upcoming agenda. Tosiwo Nakayama was a
member of the western subcommittee that visited Palau, Yap, and Truk.[29] In
the words of P. F. Kluge who had worked with many of them, the congressmen were interesting, complicated men torn or caught between two worlds.[30]
Among their ranks was a very competent core committed to making a Micronesia. They knew they would have to deal with each other and with the administering authority through a colonial structure, especially in areas involving
power and money. Their willingness to engage each other as Micronesians and
largely through the language of the colonizer evidenced a practical engagement
with the social, economic, and political circumstances of their predicament.[31]

Congressional leaders did have considerable legislative success in those
early years. The Merit System Act that provided Micronesians with pay equal
to the American administrators with whom they worked or replaced was an
early triumph[32] as was the creation of a social security system for Trust Territory residents,[33] and a Law of the Sea Committee to assert control over the
territory's marine resources.[34] The Congress also showed itself able at times to
do the difficult thing. The Congress was able to pass unpopular legislation that
levied a 3 percent tax on the wages and salaries of its citizens and a 1 percent
tax on gross business revenues.[35] An editorial in the 18 August 1966 edition of
the *Honolulu Star-Bulletin* called the members of the Congress of Micronesia,

> men who almost without exception regard the future good of the Trust
> Territory as more important than the immediate good of their local
> constituents. They are more concerned with the impression they are
> making on the world and on the future of their people than with the
> impression they make on the voters they (will) face.... They show a
> statesmanship rare in politics anywhere, and almost incredible in a
> people who have emerged within their own memory from a stone age
> society.[36]

## Nakayama, the Legislative Navigator

As Senate president, Tosiwo Nakayama played a major though somewhat invisible role in the success of the early Congress. He devoted most of his time and energy to managing the Senate's business. His speeches before the full Senate were few, and were usually given at the opening and closing ceremonies that bookended the sessions. His background in parliamentary procedures came strongly into play. He used his skills as a parliamentarian and consensus builder to manage complex, sometimes controversial pieces of legislation. At the same time, he did not cast his vote to appease others or win support for his own causes. His appreciation for the technicalities of legislation and the problems with legally or structurally flawed bills led him to oppose measures that on the surface seemed right or good.[37] He also sought to keep the Congress independent, self-supportive, and as close to its constituents as possible. During the Second Regular Session, he voted "no" on a bill to appropriate additional funds in support of congressmen's travel to conferences. He also opposed two joint resolutions at that session, one asking the high commissioner to fund the operational and contingent costs of the Congress of Micronesia with U.S. grants and the other raising the compensation of congressmen.[38]

**Fig. 4.3.** Senator Tosiwo Nakayama speaking with Bailey Olter of Pohnpei (Trust Territory Photo Archives, Pacific Collection, Hamilton Library, University of Hawai'i, Mānoa).

From his position as president of the Congress of Micronesia Senate, Tosiwo Nakayama offered an assessment of the Congress after its first two years that was as insightful as any. In his closing address to the second special session of the First Congress he argued, in response to critics, that the accomplishments of the Congress were best measured not by the quantity but the quality of the bills it passed. Noting the varied cultural backgrounds and divergent interests of peoples spread over more than three million square miles, Nakayama expressed encouragement at the progress made, and the maturity and sophistication achieved by Micronesians in such a short period of time. The Congress of Micronesia was testament to that. Nakayama conceded that the way in which the Senate conducted its business might seem too relaxed to some outside observers. He stressed, however, the importance of conducting deliberations in a well-balanced atmosphere and with a sense of proportion. At the same time, he realized the need for constantly demonstrating to the United States that Micronesians were capable and able to take on the responsibilities of self-government. He closed his remarks by stating his intention not to run for re-election as Senate president.[39]

As the holder of one of the two at-large Senate seats from Chuuk and not up for re-election for another two years, Nakayama returned to the Congress the next year. True to his word, he chose not to seek re-election as Senate president. The reasons for his stepping down remain unclear. Plans to return to Hawai'i to complete his bachelor's degree most likely informed his decision. John Ngiraked of Palau was chosen president of the Senate, thus easing the sting of his loss to Nakayama in the previous election. Despite his reduced role, Nakayama remained highly engaged in the legislative process during the third regular session of the Second Congress that ran from 15 July to 8 August 1967. His legislative concerns were immediate, practical, and with an eye to self-government and the long-term development of the Trust Territory's basic infrastructure. He sponsored a resolution calling for a feasibility study on the establishment of a publicly owned Bank of Micronesia. With Andon Amaraich, the other senator from Chuuk, Nakayama co-sponsored a bill to provide the right of additional appeal on decisions from the Trial Division of the High Court. The two also introduced a resolution in the Senate urging the high commissioner to conduct an exhaustive study on the feasibility of establishing a major international shipping port for the Trust Territory. Nakayama supported a resolution expressing dissatisfaction with the service provided by the Micronesian Shipping Line and urging a review of existing conditions and practices. He later served on the committee charged with that review. Outside of the Congress, he lobbied strongly in behalf of Continental Air Micronesia's bid to provide air service to the Trust Territory.

Land issues were of primary concern for Nakayama, who believed that the Trust Territory government had to return those large tracts of public land that had been lost during German and Japanese colonial times. Nakayama's commitment to a greater Micronesia was on display here as the public lands issue most immediately affected districts such as Pohnpei, Palau, and the Marianas. The percentage of public land in Chuuk was actually quite small. In the pursuit of this objective, Nakayama supported a bill before the third regular session of the Third Congress to create land boards in each district to facilitate the return of public lands.[40] In a joint conference on the last night of the session, Nakayama argued that the threat of veto by the high commissioner should not be a reason to dilute or defeat the bill. Nakayama and Amaraich sought to counter the reservations of those who thought the measure futile given the likelihood of a veto. Local control was also a concern as representatives from the Marshalls preferred to deal with the land issue internally rather than entrust it to an external body such as the Congress of Micronesia. Despite these objections, Nakayama believed passage of the bill was the right thing to do. The Senate concurred and voted 6–1 in favor of the bill that came out of conference, with five abstentions that were later marked "yes." The House agreed and the bill was signed into law. Though vetoed by the high commissioner, Nakayama and the Congress had made their point. Nakayama's insistence on passage of the bill foreshadowed his resolve over the issue in later political status negotiations with representatives of the United States government who sought some form of eminent domain over Micronesian lands. Nakayama's quiet ways and reserved demeanor often hid his determination. Those who saw him as compliant or detached misjudged him badly.

At school in Hawai'i, Nakayama was absent for the entire fourth regular session of the Second Congress of Micronesia, which met on Saipan from 10 July to 8 August 1968. Having won re-election from afar and completed his two years of studies in Hawai'i, Nakayama returned to the Senate in 1969. He was named temporary president but declined to run for the office, and supported instead the candidacy of Amata Kabua of the Marshalls. Nakayama did accept the position of floor leader, and thus had responsibility for the orderly and effective management of all legislative business in the Senate. His commitment to Micronesia showed itself in a brief speech he gave on the Senate floor regarding the use of the term "Micronesian." The speech was given in support of a bill requiring the high commissioner to provide legal services for Trust Territory citizens living on Guam. Nakayama remarked that while in Hawai'i, he had encountered students from Papua New Guinea who were identified as "Papua New Guineans," and not simply as residents of the then Australian trust territory. Nakayama argued that Micronesian was a more accurate designation than Trust Territory when referring to the citizens of the Caroline, Mariana, and Marshall Islands.[41]

## President of the Senate Again

The first regular session of the Fifth Congress met back on Saipan from 8 January to 26 February 1973. The session was marked by the election of Tosiwo Nakayama as president of the Senate. He defeated incumbent Amata Kabua of the Marshalls for a complex of reasons that included general unhappiness with Kabua's management of Senate affairs; his advocacy of legislation providing the Marshalls with 50 percent of the local tax revenue generated within its boundaries; and his increasingly public support for the separation of the Marshalls from the rest of the Trust Territory. Ambilos Iehsi of Pohnpei and Luke Tman of Yap approached Nakayama over breakfast at the Royal Taga Hotel before the start of the session and convinced him to run. Although Nakayama himself voted for Kabua, the election results placed a severe strain on the relationship between the two men that would continue throughout their public careers.

Putting aside the personal discomfort caused by his victory, Nakayama used his return to the Senate presidency to speak forthrightly, even critically, about the need for self-government. In his opening day address, he noted that Micronesians had been sleeping and dreaming, and as a result had lost the habit of doing things for themselves.[42] He urged Micronesians to start doing things for themselves again, and to think of their future, their families, and their children. It was, for Nakayama, a long and impassioned speech that emphasized the importance of reclaiming self-dignity, self-respect, and self-reliance. He talked about the virtues of hard, honest work, the need for economic development, and the necessity of legislation for the convocation of a constitutional convention as a first step in the realization of self-government. He expressed the opinion that members of Congress suffered from the sin of pride in their affinity for American ways. He asked members of Congress to get closer to their people, set a good example, and commit to the truly important work needed to develop a self-supporting, self-governing Micronesian nation. He also criticized the United States. Toward the end of his address, he stated:

> It is time for America to stop trying to put its ways upon Micronesia. It is like trying to make a person wear clothes which do not fit him. It is also time we stopped taking ideas from the United States for granted. We must start changing American patterns to fit our own. We must stop changing ourselves and our ways to fit American patterns. Now we must do things ourselves.... Micronesians, wherever you are, it is

time to stop sleeping. It is time to stop dreaming. Let us roll up our sleeves and build a proud and self-reliant nation. Wake up! Let's sleep and dream no more![43]

It could be argued that Nakayama was working to create a Micronesian nation through the Congress of Micronesia. He began to downplay the differences that separated the islands, instead focusing on what they had in common. In an interview with the *Micronesian Reporter,* he described himself "as one of those who do not recognize the existence of a multi-culture Micronesia."[44] He viewed language as the only real difference and an easy enough one to overcome through the use of English as the national language. Nakayama also linked an emerging Micronesian identity to the issue of economic development. He offered a vision of Micronesia's economic future that stood in stark contrast to the prescriptions of development planners and consultants who underscored the islands' limitations. Addressing a gathering of island leaders from the Upper Mortlocks on 13 July 1973, Nakayama remarked on the ways in which Micronesians had been led by outsiders to believe they had little to develop:

They tell us we have nothing to gain from the land, and practically nothing to gain from the sea. These people are a bunch of liars. They lie; they fool us.... In Japan, they bottle and sell Fujiyama air. Things will change. Air will become very precious. Sunshine might become like medicine.[45]

Bottled air and sunshine—here was a very distinctive sense of economic development that flew in the face of conventional expertise and the limitations that expertise attempted to impose on Micronesian peoples' imagination and their future.

For Nakayama, the impediments to development lay within as well as beyond the islands. In an address to the Senate in 1973, the senator from Chuuk spoke of a cultural intimidation so deep that Micronesians were made to feel ashamed of their customs, traditions, and cultures. Micronesians, argued Nakayama, were in danger of losing the ability to do things for themselves. He also pointed to the involvement of "ignorant men" who thought their ways were better than those of Micronesians. It was time, said Nakayama, for Micronesians to work, stop complaining, lay the foundations for a strong government and economy, and cooperate with other Micronesians. Despite the complexities of the problems that he addressed, Nakayama evidenced a decidedly different view of economic development, a view of development as

a means by which Micronesians might prove their worth to dominant groups
of foreigners in ways those foreigners would understand, and at the same time
develop a more self-confident national identity that allowed for the attainment
of independence.

## Election Wins and Losses

Tosiwo Nakayama's vision of a unified, self-governing Micronesia depended
upon his ability to win re-election to the Congress of Micronesia. Elections
posed no problem for him in the first decade of his congressional career. He
had never really been challenged. His elections to the Truk District Congress,
the Inter-District Advisory Committee, and the Council of Micronesia were
more by acclamation than vote. His first three elections to Congress in 1965,
1968, and 1972 were not even close. The 1965 electoral contest had affirmed
the recommendation of the district legislature; he and Andon Amaraich were
the top two finishers with 4,205 and 3,733 votes, respectively.[46] In 1968, for the
Senate term beginning the following year, he received 4,563 votes and easily
defeated Tadasy Wainit of Tol and Machime O'Sonis who garnered 619 and
589 votes, respectively.[47] In 1972, he ran in effect unopposed while earning
5,186 votes.[48] Indeed, the most difficult election for Tosiwo Nakayama to this
point in his career proved to be one in which he was not even a candidate; it
was the 1974 election for the second Chuukese Senate seat. That electoral contest witnessed the defeat of his most trusted ally, colleague, and friend in the
Senate, Andon Amaraich.

Amaraich hailed from Ta in the Mortlocks.[49] He entered PICS in 1953,
the same year that Nakayama graduated from the school. Upon completing his
studies at PICS, Amaraich resumed his career as an interpreter and clerk with
the Truk District Court. Over time, he rose to the position of assistant clerk
of courts and later public defender. Like Nakayama, Amaraich developed an
expertise and facility in the ways of government, especially the judicial branch.
A year of study at the College of Guam and participation in a series of legal
workshops supplemented his on-the-job training. His attention to detail and
his passion for his work impressed many Americans and Micronesians alike.
In 1968, John Ngiraked, president of the Senate said, "you may not be a speech
maker, Senator Amaraich, but I think everyone in the Senate is aware that most
of the successful work of the Senate is attributed to your very hard and careful
work."[50] American officials came to refer to him as "Buddha-like" because of
his quiet, calm, and poised manner.[51] If Nakayama was the visionary, Amaraich was his strategist, tactician, and legislative assistant. They accommodated
and complemented each other nicely. In 1965, he had run for one of Chuuk's

two at-large seats in the Congress and came in a comfortable and successful second to Nakayama. Under the provisions of the secretarial order that chartered the Congress, the terms of the Senate seats were to be staggered so as to minimize the disruption caused by changes in elective personnel. Amaraich ran again in 1967, this time for a four-year term. He handily defeated Nick Bossy and Sasauo Haruo, Nakayama's brother-in-law, in that 1967 election,[52] and won a second four-year term beginning in 1971.[53]

Amaraich proved a steady critic of the Trust Territory administration. The Trust Territory government's belated efforts to place more Micronesian citizens in positions of authority did not impress him. During the first regular session of the Fourth Congress in 1971, Amaraich spoke against the pitfalls of too hasty a "Micronesianization" process that placed local citizens in positions of leadership for which they were not yet qualified and in which they had little chance of success.[54] At the Congress' next regular session, Amaraich submitted a statement to the Senate criticizing the high commissioner's veto of a bill that would have waived the sovereign immunity of the Trust Territory government and thus allowed citizens the right to bring suit against the government.[55] He criticized as groundless the high commissioner's reasons for the veto that included the misuse of congressional power, the lack of funds to cover any judgment against the Trust Territory, and the adverse effects of such a bill on the ability of the government to function. Amaraich had also criticized the administration for its failure to move more quickly in permitting foreign investment within the Trust Territory. He noted that the Congress of Micronesia had passed a foreign investment bill in 1969; that first effort and subsequent versions had been vetoed on the grounds they exceeded the Congress' authority and countered the policy of the United States government. Johnston's eventual signing of a 1970 foreign investment bill was in line with the United States Department of the Interior's recently revised policy to give Micronesians more voice in the economic development of their islands. Amaraich, then chairman of the Senate Committee on Judiciary and Governmental Operations, said such a commitment to greater Micronesians input "should have been done a long time ago."[56]

Like Tosiwo Nakayama, Amaraich had been chosen to sit as the Micronesian representative when the American delegation delivered its annual report to the United Nations Trusteeship Council in New York City. He had followed Nakayama in that role in 1962, and then again in 1972. Addressing the council in 1972, he remarked upon the sad state of the Trust Territory administration, and the American dominance of the executive and judicial branches of government.[57] He also spoke of the need for Micronesians to control their lands and seas. With specific reference to the United States govern-

**Fig. 4.4.** Andon
Amaraich (Trust
Territory Photo
Archives, Pacific
Collection, Hamilton
Library, University of
Hawaiʻi, Mānoa).

ment's refusal to recognize Micronesia's territorial and resource claims under
the Law of the Sea Treaty, Amaraich argued that Micronesians must never
again be the victim of American diplomatic policies that denied them jurisdiction over their natural resources. He criticized the slow pace at which expatriate personnel were being replaced by competent Micronesians, the growing
size of the bureaucracy, and the large percentage of the Trust Territory budget
that went to expatriate salaries. He called self-government "a mere illusion,"
and pronounced the administration's political education program a failure,
saying little had actually been done to educate the people of Micronesia for
the awesome responsibilities of self-government. In summarizing the current
state of future political status negotiations with the United States, Amaraich
remarked that there remained many troublesome areas in which agreement
had not yet been reached. He lamented the American defense interests that
were playing such a large role in the negotiations, and the memories of war and
nuclear testing that they evoked in Micronesians. The promise of the return
of Bikini and Enewetak was certainly welcome but, in truth, these atolls were

never the United States' to take or give back. Amaraich returned to address the UN Trusteeship Council in 1973 and reiterated that the United States was continuing to ignore Micronesians' desire for self-government.[58]

Tosiwo Nakayama and Andon Amaraich were regarded as a very formidable and effective pair of legislators. Their shared vision of a unified, self-governing Micronesia upset some people within and beyond the islands. There were those in the Marshalls, the Marianas, and Palau who wanted no part of a united Micronesia and sought a separate political status for their respective districts. Others within Chuuk, especially the Faichuk area of the Chuuk Lagoon, resented Amaraich because he was Mortlockese; they thought his Senate seat belonged more appropriately to a resident of Chuuk Proper. In short, Amaraich's candor, honesty, hard work, and forthrightness had earned him a goodly number of adversaries in both the Congress and the administration. At the close of the first special session of the Fifth Congress meeting on Saipan in April 1974, Amaraich, sensing that he would not win re-election to the Senate, gave a farewell address of sorts in which he told the story of a man who could not see because of the two one-dollar coins placed over the lens of his glasses.[59] The senator likened the Congress of Micronesia to that man.

Amaraich did indeed lose his Senate seat but not in a way that he or anyone else expected. The first regular session of the Sixth Congress of Micronesia met from 13 January to 3 March 1975. One of its first and most contentious orders of business was the dispute over the election for senator in Chuuk between Nick Bossy and Andon Amaraich. Bossy grew up on Weno as the son of a prominent family and a member of the island's highest-ranking clan, the Sópwunupi. His uncle was Fujita Bossy, a mayor of Weno who would serve with distinction as a delegate to the 1975 Micronesian Constitutional Convention. Bossy was also a distant relative of Miter Nakayama, a fact that would make for complex family dynamics when he and Nakayama later opposed each other in the 1979 election for one of the two at-large Senate seats in the Congress of the Federated States of Micronesia.

Bossy had attended school in Hawai'i for a year. He became known over the course of his public career as a strong advocate of Weno's interests and as someone who was favorably disposed toward a close, long-term relationship with the United States. The official count of the 1974 election showed Bossy to be the winner by a very slim margin, but Amaraich contested the outcome of the election on the grounds that there had been voting irregularities and fraud. Privately, both Amaraich and Nakayama believed the election had been stolen with the help of Truk District Administrator Juan A. Sablan who was acting on orders from High Commissioner Edward Johnston.[60] Amaraich was an outspoken critic of the Trust Territory administration. As chair of the Committee on Judiciary and Governmental Relations, he had blocked on two recent occasions the administration's nominees for important posts, while taking the opportunity to criticize the high commissioner's methods and motives. Bossy, then, was the administration's preferred candidate.

While legislative measures involving future political status, unity, and preparations for the Micronesian Constitutional Convention waited, the first days of the Sixth Congress were taken up with the dispute over the election in Chuuk.[61] A congressional investigation conducted by a special credentials committee upheld Amaraich's charges. A recount done by the investigating committee actually showed Amaraich to be the winner. A minority report authored by Senator Roman Tmetuchl of Palau offered a different opinion, however. Tmetuchl's report argued that the burden of proof rested on the plaintiff and that the investigation into Amaraich's charges had not satisfied this burden of proof. The minority report went on to argue that the author of the special credentials committee's report, staff attorney Fred Ramp, had worked closely with Amaraich on the Joint Law of the Sea Committee. Tmetuchl's report argued that any registration irregularities resulted not from deliberate fraud but from the failure of the Chuuk District government to properly oversee voter registration. Moreover, the denial of voting rights to eligible voters could not be confirmed by the simple attachment of names to the committee report; other hard evidence in support of the charges was similarly lacking.

The chair of the special committee, Olympia Borja of the Marianas, summarized the majority opinion for the full Senate. Borja noted that 12,388 persons had voted; 6,382 or 51.5 percent had voted for Bossy while 6,006 or 48.5 percent had voted for Amaraich. The difference between the two vote totals was 376. Given that the majority of committee members believed there to be strong evidence in support of the charges of fraud and voting irregularities, the outcome of the election could not be said to accurately reflect the will of the people of Chuuk. The majority report closed with a set of recommendations. These included a declaration that the election be declared null and void; that the Senate decline to seat either candidate; and that the high commissioner appoint a temporary replacement senator while making preparations for a special election to fill the vacancy.

In a surprising and unprecedented move, the full Senate voted to accept both the majority and minority reports. There followed considerable confusion among senators as to what the votes to accept both reports actually meant. Responding to the situation, Senator Petrus Tun of Yap, in a speech on the Senate floor, noted the dislike of several senators for Andon Amaraich and their desire to see him removed.[62] Tun accused Senator Tmetuchl of play-

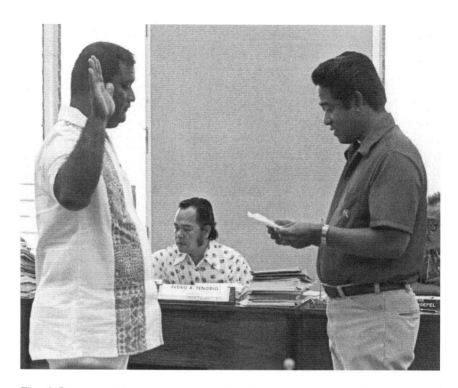

**Fig. 4.5.** Tosiwo Nakayama swearing in Nick Bossy as a member of the Congress of Micronesia Senate, 1974 (Trust Territory Photo Archives, Pacific Collection, Hamilton Library, University of Hawaiʻi, Mānoa).

ing to this sentiment. He underscored the preponderance of evidence in the majority report that pointed to widespread voting irregularities, and asked that the Senate adopt the majority report and its recommendations. A secret ballot vote was ultimately taken on the majority report and its recommendations were defeated by a vote of 6 to 5. In a spirit of reconciliation, Petrus Tun motioned and Bailey Olter seconded that Nick Bossy take his seat as the second senator from Chuuk. A secret ballot vote on the motion came out 8–3 in favor of seating Bossy. The 1974 congressional election in Chuuk then cost Tosiwo Nakayama a close friend and ally in the Senate. Amaraich left the Senate but continued to work for the Congress. He eventually became the executive director of the Joint Committee on Future Status, and played a major role in negotiations with the United States that ultimately eventuated in the Compact of Free Association. Following the inauguration of the Federated States of Micronesia, he became the secretary for external affairs and later the first Micronesian chief justice of the nation's Supreme Court.

## Personal and Personnel Matters

Nakayama's rise to public prominence in the 1960s took him to places far from
Chuuk. There were conferences, workshops, the Inter-District Advisory Com-
mittee and Council of Micronesia meetings on Guam, and the Congress of
Micronesia sessions on Saipan and later in the different districts of the Trust
Territory. Of all of these early journeys perhaps the most notable was a trip to
Japan in search for his father Masami who had been repatriated in 1946 following the end of the war.[63] In preparing for his 1961 trip to testify before the
UN Trusteeship Council, Nakayama learned from John de Young, the then
program officer and conference coordinator for the Council of Micronesia,
that he could for a relatively minor fee return home on eastbound flights from
New York City, making whatever stops he chose and completing what was
in essence a trip around the world. Following de Young's advice, Nakayama
adjusted his return ticket to include a stop in Tokyo. The reason he gave for
his journey was not at all complex; he simply wanted to find and speak again
with his father.

Nakayama stated that one of his reasons for attending school was to
learn enough English to travel in search of his father. Responding to Nakayama's personal request, Americans working for the Trust Territory government in Chuuk managed to locate Masami during the course of their travels
to Japan. The son then wrote a series of letters to the elder Nakayama at the
address provided to him by his expatriate co-workers. One letter elicited a
written response from Nakayama Masami, saying that he had failed his
Chuukese family. When subsequent letters to his father went unanswered,
the younger Nakayama decided to take advantage of the opportunity afforded
by his UN trip. Landing in Tokyo in early 1961, Nakayama made his way to
a hotel where a bellhop took an interest in him. They struck up a conversation in English, and Nakayama informed the man of his reason for being in
Japan and what he knew of his father's family. The bellhop offered to help
and took Nakayama by taxi to the Tsurumi section of Yokohama where they
sought assistance at three different police stations. They secured an address
from the third police station, but had a difficult time locating the place amidst
the crowded, narrow, and hidden backstreets of Tsurumi. They were eventually directed to a small building by a local resident who thought its occupant
matched their description.

Nakayama knocked on the door and soon found himself face-to-face
with Masami who said simply "you've come." After several awkward moments
of conversation, Nakayama Masami took his son to the family home for an
introduction and then a tour of Yokohama. Later that day they returned to the

home for a formal family gathering where Tosiwo had the opportunity to meet his two surviving uncles, Tosiwo and Hiroyoshi, his aunt, their spouses, and other family members. Before that time, he hadn't realized that he'd been named after one of his uncles. During the gathering, Tosiwo also learned that Masami had not remarried following his return to Japan, but had been adopted as family by two older women whom he assisted in return for his food and lodging. He had changed his last name to theirs and was now Ozeki Masami. His ability in English eventually secured him employment at the large American military base in Yokohama where he helped manage a social club. After the gathering and before a hurried trip to a local shrine to pay respects to family ancestors, Tosiwo asked his father to return with him to Chuuk. Masami replied that he would but that there was still work in Japan he needed to do first.

Nakayama Masami did return to Chuuk in 1972; he arrived not too long before the passing on 15 August of his wife Rosania who had married a man from Tamatam in the intervening years.[64] His last years in Chuuk were much like his first, though on a considerably more modest scale. He managed the family's small store on the grounds of their residence in the village of Mwan. Becoming slightly senile in his last years, Masami proved a popular store clerk as he often returned people's money with their purchase. On 16 August 1979, a little more than a month after his son was inaugurated as the first president of the Federated States of Micronesia, Nakayama Masami passed away in the Chuuk state hospital after what was described as a long illness. He was buried in front of the Nakayama family home at Mwan near the shore. Nakayama's trip to Japan to find his father was but the first of many to that country over the next thirty years. Long-distance travel would prove commonplace in Nakayama's life. By the mid-1960s, he was already a well-traveled individual; the security clearance form that he completed in support of his appointment as assistant district administrator for public affairs in 1964 listed the United States, Lebanon, the United Kingdom, Hong Kong, Holland, Australia, and the Philippines as other countries he had visited to that time in his life.[65]

The year 1961 had marked the reunion of father and son; the following year, 1962, brought sad news. Napoleon DeFang who had been a friend, supporter, and advocate of Tosiwo Nakayama died in a vehicular accident.[66] DeFang was returning to his home in Iras from church in Tunnuk on a Sunday morning. He was driving along the airstrip that was often used by vehicular traffic as a road to access the village. DeFang suddenly found himself facing a helicopter that was preparing to take off. He swerved to avoid a collision. The jeep overturned, killing him and injuring several family members. Eleven years Nakayama's senior, DeFang was forty-two years old at the time of his death and held the position of assistant educational administrator for Chuuk

District. Like Nakayama, DeFang's father was Japanese. Their mothers had become promised sisters in the Mortlocks—this meant the two boys were like brothers. It was DeFang who had introduced Nakayama to Thomas Gladwin and later helped him secure admission to PICS. DeFang and Nakayama had worked together to translate numerous legal and legislative documents from English into Chuukese at a time when the Trust Territory administration was promoting the establishment of local representative government at the municipal and district levels. Now he was gone. Nakayama felt the loss deeply even as his public and political career advanced.

Nakayama's rise up the district administrative ladder brought him compensation and benefits not available to most Chuukese or other Trust Territory citizens at the time. Material conditions had improved since the scarcity and shortages of the immediate postwar period. The effects of rapid increases in appropriations from the U.S. Congress that began in 1963 could be seen in district centers such as Weno; there were more stores that offered an expanded inventory of rice, canned goods, cloth, tools, household items, cigarettes, and alcohol, much of it from Japan.[67] Cars and pickup trucks now motored over restored roads lined by new businesses, gas stations, and enhanced private dwellings. Still, the Nakayamas fared better than most. His promotion to assistant district administrator entitled him and his family to government housing that cost $10 a month in rent.[68] The cement-block structure that Tosiwo Nakayama and his family of seven occupied beginning in May 1964 had three rooms, electricity, running water, and a tin roof. It had a refrigerator, stove, washing machine, water heater, and furniture. Nakayama had his own car as well as access to government vehicles. In 1965, he owned a new light blue, four-door Contessa sedan. His salary had increased accordingly—his days as a clerk in the Island Affairs section earned him $30 a month; now he received a yearly salary of $5,300 as an assistant district administrator for public affairs.

Professional advancement meant more and more time away from home and family. Nakayama was nominated for the Parvin Fellows Program at Princeton University in early 1967; he ended up accepting an East-West Center Fellowship at the University of Hawai'i, Mānoa, for the 1967–1969 academic years, but was not completely free from congressional business, future political status issues, and related travel.[69] He continued to receive his government salary, though the $60 in additional monthly support for his family that he was promised never materialized. A much greater source of aggravation was the eviction of his family from government housing in January 1969 while he was away. By special provision, the secretarial order creating the Congress of Micronesia permitted employees of the Trust Territory government to run and, if elected, serve in the Congress. This was a special four-year exemption that ran until January 1969, and was designed to draw upon the expertise and experience of government employees at what was perceived as a critical moment in the development of self-government for the islands. Leave without pay was granted to government employees to enable them to run for office and, if elected, to serve in the Congress. After the end of the four-year exemption period, islanders holding positions in the executive and judicial branches of the Trust Territory government or serving in district legislatures were no longer able to serve simultaneously in the Congress.[70] They would now have to resign from their employment with the government to hold elective office.

Nakayama had no trouble with the policy, but resented the way in which his wife and now eight children were forced to move from their government housing on short notice and while he was away. In a letter dated 15 January 1969 to the high commissioner, he called the removal of his family disheartening and a personal affront. Nakayama sent a copy of the letter to Chuuk district administrator Jesse R. Quigley, the local enforcer of the policy, with a curt note saying that he would be in touch again soon on the matter.[71] Andon Amaraich was also asked to vacate his government housing under similar circumstances, and he made his dislike known in an interview with the *Truk Review*.[72] He made reference to the Nakayamas' situation, calling Miter Nakayama a "sickly woman" whose displacement with her children from government housing to temporary quarters at the back of a local bakery was "completely unacceptable." With these privileges and material advantages, Tosiwo Nakayama lived a life that was personally and professionally demanding. The momentum building toward self-government for the Trust Territory would only increase those demands.

## Negotiating Political Status

The two most serious and intricately linked issues that confronted the Congress of Micronesia throughout its fourteen-year life were unity and political status. Less than two years after its opening, the Congress found itself confronting the issue of future political status. Some within the Congress, like Bailey Olter of Pohnpei, thought the question to be premature for a people struggling to cope with modernization, development, and new forms of representative government. Not Tosiwo Nakayama. He had made his position on self-government clear before the UN Trusteeship Council meeting in 1961. Supported by others in the Congress and aided by developments beyond the Trust Territory, Nakayama pressed the issue. Encouraged by the Trusteeship Council, the Congress of Micronesia, during its second regular session in 1966, passed a resolution requesting that President Lyndon Johnson create a commission "to study and critically assess the political alternatives open to Micronesia."[73] When the United States government failed to respond, the Congress of Micronesia formed its own six-member political status commission.[74]

At its first formal meeting in 1967, Lazarus Salii of Palau, Nakayama's friend from their student days in Hawai'i, was chosen chair. The committee immediately began planning a tour of island states and territories in the Pacific and the Caribbean to identify and evaluate different political options. Tosiwo Nakayama was a member of the commission, having been chosen by his Chuukese colleagues to replace Petrus Mailo who had retired from the Congress in 1966.[75] Nakayama's fellowship at the East-West Center did not prevent him from traveling with the commission and participating in its meetings. Among the commission's travels, Nakayama was particularly impressed by the visits to Papua New Guinea and Australia. In Canberra, members of the commission asked to meet with Sir William John Aston, the Speaker of the Australian Parliament's House of Representatives. Australian government representatives told the commission members that the Speaker was traveling and thus unavailable. Nakayama then contacted John Kaputin, a friend from the East-West Center who was in Canberra at the time and well connected to Australian politicians. Kaputin would later go on to serve as Papua New Guinea's foreign minister on two separate occasions in the 1990s. In a phone conversation, Kaputin told Nakayama that the commission members were being lied to; the Speaker was in fact in Canberra. Kaputin went ahead and set up a meeting at which the Speaker advised the Micronesian congressional delegation to get rid of the *palangis* or outsiders; until they did, they would never control their own government.[76]

The June 1968 interim report of the commission identified four relevant options: independence, a state of free association or protectorate status, integration within a larger sovereign as either a territory or a commonwealth, and the continuation of Trust Territory status.[77] The report also considered the creation of a larger regional grouping that would include Guam as well as a division into smaller governmental entities based on cultural features. In 1969, the commission issued its final report, endorsing a relationship of free association with the United States.[78] Salii was a particularly strong and vocal proponent of this option. Congress voted to accept the final report and approved the creation of a ten-member Future Political Status Commission. Members were authorized to fly to Washington, D.C., later that year and begin status negotiations with an American team of negotiators headed by Harrison Loesch of the Department of the Interior. Initially, Nakayama supported Salii's advocacy of free association. He said upon the commission's return from its fact-finding tour of the region:

> We have been under the American system for 20 years, but we can't
> prolong the issue for another 20 years. With this associate free state,
> we will have a goal that Micronesians know about and the United
> States knows about. It's time we involved the people in discussions.[79]

He added, however, that he still wanted to be "labeled as the person for independence," and affirmed that if an agreement of free association could not be
reached, independence was the only other alternative.[80] His place on the negotiating team would allow him to pursue that option.

As a result of World War II and the Cold War that developed in its aftermath, the United States had strong and deep strategic interests in the Trust
Territory. The 1947 award of a United Nations strategic trusteeship was recognition of those interests. The political, social, and economic costs of the
Korean and Vietnam Wars, coupled with increasing unrest and anti-Ameri-
can sentiment elsewhere in East and Southeast Asia, added to American per-
ceptions of an increasingly hostile and dangerous world. In 1969, President
Richard Nixon had declared in a speech on Guam what became known as the
Nixon Doctrine, a new policy that called for a shifting of the American defense
perimeter from contested bases in Japan, Okinawa, and the Philippines toward
more secure sites in the American Pacific, most notably Guam and the Trust
Territory.

Emboldened by the Nixon Doctrine and the circumstances that
informed it, Micronesian negotiators headed to Washington with a list of
eleven demands. These included the right to draft a constitution; undisputed
control over all public land taken by past colonial regimes; access to the United
States for Micronesians and their exports; the settlement of all war claims; and
the guarantee of long-term financial assistance. In return, the islands would
consent to the construction of American military bases and the exclusion
of foreign military forces from Micronesia's lands and surrounding waters.[81]
The lack of access to necessary records prevents at this time a thorough and
nuanced history of the negotiations between Micronesians and Americans.
Still, the contours of those encounters are clear, and Tosiwo Nakayama was at
the heart of them.

Caught off guard by the boldness of the Micronesian position, the Americans did little more at this first formal session than acknowledge the Micronesian presentation. At the second negotiating session on Saipan a year later,
American representatives countered by extending an offer of commonwealth
status, with the United States holding full sovereignty over the islands. In a
speech before the Congress of Micronesia, Lazarus Salii gave his understanding of what commonwealth status would mean for the islands: "Micronesians

would become the newest, smallest, the remotest non-white minority in the United States political family—as permanent and as American, shall we say, as the American Indian."[82]

Calling the offer of commonwealth status unacceptable, the Congress of Micronesia charged its Future Political Status Commission with investigating the option of independence. The change resulted in part from a crescendo of discontent with the Trust Territory administration, and the willingness of an increasing number of congressmen to seriously consider independence as a viable political option for the islands. Congressmen Hans Williander from Chuuk and Henry Samuel of the Marshalls were particularly vocal advocates of independence. Samuel, in a speech on the House floor, said that the U.S. offer "assumes that America knows what is best for Micronesians." He went on to decry "the myth that our government can only be maintained through America's charity and the myth that America's standard of living is superior to our own."[83] For a goodly number in the Congress, including Nakayama, independence now became the preferred future status position. At the closing Senate session of the Third Congress in mid-1970, Nakayama gave a short, seven-word speech: "Mr. President and Honorable Members of the Senate, Micronesia ought to be an independent state."[84] He later defined independence as simply the ability to decide for oneself "without asking for permission of another person. In other words, it is independence in all areas of human endeavor."[85] On 10 May 1971, Hans Williander announced the formation of an independence coalition designed as a counterweight to the status commission and its endorsement of free association. Members of the coalition included the entire Chuukese congressional delegation comprised of Tosiwo Nakayama, Andon Amaraich, Endy Dois, Sasauo Haruo, Masao Nakayama, Raymond Setik, and Hans Williander, along with Ataji Balos and Henry Samuel of the Marshalls, Heinrich Iriarte of Pohnpei, and Roman Tmetuchl of Palau.[86]

Trust Territory citizens studying abroad also became quite vocal. Students in Hawai'i published a newsletter entitled the *Young Micronesian*. Its articles and editorials advocated self-reliance as a path to independence and demanded that the United States refrain from building military bases in the islands. Students on Guam published a similar newsletter, the *Surviving Micronesian* that, among its editorial purposes, sought to counter the negative and politically harmful stereotypes of people from the Trust Territory as backward and primitive.[87] Adding impetus to the cries for independence was the unauthorized release of parts of the Solomon Report, a 1963 study commissioned by President John F. Kennedy that specified the ways in which the islands could be moved toward permanent affiliation with the United

States.[88] The report smacked of conspiracy and subversion to some people. *The Young Micronesian* published in its March 1971 issue the excerpts from the report that had been provided to its editors by Tosiwo Nakayama.[89] While talk of independence increased, the majority of congressmen still viewed it as a fallback position. In the end, the Congress agreed to reaffirm the four basic principles upon which all future negotiations with the United States would be founded. The United States had to recognize Micronesia's political sovereignty, its right to self-determination, its right to adopt its own constitution, and the right of either party to unilaterally terminate a compact of free association.

Over the next two years, negotiations bogged down over disagreements regarding the levels of American financial assistance, the length of an agreement, and the procedures for any early termination of that agreement. On the American side, the transfer of responsibility for the conduct of the negotiations from the Department of the Interior to an interdepartmental task force, titled the Office of Micronesian Status Negotiations, added to the delay. Hayden Williams, a former president of the Asia Foundation, headed the office and held the rank of ambassador. The Micronesian side also made changes, adding four new members and changing the name of the commission to the Joint Committee on Future Status. Lazarus Salii remained its chair. The Congress hired Eugene Mihaly of the Institute of International Studies at the University of California at Berkeley and James Davidson of the Australian National University as consultants to the committee.[90]

Negotiations resumed in October 1971 at Hana, Maui with the U.S. team signaling its willingness to take the Micronesian position seriously. It offered a relationship of free association based on a negotiated compact to be approved by the Micronesian people in a sovereign act of self-determination and subsequently recognized by the international community. Americans conceded the right of Micronesians to draft their own constitution and to control all land except that set aside for military use under the terms of the compact. For its part, the United States would assume responsibility for Micronesia's foreign affairs and defense. The United States continued to insist that the compact could be revoked only by mutual consent.

After much haggling, Micronesian negotiators accepted for the time being the point that unilateral termination of any compact would leave American military bases extremely vulnerable. They compromised by agreeing to an initial period in which any termination would require mutual consent followed thereafter by the right of either government to terminate unilaterally after providing appropriate notice. No financial terms were discussed, though the United States' representatives did identify Kwajalein, Palau, and Tinian as being the focus of the military's land needs.[91] Kwajalein was the site of a major weapons testing and missile tracking station; American negotiators considered it essential and also sought to acquire use rights in Enewetak and Bikini. A large tract of land on Babeldaob for training maneuvers and a landing strip for jet airplanes, along with acreage for a support facility on tiny Malakal Island at the tip of Koror, comprised American military land needs in Palau. Discussion over military land needs on Tinian became mute as the Marianas and the United States had commenced separate political status talks.

The Congress did not respond well to the draft compact placed before it by the Joint Committee on Future Status. Congressional critics felt the compact gave up too much for too little. Representative Timothy Olkeriil of Palau called it a "serious mistake"; Sasauo Haruo of Chuuk termed the draft compact "a stinking idea with ominous implications."[92] There was also growing displeasure with Lazarus Salii who limited the participation of his fellow committee members in the talks and seemed at times to be negotiating with the Americans by himself. Nakayama in particular became discouraged over the direction of the talks and the ways in which his friend Salii was mishandling the Micronesian side. As a result of these concerns, the Congress withheld approval of the draft compact and ordered its political status committee to begin negotiations for independence even as it continued discussions over free association. This was a concession to members of the Micronesian Independence Coalition. The Americans refused to discuss independence at the sixth round of talks in September 1972 and negotiations broke off for a year.

Adding to the tensions that surrounded the negotiations were congressional concerns over American interference and surveillance. During the first regular session of the Fifth Congress in early 1973, there arose debate about a press release from the Congress of Micronesia that criticized the Trust Territory government for restricting the access of congressmen to members of the UN Visiting Mission.[93] Some like Senator Edward Pangelinan of the Marianas felt the press release was in error, and that there had been no such interference on the part of Trust Territory personnel. Addressing the Senate, Nakayama conceded that there may have been times when access was limited because of time constraints and the number of congressmen wishing to speak with UN officials. He expressed the belief, however, that the chairman of the UN Visiting Mission, Mr. Tang, had been abruptly hurried away by a high American official before he had the chance to finish his conversation with Andon Amaraich, one of the Congress' most vocal critics of the American administration. Nakayama noted too that at a special luncheon for the UN Visiting Mission, Mary Vance Trent, a liaison officer with the United States Department of State, had shown up unexpectedly and seated herself between Mr. Tang and Bethwel Henry, the Speaker of the House of Representatives. Nakayama politely intervened to have Trent moved to another table away from any conversation between the House Speaker and the UN Visiting Mission head.[94]

When negotiations started up again in September 1973, financial assistance proved the major negotiating point. Micronesian representatives requested $100 million annually; the United States offered $39 million. More critical, however, was how the money was to be distributed. The United States calculated its contribution on the assumption there would be five states; the Micronesian negotiators insisted that they still held responsibility for the Marianas. It would be three years before all sides would meet again and come to a mutually acceptable formula for financial assistance. During this time, Nakayama and other members of the Joint Committee on Future Status worked to keep people informed of the negotiations and the myriad of issues involved. In June 1973, Nakayama participated in a weeklong conference sponsored by the Micronesian Seminar on Pohnpei that addressed moral issues related to the choice of political status.[95] The next month, he traveled as a member of the Joint Committee's Eastern District Subcommittee to Chuuk, the Marshalls, and Pohnpei to ascertain people's views and preferences on a future political status for the islands.[96] His commitment and patience were on full public display at all of these gatherings and venues.

## The Lack of Unity

While academics have debated the coherence and integrity of the Caroline, Mariana, and Marshall Islands as a single cultural area known as Micronesia, the inhabitants of these islands saw themselves as distinct from one another. The divisions were evident during Territory-wide meetings prior to the creation of the Congress of Micronesia and intensified dramatically over time. Separatist sentiments showed themselves early in the Northern Marianas.[97] A 1961 referendum conducted there showed two-thirds of voters supporting integration with Guam and nearly all of the rest voting for direct annexation by the United Sates. Over the years, visiting UN delegations listened to ardent pleas from citizens of the Northern Marianas asking to be allowed to separate from the rest of the Trust Territory. Senator Francis Palacios, a member of the Congress of Micronesia from Saipan, told the UN Trusteeship Council in 1967 that the Marianas were ready to become a territory of the United States. He termed the denial of that desire reversion "to a colonial mentality."[98]

In late 1969, the Marianas held another plebiscite in which 65 percent of voters expressed a desire for annexation by the United States. When the United States made an offer of commonwealth status to the entire Trust Territory, the Marianas congressional delegation protested the rejection of that offer by the Congress of Micronesia. The depth of resentment in the Northern Marianas showed itself in a resolution passed by the district legislature on 19 February 1971 threatening to "secede from the Trust Territory...by force of arms if necessary, and with or without the approval of the United Nations."[99] The Northern Mariana Islands had experienced a very different, much longer, and more heavily Spanish colonial history than either the Carolines or the Marshalls. Chamorros chafed at the thought of inclusion in a political entity comprised of other islanders they considered less developed and sophisticated than themselves. This point was underscored dramatically when arson badly damaged the Congress of Micronesia's building on 20 February 1971, forcing the abrupt termination of the current session and the temporary relocation of the Congress' meeting to Chuuk.[100] To underscore their resolve, members of the Marianas congressional delegation deliberately arrived several days late for the Chuuk session.

Separatist sentiment also showed itself in the Marshalls and Palau. Money, power, and cultural identity fueled the Marshalls' desire to create for itself a political status apart from the rest of the Trust Territory. The debate over revenue sharing proved the most public catalyst. At the 1972 regular session of the Congress of Micronesia, Representative Charles Dominik proposed that half the tax money collected by the Congress be returned to the districts from which the revenue originally came. Largely because of the heavy commercial activity in and around the Kwajalein missile testing facility, the Marshalls accounted for over half of the total revenue collected by Congress and thus stood to benefit most from the legislation proposed by Dominik. As Hezel notes, Marshallese leaders felt that their district, which had turned over whole islands to the military including Kwajalein, Bikini, and Enewetak, was being asked to shoulder more than its share of the burden by in effect subsidizing congressional projects in the poorer districts.[101] When Congress balked, Dominik introduced another bill authorizing each district to establish its own political status commission. That bill was also defeated.

At the next regular session of the Congress in 1973, the Marshallese delegation again introduced the revenue sharing bill and with the threat that if it were not passed, the Marshalls would begin separate status talks with the United States. When Congress killed that bill, the Marshallese delegation staged a temporary walkout. Said Amata Kabua: "Our fear is now greater with respect to other Micronesians than with the United States."[102] Kabua's anger was also fed by his loss of the Senate presidency to Tosiwo Nakayama. Congress sought compromise by ultimately passing a bill that mandated 20 percent of tax revenues generated within a given district be automatically returned to that district.[103] The Marshallese would have none of it. When the tax bill failed again in 1974, the Nitijela or Marshallese legislature announced that it "is unwilling and unable to be a member of the political family of Micronesia after the termination of the trusteeship agreement." It was now *Majol Mokta,* "the Marshalls First."

Divisions within Palau between political parties that identified themselves as "Liberal" and "Progressive" affected the operations of the Congress in the form of electoral challenges and issues involving future political status. Throughout the first week of the Fourth Congress' first regular session in 1971, the credentials committee of both houses met to consider challenges to the election of Senator Roman Tmetuchl, and Representatives-elect Timothy Olkeriil, George Ngirarsaol, and Tarkong Pedro.[104] The challenge to the election of these Liberal Party members came from Palau's Progressive Party whose members were increasingly espousing political separation from the rest of the Trust Territory. Tmetuchl survived the challenge and was seated by the Senate; the three representatives-elect were denied their place in the House but two eventually reclaimed their seats in a special election. Only George Ngirarsaol, who lost to Polycarp Basilius, failed to return.[105]

In September 1972, the leadership in Palau, consisting of chiefs, local magistrates, and legislators, endorsed a resolution registering their opposition to any land use by the U.S. military.[106] The resolution was aimed primarily at Lazarus Salii and the draft compact he had negotiated with the Americans at Hana; the resolution also reflected the genuine sentiment of a number of Palau's leaders. When it became clear the United States had strong land interests on Babeldoab and Malakal Islands, Palau's leaders realized they were one of the "have" districts with a strong bargaining chip in any negotiations with the United States. Aware of the developments in the Marianas and the Marshalls, Palau's Progressive Party now turned toward separation, fueled in part by a proposal from Japanese business interests to establish a half-billion dollar supertanker port and oil storage facility in Palau.

Questions of unity and future political status loomed large as the convocation of the Micronesian Constitutional Convention approached in July 1975. The Marianas had already entered into separate political status talks with the United States, and the Marshalls and Palau were now asking to do the same. Micronesia was about to hold a constitutional convention just as "the political myth of a unified Micronesia was being shattered."[107] Tosiwo Nakayama who had committed heavily to unity, self-government, and independence, would assume center stage. The success of the convention hinged on his ability to forge consensus among district delegations that were showing themselves to be increasingly divided over a host of issues relating to the future political status of the islands.

CHAPTER 5

# Constituting a Nation

TOSIWO NAKAYAMA stood before the assembled delegates to the Micronesian Constitutional Convention on 12 July 1975 and stated that the time to create a constitution for a Micronesian government was "now or never."[1] He believed firmly that the convention offered the only real opportunity to create the foundations for an independent, self-governing entity for islands too long under the control of other countries. The obstacles facing delegates at the start of the convention were enormous, and would be compounded by events and developments over the ninety-day life of the gathering. Divisions among the different island groups threatened to undermine the drafting of a constitution. Equally contentious were debates over the role of chiefs and the place of tradition in a new national government; the structure of the executive and legislative branches; the distribution of power between the national and state governments; and more specific issues involving land, eminent domain, secession, and the location of a capital for the new government. These were all issues that seemed to undermine the possibility of consensus. In the words of one advisor, the Micronesian Constitutional Convention was a time of high drama and uncertainty.[2]

There had been some speculation that the Congress of Micronesia's Joint Committee on Future Status might do the actual drafting of a constitution that would then be submitted to a countrywide referendum. This scenario gave way to the belief that any draft constitution required the input of independent delegates representing as broad a spectrum of the population as possible. The ultimate success of the convention in approving a draft

128

constitution resulted in no small part from the efforts of the man chosen to be its president, Tosiwo Nakayama. He was not just overseeing the drafting of a constitution but actually helping to constitute a nation based on shared historical experiences and cultural connections. As he had in the Congress of Micronesia's Senate, Nakayama adopted a quiet, humble but persistent and strategically effective approach that sought consensus for larger goals and the greater good through compromise and concession. The stakes now were much higher and the impediments almost overwhelming. In the end, the success of the convention was a testament to Nakayama's initiative, will, and vision; it was perhaps his greatest achievement as a political leader. Its story is his story.

## Planning and Preparations

Chosen as chair of the Congress' Pre-Convention Committee, Nakayama found himself confronted with a host of issues that required careful resolution if the convention were to proceed let alone succeed. Not the least of these problems were the deficiencies in the law chartering the convention.[3] Errors and inadequacies in the enabling legislation required numerous amendments in a variety of areas that ranged from apportionment, finance, and timing to the size of district delegations. The latter issue proved particularly complex and fraught. In the end, Yap was allocated three elected representatives, the Marianas four, Palau five, the Marshalls and Pohnpei nine each, and Chuuk twelve.[4] In addition, a member of Congress was chosen to sit on each district's convention delegation. Chiefly representation on the district delegations was an even more sensitive issue. After much debate, it was decided that two chiefs from each district were to be chosen as delegates to the convention by the determination of their fellow chiefs.[5] To deal with the lack of chiefs in the Marianas, the district administrator there was asked to appoint the equivalent of a chiefly or community leader and the district legislature another.[6] The assumption was that one of the two chiefly representatives would come from the *Re Falawasch* or Carolinian community in the Marianas.

The enabling legislation also left it to the convention to adopt its own rules of procedure, and said nothing about attempting to produce a document in accord with the draft compact of free association that had emerged from negotiations between Micronesian and American representatives.[7] Eligibility criteria for both voters and delegate candidates also fell to the convention, which was identified as the sole judge of elections results and the qualifications of the delegates elected.

Ratification of any draft constitution loomed as another critical matter around which there swirled intense, potentially disruptive politics.[8] There were no approval majorities stipulated in the enabling legislation, only the provision that the high commissioner would set the date for a referendum on the draft constitution produced by the convention. At its 1975 regular session, the Congress passed a bill specifying two criteria necessary for passage of any draft constitution—a Territory-wide majority vote and a two-thirds approval vote in the individual districts.[9] The options open to any district that rejected the constitution went unspecified. The stringent requirements were at the insistence of those congressional delegations whose districts were contemplating political separation from the rest of the Trust Territory. Later, during the 1975 special session, the members of Congress reduced these two-tiered approval requirements to a simple majority vote in each of the districts with the results to be binding on all.[10] The revised requirements resulted from a desire to prevent the now certain separation of the Marianas and the possible defection of Palau and the Marshalls from undermining approval of the constitution. In his role as president of the Senate, Nakayama was the architect of many of these pragmatic and necessary adjustments.

The voting rights of the chiefly or traditional leader delegates required reconsideration and amendment. In its original form, the enabling legislation gave traditional chiefs the right to engage in debate but not vote. Proponents of this approach argued that it afforded the chiefs the opportunity to participate in a manner befitting their rank, but without the risk of public embarrassment when being on the losing side of a vote. Critics charged that the chiefs were being excluded so that Congress could institute a more modern form of government closer to its liking and interests. Faced with these objections, the first regular session of the Sixth Congress of Micronesia voted in early 1975 to amend the enabling act so as to remove all restrictions on the participation of the chiefs.[11] This change necessitated other amendments involving quorums and the vote requirements for approval of formal actions. The quorum needed to conduct business was raised from thirty-six to forty delegates. At the same time, the minimum number of votes needed for the convention to take action was raised from two-thirds to three-fourths of the delegates present.[12] This latter adjustment was in effect a compromise that sought to counter Palauan demands that delegations vote as a single unit on all convention business, a requirement that would have meant gridlock and stalemate given the strong separatist sentiment in three of the six districts.

It fell to Tosiwo Nakayama as chair of the Pre-Convention Committee to oversee preparations for the convention. The Congress had created the committee in the convention's enabling legislation, and given it sufficient powers to take whatever action it deemed necessary. The committee faced numerous, potentially disruptive, and defeating issues, not the least of which centered around the organization of the district delegations whose designated chairs automatically became members of the Pre-Convention Committee. The Marshalls near-total boycott of the July 1975 status referendum and the elections a year earlier to choose convention delegates threatened to deny the district representation on the Pre-Convention Committee. With the district delegation unable to organize, the Pre-Convention Committee invited Carl Heine, the largest vote getter in the Marshalls' limited delegate elections, to sit as the Marshallese representative on the committee.[13] The most difficult decisions facing Nakayama's Pre-Convention Committee were the determination of the start date and the site for the convention.[14] Saipan was chosen for reasons of convenience and economy, though there were those who wondered how appropriate and hospitable a site Saipan would prove given the Northern Marianas' already clear decision to leave the rest of the Trust Territory. A serious effort to relocate the convention to Palau had been defeated only on the last day of the 1975 regular session of the Congress.

Nakayama and members of the Pre-Convention Committee acknowledged concern about how ready the citizens of the Trust Territory were to decide upon the weighty matters of self-government and future political status. The Trust Territory government's Education for Self-Government program was proving to be of limited effectiveness. The committee considered drafting a constitution in advance of the convention that would serve as a working document from which to begin. In the end, however, members decided to let the individual delegations present the views of their constituents at the convention and trust in whatever consensus emerged.[15] The committee itself did not make any formal recommendations on the form and content of a constitution. What members of the committee did do was to travel to the different districts to meet with the individual delegations to review preparations, answer questions on procedures, address objections, and ensure that the timing of the convention did not conflict with important events in the district. All of these early and critical decisions reflected the personal imprint and influence of the Pre-Convention Committee's chairperson.

The setting of a date for the convention proved complicated. The election for convention delegates had taken place in June 1974; 1975, however, was looking to be a very crowded political year. The Congress of Micronesia's regular session; the Territory-wide political status referendum; the Marianas' plebiscite vote on the offer of commonwealth from the United States; the challenge to the Marshallese delegate elections; and the belatedly recognized need to hold a special midyear session of Congress were all scheduled for 1975. So crowded did the 1975 political calendar look that the Congress of Micronesia contemplated for a time postponing the convention until 1976. Lazarus Salii, the chairman of the Joint Committee on Future Status, advised the Pre-Convention Committee to seriously consider postponement.[16] Others feared that the increasing friction among the districts would turn any convention into a debacle. Some legal observers countered that a reduced federation of Micronesian states constituted a viable and practical alternative. Nakayama, however, was reluctant to abandon the goal of unity. Ever the optimist, he urged that planning for the convention proceed on the assumption that all districts would attend and participate.

The committee finally settled on 12 July 1975, the ten-year anniversary of the opening of the first Congress of Micronesia, as the start date of the convention. Given the differences and the complexity of issues, it became painfully clear soon after the start of the convention that the delegates would be hard-pressed to complete their work within the mandated ninety days. Nakayama had thought six months a more appropriate time period for the convention but found few supporters for his position in the Congress.[17] Complicating matters even further were elections for the Palau District Legislature; they were scheduled during the life of the convention and posed a serious threat to the convention's ability to complete its work on time. Fortuitously as things turned out, the Congress at its 1975 special session amended the enabling legislation to allow for up to thirty days of recess, and to provide funds for delegates' interim travel and the ongoing work of the convention and its staff during the recess.[18]

The selection of a site for the convention presented yet another confounding matter.[19] Unable to locate any suitable public facility on Saipan, the Pre-Convention Committee considered the InterContinental Hotel's main dining room for the plenary sessions of the convention, and the rooms immediately above it for supporting staff and committee meetings. Negotiations broke down over the convention's need for the continuous and exclusive use of the facilities. The committee then turned to the White Sands Hotel and signed a lease with its owner, the South Seas Corporation. The hotel was still under construction, and there developed acute concern over whether the facilities would be ready in time. Complicating the situation further was a lawsuit against the South Seas Corporation that contested the ownership of the hotel. All parties to the lawsuit did agree to honor the contract signed with the Pre-Convention Committee, and construction proceeded. While completion of the main hotel building and surrounding lodges allowed the convention staff to move in, legal challenges and counter-challenges associated with the lawsuit made the possibility of eviction a real and constant threat throughout the convention. There were also delays in completing the electrical and air-conditioning systems of the hotel without which the convention could not proceed.

The withholding of fuel for the hotel's generator as a tactic to settle the lawsuit forced the pre-convention workshop to move for a day to another location; the very next day the fumes from the asphalt paving of the hotel's driveway again forced the delegates from the site.

The Congress of Micronesia's House of Representatives had estimated the total cost of the constitutional convention at $550,000, with $450,000 of that sum being covered by the Trust Territory government using special funds appropriated by the U.S. Congress.[20] This left the Congress of Micronesia to cover the balance of $100,000. This figure proved to be a gross underestimate as the Congress was eventually forced to appropriate $600,000 in support of the convention. Delegate travel, per diem and supplemental support, staff salaries, and adjusted compensation for those government employees on loan to the convention accounted for the major share of these expenditures. Again, Nakayama's roles as Senate president and chair of the Pre-Convention Committee enabled him to help secure the additional funds.

As mentioned earlier, the Congress, in its efforts to seek broader representation, had agreed to the appointment of two traditional representatives and one congressional member from each district. This raised the total number of convention delegates to sixty. Particularly critical was the decision to amend the enabling legislation to allow other congressmen to run for election as delegates. Planners had come to realize the importance, even necessity, of having among the ranks of the delegates those trained in legislative procedures. This adjustment led to the addition of three incumbent congressmen to the six already appointed as the congressional representatives to their respective delegations. Among the three congressmen elected under this 1974 amendment was Tosiwo Nakayama.[21] Without the amendment and consequent election that gave Nakayama a formal place at Saipan, it is highly doubtful that the convention would have succeeded.

In addition to the nine congressional delegates, another fourteen elected delegates had either served as congressmen or worked as congressional staff members.[22] Twenty-three of the sixty convention delegates thus had congressional experience, a fact that was to prove critical in explaining both the successes and fissures that resulted over the course of the convention. Notable too was the overall youth of the delegates—two-thirds were between the ages of twenty-five and thirty-five, and four delegates were under the age of thirty. Nakayama himself was thirty-four. Whereas employment as educators had been a characteristic of earlier representative groups in the region, only a third of the delegates brought a professional background in education to the convention. Experience in government and private business distinguished a number of participants. As the delegates convened in Saipan, there emerged concern about American dominance of the convention.[23] The U.S. Congress had shouldered a major portion of the convention's expenses, and the technical support staff was overwhelmingly American. American principles, structures, and procedures heavily informed the gathering, and there was too the political socialization of the delegates under the American Trust Territory government. There were those who doubted the possibility of a unique, truly Micronesian constitution. The convention and the draft constitution that it produced proved anything but "American made," however.

The Pre-Convention Committee had opted for a committee structure as the way to best promote active dialogue and delegate input.[24] To this end, two committees emerged with broad commissions: the Functions Committee that considered the entire range of functions for the government to be chartered by the constitution; and the Structure Committee that held responsibility for determining the form of the new government and its component parts. In addition to these two committees, there were three other committees charged with addressing more specific areas of governmental authority: the Public Finance Committee, the Future Political Status and Transition Committee also known as the Committee on General Provisions, and the Civil Liberties and Traditional Rights Committee. Finally, a Style and Arrangements Committee reviewed all approved proposals coming out of the five major committees to ensure that they were written in a language that was legally consistent and correct. Eugene Mihaly, a constitutional consultant from the University of California at Berkeley, worked closely with this committee.[25] Norman Meller, University of Hawai'i professor and legal advisor to the constitution, described the convention's procedures as follows:

> Upon a committee report and proposal being delivered to the convention, the latter would receive nominal First Reading, and no sooner than the following day, go to the Committee of the Whole. Securing approval there by a majority vote, the proposal would next receive the attention of the Style Committee, which in turn would report upon it, together with any amendments believed required. At this stage, the Convention now in the more formal Plenary Session, would consider the proposal, and a three-quarters vote would be requisite for passage on Second Reading. This hurdle past, once again the proposal would be referred to the Style Committee, including all amendments which might have been added, there to be held and incorporated into a complete draft with all the other proposals so received. The ultimate act would be the resubmission of the whole constitution to the Plenary Session for formal adoption.[26]

Convention rules stipulated time limits for discussion; the scheduling of the different procedures detailed above was ordered in such a way as to avoid last minute actions that could derail, disrupt, and confuse the overall process. Other convention rules allowed the president to allot parts of lengthy, complex delegate proposals to different committees. Minority reports were treated as amendments and the roll call for the Committee of the Whole was prohibited in the interests of saving time and avoiding delegate embarrassment. Despite the seemingly foreign nature of these procedures, they proved flexible enough in accommodating the more personal, informal, and relaxed interaction among delegates that came to be called the "Micronesian Way," a more localized version of the term "Pacific Way" used to describe the consensus-seeking manner of decision making in the larger region.

The Pre-Convention Committee's work included staffing for the convention. Here, Nakayama called on both personal and familial relationships, and to good effect.[27] Victorio Uherbelau of Palau was hired as executive director of the Pre-Convention Committee and later became convention secretary.[28] Uherbelau had first met Nakayama in 1966 when he worked as a management intern with the Trust Territory government's Public Information office on Saipan. Nakayama was impressed by the young Palauan and recruited him to serve as the clerk of the Congress of Micronesia Senate later that year. The two were together for a short time in Hawai'i during the late 1960s; Nakayama was at the East-West Center attempting to complete his bachelor's degree when Uherbelau attended a two-month training session there on legislative procedures. Uherbelau had majored in English literature as an undergraduate and later earned a law school degree before assuming his convention duties. Asterio Takesy, a nephew of Nakayama, was hired as assistant convention secretary. Both men performed admirably, and would later be entrusted with key responsibilities in the transition period between governments. Uherbelau at times came under strong criticism from the Palau delegation for his strong pro-unity sentiments at a time when that delegation was becoming increasingly committed to separatism. This did not affect the impartial discharge of his responsibilities as convention secretary, though Nakayama at times had to intervene in Uherbelau's behalf against his critics.

Uherbelau and Takesy worked with a staff in the convention president's office whose members served as sergeant-at-arms, journal clerks, and floor runners.[29] A staff of eighteen manned the administrative section of the office and dealt with records, disbursements, and travel arrangements. A small public relations section of four issued press releases, released public information as requested or scheduled, and sometime wrote speeches. The research and drafting section was by far the largest with a staff that at one time or another numbered twenty-six; it dealt with all matters pertaining to the writing of the constitution. Seven attorneys and six law clerks interning in the Trust Territory from the University of California at Berkeley assisted the convention's legal advisor, Prof. Norm Meller of the University of Hawai'i, who had been deeply involved in setting up the Congress of Micronesia ten years earlier. Nakayama and Meller knew each other from Hawai'i and worked well together.

The Pre-Convention Committee's preparations gave way to a four-day convention workshop that began on 8 July 1975.[30] The workshop addressed the many administrative and procedural issues involved in a gathering of delegates charged with drafting a constitution for a would-be Micronesian nation. There was the introduction of staff; a review of logistical matters involving dress, the daily calendar, and the opening ceremony; an explanation of congressional amendments to the original enabling legislation; a summary of funding sources for the convention; and an overview of convention procedures. Near the end of the workshop, delegates broke up into assigned groups to examine and make rule recommendations. The delegates also received a briefing on the Special Conference Committee, a body consisting of two delegates from each district and created for the purpose of considering and recommending "solutions to such fundamental jurisdictional and substantive questions as are referred to it by the President of the Convention."[31] The Special Conference Committee occupied a prominent role at the convention; in the end, however, the convention's most difficult issues would be handled through an ad hoc special committee chaired by Tosiwo Nakayama.

## The Convention Begins

Despite the incredible impediments, complications, and doubts that preceded the day, the Micronesian Constitutional Convention began at one forty-five on the afternoon of 12 July 1975. Following opening prayers, the convention delegates were addressed by Congress of Micronesia Senate president Tosiwo Nakayama, Acting President of the Convention Mayor Vicente D. Sablan of Saipan, and Trust Territory High Commissioner Edward E. Johnston. Despite invitations to dignitaries in Washington, D.C., and at the United Nations, only local Saipan officials showed up. Nakayama's words were by far the most poignant and are worth repeating here. The speech was pure Nakayama— clear, concise, to the point, honest, and hopeful.

> High Commissioner Johnston, honored guests, fellow Delegates: The writing of a constitution is an important event in the history of any land. To be brought together like this; to draft the supreme law of the

land; to plan our future; to know our success or our failure may follow us for the rest of our lives—all this makes the writing of a constitution a crucial event. In Micronesia, however, the writing of a constitution becomes even more important—it becomes a matter of national life and death.

Many people have commented on the problems facing this convention. There are old customs and new, problems of unity, problems of political status. We all know what these problems are—we have been living with them. They make it all the more important for us to do our jobs as best we can. There are some who expect we will fail here. And the consequences of such failure would be profound. If we fail, the idea of Micronesia may die. If we do not produce a constitution or if the constitution we produce is a meaningless piece of paper, this failure will echo in these islands for years to come.

Now, having the problems we face, having discussed the consequences of failure, it is only fair to discuss the consequences of <u>success</u>. If, against heavy odds, we can work together here and produce a constitution which works for Micronesia, then the idea of Micronesian unity will be given new life. If this convention, day by day, meeting by meeting, issue by issue, detail by detail, can build a constitution in which we believe and in which our people believe, then we can have renewed faith in the future of Micronesia.

We have a long ninety days before us. After these ceremonies are over, after our officers have been elected, after we have all made speeches, there will be weeks and weeks of hard work. As we go about our work, let us keep one main thought in mind: that we are writing a constitution <u>for Micronesia</u>. No matter who has guided us in the past, no matter who assists us now, this is to be a <u>Micronesian</u> constitution. If we face problems, we should face them in a Micronesian way, searching for our own traditions and resources for the answers we need. We can accept help when we feel we need it, we can work with outsiders, but we must remember that what we do here, we do as Micronesians for Micronesia. We will be living with this constitution when our friends are gone. Our Micronesian children will be living with this constitution when we ourselves have departed.

What is Micronesia? It began as an accidental discovery by outside explorers. Then it was a proving ground for <u>outside</u> missionaries and traders. After that, it was an arrangement for <u>outside administrators</u>, Japanese and American. Thus, until very recently, the idea of Micronesia has been a foreign-imposed one. It will be the task of this

convention to decide whether this idea of Micronesia is an idea which
our own people can live with. Now is the time of testing for Micronesia. Not just testing, but final examination. It is now—or never—for
Micronesia. Let it be <u>now</u>. Thank you.[32]

With formalities completed, the convention rules were quickly adopted
and nominations were taken for the post of convention president.[33] Leo Falcam
of Pohnpei, Tosiwo Nakayama of Chuuk, and John Ngiraked of Palau were
nominated. Those supporting Nakayama showed themselves to be politically
and culturally astute by having a delegate from the Marianas, Louis Limes,
place his name in nomination.[34] The vote for convention president mirrored
the election ten years earlier in which Nakayama, nominated by an individual
from the Marianas, contended with John Ngiraked for the presidency of the
Senate of the Congress of Micronesia. As in 1965, Nakayama was a less than
willing candidate. He had reluctantly agreed to have his name listed after he
was told it would be written in on the ballot regardless of whether he approved
or not.[35] Given all that he had done in behalf of self-government and despite
his reluctance, Nakayama was assured of victory. The vote was thirty-two
for Nakayama, twelve for Falcam, and six for Ngiraked. Unlike Nakayama,
Ngiraked and Falcam had been active candidates. Ngiraked had not helped
his candidacy when in an interview a year earlier, he had speculated that the
success of the convention could well depend on the election of its president.
Falcam had an exceptionally strong personality, and his many years working
for the Trust Territory headquarters on Saipan led delegates to see him as too
close to the high commissioner.

With the convention president determined, the rules were then suspended and the district delegation chairmen were recognized as vice presidents. In the absence of any competition, Luke Tman of Yap received the
convention's endorsement as floor leader. Following Tman's selection, the
convention adjourned for food and drinks, a seemingly modern practice that
also carried heavy Micronesian content having to do with respect, welcome,
and hospitality. The most singular aspect of the election for convention officers was the prominence of individuals with legislative experience.[36] Of the
eight top officials, five had experience in the Congress of Micronesia. Congressional experience also proved a notable characteristic of those elected to
be committee chairs and vice chairs. While Nakayama had sought to ensure
fair, equitable, and balanced assignments, some committees did lack symme-
try. Half of the members of the Civil Liberties Committee came from the ranks
of the traditional chiefs, a harbinger of the sharp debates to come over traditional rights in a modern government.[37] As the individual committees met to

**Fig. 5.1.** The delegates to the 1975 Micronesian Constitutional Convention on Saipan. Tosiwo Nakayama is standing at the far left (Trust Territory Photo Archives, Pacific Collection, Hamilton Library, University of Hawai'i, Mānoa).

organize, it became clear that the delegates from Palau aspired to leadership roles and were not interested in chairing any subcommittees.[38] Those elected as subcommittee chairs, such as Johnson Toribiong and Tosiwo Nakamura, promptly resigned.

In a gesture that demonstrated his diplomatic skills, Tosiwo Nakayama nominated Jacob Sawaichi to chair the Special Conference Committee.[39] Nakayama offered this nomination as a conciliatory gesture to the Palau delegation, knowing that Sawaichi had placed John Ngiraked's name in nomination for the position of convention president. He also hoped that a Palauan as chair of this potentially very important committee would lead other members of the Palauan delegation to reconsider their refusal to serve as subcommittee chairs. Only John Ngiraked responded to Nakayama's gesture, agreeing to serve as chair of the Structure Committee's legislative subcommittee. Noticeably absent from any committee chairmanship was Lazarus Salii. Nakayama himself accepted an offer to chair the Administration Committee, a strategic, very important decision as things turned out.

Communication showed itself to be a problem at a number of levels. Delegates received little input from their constituents back in the districts who did not grasp many of the more complicated issues and procedural technicalities of the convention. Media coverage was limited and distorted, tending to focus on the convention's difficulties and delays. In a 12 August 1975 interview with the Education for Self-Government Task Force, Nakayama complained that much of the coverage about the convention was not correct and grossly incomplete.[40] The careful and conscientious deliberations going on in committee went unreported. Nonetheless, the convention had opened and was functioning. While decidedly Western in form, convention procedures would be affected by more local, culturally contexted ways of negotiating and reaching agreement known as the Micronesian Way, a process that would frustrate some outside observers, and be the cause of derision and ridicule from others.

## The Palauan Proposal

The most shocking and discouraging development of the early convention was the Palauan delegation's presentation of its seven non-negotiable demands that disguised, and not very subtly, the district's increasingly public desire for separation from the rest of the Trust Territory. On the seventh day of the convention, Lazarus Salii presented the conditions under which Palau would accept Micronesian unity.[41] Norman Meller saw in this presentation the essence of *Tuich el Kululau,* a Palauan challenge strategy that delivered a veiled, unexpected threat with *Ideuekl chemaidechedui,* a quiet confidence designed to surprise, confuse, and intimidate.[42] The Palauans demanded that any central government chartered under the constitution have only those powers specifically granted to it, with all other powers belonging to the districts or states. Their other demands were for a unicameral legislature with equal representation from each district; district or state control over landownership and land use; the equal division of all foreign aid among the constituent districts or states; equal district or state contributions to the central government; the right of each district or state to withdraw from the central government for a set period of years; and the designation of Palau as the seat of government for the central government. This last demand was thought to exemplify *Mengar ma Mecherochr*, a strategy designed to have one's opponents taste the bitterness of salt.

These demands, identified as non-negotiable, ensured that the Micronesian Constitutional Convention would be a tense gathering. The petition in effect offered the convention the outlines of what for Palau would be an acceptable constitution. The implied threat was that, if its terms were not met, Palau would go its own way. The convention response to the demands was slow, deliberate, and evasive. On the eleventh day of the convention, after the petition had been duplicated and referred to the Functions Committee, the chairman of that committee, Hiroshi Ismael of Kosrae, requested in accordance with convention rules that the document be divided into parts and referred to three other standing committees.[43] The shrewd move blunted for a time the force of Palau's proposal.

Palauan delegates became impatient with the slow response from the three committees to which their petition had been referred, and countered with what quickly became known as Delegate Proposal No. 100, in effect, the Palauan version of a constitution for Micronesia.[44] The proposal fleshed out the seven demands made in the earlier petition and was in actuality one of the two draft constitutions considered earlier that year by Palau's own constitutional convention. Reserve and moderation characterized the response of the larger convention. No district delegation offered a counter constitutional proposal; committee deliberations were cautious in their probing of the Palauan draft constitution and the resolve that underlay it. As things turned out, the convention and its various subcommittees never took action on Delegate Proposal No. 100. Ironically, however, the draft constitution ultimately approved by the convention borrowed heavily from the Palauan proposal.

Things moved haltingly at first. There was the adjustment that delegates need to make in working with each other. The styles of committee chairmen also varied; some, like Carl Heine of the Civil Liberties Committee, introduced proposals on their own initiative to get issues before their respective committees, while others like Heinrich Iriarte of the Structure Committee waited. All convention actions occurred within a constraining paradigm of language and law with which most delegates struggled. English was still very much a foreign language, and American legalese even more so. The law of the land was to be Micronesian but it was being expressed in English, and drew heavily upon a corpus that reflected British and American legal history and concepts.

## Vexing Issues

The convention through its committees grappled with a host of complex and confounding issues. These included the constitution's relationship to the future political status of the nation, questions of basic individual freedoms and human rights, the concept of federalism, eminent domain, taxation, and land rights. Delegates also spent a great deal of time debating the structure and power to be accorded the executive branch, and the organization and authority of a national legislature. Some saw the convention as an ultimate struggle between the idealism of those seeking to institutionalize democracy and others wishing to perpetuate or at least reaffirm the islands' chiefly hierarchies and stratification. Norman Meller came to characterize the convention as being about a "radicalism of restoration," which ultimately sought to fit traditional chiefly powers and local cultural practices into an introduced system of Western law and government.[45] Tosiwo Nakayama saw more complement than uncomfortable fit in the relationship between modern and more traditional forms of government. To the second conference of Micronesian traditional leaders meeting on Chuuk in November 1974, he had said:

> While I am not a chief or traditional leader myself, I have always respected the traditions and customs of the people of Micronesia, and the important work carried out by its traditional leaders both in regard to the customary practices, but also in helping to make decisions on matters which involve new ideas and problems brought to us from the outside.... Some people say the two systems cannot work together, I believe that is not correct, in fact, I believe they work together very well. It is my belief that both systems can and should continue to work together in helping all of the people of Micronesia, and that both systems should complement, and assist each other.[46]

On the surface, there appeared to be little progress. The complexity of issues, coupled with the convention's rules of procedure and many of the delegates' unfamiliarity with them, made for a very slow process. Not one committee proposal had been approved by the convention prior to the recess that began on 22 August, the forty-second day of deliberations. The issue of a recess was not without its own conflicts and problems. The Congress of Micronesia at its 1975 special session had passed an amendment to the convention's enabling legislation that permitted the convention to extend its life by recessing.[47] While the ostensible reason for the recess was to allow delegates to travel to their home districts for consultation with their constituents, the fundamental motivation lay in dealing with the Palauan delegation's demand to return home for the district legislature elections.

In late July, the Administration Committee addressed the length of the recess. Tosiwo Nakayama found himself at the center of these negotiations. John Ngiraked had proposed the recess begin on 14 August and last for a period of twenty days.[48] Fearing that returning delegates would not have enough in the way of progress to show their constituents, Nakayama requested that the start of the recess be delayed until 22 August and that it end on 14 September.[49] A provision in the draft recess resolution urging the delegates to return to Saipan eight days prior to the reconvening of the convention for purposes of preparation and planning failed as did a request from the Administration Committee to relocate the convention. The public reaction to the convention's recess deliberations was quite negative. A headline in the *Guam Daily News* read "Recess Decision ConCon Biggest Step in Three Weeks."[50]

The agreement to recess in late August did not appease the Palauans. Frustrated over the failure of the convention to address seriously their draft constitution and the general lack of progress, an angry Lazarus Salii addressed the convention on the last day of business before the recess. "In forty days, we have accomplished a great deal of nothing."[51] He criticized the delegations, staff members, and the rules of the convention. The only way to salvage the convention, he argued, was to abolish all standing committees, purge the staff, create a single drafting committee, and use the Palauan draft constitution as a model for the convention constitution. "Unless these steps are taken, Mr. President, you and the rest of us might as well forget it." Salii's words were not the only critical remarks to emerge from the ranks of the convention delegates. Tipne Philippo of the Marshalls remarked publicly that the standing committees looked more like sitting committees. Jose Cruz of the Marianas thought the rules too complex and inhibitive of the kind of discussion and consensus building he understood to be the basis of the Micronesian Way.[52] Jack Fritz and Gideon Doone, two young translators for the Chuuk delegation, were particularly critical of Nakayama's leadership.[53] They would later emerge as strong public critics of Nakayama in the earliest years of the Federated States of Micronesia.

**Fig. 5.2.** Lazarus Salii
of Palau (Trust Territory
Photo Archives, Pacific
Collection, Hamilton
Library, University of
Hawaiʻi, Mānoa).

The situation was not as hopeless as some suggested.[54] The standing committees had concluded much of their preliminary work, and would be ready to act upon the specifics of the proposals before them when their members returned from recess. In planning for the delegates' return, convention officers were encouraged to exert stronger leadership in moving the convention along and to pressure those committees that were lagging behind in their work. Rather than single out individual committees and thus risk the alienation and embarrassment of their members, Nakayama's Administration Committee set collective deadlines.[55] While the convention was in recess, the research and drafting section put the break time to good use by preparing digests with indices for all of the paperwork that had been generated by the convention. Necessary background research was completed and memoranda prepared on matters not yet resolved by the committees. Most important of all, staffers created a mock-up of the constitution showing those areas that had been addressed as well as those that were still in need of attention.[56] The provisional outline of a constitution as mapped by the members of the Research and Drafting Committee was beginning to take shape. This mock-up was meant as a psychological prop designed to encourage the convention's leaders and to show them that the achievement of the convention's goal, a constitution, was not impossible despite the delays, challenges, and complications encountered. With delegates trickling back slowly from recess, the reconvening of the convention was delayed. The convention did not resume until 16 September. Greeting the delegates upon their return to Saipan were the election results from Palau.

The Liberal Party headed by Salii and Roman Tmetuchl lost its majority to the Progressive Party and aligned independents.[57] Among the eight members of the Progressive Party to win election to the Palau District Legislature were convention delegates Tosiwo Nakamura, John Ngiraked, and Jacob Sawaichi. Palau's Progressive Party began flexing its muscle as the convention reconvened, at the particular expense of Lazarus Salii who found his position undermined by the increasing sentiment for separatism in Palau and those who promoted it. A petition reached Saipan calling for the removal of Salii as the congressional representative to the Palau delegation. The request was viewed by some as yet another example of ulterior motives that had more to do with politics in Palau than any effort at nation building in Micronesia. Salii was in Japan at the time but received the support of his longtime friend Tosiwo Nakayama who dismissed the attempts to unseat him as "ineffective."[58] His once strident voice now muffled, Salii remained a convention delegate, adopting a more constructive, pro-constitution stance in the latter half of the convention. The convention's problems with Palau did not stop, however.

Those members of the Palau delegation who had won election to the district legislature now requested that they be absented from the convention to attend the convocation of the Palau District Legislature. Had the Palauans been allowed to return home, convention business would have come to a halt. Nakayama managed this potential problem deftly by asking the acting high commissioner to postpone the start of the Palau Legislature.[59] The postponement kept the Palauans in Saipan and allowed the convention to proceed.

The absence of traditional leaders from the Marshalls at the convention constituted a lingering and serious matter. Just prior to the recess, the traditional leaders of the Pohnpei delegation introduced a resolution inviting the participation of the Marshallese chiefs. Carl Heine spread word of the resolution among the convention's supporters back in the Marshalls. In response, two young Marshallese chiefs, Iroij Litokwa Tomeing and Iroij Jeltan Kanki, volunteered to represent the Marshallese traditional leaders at the convention. This action raised an immediate protest from the strong and sizeable Kabua faction in the Marshalls that remained adamantly opposed to the convention and any constitution that might come from it. Representing this faction, seven *iroij laplap*—paramount chiefs—sent a cable of protest to Saipan in which they expressed outrage that two minor chiefs "were unilaterally selected by Carl Heine without any notice to a single Marshallese paramount chief or to [the] Nitijela."[60] A letter to Tosiwo Nakayama from nine *iroij* and *leiroj,* or female chiefs, supporting the selection of Tomeing and Kanki, countered the cable.

It was clear that the Marshalls were seriously divided over the appointment and that any chance the constitution had of passing in the Marshalls was at risk. Given the delicacy of the situation, a resolution was crafted for consideration by the convention upon its return from recess.[61] The ultimately successful resolution welcomed the two Marshallese chiefs, acknowledged their presence, awarded them seats and committee assignments, and encouraged their input. Their attendance did not count toward a quorum and their votes on issues were not formally recorded. With these compromises, the crisis that had developed around Marshallese chiefly participation thus abated.

Another issue to emerge during the break was the misinformation and lack of information about the convention in the districts. The lack of unity at the convention and its impending collapse were the most prevalent impressions.[62] Despite Nakayama's earlier protest, media coverage continued to give little attention to more substantive, nation-making matters. While the convention's information officer prepared daily summaries to be distributed through the Micronesian News Service, convention news was often not broadcast in the districts away from Saipan. Compounding the lack of information about the convention was the failure of the Trust Territory government's Education for Self-Government Task Force to provide instructional materials to district citizens on the convention process.

Hanging over the conference from the outset was the relationship of any draft constitution to the future political status of the islands. Nakayama and others, including the convention's chief legal advisor Norman Meller, argued successfully for the creation of a constitution before any formal decision on a compact of free association. For any government to be viable, its constitution had to be the law of the land and preeminent over any and all subsequent agreements with other nations. At a pre-convention meeting in September 1974 with traditional leaders, Kintoki Joseph of Chuuk had inquired about the relationship between the constitution and what was then the draft Compact of Free Association. Tosiwo Nakayama replied:

> It will be best to draft a constitution without knowing what is in the draft compact because in working on the constitution, we are dealing with the interests of the people of Micronesia and we should not be

concerned with trying to protect the interests of someone outside of Micronesia.[63]

The commitment to the constitution as the supreme law of the land marked an extremely critical guiding principle of the convention, one that allowed it to move successfully toward the drafting of a constitution without undue external pressure or influence.[64]

There were other, more immediately practical and political reasons for disentangling the constitution from the question of future political status for the islands. A Trust Territory referendum to determine people's preferences on the question of a future political status had been conducted on 8 July 1975, the same day as the start of the pre-convention workshop. The results of the referendum were ambiguous, confusing, and ominous.[65] The Education for Self Government program that had sponsored the referendum provided flawed vernacular translations for the six options being offered: independence, commonwealth, free association, statehood, present status, and other. In addition, there resulted considerable confusion over voting instructions. Individuals could vote "yes" or "no" on any or all of the four propositions; voters could thus endorse all, some, or none of the options offered. There was no way to prioritize the choices on those ballots that endorsed or said "yes" to more than one option. The confusion was compounded by the near-total boycott in the Marshalls of the status referendum, and all initiatives sponsored by the Congress of Micronesia relating to the constitutional convention. In Palau, Senator Roman Tmetuchl, together with members of the district legislature, advised people not to vote. The Marianas also did not participate, having formally approved a negotiated offer of commonwealth in a referendum earlier that year.

Approximately half of the Trust Territory's registered voters exercised their franchise. A majority of those casting ballots clearly rejected statehood and commonwealth. "Present status" (10,148) drew the largest affirmative vote, followed by strong, almost equal support for both free association (7,705) and independence (7,486). Those who did vote in the Marshalls tended to endorse the status quo; free association appeared to be the Yapese choice by a slight margin, while in Palau, Pohnpei, and Chuuk, voters opted for independence, free association, and the status quo but with no overwhelming preference for any of the three options. In short, the results of the vote gave convention delegates no clear mandate on the issue of a future political status.

In Washington, D.C., Fred M. Zeder, director of territorial affairs within the United States Department of Interior, wrote to Tosiwo Nakayama during the convention. In that letter, he stated that "We in Washington...have not taken any part in the [Convention] proceedings, feeling rather that the work you are doing toward the formation of a future Micronesian government is a matter for the people and leaders of Micronesia themselves."[66] Despite the platitudes, American negotiators had insisted that a constitution that in any way infringed upon a compact of free association would be unacceptable.

The Committee on General Provisions had reported out Committee Proposal No. 11 stipulating the constitution as the supreme law of the islands. After considerable debate and in an atmosphere of tension and anxiety, the proposal barely garnered the three-fourths vote necessary for adoption. Opposition was scattered throughout the convention and reflected not just the separatist intentions of the Marianas, Marshalls, and Palau but more general uncertainty over a future political status for a Micronesian nation. In an effort to address the anxieties over the future political status of the islands, the convention approved a "status hinge" for the constitution.[67] This status hinge stipulated the approval of two-thirds of the district legislatures for the ratification of any treaty with a foreign government. The advantage of this hinge was that it diffused any disruptive debate over future political status among the delegates, and allowed them to focus on the drafting of a constitution.

As the pace picked up, so too did the importance of the issues being addressed by the convention delegates. The form of federation, more particularly the powers allotted to the national government as opposed to those reserved for the states, proved a topic of intense debate.[68] In the end, the convention opted to carefully delineate the powers of the national and state governments. National defense and foreign affairs, the regulation of foreign and interstate commerce, patents and copyrights, the issuance of currency, and the authority to identify and punish major crimes were identified as areas of jurisdiction for the national government. Matters concerning citizenship, naturalization, immigration, and emigration also fell under national jurisdiction. Left unresolved was the question of whether or not naturalized citizens could own land; the deferral of this issue to a national Congress for decision at a later date reflected the extreme sensitivity that Micronesians held toward land and also their fear of its alienation. State powers included authority over everything not expressly delegated to the national government or prohibited to the states. Concurrent power between the national and states governments included health, education, and welfare, the establishment and administration of public welfare and social security systems, the appropriating of funds, and the borrowing of money.

While progress was being made, deadlines were becoming more pressing. Nakayama's Administration Committee set 2 October as the date for all standing committees to submit their proposals for consideration to the full convention; the deadline was later extended by a week.[69] On 13 October, a very rough draft of the constitution was delivered to all delegates with the admonition that the version before them was preliminary and subject to change.[70] Legal consultant Norman Meller did the arithmetic and became concerned that the convention was running out of time. The 8 November deadline loomed ominously as various committee proposals still needed to be reviewed and approved by the convention in plenary session. The Style Committee needed time for its editing work, and there was also the review, debate, and resolution of any inconsistencies in a full draft constitution, and then the double-checking, proofreading, and approval of the final version. A worried Meller did not anticipate the distinctive, deliberate, and ultimately successful way that the convention dealt with outstanding issues. The highly risky, ultimately successful approach entailed the continual deferral of sensitive decisions and the compression of the final adoption of the constitution into a few short hours. It would be Tosiwo Nakayama who would masterfully manage and negotiate the convention's final days.

The ultimate success of the convention and the constitution it sought to draft continued to hinge on the issue of unity. John Ngiraked had initially disturbed many delegates with his proposal that the convention adopt the name the "Federated States of Micronesia" for the government whose constitution was in the process of being drafted. It was the name used in Delegate Proposal No. 100. The name eventually gained widespread currency among the convention delegates as did the Palauan proposal's preamble, a very powerful, eloquent, and moving statement about the desire for self-government. As a way to underscore the unity and purpose of the convention, Nakayama had the Palauan preamble read to open the plenary session on 16 October and then at the start of each remaining day of the convention.[71] The constitution taking shape on Saipan was coming to resemble strongly the version the Palauans had brought with them and introduced to the convention as Delegate Proposal No. 100.

## The Role of Chiefs and the Place of Tradition

Aside from unity, no issue more threatened the success of the convention than the role to be allotted for Micronesia's traditional leaders in the new government. Heinrich Iriarte, a delegate from Pohnpei and the brother of one of its traditional representatives, Nahnmwarki Max Iriarte, opened the seventy-sixth day of the convention with the following statement:

> I know that all of us are born on this earth and we are the same. However, some of us are born to rule and some of us are born to serve. Mr.

President, among us there are some people who were appointed by
God by virtue of our birth and tradition.[72]

With this statement, the convention now found itself faced with the long
building confrontation between the supporters of island cultures and traditions, and those who looked to a more modern polity based on the principles
of representative government.

An earlier report from a Senate subcommittee within the Congress
of Micronesia had acknowledged the historical and cultural significance of
Micronesia's chiefs. The statement, which bore the wise and conciliatory
hand of Andon Amaraich, who was now working with the convention's legal
staff, read:

> The traditional leaders of Micronesia occupy a very important place
> in our culture and traditions, and therefore, to a certain extent, to
> deny them the power to assist in the shaping of our future political
> destiny is to deny, not only their great wisdom and insight, but in a
> certain sense, our own cultural heritage as well.[73]

As true as that statement rang for many, it elided the varied histories, structural and functional differences, and the changing status of chieftanship within
the Trust Territory of the Pacific Islands. To be sure, chiefly systems differed
within Micronesia; Yap's chiefs retained their full authority, while those in the
Marshalls had leveraged the American military presence at Kwajalein to reas-
sert some of their former prominence. Chiefs on Pohnpei and to a lesser extent
Palau still wielded considerable cultural influence even if their governing powers had waned significantly. Even in earlier times, Chuuk's chiefs had served as
facilitators in a decentralized polity rather than powerful rulers. In Kosrae and
the Marianas, the indigenous chiefly systems had disappeared. Compounding
the varying demographics of chiefly rule in the region called Micronesia was
the diffuse sentiment among those chiefs gathered on Saipan. Traditional representatives brought varying skills and comfort levels to the convention. Most
depended heavily on interpreters or congressmen to express their views. It was
not always clear if the views being expressed were those of the chiefly delegate
or the person speaking for him.

No one opposed a role for the chiefs in the new government. Even those
most committed to a more modern, representative form of government conceded the need to recognize custom and tradition. No delegate wished to give
offense, and there was the very real fact that chiefly support was necessary to
secure approval of the draft constitution at the convention and in the popu-

lar referendum to follow. Early on, the chiefly caucus had made a display of unanimity and influence by requesting an increase in the per diem for their interpreters "as extremely reasonable and fair in light of the circumstances surrounding the convention."[74] The petition said nothing about delegation staffs whose members would have to be accorded comparable support under the argument being made. Eventually, the Administration Committee, chaired by Nakayama, reached a compromise solution based on the availability of funds; all parties would receive an increase in their per diem, though not as much as had been requested. On the surface, it was a seemingly minor matter; Nakayama, however, possessed the wisdom and foresight to understand how important this conciliatory gesture would be to the success of the convention.

Some sought a greater role for chiefs at the convention. The two chiefly representatives from Pohnpei had proposed a rule that required one of a delegation's two members assigned to each of the convention's five major committees to be a traditional leader. The proposal came early in the convention, and was quickly defeated, though twenty-two delegates chose not to vote as a way to avoid giving offense to the chiefs present.[75] A far more serious matter arose when Heinrich Iriarte of Pohnpei, the chair of the Structure Committee, asked for a closed-door meeting with all traditional leaders.[76] At that meeting, Iriarte informed those present that he did not feel it proper that his committee decide on the role of the chiefs in a future government. He thought that decision best left to the chiefs themselves. After an exchange of views, the chiefs indicated their desire to consider the matter further among themselves and at a separate meeting. The question of who would chair the meeting of chiefs immediately arose. The more sensitive issue behind the question was how to determine seniority among the region's chiefly systems. Tosiwo Nakayama solved the dilemma. He presided over the initial meeting, and suggested that the traditional leaders take turns chairing subsequent meetings in an order to be determined by the drawing of names.[77] The chiefs accepted Nakayama's proposal.

Civil liberties exposed the convention's deep divide over the place and practice of Micronesian tradition and custom in a new constitutionally chartered government. Was, for example, freedom of expression to be protected if it violated the customary practice of a particular state or district? Should the constitution's Bill of Rights contain a provision protecting Micronesian customs, traditions, and morality? After much debate and maneuvering, the Civil Rights Committee reported out an amended proposal that permitted legislative action in the defense of custom for compelling social reasons.[78] Eminent domain was another issue that created controversy at two levels. As one delegate put it, "Micronesians need their land more than they need civil liberties."[79]

There were those who saw as threatening the power of the national government to seize land; due process and just compensation did not ease that threat for those opposed to the national government's possession of such a power. Chairman Hiroshi Ismael, and a majority of his Functions Committee, supported the position that eminent domain was a power necessary in a democratic government and that it should reside with the states because of the importance of land to local custom and tradition.[80] A minority report argued that the national government and the states should hold concurrent authority in the matter of eminent domain. Nowhere in the debate, however, did there appear consideration of the central government's need to condemn land to meet commitments to the United States under a future status agreement. Repeated attempts to address the issue through varied amendments to the Government Functions Committee's proposal failed. In the end, the constitution remained silent on the issue of eminent domain.

Meanwhile, the debate over the place of chiefs in the future government intensified. With the chiefs having formed their own caucus, the Structure Committee waited on their proposals before submitting its final report to the full convention. There were, however, a number of factors inhibiting a single or unified response from the chiefly caucus. The chiefs were in an environment and operating under procedures that were unfamiliar and alien; language too proved an impediment for many chiefs who were not facile in English, and had to rely on interpreters and fellow delegates for translations and explanations. The group itself lacked cohesion as there were significant differences of opinion about the role and place of chiefs in a modern government.

Frustrated by the chiefs' lack of consensus and pressured by the larger convention, the Structure Committee submitted its final report.[81] Committee Report No. 24 provided an entire framework for a central government and its component parts; the report also contained structural recommendations for the system of state government. The report underscored the significance of Micronesia's chiefs, gave them roles in both the national and state governments, and confirmed their eligibility to seek and hold elective office. The committee's report also called for the establishment of special state courts with jurisdiction over land and matters pertaining to traditional laws and customs. The convention as a whole evidenced little support for this attempt to incorporate traditional leaders within the national government. Having reminded the convention delegates earlier that some were born to rule and others destined to serve, Iriarte attempted to alleviate the divisiveness of his remarks by offering an amendment that would have allowed for rather than actually created a chamber of chiefs.[82] The amendment left to national legislation the actual creation of the chamber and the delineation of its functions. The amendment passed and found its way into the draft constitution as section three of Article Five on traditional rights.

The Style and Arrangements Committee's work on the Bill of Rights had made clear and more palatable the sections on the protection of traditions and the freedom of expression and assembly. Some delegates took exception to a clause dealing with protection against discrimination; they viewed it as impugning custom, negating the special provision for traditional leaders, and precluding the placement of chiefs within the formal structure of government.[83] At the request of the Committee of the Whole and before the vote on the prohibition against the discrimination clause, the Functions, Structure, and Civil Rights Committees met with the traditional leaders. This meeting in effect involved about half of the convention delegates. The result of the meeting was an amendment offered in behalf of the traditional leaders that declared:

> Nothing in the Constitution takes away a role or function of a traditional leader as recognized by custom and tradition, or prevents a traditional leader from being recognized, honored, and given formal roles at any level of government as may be prescribed by this Constitution or by Statute.[84]

This amendment became a part of the Bill of Rights proposal and eventually won incorporation into the final version of the draft constitution. Not without a fight, however.

On Thursday, 23 October, the Committee of the Whole fell short of the three-fourths majority vote required to approve the proposed Bill of Rights with its anti-discrimination provision and its statement on the role of chiefs in government. A second vote also failed. Acting in behalf of the two traditional leaders of Palau, John Ngiraked called for a meeting of all traditional leaders.[85] An announcement followed that meeting; the chiefs had decided to remain away from the convention until after they met on the following Monday. There were rumors of a formal boycott and of some traditional leaders planning to return home. On the next day, eight traditional leaders failed to answer the roll call. Their absence spurred the convention to act on a special resolution. Echoing the sentiments of the earlier resolution considered by the three committees, this special resolution affirmed the honor and respect to be accorded traditional leaders, and stated that nothing in the constitution of the Federated States of Micronesia was intended to detract from their roles and functions as leaders.[86]

Intended as an apology to the chiefs, the resolution quickly won passage in the Committee of the Whole. Delegate William Eperiam of Pohnpei then asked that a letter be sent to all traditional chiefs inviting them to return to the convention.[87] As convention president, Nakayama played the role of mediator. He responded to Eperiam's request by noting that customs varied throughout the islands and that in Chuuk such a letter would be considered inappropriate.[88] He urged instead that each delegation meet with its traditional leaders and in a manner deemed fitting. The convention was stalled as it waited for the traditional leaders to return. Meanwhile, radio broadcasts spread word of the walkout.

But was there really a boycott taking place? According to Norman Meller, the walkout was an event staged by a few and used by still others to achieve objectives that had more to do with separatism and personal ambitions than the defense of tradition. There was no real unanimity among the chiefs over a boycott. At the roll call for the plenary session on Monday, 27 October, only two chiefs were missing.[89] The fact still remained, however, that the support of traditional leaders was vital to the success of the convention, its constitution, and the cause of Micronesian unity. Delegate Petrus Tun of Yap, himself a chief, stood to give the Yapese delegation's understanding of things.[90] He stated that while some chiefs may have boycotted convention proceedings as a display of their dissatisfaction, the Yapese traditional leaders were not among their number. Expressing respect for the opinions of others, Tun went on to say that the power and authority of Yapese chiefs were not dependent upon laws, constitutional clauses, or legal precedents. Yapese chiefs knew their place and so did the people of Yap. They did not want their powers debated and confirmed by legislation. They did not seek a corner of the national government to inhabit, and did not feel threatened by the passage of a Bill of Rights. They were, however, willing to compromise in the interests of Micronesian unity. The statement by the future first vice president of the Federated States of Micronesia allowed the convention to move on with the understanding that it would fall to future legislation to determine the role of chiefs in the national government and at the state level.

Equally threatening to the ultimate success of the convention were issues involving the structure of government: more particularly, the nature of the executive branch, the issue of proportional representation in the national legislature, and whether that legislative branch of the central government would be a unicameral or bicameral body. Many of the proposals before the Structure Committee advocated a plural executive. Again, the Palauan draft constitution loomed large over the proceedings with its stipulation for a loose federation, a unicameral legislature, a single but limited chief executive, and equity in revenue sharing between the national and state governments. The debate over these matters became prolonged, and Tosiwo Nakayama worried that disagreement over these issues could defeat the convention. With the convention on its eighty-fifth day and time running out, Nakayama's Administration Committee entertained and approved a proposal to have the convention meet in a closed-door session.[91] The meeting resolved little, but did allow for a more relaxed discussion of differences that served to reduce tensions and reinforce in many delegates' minds the advantages of the Micronesian Way. The straw votes taken in this closed-door session indicated a slight preference for a single rather than plural executive, and a sharp division among the delegates on the structure of the national Congress and the issue of proportional versus equal representation.

## Closing Days and the Special Committee

There also resulted from the closed-door meeting a recommendation that these sensitive matters be addressed by an ad hoc special committee, different from the Special Convention Committee chaired by Jacob Sawaichi, and comprised of two delegates from each district, one being a traditional leader or his designated substitute.[92] The intent here was to work toward consensus through private committee deliberations, and with Micronesia's traditional leaders present and helping to mediate the discussions. Staff lawyers were excluded from the special committee meetings for the purpose of facilitating discussion among delegates and avoiding the excruciatingly detailed legal haggling that had come to frustrate and inhibit so many participants at the convention. The presence of the chiefs had a very salutatory effect. Nakayama, chosen to chair the special committee, deliberately turned to chiefly members for their counsel and advice when discussions became intense or wandered.[93] The conferees decided upon a single congressional house; successful legislation required a two-thirds vote of the members upon first reading and approval from two-thirds of the state delegations for final passage.[94] The unicameral legislature was to be made up of one representative from each state elected to a four-year term; the number of other representatives from the states was to be determined by population and elected to two-year terms. Only representatives elected to the four-year seats were eligible for election to the positions of president and vice president by the members of the Congress. The committee also dealt with the issue of traditional leaders' involvement in the new government. In addition to the resolution agreed to earlier in the convention, the committee endorsed a proposal that allowed a state to award one of its two-year apportioned seats to a traditional leader. The method of selection fell to the states, with the requirement that the congressional districts for the remaining two-year seats be reapportioned to ensure as adequate a representation as possible for the state's population.

The report that emerged from the special committee was greeted with relief and approval. Delegates who held opposing views on the positions endorsed by the committee found themselves inclined or pressured by their delegations to vote for the report. So pleased were delegates with the committee's work that they asked it to resolve the two remaining and extremely sensitive issues facing the convention: the right of unilateral secession and the location of the new government's capital in Palau.[95] The Palauan position had been adamant on the right of individual states to unilaterally secede from the central government. Pro-unity delegates from other districts had insisted on denying the right of state withdrawal from the national government. Nakayama's special committee took a somewhat indirect approach and opted for an amendment ultimately included in the constitution that required the national and state governments to uphold the provisions of the constitution and to advance the principles of unity on which it rested.

The last issue before the special committee involved the designation of Palau as the capital of the Federated States of Micronesia. Accounts of the closed-door meeting called to address the issue described it as tense and acrimonious with especially strong words spoken on different sides of the issue by delegates Ngiraked and Falcam.[96] Sitting between the two in closed-door session, Nakayama, more personally comfortable and familiar with the Pohnpeian, at times stepped on Falcam's foot to calm him down and let Ngiraked have his say.[97] The under-the-table maneuver worked. On the eighty-ninth day of the ninety-day convention, members of the special committee agreed to eliminate all mention of the capital from the constitution. What also came out of the committee was a resolution recommending Palau as the site for the new capital. The resolution, meant to be conciliatory, caused confusion and anxiety. It became the focus of intense debate on the evening of the convention's last day. Lazarus Salii announced with emotion that the convention's vote on the capital resolution would influence his vote on the constitution.[98] Sensing a threat from Palau that could still defeat the draft constitution, the delegates engaged in an hour-long debate that included two recesses. In the end, they adopted a revised version of the resolution that identified Palau's offer as the first to be considered when time came for the selection of the new capital. With that vote, the convention concluded its review of all reports, proposals, and resolutions, and was now ready to consider the full draft constitution that was the product of its deliberations.[99]

## Approval and Afterward

There still remained a great deal of last-minute work to be done. In an atmosphere of organized confusion, the final language of the concluding compromises had to be drafted, and then all of the various sections of the constitution put together in a cohesive whole, with grammar, syntax, spelling, and consistency checked and double-checked. All documentation was scrutinized carefully to see that no constitutional detail agreed to by the convention had been omitted. Technical errors were still being found and corrected up to the last minute. At 12:50 a.m. on the ninetieth and last day of the convention, the draft constitution was ready for presentation to the delegates.[100]

The rules called for delegates to vote article by article. After the approval of the Preamble with forty-five affirmative votes, no negative votes or abstentions, and all delegations in accord, the convention suspended its rules and adopted the remainder of the constitution with forty-three votes in the affirmative and two abstentions. Celebration followed.[101] Individual delegates gave congratulatory speeches. The only woman delegate to the convention, Mary Lanwi from the Marshalls, was asked to lead the delegates in the singing of the Micronesian anthem. In the afternoon, the convention reassembled for the closing ceremonies.[102] After the invocation, each of the delegations walked to the front of the hall where individual members affixed their signatures to the document. Yap, being the smallest delegation, was first. Each delegation chairman made remarks before members signed the constitution. There was an address by High Commissioner Edward Johnston and then a closing benediction. It was done. Tosiwo Nakayama was emotionally drained and totally exhausted; he cried at the closing ceremonies and then left the White Sands Hotel for the home of Joe Lafoifoi, a member of Saipan's *Re Falawasch* community whose founders had journeyed to the Northern Marianas from Namonuito and other Central Caroline islands in the nineteenth century.[103] Among family and kin, Nakayama spent the next three days resting and recovering from the ordeal of constitution making in Micronesia.

With the convention ended, the constitution approved, and the delegates leaving Saipan, Victorio Uherbelau, the convention secretary, was cleaning out a desk in his office when he found half a coconut shell, its meat partially charred and with a brown liquid poured over the handful of leaves that rested in the concave hollow of the shell.[104] It was magic, strategically placed to affect the outcome of the convention. But was it good or bad magic? Perhaps, the successful outcome of the convention had been assured all along. Regardless, Tosiwo Nakayama, as always, had faith that things would work out. They did this time, but it had been close, with failure a possibility right up until the very end. Had the convention failed, reflected Nakayama, that would have been it.[105] He wasn't sure what would have followed, but it wouldn't, he was sure, be self-government for the Federated States of Micronesia.

About a month before the end of the convention, Tosiwo Nakayama had written a note to Norman Meller asking what was to be done in the event the convention could not reach an agreement on the constitution.[106] Two weeks later, when faced with the possible boycott of the traditional leaders, Nakayama inquired if Meller had prepared the requested contingency plan. Meller replied that he had, but wanted to avoid revealing it for fear that it might affect the resolve of the convention. Meller's plan to have the draft constitution referred by resolution to the Congress of Micronesia for completion, was not needed.

The approval process would, by necessity, have to be multitiered and would entail a Territory-wide voter education program followed by a popular referendum on the draft constitution. The establishment of an autonomous, self-governing Federated States of Micronesia also depended upon a political status agreement with the United States that was compatible with the constitution. There was, in short, much work still to be done. The inauguration of a new government and the continuation of status negotiations with the United States would require an enormous amount of time, energy, effort, and patience. As had been the case with the constitutional convention, Tosiwo Nakayama would stand quietly but firmly and effectively at the center of things.

# One Canoe

On 27 May 1976, High Commissioner Edward E. John-ston formally presented Tosiwo Nakayama with the pen Nakayama had used to sign the draft constitution. The historically significant pen was mounted in a glass frame; it came with the inscription "Pen Used by Honorable Tosiwo Nakayama, President of the Constitutional Convention as final signer of the Constitution for the Federated States of Micronesia, November 1975."[1] It was an odd, awkward moment that revealed a dominant colonial presence seeking to assert its continuing presence and to add its imprimatur to political change. Johnston was in the final days of his tenure as high commissioner. He had accepted the position of executive vice president of the Pacific Area Trade Association, a San Francisco–based company that worked to promote tourism in the Pacific. "It's good to present you the pen before I leave the Trust Territory," Johnston said to Nakayama. Johnston would be leaving the islands soon, but not the government he had represented for the last seven years, not yet.

The road to self-government remained long, arduous, with much to do, and many impediments to overcome. The withdrawal of the Marianas and the increasingly likely departure of Palau and the Marshalls complicated negotiations over the draft compact of free association, and threatened the very prospect of self-government for the remaining islands. There were also the major differences with the United States over the relationship of the draft compact to the constitution as well as a myriad of legislative, administrative, and logistical matters involved in transitioning from a trust territory to an autonomous, self-governing entity. Tosiwo Nakayama urged his fellow citizens to "sail one canoe

**Fig. 6.1.** High Commissioner Edward Johnston presenting to Tosiwo Nakayama the pen that Nakayama had used to sign the draft constitution of the Federated States of Micronesia, 1975 (Trust Territory Photo Archives, Pacific Collection, Hamilton Library, University of Hawaiʻi, Mānoa).

together through time and history."² In Nakayama's eyes, the metaphor of the canoe linked past, present, and future. The canoe of state, however, faced challenges and changing circumstances radically different from those encountered and successfully met by ancestral and immediately preceding generations. "We have to sail as one," he said, "... in order to have a visible and viable place among the world's community of nations."³

## Separation and Association

Earlier in 1976, Nakayama had addressed the second regular session of the Sixth Congress of Micronesia on Saipan.⁴ Despite the specter of separation hanging over the legislative body, Nakayama pointed to the success of the constitutional convention; he noted as well all the work needed to be done in preparation for self-government, work that ranged from a Territory-wide voter education program and a plebiscite on the draft constitution to continuing negotiations with the United States over a compact of free association.

With an eye to a more self-sufficient future, Nakayama called upon the Congress to pass specific legislation to promote economic development, encourage greater foreign investment at the local level, and create selective tariff and import restrictions designed to foster local industries.

In an interview on 29 January, Nakayama reiterated that 1976 was a crucial year for Micronesia.[5] He called attention to the dissolution of the Joint Committee on Future Status and the creation in its place of the Commission on Future Political Status and Transition. He noted that Micronesian negotiators had been instructed to bring the compact into line with the constitution, not the other way around as Trust Territory officials and American negotiators desired it. Nakayama wanted the referendum on the constitution to be held within a year's time, though he had yet to receive any official reaction to the constitution from the American side. He also expressed the hope that the Congress would make a decision soon on the location of a new capital and that the U.S. Congress would move ahead with a review of all laws and treaties affecting the islands under a changed political status.

The most pressing issue facing Nakayama and the proponents of the constitution remained unity. In early 1976, members of the Marianas delegation, waiting for the inauguration of commonwealth status, let it be known that they would no longer be participating in the Congress of Micronesia. Their absence was not at all surprising or unexpected given the Marianas' overwhelming vote to accept the offer of commonwealth from the United States in July of the previous year. Much more ominous were the comments being made on the House and Senate floors by representatives from the Marshalls and Palau, comments that were reinforced with calculated, sometimes prolonged absences by congressmen from the two districts. Members of Palau's congressional delegation made it known that the failure to select Palau as the capital for the new central government would lead to Palau's secession. Despite the intimidation, the Congress of Micronesia ultimately designated Pohnpei not Palau as the seat of the new government. The following year, in 1977, the Palau congressional delegation boycotted the first special session of the Seventh Congress of Micronesia. Delegation members said that the session "could only aggravate and perpetuate the present political deadlock" between Palau and the Congress, and that the legislative body's agenda was "totally secondary and subordinate to the paramount issues of future political status."[6]

Lazarus Salii's changing views and declining fortunes in the Congress also hurt the cause of unity. At the special session of the Sixth Congress of Micronesia that met from mid-July to early August 1976, Salii took the floor amidst all of the debate around a future political status for the islands and proclaimed that free association with the United States remained the best option for Micronesia.[7] He acknowledged, however, that things had changed considerably from the late 1960s. Salii recognized the intense desire of Palau and the Marshalls to separate, and urged the Congress to do the same. He called upon the leaders from those two districts to be more specific about their plans. Salii took the opportunity to support the Marshallese request for a greater share of the revenues collected in their district. The sufferings caused by the American occupation of Kwajalein earned them the right to enjoy whatever economic or monetary benefits came their way. Salii's speech foreshadowed his later departure from the Congress and the chairmanship of the Commission on Future Political Status and Transition. His commitment to unity and free association had been compromised by the growing forces of Palauan separatism, and by the desire within the core of the Congress for a form of free association that more explicitly affirmed the islands' sovereignty and independence.

The Congress was not the only arena for the articulation of Palauan dissent. During the course of the congressional session, Nakayama addressed the controversy caused by an article that had appeared in the 20 February 1976 edition of *Marianas Variety*.[8] The article stated that the Congress of Micronesia leadership had requested the high commissioner to fire all Palauan directors within the Trust Territory government for their advocacy of separation. In a joint statement with House Speaker Bethwel Henry, Nakayama acknowledged the concern over the reports of Palauan officials within the Trust Territory government urging separation. Nakayama insisted, however, that no such request to remove them had been made or even considered by the congressional leadership. Later in 1976, three key members of the Palau District Legislature, two of whom, John Ngiraked and Johnson Toribiong, had been delegates to the constitutional convention, introduced a resolution seeking separate status negotiations for Palau.[9] The resolution cited as reasons for separation the loss of confidence in the Congress of Micronesia and the increasingly dismal prospects for Micronesian unity, given the incompatibility between the draft constitution and the desire of the majority of Palauans for a loose federation. The resolution characterized the trend toward separate status as irreversible.

The Marshalls' congressional delegation was equally assertive in its advocacy of separation. During the first regular session of the Seventh Congress in early 1977, Amata Kabua explained the Marshalls' decision to seek a separate political status.[10] He denied that the Marshallese desire for separation had been at all influenced or encouraged by external forces as some within Congress had suggested. He called the money spent on the constitutional convention and the political status negotiations a waste, and dismissed Micronesian unity as a cover for Americans seeking a quick, long-term deal for continued use of Kwajalein Atoll as a missile testing site. Kabua concluded his remarks by asking the Congress to respect the wishes of the Marshall Islands for separate political status negotiations. Kabua's speech, like all of the other statements against unity on the Senate floor, began with the words, "Mr. President." The salutations were more than a mere formality of address. They were aimed specifically at Tosiwo Nakayama who stood as the foremost proponent of unity. Nakayama took them seriously, but not personally.[11] In so doing, he left room for further dialogue in a contentious present and an uncertain future.

## Constitution and Compact

The United States' official response to the draft constitution, when it finally came, did little to encourage a belief in the viability of the document or the unity it sought to create. After a review that took eight months to complete, Ambassador Hayden Williams, head of the American negotiating team, stated that the United States could not accept the draft constitution as the supreme law of the land: "Free Association as envisioned by the compact is clearly inconsistent with the sovereign independent status called for in the constitution. We have further concluded that the mere revision of the compact will not alter this basic fact."[12] Micronesian negotiators responded to Williams' 1976 comment by saying that "while the constitution may be inconsistent with your interpretation of free association, it is not inconsistent with ours."[13]

American negotiators saw the Compact of Free Association as being a free, voluntary, and terminable relationship between a self-governing territory and a fully independent state. The American side argued that free association by definition was not a relationship between equals. In addition, the United States objected to Micronesian claims of jurisdiction over ocean waters and the power of the FSM government to claim new territories. United States reviewers described the ratification process of the draft compact under an already approved constitution as being overly complex and prolonged. They took strong exception to the provision prohibiting the testing, storage, or transfer of radioactive materials and toxic waste without the consent of the government of the Federated States of Micronesia. The Americans also deemed unacceptable the prohibition on indefinite land leases and the required renegotiation of existing ones because the provisions threatened the U.S. military's access to Micronesian land and waters. At the same time, U.S. representatives questioned how effective the FSM national government could actually be in light of the constitutional limits on the extent of its powers as delineated in the draft constitution.[14]

For Ambassador Williams, the solution was clear. He urged the insertion into the draft constitution of a phrase declaring that the constitution and laws of Micronesia were not to infringe upon the rights and responsibilities vested in the United States by the compact.[15] Williams argued that support for the constitution meant the favoring of independence; this raised the question of how much, if any, American financial support there could be for the new Micronesian nation. Similarly, Acting High Commissioner Peter Coleman, in his 1977 "State of the Territory" address, urged the Congress of Micronesia to ensure that the draft constitution was compatible with the Compact of Free of Association before submitting it to the people for approval.[16] As Norman Meller noted, the positions advocated by Williams and Coleman erroneously presumed that the Congress of Micronesia had the power to simply amend the constitution at will.[17]

Williams' words troubled many, and were quoted by proponents of separation in both the Marshalls and Palau as yet another reason to avoid inclusion in an integrated Micronesian nation. The position of the United States government in this period came across as self-serving if not duplicitous. Until his resignation in July of 1976, Ambassador Williams publicly espoused the unity of the Caroline and Marshall Islands.[18] Despite this and other like statements, the United States did not actively discourage the possibility of separate negotiations. The seeming contradiction actually reflected the dilemma that the American government faced in the region. A divided Micronesia posed significant complications for American security interests in the region. At the same time, concerns about the incompatibility of the constitution with the compact comprised a different but equally serious challenge.

Other factors contributed to the slowdown in negotiations. The 1976 American presidential elections and the subsequent change in administrations resulted in a prolonged delay between negotiating sessions as did a published account in 1976 on CIA surveillance of the Micronesian negotiating team.[19] A *Washington Post* article, written by Bob Woodward whose in-depth investigation into the Watergate burglary helped bring about the resignation of President Richard Nixon, reported that the United States Central Intelligence Agency had been conducting electronic surveillance on Micronesian negotiators over the last four years.[20] Other intelligence gathering techniques included the recruiting and paying of Micronesian citizens for information; among this group was a staff member on the Commission for Future Political Status and Transition.[21] Reports of the surveillance drew the condemnation of the United States Senate Intelligence Committee. One member of the committee called the spying "one of this country's most shabby operations in modern time...it is deplorable to even contemplate what we did."[22] As a condition to the resumption of the status talks, the Micronesian side insisted on an immediate apology and the names of those citizens who had cooperated with the CIA. Their demands were ultimately honored.

In private, Micronesian negotiators were more sanguine. Andon Amaraich, who had replaced Lazarus Salii as the chair of the Commission on Future Political Status and Transition, acknowledged that the Micronesian side had been aware of the spying for quite some time, and had taken precautions accordingly.[23] The surveillance was, he said, crazy, unnecessary, and more annoying than anything else. Amaraich recounted how, to avoid American eavesdropping, he had to sometimes travel to more neutral sites outside of the Trust Territory to communicate by phone or radio patch on matters relating to the negotiations. American efforts to gather information clandestinely were less than completely successful, and sometimes humorous in their failings. On one occasion, an American official gave Tosiwo Nakayama a lamp in which was concealed a listening device.[24] Suspicious of the gift, Nakayama passed it on to a family member from Onoun. This individual took the lamp with him back to the atoll where he sometimes used it for light at night when his electric generator was turned on. Intelligence gatherers learned a great deal about life on Onoun and little else.

In January 1977, Nakayama headed a delegation from the Congress of Micronesia that traveled to Washington, D.C., to meet with Jimmy Carter's secretary of state–designate Cyrus Vance.[25] Vance and Secretary of the Interior Cecil Andrus followed up that meeting by sending a letter to Nakayama and Speaker of the House of Representatives Bethwel Henry assuring them of the United States' interest in a close relationship with Micronesia and their confidence in negotiating an agreement on a future political status that would serve the interests of the people of Micronesia and the United States.[26] As preface to the renewed negotiations, scheduled for Guam in July of 1977, Vance and Andrus suggested a discussion in Honolulu designed to give Micronesian negotiators the opportunity to discuss with representatives from different federal agencies the changes a new political status for the islands would bring. The most significant outcome of that meeting, however, proved the articulation of strong separatist views from the Marshallese and Palauan representatives. At American Ambassador Phillip Manhard's request, the roundtable ended with all participants gathered in a circle and holding hands as a sign of unity and equality.[27] The circle gave lie to what actually happened at the talks. The expression of Marshallese and Palauan grievance dashed publicly and completely any last hope of Micronesian unity.

At the opening of the formal negotiating session on Guam later that year, Andon Amaraich spoke of the frustration caused by the long thirteen-month delay in the talks. He criticized the scheduling of this latest round of negotiations as too soon after the just concluded discussions in Honolulu. The rushed timing had left Micronesians without "sufficient time for these issues to be discussed in a truly Micronesian way and also to ensure the greatest possible representation of Micronesian views."[28] The Congress of Micronesia remained committed to unity, but circumstances had thus far precluded a full and frank discussion among Micronesians concerning the benefits of unity and of the steps to be taken to mitigate the concerns expressed by those who opposed it. Amaraich likened the constitutional convention to the framing of the United States constitution two hundred years before. He noted the pessimism that preceded the Micronesian Constitutional Convention, the "non-negotiable" demands that had to be overcome, and the compromises made in a unique Micronesian way that allowed for the formulation of the first truly Micronesian government. Anticipating the American decision to enter into multiple negotiations, Amaraich asserted that there could be "no greater transgression against the inherent sovereignty of the Micronesian people than an act by the United States which denied any of those people the right to express their opinion on the draft constitution."[29] Despite the Micronesian negotiator's plea, U.S. representatives made explicit their government's willingness to negotiate separately with the Marshalls and Palau. The Congress of Micronesia later protested, contending that negotiations with separatist factions violated United Nations' precedents on the territorial integrity of a non-self-governing territory. The protest was to no avail, however.

With the inauguration of Jimmy Carter as president, Peter Rosenblatt replaced Hayden Williams as the chief American negotiator. Like Williams, Rosenblatt believed the compact and the constitution to be incompatible. His suggestion, however, was not to amend the constitution, but to attach a rider to the constitutional referendum that stipulated the supremacy of the Compact of Free Association.[30] Nakayama vigorously opposed Rosenblatt's suggestion that a rider be attached to the constitution.[31] He regarded much of the discussion over compatibility as premature, unnecessary, and confusing; he argued that it was first imperative to define clearly what was meant by "free association." Nakayama argued against Rosenblatt's comment that a "yes" vote on the constitution would mean Micronesia had opted for independence, and took exception to Williams' veiled threat about the effects of a vote for independence on American financial support. Though his own preferences were quite clear, Nakayama argued that approval of the constitution "would actually mean nothing more than that the people would be given the opportunity to form their own government."[32] He urged the people to listen to their representatives and not the ambassador, and disagreed strongly with Rosenblatt's contention that the constitution and the draft compact of free association were not compatible.[33]

The persistence of Nakayama and others brought a breakthrough, with concessions from the American side that proved acceptable if less than optimal. The Hilo Accords, signed on 9 April 1978 at the Lagoon Hotel in Hilo, Hawai'i, brought greater definition and clarity to the political status talks, and provided a framework for what ultimately became the Compact of Free Association between the United States and the Federated States of Micronesia. Present and representing their respective constituencies were Ambassador Peter Rosenblatt, Bailey Olter from the Congress, Roman Tmetuchl of Palau, and Amata Kabua of the Marshalls.[34] The document stated that an agreement of free association would be negotiated on a government-to-government basis and executed before the termination of the Trusteeship Agreement. The resulting compacts would then be put to a United Nations–observed plebiscite. The constitutions of the three Micronesian entities were to be in accord with the political status of free association as set forth in the principles. The people of Micronesia were to enjoy full internal self-government, and have authority for their foreign affairs, including marine resources. The United States was to have responsibility for security and defense matters, including the establishment of necessary military facilities and the exercise of appropriate operating rights. Unilateral termination of free association was permissible under the terms and procedures outlined in the compact itself; mutually agreed-upon termination would not prevent the continuation of U.S. economic assistance as negotiated by both parties. Unilateral termination by the United States would not disrupt the flow of economic assistance at the levels and for the time period previously agreed upon.

## Criticisms from Within

Nakayama was not without his critics among those in support of unity and the draft constitution. John Mangefel of Yap had been a strong ally and supporter of Nakayama within the Senate. Like Nakayama, Mangefel had attended the University of Hawai'i. There, he had demonstrated strong creative writing skills. Witty and thoughtful, the future first governor of the state of Yap often read into the congressional record self-authored letters from his imaginary cousin Ngabchai that criticized the American administration for its ineptitude. Mangefel also criticized the Congress of Micronesia for its lack of productivity and its aping of American practices, including the wearing of neckties during congressional sessions. His version of the Lord's Prayer spoofed Micronesia's increasing dependence on American aid. He also targeted the negotiations. Mangefel charged that the Congress of Micronesia had spent too much money "year-in and year-out" in dealing with the question of future status. He argued that the money would have been better spent on the development of the islands' economy. Nine years of negotiations with no results and enormous spending was "just too much," he concluded. He saw unity as threatened not by external forces but from within: "If Micronesian unity collapses, it is because we failed to understand each other and to accommodate each other's particular wishes, not because of some American secretary or ambassador, or high commissioner, or CIA agent. We have found the enemy and they are ourselves."[35]

Nick Bossy, Nakayama's severest critic and chief political adversary, did not hesitate to criticize the status negotiations. During a special session of Congress in August of 1977, Bossy introduced a joint resolution directing the Commission on Future Political Status and Transition to resume negotiations with the United Sates forthwith.[36] Bossy claimed that he was expressing the consensus of his constituents over the delay in negotiations. He noted too that 1981, the year designated by the United States for the termination of the Trusteeship, was fast approaching. The United States, he said, had formally apologized for the CIA's surveillance of the Micronesian negotiating team and given the assurance that it would not happen again. Bossy expressed satisfaction with the apology, and said the commission had used the incident as an excuse not to negotiate. Bailey Olter of Pohnpei took exception to Bossy's remarks.[37] The negotiations had not resumed sooner because the United States government had not made good on its promise to reveal the names of those Micronesians who had collaborated in the surveillance. Olter added that the commission had also been waiting for the U.S. response to the Micronesian position on the Law of the Sea Treaty, something that had been promised by Ambassador Hayden Williams back in June of 1976.

Tensions between Tosiwo Nakayama and Nick Bossy continued over more local issues and in congressional elections. Nakayama had supported the complaints of people in the villages of Iras and Mechitiw whose lands and access to reef resources were being adversely affected by the expansion of the Chuuk Airport.[38] Nakayama felt strong ties to the residents, most of whom were originally from islands beyond the Lagoon. Nakayama's own mother Rosania had grown up in Iras. Given his Weno origins, Bossy was less sympathetic and stressed the importance of the airport's expansion to the economic development of greater Chuuk. The destructive impact of dredging, paving, and construction on important cultural and historical sites added to the dispute. At the urging of Nakayama and other members of Congress, High Commissioner Adrian Winkel ordered in 1979 the dredge area changed, and signed a charter for cooperatives designed to help the residents of the two villages develop other food sources to make up for the loss of land crops and marine resources due to the airport's expansion.[39]

Bossy's criticisms of Nakayama could be barbed and his self-effacing comments deceiving. Near the end of the Congress' early 1978 session, Bossy criticized Nakayama for the absence of the Micronesian flag from the president's podium. He refused to concede that the absence of the flag was an innocent error caused by the temporary need to rearrange the furnishings on the podium. Alluding to Nakayama's foreign ancestry and lighter skin color, Bossy called attention to his own dark skin color and his pride in being Micronesian.[40] The flag, he implied, was an important reminder of what it meant to be Micronesian. At the end of the session, he noted that if it turned out that he would have to run against Nakayama for the single four-year, at-large seat in the Interim Congress of the Federated States of Micronesia, he would not do so but instead return to being a fisherman and a farmer.[41] He later went back on that promise and did indeed challenge Nakayama for the at-large seat in a bitter and ugly campaign that differed markedly from the more relaxed, personal, and informal campaigning of earlier years. Fragmentation within the core districts supporting the constitution also posed a host of complications that affected the move toward self-government. The people of Faichuk and the Mortlocks held a referendum in November 1977 to vote on administrative separation from Truk district. Both districts voted overwhelmingly for the separation.[42] While nothing of immediate consequence resulted from the vote, Faichuk's persistence in seeking to break away from Chuuk State would create the greatest crisis in Nakayama's later presidency.

Differences over unity and future political status also informed the expulsion of Roman Tmetuchl from the Senate.[43] During a regular session of the Seventh Congress in early 1978, Senate Resolution 7–5, introduced by Nakayama, called for the censure and expulsion of Senator Tmetuchl for his neglect of duty and violation of oath. In the speech introducing the resolution, Nakayama noted that the presiding officer of the Senate had few prerogatives and many responsibilities, one of which was to ensure that members adhere to the rules of the chamber and honor their oath of office. He told his fellow senators that there was nothing personal behind the resolution and that it was not an easy task. He also denied that his motivation was political: "If differing political views were the criteria for expulsion and censure, then we could not have a legislative body."[44] He noted that Tmetuchl had only attended twelve days of the first regular session of the Seventh Congress, did not attend the first special session at all, and had not yet shown up for the current session that was now in its thirty-sixth day. "Clearly," he said, "the people of Palau are not being fully represented in this Senate and in this Congress."[45] Tmetuchl characterized the expulsion as a personal and vindictive reaction of the Senate president against him, but a special committee report supported it.[46] The full Senate voted 8–2–2 for the resolution with Senators Kaleb Udui of Palau and Wilfred Kendall of the Marshalls voting no, and Senators Amata Kabua of the Marshalls and Roman Tmetuchl of Palau not present to vote.[47] In his closing remarks at the end of the session, Nakayama expressed his thanks to the members of the Senate for their patience and understanding during what for him was "this most difficult and painful session."[48] Though difficult and distracting, the expulsion of Tmetuchl only affirmed what was already obvious to all within the Congress—Palau would not be a part of any Micronesian union. Tmetuchl's characterization of the censure as a personal and vindictive action on the part of Nakayama was overly dramatic. The two men remained on relatively cordial terms throughout the balance of their lives.[49]

## Sea and Sky: Working for Micronesia

Nakayama was also a leading advocate of full Micronesian participation in the international Law of the Sea Treaty, a key and controversial issue in political status negotiations with the United States. During its 1974 regular session, the Congress of Micronesia had passed a joint resolution proclaiming Micronesia to be an archipelagic state.[50] As such, Micronesia was entitled to define its territorial baselines in such a way as to include its outermost islands and to claim internal sea jurisdiction over a 200-mile economic zone measured outward from those baselines. Given the unlikelihood of securing international recognition for the position while still under the Trusteeship Agreement, the Congress' delegation to the United Nations Law of the Sea Conference had focused its efforts on the 200-mile economic zone as a first step in the exercise of its territorial sovereignty. In preparation for the next meeting of the conference, Nakayama, as head of the Micronesian delegation, convened the first Micronesian Law of the Sea Convention in November 1976 at the Christopher Inn on Weno.

The purpose of the convention was "to formulate and develop a unified position on the Law of the Sea...for the future island nation of Micronesia."[51] The 1976 convention helped make possible the passage of a bill to create a 200-mile economic zone for the nation-to-be. Acting High Commissioner Boyd Mackenzie had vetoed the bill passed by Congress because it did not include necessary amendments required by the Trust Territory administration and the United States government.[52] The version that ultimately passed and was signed into law later in 1977 did establish a 200-mile fishery zone and provided for the regulation of living resources within the zone.[53] The bill had been amended to bring the Micronesian jurisdictional claims within the parameters of international law and in accord with the Trusteeship Agreement and the responsibilities of the administering authority. The bill also called for the creation of a Micronesian Maritime Authority (MMA) whose members were drawn from both the Congress and the Trust Territory administration. The MMA was charged with making direct contact with fishing companies, issuing permits for fishing, and establishing and enforcing regulations for the regulation and conservation of various species of marine resources found in Micronesian waters.[54] As much symbolic as practical, the bill nonetheless underscored the desire of its advocates to assert control over their natural resources, win international recognition, and secure a local source of revenue for their future government.

Nakayama also acted in behalf of the territory's interest in more regional matters involving transportation and economic development. In November 1976, he and Bethwel Henry traveled to Japan where they spent four days endeavoring to repair the breakdown in talks between the United States and Japan over the renegotiation of an air transport agreement that involved the Tokyo-Saipan route.[55] Negotiated in 1969, the agreement allowed Japan Airlines and a U.S. carrier to serve the same route. On 24 June 1976, President Gerald Ford authorized Continental/Air Micronesia as the American carrier

**Fig. 6.2.** Tosiwo Nakayama speaking at a meeting on Saipan. Bethwel Henry is seated to Nakayama's right (Trust Territory Photo Archives, Pacific Collection, Hamilton Library, University of Hawai'i, Mānoa).

for the route. The Japan Civil Aeronautics Board, however, refused to allow Continental/Air Micronesia to begin service, claiming there was a shortage of terminal space at Tokyo's Haneda International Airport and, more tellingly, that the 1969 agreement gave the U.S. carrier too large a share of the market.

Nakayama and Henry met with representatives of all parties concerned as well as gave interviews to six Japanese newspapers and periodicals. Arguing for the implementation of the 1969 agreement, the two stressed the economic and political hardships that further delay would cause Micronesia. They likened the situation to World War II when Micronesia was caught between the two nations and suffered as a consequence. They requested that a compromise be reached and pointed out the economic stakes for Continental/Air Micronesia, its local owners, and the islands' economy. Continental/Air Micronesia had invested some $32 million in Micronesia, and had lost $10 million in the past eight years. Moreover, a multi-million dollar international airport had been built on Saipan in expectation of the Tokyo route. Micronesian citizens owned a majority interest in the airline through the United Micronesia Development Authority or UMDA, and many hotels and other businesses stood to suffer major losses if service were delayed further. Noting the changes to come in Micronesia's future political status that would place governing authority and decision making in the hands of Micronesians, the two pointed out the importance of maintaining good relations between the two countries. The statement played on the historical relationship between Japan and the islands as visibly and personally manifest through Nakayama's paternal ancestry.

Nakayama and Henry left Japan feeling that they had been effective in stating Micronesia's case and were optimistic about the possibilities of a settlement. With delays continuing, however, the two sent a cable to both sides asking for a Micronesian representative as either a participant or observer in future talks.[56] In their cable, Nakayama and Henry again reviewed the history of the dispute and the injury it was causing to island businesses. They noted that Japan's demand for an equivalent American city destination should not be used as an excuse to delay implementation of the 1969 agreement as neither Saipan nor the other five districts were "American cities."[57] Nakayama and Henry later sent a letter of protest to Japanese foreign minister Hatoyama Ichirō and Yamaji Susumu of Japan's Civil Aviation Bureau. They wrote that a "delay of one year may be insignificant in terms of long-range national interests of Japan and the United States, but it represents a serious economic step backward for our islands, which are scheduled to become the newest self-governing area in the Western Pacific four years from now."[58] It was clear to them that the route was being held "hostage" to Japan's bargaining strategy with the United States. The interventions by Nakayama and Henry certainly helped as an accord was reached later in the year. Nakayama and Henry were on board the first inaugural flight that landed at Haneda International Airport on 2 October 1977.[59]

Nakayama and Henry again visited Tokyo, this time in December 1977, to meet with Japanese Prime Minister Fukuda Takeo, his top aides, cabinet ministers, and members of the Japanese Diet.[60] Susumu Aizawa, Nakayama's boyhood friend and now the chief magistrate of Tol, traveled with the two and served as their interpreter. Aizawa had left Chuuk at the end of the war with his father, played professional baseball in Japan, and became proficient in the language before returning to the islands in 1958. The focus of these 1977 meetings was the current and future relationship between the two entities, and Japan's contribution to the economic development of the islands. Nakayama underscored the importance of Japan to the islands' future and looked forward to the day when formal diplomatic relations could be established between the two island countries. He called the meeting a miracle, the first of its kind, and said he and Henry would be returning to Japan with a "long shopping list" after the completion of the current congressional session.

The two trips to Japan also displayed the extremely close and effective relationship between Tosiwo Nakayama and Bethwel Henry. Aside from Andon Amariach, there was no one in or around government whom Nakayama trusted more. Born on the outlying island of Mokil, also called Mwoakilloa, in 1934, Henry had attended the University of Hawai'i from 1955 to 1959 after working as a junior clerk for the district administration on Pohnpei.[61] He returned from Hawai'i and took a teaching position at the Pacific Islands Central School. That same year, he served as an advisor to the U.S. delegation in its annual presentation before the UN Trusteeship Council, and won election to the Ponape District Congress where he served at different times over the next six years as that body's president and vice-speaker. In 1965, Henry ran successfully for a two-year seat in the Congress of Micronesia's House of Assembly, later known as the House of Representatives, and became that legislative body's first and only Speaker. He also served as Speaker in the Congress of the Federated States of Micronesia, an office he held from 1979 until he lost a race for Pohnpei's four-year, at-large seat to Leo Falcam in 1987.[62] Known for his honesty, fairness, effectiveness, and calm demeanor, Henry managed the flow of legislation in the Congress, and participated actively in a host of negotiations involving the economic development and future political status of the islands. Along with Nakayama and Amaraich, he played a pivotal role in helping bring the Federated States of Micronesia into existence.

## The Referendum on the Draft Constitution

A delegation from the convention had visited the Trust Territory high commissioner Edward Johnston soon after the conclusion of the convention and presented him with a copy of the draft constitution.[63] The high commissioner subsequently proposed June 1976 as the time for a referendum on the constitution. The convention leaders considered this too soon; their plan was to hold the referendum five months later in conjunction with the November congressional elections. Johnston felt that a dual-purpose election might deflect voter attention away from the constitution and disallowed the proposed date. The debates over unity, separatism, and compatibility between the draft constitution and the Compact of Free Association further delayed the vote. With the necessary authorizing legislation passed and funds appropriated, the referendum was finally set for mid-1978. The day agreed upon was 12 July, the same date for both the opening of the first Congress of Micronesia in 1965 and the convening of the 1975 Micronesian Constitutional Convention.

With the date for the referendum set, there developed a two-pronged program to educate voters on the draft constitution and the many issues it encompassed. The Trust Territory government deployed the resources of its Education for Self-Government program, while the Congress of Micronesia through its Commission on Future Political Status and Transition sponsored their own advocacy teams that included a large representation of traditional leaders. Concerned about the quality and bias in the aforementioned efforts, the Catholic Church on Chuuk and Pohnpei conducted studies and sponsored gatherings on the draft constitution. Public consideration of the constitution included rallies, meetings, radio broadcasts, television shows, motor vehicle caravans, and the display of public posters.

Different islands raised different concerns about provisions in the constitution.[64] Some voters on Kosrae, once a part of Pohnpei but now a separate district as the result of popular pressure leading to a 1976 administrative order, expressed reservations about the provision for freedom of religion. These reservations reflected the dominance of the Kosraean Congregational Church over life on the island. On Pohnpei, land proved an emotional issue as opponents of the constitution argued that the national government would take charge of all public lands and with no assurances they would be returned to the states. The majority of residents in the Marshalls remained hostile to the constitution and the national government that it chartered. The division in Marshallese politics between the Kabua and Heine factions figured prominently in the referendum, with the Kabua faction decidedly opposed to the constitution while the Heine group supported the pro-unity Voice of the Mar-

**Fig. 6.3.** Opposition to Micronesian unity in the Marshalls (Trust Territory Photo Archives, Pacific Collection, Hamilton Library, University of Hawai'i, Mānoa).

shalls party. The struggle for power between Palau's two major political parties impinged upon the referendum in Palau, though both parties were by now pursuing separation. In Chuuk, the elections for governor that were scheduled for a month after the referendum had the effect of focusing the electorate's attention on personalities and away from the constitution and its provisions.

On 12 July, 55,000 out of the 60,000 total registered voters in the Trust Territory went to the polls under the watchful eye of the largest United Nations Visiting Mission ever. In the words of Norman Meller, the results of the referendum both vindicated the work of the convention and undermined most of the compromises so laboriously reached for the sake of unity.[65] Kosrae's elevation to the status of district proved extremely fortuitous as a majority of voters there as well as in Chuuk, Pohnpei, and Yap assured the required two-thirds majority needed for establishment of the government of the Federated States of Micronesia. The Marshalls and Palau did not approve the constitution. The vote in Palau proved closer than expected with the margin of victory for the anti-constitution forces being only 310 votes. In the Marshalls, the strong opposition of Kabua and other leading chiefs, or *iroij,* resulted in two-thirds of the voters rejecting the draft constitution. So there was to be a Federated States of Micronesia, but what next? Following the certification of the vote, transition plans moved ahead as did negotiations over future political status and the establishment of separated governments for Palau and the Marshalls. The Trust Territory government was to be largely dismantled and its functions and supporting staff divided among the three emerging polities.[66] The administering authority did retain executive power over financial matters, foreign affairs, and other areas of responsibility required of it by the UN Trusteeship Agreement. The Trust Territory High Court reserved jurisdiction over a number of sensitive areas until the governments of the three Micronesian entities had established their own court systems. Transition would be ongoing as would negotiations over future political status and the actual establishment of the Federated States of Micronesia government.

## The Election of 1979

Tosiwo Nakayama appeared as the most likely choice to become the first president of the Federated States of Micronesia. The leadership he had demonstrated as the president of the Congress of Micronesia's Senate, his role in the Micronesian Constitutional Convention, his deep involvement in the political status negotiations with the United States, and the high regard and respect accorded him by his peers made his selection seem inevitable. First, however, he had to win Chuuk's at-large seat in the first regular Congress of the Federates States of Micronesia. In hindsight, the elections for the first regular Congress of the Federated States of Micronesia were more momentous than commonly acknowledged. Given the constitution's stipulation that the president of the FSM be chosen by members of Congress from among the four at-large senators, the election for the at-large seat from Chuuk was particularly important; the future of the larger, would-be nation was quite literally at stake. Nakayama and Nick Bossy were the two senators from Chuuk in the last Congress of Micronesia, each holding a district-wide, four-year seat. They both carried their seats into the interim or transition session of the Congress that met in July 1978. As noted previously, Bossy had announced at the closing session of the Interim Congress of the Federated States of Micronesia that he would not run against Nakayama for the single, four-year, at-large seat in the new Congress. He soon changed his mind, however, and did in fact oppose Nakayama for the seat in the 27 March election of the following year.

Victory had always come easy for Nakayama in previous elections. He campaigned little if at all, and relied instead upon his reputation, name recognition, experience, and family and clan connections. While campaigning had become a somewhat more proactive process over the life of the American-administered Trust Territory, elections remained relaxed, informal affairs. The

Chuuk elections of 1979 changed this pattern dramatically as the competition between Nakayama and Bossy was intense, ugly at times, and marred by rumor, innuendo, and, in places, voter intimidation.[67] Aside from the clan, family, and regional affiliations that distinguished them, the two men held decidedly different positions on the issue of a future political status for the islands. Nakayama had moved from his advocacy of independence to support for free association with the United States that he understood as ultimately being a relationship between two sovereign and independent nations. Bossy, on the other hand, advocated commonwealth status with the United States as being a more secure and realistic option for small, resource-poor islands that had only their strategic location as an asset with which to bargain. The two men had clashed repeatedly in the Congress of Micronesia's Senate with Bossy being critical of Nakayama on matters that were often more about appearance and style than substance. Bossy's first election to the Senate in 1974 had come at the expense of Nakayama's friend and ally Andon Amaraich, and involved questionable practices, claims of interference by the Trust Territory government, and charges of voter fraud. The election of 1979 would be more of the same.

Rumors began circulating that Nakayama had enriched himself as a public servant, used his connections and contacts to enter into lucrative agreements with foreign businessmen, and grown distant and indifferent to the needs of Chuuk and its people.[68] He and his wife Miter traveled to Toloas where the rumors were proving particularly strong. Miter's presence was purposeful as it emphasized her husband's connection through marriage to Weno and the larger Lagoon area. At a community meeting, Nakayama spoke directly to the accusations, declaring that he was not a rich man and had never taken money from foreign businessmen. To reach Toloas, he said, he had borrowed a boat and engine from his brother-in-law Sasauo, who by this time had changed his last name from Haruo to Gouland. The watch on his wrist and the rubber slippers on his feet were loaned by another relative. Nakayama later claimed that he spent less than a thousand dollars on his 1979 election campaign with most of the money going to buy donuts and soft drinks for those who gathered to hear him speak. There were other rumors, emanating from the Bossy camp that claimed a deal had been struck between the two candidates. Bossy was to back Nakayama in the current election in return for the latter's support in the special election to fill the vacancy anticipated by Nakayama's election as president of the FSM. Nakayama was embarrassed and caught off guard during a campaign visit to Uman when Bossy took the opportunity to make a public denunciation of the alleged agreement on local radio.

Opposition to Nakayama also provided common ground for people who otherwise opposed one another. The Faichuk area, led by its controversial representative in Congress Kalisto Refalopei, was seeking recognition as a second Chuukese state separate from the Lagoon and the outer island groups. Faichuk, however, joined those in the Lagoon area who supported Bossy, as Nakayama was seen as an opponent of Faichuk statehood. So widespread were the rumors circulating in Faichuk that Nakayama and his wife Miter traveled to Tol on election day to confront the people promoting them. Nakayama and his wife reached Tol at nine o'clock in the morning only to learn that most of the island's residents had already voted. They proceeded to Refalopei's home where they were received cordially and offered lunch by his parents, brother, and other relatives. Refalopei eventually showed up carrying a rifle, and quickly proclaimed that there were no votes for Nakayama on Tol. The congressman made it quite clear that he had used his rifle to ensure that voters marked their ballots for Bossy. Nakayama responded that he had not come seeking votes and already knew that he would lose Faichuk. He came instead, he said, to clear his name. He proclaimed that he was not a wealthy man, owned no businesses, and had never accepted money or gifts from any foreign company. There were people on Tol who believed him. Despite Refalopei's claim, Nakayama actually did receive a fair number of votes from the Faichuk area, nine of which were cast in the congressman's home precinct. Nakayama believed those nine votes came from members of Refalopei's immediate family who remembered the kindness he had extended to their mother several years earlier when she was sent to Hawai'i on medical referral while he was a student there.[69]

Tosiwo and Miter Nakayama returned to Weno that day to await the election results. Given the time needed to collect and count the votes from Chuuk State's more distant islands, it would not be until 16 April that the final results were announced. The wait was made even more awkward by the fact that only thirty feet separated the Nakayama and Bossy homes in Mwan village.[70] The early results from Weno and Faichuk had Bossy in the lead, a fact that caused those gathered at the Bossy home to celebrate loudly. The gaiety disappeared as the count proceeded. Nakayama actually won Weno and its absentee ballots by a 278-vote margin.[71] When the entire Lagoon vote had been counted, Bossy trailed Nakayama by almost 1,600 votes.[72] Given Nakayama's electoral strength in the outer islands where the vote had yet to be reported, the election was for all intents and purposes over. The final statewide tally showed Nakayama with 9,044 votes or 58.6 percent of the total; Bossy finished with 6,297 votes or 41.4 percent of all votes cast.[73] A third candidate Niko Meris had also run but received so few votes that his name was not included in the high commissioner's tabulations.[74]

Nakayama's victory was decisive, but also personally painful and diplomatically troubling. Several members of Miter's family had publicly supported Nick Bossy. This was not completely surprising given the fact the Miter and Nick Bossy were related. More disappointing for Nakayama was the fact that members of his own family on the Mori side had voted for Bossy.[75] The most ominous aspect of the 1979 congressional election in Chuuk revolved around charges of American interference in support of Nick Bossy. A published account in the *Micronesian Support Committee Bulletin* alleged that Jim Berg, an aide to Ambassador Peter Rosenblatt in the Office of Micronesian Status Negotiations, had offered Susumu Aizawa a large sum of money to enter the senatorial race as a third candidate.[76] The thinking behind the offer was that Aizawa would draw enough votes away from Nakayama to ensure a victory for the more America-friendly Bossy. Berg vehemently denied the accusation, terming it "pure rubbish"; Bossy called the charge "an outright lie."[77] Nakayama found the accusation quite plausible and Aizawa himself insisted that it was true.[78] There were, however, far more pressing matters ahead. With his seat assured, Nakayama now turned his attention to the organization of the new FSM Congress and governmental transition issues, not the least of which was the selection of leaders for the new country.

## Pohnpei Me Kak Apwal

Nakayama's election to the presidency of the FSM proved a foregone conclusion. With Petrus Tun as his vice president, Nakayama took the oath of office on 15 May 1979. The baseball field between the governor's office and the old Ponape State Hospital provided the venue. Nakayama's inauguration in May 1979 proved a humbling experience. He and his wife Miter drove to the inauguration grounds by themselves in a beat-up rental car with her long dress caught on the passenger side door.[79] The train of her gown was dragged along the road as they made their way to the inauguration site. Once there, Miter Nakayama found herself forced to sit alongside dignitaries in the front row of the review stand with a dress whose hem was torn and tattered. In yet another, even more humbling moment at the 1979 inauguration, the United States high commissioner of the Trust Territory of the Pacific Islands Adrian Winkel was accorded greater recognition and deference than the president of the nation whose inauguration he had come to observe.

*Pohnpei me kak apwal* is a phrase that translates from Pohnpeian into English as "Pohnpei can be difficult." The FSM government's initial relationship with the state of Pohnpei certainly required forbearance. The second special session of the Sixth Congress of Micronesia had formally designated Pohnpei as the capital of the new government in 1976. Plans for the relocation of the Congress' offices and the development of national government facilities were finalized in June 1977.[80] Despite the feasts, speeches, and general festivities that marked the inauguration of the new government, Pohnpei did not prove a particularly welcoming home for the new government in its very first years. The logistics of establishing a new government were formidable and entrusted to young energetic men such as Asterio Takesy, the capable nephew of Tosiwo Nakayama, and Sabo Ulechong, the clerk of the Senate.[81] Takesy had served as the clerk of the Congress of Micronesia's House of Representatives from 1970 to 1977, and the assistant convention secretary to the Micronesian Constitutional Convention in 1975; he would go on to have a distinguished career in government, holding posts that included secretary of external affairs and FSM ambassador to the United States. Takesy's and Ulechong's immediate task on Pohnpei was to locate office space and housing for the incoming government. As advance agents, the two negotiated for the renovation of buildings and arranged for the procurement of equipment, supplies, and vehicles necessary for the functioning of the fledgling government. The task was made difficult by the sometimes-heated competition with the state government for resources, and by the demands of landlords who charged high rents for the most dilapidated of buildings or rooms.

The executive branch's first home was the old district hospital complex in Kolonia that lay atop a hill overlooking the harbor and bordered the inauguration site.[82] A baseball field, the remnants of the old Spanish Wall, and the state governor's office were nearby. The Kaselehlia Inn just down from the governor's office provided temporary meeting and office space for the FSM Congress. The executive complex had been renovated at a cost of $360,000. Work began in September of 1979 and was completed by May of the following year. One of the buildings housed the Social Services Department, and the offices of the attorney general, public defender, and budget director. Another building was home to the offices of the president and vice president, their special assistants, and the Departments of External Affairs, Resources and Development, and Finance. The FSM Personnel Office occupied the third and smaller building. To promote the relationship between the people and their government, Nakayama ordered that an open house be held, and that there be tours of the renovated buildings by guides who spoke Pohnpeian and could explain the functions of the different government offices.[83] Other offices were scattered about Kolonia in structures or spaces leased from private businesses and homeowners. The diplomacy helped but did not necessarily ease the tension that existed between the new government and the host state.

Leo Falcam from Uh was the first elected governor of Pohnpei. He had served as district administrator of Pohnpei prior to his election, and had extensive experience as an administrator in the Trust Territory government. He had also served as the head of his state's delegation to the Micronesian Constitutional Convention in 1975. His prior service and his status as Pohnpei's first elected governor had led the paramount chiefs of the island's five chiefdoms to award him the title of *Luhk Pohnpei,* the only island-wide title in existence. Falcam believed that the island should enjoy precedence in all ceremonial matters involving Pohnpei State and the FSM. He insisted on protocol in any ceremonial or state occasion that recognized Pohnpei and its governor first, and the FSM and its president second. To his credit, Nakayama ignored the slights with patience and dignity, and with an eye toward maintaining good relations among his national government, its host state, and the fading but still engaged Trust Territory government.

Power outages on Pohnpei proved a constant problem for the FSM national government throughout the Nakayama years as the island's generators were old, outdated, frequently broke down, and could not meet the extra demands now being placed on them by the national government.[84] Land proved a particularly contentious, more threatening issue for the new national government. A 22 December 1978 memorandum of understanding between Nakayama and Bethwel Henry and the Pohnpei Public Land Authority had set aside two hundred acres of land for the purpose of constructing a capitol complex at Palikir.[85] The Pohnpei State Legislature had agreed earlier to deed two hundred acres in the Palikir area of Sokehs municipality for construction of the FSM national capitol.

Reservations developed in the Pohnpei State Legislature about the agreement and the legislation that gave it legal force. Speaker of the State Legislature Edwel Santos stated in a speech broadcast on local radio that the state had never agreed to the use of the land in Palikir for staff housing; that housing, argued Santos, should be built by local businessmen with loans from funds set aside for the purpose of economic development on the island. A second bill passed by the state legislature in January 1982 sought to resolve the differences in understanding by clarifying the kinds of structures that the federal government could build at Palikir. The dispute continued, however. The unease among Pohnpeians led to a resolution from the FSM Congress that mandated Nakayama to form a task force on the deed to the Palikir site. After a series of meetings, the task force filed a report reaffirming Palikir as the capitol site, but with provisions that sought to mitigate the effects of site development upon the surrounding environs. No commercial operations were permitted on the site and any staff housing built was to be beyond the control of the national government.[86] It would not be until January 1985, however, that the Palikir deed was actually transmitted to the FSM government.[87]

The presence and activities of the new government gave rise to fears and rumors. There were those who worried about the loss of land and the influx of people from elsewhere; others argued that Pohnpeians were being discriminated against when it came to hiring and that foreign businesses were being prevented from establishing themselves on the island by the national government. In light of this unease, a bill, number 327–82, was introduced in the state legislature that provided $20,000 for a referendum on whether or not Pohnpei should remain in the FSM.[88] Governor Falcam was quick to criticize the bill, calling the concerns that motivated it unfounded and "childish." Declaring himself a strong supporter of unity, Falcam said there was no evidence to suggest that the FSM government was taking land away from Pohnpeians or keeping business away from the island. He considered the national government's hiring practices more than fair; if anything, there were too many Pohnpeians being hired by the national government. He was right. As of March 1982, Pohnpeians held 126 of 282 or 45 percent of all national government jobs.[89]

During the early years of his administration on Pohnpei, Nakayama had found himself at odds with the elected leadership of the island over issues involving land, power, precedence, and jurisdiction. On more than one occasion, the island's chiefs came to his assistance. Somewhat ironically, a man committed to a modern agenda of change and development relied on earlier, established sources of power under stress from that very agenda. During the controversy surrounding the deeding of land in Palikir to the FSM government, the *nahnmwarki* of Madolenihmw, Samuel Hadley, and Johnny Hadley, the *nahnken* of Madolenihmw, had written in support of the Palikir deed. In a 3 November 1981 letter to the leaders of the FSM government, the Hadleys urged that plans proceed with the development of the Palikir site. They expressed their displeasure with those in the legislature who were "easily forgetting our original pledge to support the new nation emerging from the Trust Territory government."[90]

Nakayama had chosen Johnny Hadley to head the Division of Micronesian Affairs within the Department of External Affairs. Hadley was an ordained minister of the Congregationalist Church and the son of *Nahnmwarki* Samuel Hadley, the paramount chief of Madolenihmw. As was sometimes the case on Pohnpei, the eldest son of the paramount chief or *nahnmwarki* became *nahnken,* the senior title in a secondary line of chiefs that served the *nahnmwarki*. The younger Hadley, then, was ideally situated to address two of the more prominent constituencies in the FSM: the chiefs and the churches. Nakayama also enjoyed the strong support and friendship of Benito Peter, the *nahnmwarki* of Kitti. Peter had sat in the front row of guests at Nakayama's inauguration in 1979. *Nahnmwarki* Ioanis Artui of Sokehs also proved a supporter of Nakayama and the national government; he challenged the people in his chiefdom of Sokehs to join him in supporting the FSM. In remarks translated into English from Pohnpeian, Artui, a strong proponent of unity, proclaimed: "Our success in life depends on whether or not we love our fellow men so that we can work cooperatively toward the goal to make our islands become a strong nation."[91]

Over the course of his time on Pohnpei, Nakayama would receive several honorific or *koanoat* titles from the paramount chiefs of the island. Despite his commitment to modernity, Nakayama did not actively seek the demise of the islands' chiefly systems. He appreciated the continuity of values and traditions that chiefly systems on islands such as Yap, Pohnpei, and to a lesser extent Chuuk could provide the fledgling nation, and said so on numerous occasions. An indication of improved relations between the state and national governments came in April 1983 when Resio Moses, who had defeated Leo Falcam in the election for governor and was himself a high titleholder in the chiefdom of Uh, agreed to a joint inauguration with the second Nakayama administration as a sign of unity and support.[92] Relations with Pohnpei State, however, were just one of many issues that confronted Nakayama in his efforts to establish a national government.

# CHAPTER 7

# Governing a Rainbow

IN HIS FIRST INAUGURAL ADDRESS, Tosiwo Nakayama borrowed heavily from the Preamble of the Constitution of the Federated States of Micronesia to underscore the significance of the occasion.[1] He cited the constitution as an exercise of sovereignty, and quoted the passage that affirmed the common desire of the people to live together in peace and harmony, to preserve the heritage of the past, and to protect the promise of the future. He noted too the diversity within the borders of the new nation, and the enrichment and promise that such diversity made possible. He likened the FSM to a beautiful rainbow of many different colors stretching across an ocean; shared aspirations made this new Pacific Islands nation stronger than its individual parts. Later speeches, given on national occasions including his State of the Nation addresses, came to focus on the mechanics of government and development. His first speeches, however, were more inspirational and focused on the ideals that had fed the founding of the FSM. The next eight years would prove just how hard it is to govern a rainbow as unity remained more a goal than a reality. Compounding the difficulties was the lack of experience in establishing a new government. Nakayama and associates would learn to govern by the doing of it. The task before them was to establish a functioning, internationally recognized government, while concluding negotiations with the United States on a compact of free association that would end the trusteeship, and affirm the FSM as an independent, self-governing nation.

## Transitioning to Self-Government

The transfer of administrative authority from the Trust Territory to the Federated States of Micronesia created a host of complicated, sometimes confounding problems that affected almost all areas of government. Disputes arose over the division of previously budgeted, U.S. federal funds among the different governmental entities that were in the process of emerging from the Trust Territory. The desire of FSM officials for a quick transition clashed with the reserve and caution of those in Saipan and in Washington, D.C. Within the FSM, the states' desire for as much administrative autonomy as possible ran up against national government concerns for coordination and control. There were those who thought the FSM copied too closely the administrative structure of the old Trust Territory government. To some of its critics, the new government was losing the chance for real autonomy and independence by duplicating the bureaucratic procedures that had previously controlled and dominated it. Nakayama, however, was more immediately concerned with the practical and the possible. He sought to transform an inherited system of administration with competent people who shared his commitment to the new nation.

Nakayama's first presidential order established the duties, responsibilities, and internal organization of the executive branch.[2] Underneath the president and vice president were the departments: Budget, Information, Attorney General, Planning and Statistics, Personnel, Public Defender, Resources and Development, Finance, Social Service, and External Affairs. Nakayama chose able men to head these departments. In selecting his cabinet, Nakayama sought to balance competency and experience with equitable state representation. Andon Amaraich of Chuuk headed the Department of External Affairs.[3] Aloysius Tuuth of Yap was chosen to be secretary of finance because of his past experience in the Trust Territory Personnel, Education, and Budget offices. Nakayama's selection of Tuuth met resistance from Vice President Petrus Tun who as a member of Yap's chiefly caste was uneasy with the appointment of a low caste person to such a high position.[4] Ambilos Iehsi, a congressional ally from Pingelap in Pohnpei State, was appointed to be secretary of resources and development. Del Pangelinan, also of Pohnpei, was chosen as budget officer given his extensive work in the Trust Territory government. Yosiwo George of Kosrae served as the secretary of social services, and Dan Perrin, an economist with the Congress of Micronesia who also advised the Commission on Future Political Status and Transition, headed the Office of Planning and Statistics. Fred Ramp, a former Peace Corps volunteer who had worked closely with Nakayama as a staff lawyer for the Con-

**Fig. 7.1.** Tosiwo Nakayama swearing in Vice President Petrus Tun at the inauguration of the Federated States of Micronesia government on Pohnpei, 1979 (Micronesian Seminar).

gress of Micronesia, was appointed attorney general. Kasio Mida of Chuuk served as personnel officer; Ketson Johnson of Pohnpei as information officer; and John Brackett from New York as public defender. Entrenched ideas regarding gender roles proved hard to break as no women were appointed to Nakayama's cabinet or to executive positions within the national government during his first term.[5]

## Continuing Negotiations over Political Status

Much of Nakayama's time as president of the FSM was devoted to completing negotiations over the Compact of Free Association with the United States, overseeing a popular referendum on it, and then dealing with a host of crises that arose as the draft document worked its way through multiple reviews, amendments, and revisions at local, national, and international levels. Nakayama had been a member of the Congress of Micronesia's negotiating team since 1969. As president, he remained close to the negotiations, either attending the sessions in person or through direct communication with the FSM negotiating team. Changes in U.S. presidential administrations caused delays in the negotiating and approval process of the compact. Ronald Reagan had put a hold on the negotiations in January of 1981 when he replaced Jimmy Carter as president and ordered the creation of a Micronesia Interdepartmental Group to review the draft compact. The move raised fears in the FSM that the Reagan administration would seek changes in the draft document that had been agreed to by both parties during the Carter years. In early September 1981, Nakayama received a cable from Under Secretary of State James Buckley, head of the intergovernmental review group, indicating that the United States was firm in its commitment to end the trusteeship under the terms negotiated by the previous administration.[6] Reassured by the statement, Nakayama announced his intention to lead the FSM delegation to the next round of talks scheduled to begin on 3 October 1981 in Maui, Hawai'i.

The talks in Maui took place as scheduled but bogged down when American representatives indicated that there would have to be reductions in the level of funding previously agreed to.[7] In a formal response to the American position, Nakayama noted that the recent delay in negotiations resulting from the change in American presidential administrations had been prolonged and uncomfortable. He took exception to the American side's retreat from a pledge to provide funds for a national capitol, and noted that only 50 percent of the capital improvements promised prior to termination of the trusteeship had been completed. Nakayama also protested the number of previously agreed-upon federal programs that were now being reduced or eliminated.[8]

In a formal diplomatic response to Under Secretary of State James Buckley, Nakayama argued that the proposed budget cuts would inhibit the development of a national economy. He enclosed a memorandum that detailed the critical budget and transition requirements of the FSM that had to be met before termination of the trusteeship. He added that a formal accord on long-term funding would have to be reached before negotiations on other compact issues could proceed.[9]

The negotiations did not escape local scrutiny. The Catholic Church on Pohnpei cast a particularly questioning eye on the compact talks through a series of memorandums authored by Brother Henry Schwalbenberg and distributed through the Micronesian Seminar. The memorandums were so probing and detailed that Andon Amaraich and James Stovall, an attorney with the Washington, D.C., law firm of Clifford and Warnke contracted to assist the FSM in its negotiations, had to request Fr. Francis Hezel, director of the Micronesian Seminar, for a little more patience and a little less criticism.[10] Hezel agreed to suspend the publication of the memorandums until the completion of the negotiations.[11]

Nakayama's quiet demeanor cloaked his ability as a persistent, tough-minded negotiator. This side of Nakayama showed itself when U.S. representatives proposed reductions in the Trust Territory budget during the transition period. In a letter to Acting High Commissioner Daniel High, Nakayama complained that the Reagan administration's plans to cut the budget for the Trust Territory in fiscal years 1982 and 1983 by a combined $6.5 million would "critically diminish the ability of our government to continue present operations, pursue development goals, and successfully terminate the United States Trusteeship."[12] He added that if the cuts were realized, the goodwill of the United States in its negotiations to terminate the trusteeship would be brought into question, and the compact itself jeopardized. The cuts were inappropriate, he said, at a time when the Trust Territory administration was winding down, and the FSM and its states were assuming more and more responsibilities. He argued that the overall effects of the cuts would be to reduce the FSM to a "custodian government, one without any capability to reach outside itself and accomplish change."[13] The U.S. intention to reduce dramatically the Trust Territory budget at such a critical time indicated to Nakayama a denial of the purposes and responsibilities of the trusteeship. Nakayama made the same arguments in a strong letter to Senator James McClure, chairman of the Senate Energy and Natural Resources Committee, and Under Secretary of State James Buckley.[14] To be sure, Nakayama benefited from the support of those around him, including sympathizers in the American Congress and the federal bureaucracy. His firm, persistent, and unrelenting attention to the negotiations certainly had their effect, however. In the end, the U.S. Congress restored the cuts.

A final agreement on the draft compact and its subsidiary agreements was reached on 1 October 1982 in Honolulu.[15] The parties approved a fifteen-year agreement that provided $60 million in financial assistance for the first five-year period, $51 million for the second, and $40 million for the third. Subsidiary agreements on federal programs called for another $7 million a year in support over the life of the compact. The Mutual Security Pact, a separate, open-ended agreement that Nakayama and his negotiators had originally resisted, entrusted the United States with the defense of the islands and included the authority to close FSM lands and waters to third countries for military purposes. The negotiated agreement stipulated that the compact could be terminated unilaterally or by mutual consent at any time during the life of the compact period. Andon Amaraich, head of the Commission on Future Political Status and Transition, called the compact "the best we can get under the circumstances."[16]

With the draft compact agreed to by both parties, a national plebiscite became the next priority. Nakayama submitted a bill to fund a public information campaign on the compact.[17] Newly appointed high commissioner Janet McCoy pledged the Trust Territory government's neutrality on the plebiscite and the FSM Congress soon passed the bill on 9 November.

In February 1983, members of the Commission on Future Political Status and Transition met in Honolulu with U.S. representatives to work out a mutually acceptable date for the plebiscite and to agree on the ballot language for the referendum.[18] With public information programs having begun in March 1983, Nakayama gave an address to the state legislature on Pohnpei that was filmed for distribution and broadcast throughout the FSM. Nakayama gave a history of the negotiations, a summary of the compact, and urged people to review and study it carefully. Responding to those who had criticized Amaraich's characterization of the compact as less than enthusiastic, Nakayama reassured the people about the efforts of their negotiators. He added: "The Commission's conclusion that it has negotiated the best compact that can be negotiated at this time should not be taken lightly. It is not easy for a people to start with nothing, but their intelligence and desires for a better life, and negotiate with one of the most powerful nations in the world."[19]

The plebiscite was held on 21 June 1983. As required by the FSM Constitution, 75 percent or more of the voters in three of the four states voted in favor of the compact. Only Pohnpei rejected the compact with 51.1 percent voting no. Nakayama chose to characterize the victory as "a landslide."[20] He termed the vote on Pohnpei evidence of a fair election and added: "That's the beauty about democracy, once you express your views, no one can question it." The second part of the ballot asked for citizens' preference in the event that the compact was rejected; 73 percent of those voting chose independence.[21]

On 13 July, Nakayama requested the four state legislatures to promptly review the compact and its ten subsidiary agreements in accordance with section 4 of Article IX of the FSM Constitution.[22] The constitution also required the Congress of the Federated States of Micronesia to review and approve the compact before its implementation. Things did not move as quickly or as smoothly as Nakayama had hoped, however. The Truk, Yap, and Kosrae legislatures were quick with their endorsements. Pohnpei's state legislature, however, voted 17–2 against the compact in early September 1983.[23] Interpreters of the Pohnpei vote explained that citizens there simply felt that they did not know enough about the compact to vote for it; their self-respect and honor were at stake, and they refused to be rushed or pressured by those who only "pretend to understand it."[24] The Congress of the Federated States of Micronesia voted on that same day to ratify the compact. The Pohnpeian congressional delegation did join with the other state delegations in voting to support the compact. Later, in a conciliatory gesture, a state leadership conference on Pohnpei endorsed the compact but with the request that both the United States and FSM governments address the legislature's objections.[25] Nakayama responded to the post-referendum analysis by again stating that the beauty of a review and approval process was that everyone was able to express their views. He asked all to unite behind the compact, and support the ongoing negotiations with the United States and the United Nations over the termination of the Trusteeship Agreement.[26]

In March 1984, an FSM delegation traveled to Washington, D.C., to lobby with U.S. representatives and congressional officials for quick approval of the compact.[27] The Reagan administration transmitted the compact to the U.S. Congress at the end of that month.[28] Reagan had voiced his support for the compact at the Guam International Airport during a 2 April stopover on his way to Asia. Nakayama traveled to Guam to meet with Reagan and to attend a reception for the heads of Pacific governments hosted by the American president. Nakayama reported that he was moved by Reagan's quoting from the Preamble of the FSM Constitution in his welcoming remarks, and found him to be very warm, considerate, and courteous. He came away from the meeting with the feeling that he had known Reagan for a long time.[29]

In late May, Nakayama led a delegation to Washington, D.C., where he testified in behalf of the compact before the U.S. Senate Energy and Natural Resources Committee, one of the primary congressional committees charged with oversight of the Trust Territory. Seeking congressional support, Nakayama showed his diplomatic skills as he toned down mention of sovereignty and chose instead to emphasize the strong bonds and shared governmental principles that bound the two countries. He told Chairman James McClure and other members of the committee, "The relationship of free association as embodied in the Compact serves our people's sense of need for identity. It meets our ambition after so long a colonial period to take a real place in the community of nations. But at the same time, our free choice of association with the United States allows us to accept your considerable generosity with a sense of dignity."[30]

Delays, inaction, and the number of congressional committees and subcommittees exercising jurisdictional scrutiny over various sections of the draft compact significantly slowed the review process. The U.S. Senate's Energy and Natural Resources Committee, the House Interior Committee's Subcommittee on Public Lands and National Parks, and the Asian and Pacific Affairs Subcommittee of the House Foreign Affairs Committee were among the several congressional bodies that held hearings on the draft compact. The additional House hearings and the failure of the full Senate to vote before the end of the congressional session meant that the Reagan administration was required to resubmit the compact to the new Congress that convened in early 1985.

Representative Stephen Solarz, the chairman of the House Foreign Affairs Committee's Subcommittee on Asian and Pacific Affairs, visited Pohnpei in April 1985, and told Nakayama and others at a reception in his honor at the Village Hotel that he expected to report the compact to the full House by mid-May of that year. Nakayama and congressional and state officials took the opportunity to lobby for the continuation of federal programs, funding for the national capitol and college complexes, and the satisfaction of all previously agreed-upon capital improvement projects.[31] Nakayama warned against plans to insert a "buy America" provision into the compact that would prove costly and that was not a part of the compact agreed to by both sides. Nakayama also argued for provisions that exempted American citizens residing in the FSM for more than 183 days in a calendar year from paying U.S. federal income taxes. This provision was necessary, he said, to attract skilled people to the new nation. The U.S. tax exemption on American investments, opposed by the other flag territories, was necessary if the FSM were to catch up economically. Fears of FSM citizens migrating en masse to the United States under the visa-free entry terms of the compact were unfounded, he said. Even if a deteriorating economy forced considerable movement, any percent of the small FSM population would have little impact on the United States or its territories. The concerns of the American Tuna Boat Association over licensing fees and access issues were, he argued, best left to licensing negotiations with the FSM government and its Micronesian Maritime Authority.

Nakayama later traveled to Washington to give formal testimony before Solarz' subcommittee urging quick approval of the compact, adding that the FSM anticipated a long and very close relationship with the United States. He stated: "The United States is the only nation with whom we share so completely the ideals of freedom, and thus is the only nation to whom we could entrust the defense of our freedom."[32] Officials from Guam endorsed a quick approval of the compact, but other witnesses spoke of the economic disadvantages to American flag territories that would result from the special tax incentives and lower minimum wage level given to the FSM, and also the Marshalls and Palau. To the dismay of the FSM delegation, American ambassador Fred Zeder told the committee he would be willing to support an annual review of the compact to ensure there were no other adverse effects on American territories.[33]

Nakayama did what he could to move the process along. He testified before members of the UN Trusteeship Council on 13 May 1985 urging them to help expedite the termination of the trusteeship. Meanwhile, an estimate from the Reagan administration in light of the House Foreign Affairs Subcommittee's adoption of the Compact of Free Association was now pointing to 1 October as the implementation date.[34] This estimate failed to take into adequate account the approval needed from the House Public Lands Subcommittee, the reconciliation of the House Interior and Foreign Affairs committee versions, the conferencing over the full House and Senate versions, and the final vote by both legislative bodies on a reconciled bill. There was also the public opposition of such groups as the Pacific Region of the World Council of Indigenous Peoples, the Minority Rights Group, Inc., the International League of Human Rights, and the National Council of Churches who appeared before the UN Trusteeship Council to denounce the compact and the American administration of Micronesia, and to call for independence.[35] Representatives of these well-meaning groups saw the compact as neo-colonialism by another name. With little or no direct connection to the region, its people, or their leadership, these varied organizations failed to understand the compact as an admittedly imperfect but nonetheless critically important expression of self-determination.

The situation got no better when the Subcommittee on Public Lands reported out a bill with amendments that, in Nakayama's characterization, severely restricted the concept of sovereignty and self-government as well as undermined the special measures designed to stimulate economic development in the FSM.[36] The FSM president argued that the amendments converted the negotiated version of free association into something more resembling territorial status. Nakayama and others in the FSM took strong exception to amendments that would allow American tuna boats free unlicensed access to FSM territorial waters, force the FSM to "buy America," and impose a wide range of U.S. criminal laws that would compromise the constitution of the sovereign nation. He also criticized those changes that required the FSM national development plan to be externally reviewed and approved by the U.S. Congress every five years. Over the next two months, Nakayama lobbied hard against the many and various committee amendments to the compact; he wrote Senator Robert Packwood, chair of the Senate Finance Committee, that the changes to favorable tax and trade provisions were unacceptable.[37]

Nakayama and other Micronesian representatives met with American negotiators in Honolulu on 26 and 27 August 1985 to strategize ways to defeat the tax and trade amendments. Despite assurances from Fred Zeder that the Reagan administration remained supportive of the compact approved by the voters in the 1983 plebiscite, FSM officials were described as tense and frustrated, and perhaps tired too as they had flown to Honolulu after attending meetings of the South Pacific Forum in Rarotonga earlier in that month.[38] The FSM team agreed to concessions in areas involving marine surveillance, certain tax and trade provisions, and the auditing of compact funds in return for the restoration of certain federal programs and the elimination of restrictions on the future use of compact monies as collateral. But that was it. Returning to Pohnpei after the Honolulu meetings, Nakayama announced that the FSM was not agreeing to any more compromises in the Compact of Free Association.[39] At a nondenominational retreat of Asia/Pacific Christian leaders on Pohnpei on 31 October 1985 sponsored by World Vision International, Nakayama asked those assembled to pray for the expeditious approval of the Compact of Free Association. He cited the nearly four-hundred-year old struggle to regain unity and self-determination: "we are on the verge," he said, "of either going into a new status or going into a state of confusion."[40]

Adding to the tension and frustration was the threat of a Senate filibuster by Senator Strom Thurmond of South Carolina who was seeking an amendment to the compact that would protect the domestic textile industry in his and other states by eliminating the trade incentives for the FSM contained in the compact.[41] Thurmond's threat of a filibuster was followed by Reagan's promise to veto any compact legislation that had such an amendment attached. The Senate rejection of the Thurmond textile amendment by a vote of 52–46 only added to the likelihood of a filibuster. Some progress had been made, however, as the Senate in early October 1985, approved the restoration of federal programs that included legal aid, health services, and the authorization of a transition period of up to three years during which all existing federal programs in Micronesia would be continued. At home, things became more complicated for Nakayama as the FSM Congress on 28 October 1985 over-rode his veto of a compact review bill that required congressional and state legislative approval of the Compact of Free Association as amended by the U.S. Congress. Nakayama had vetoed the bill, thinking it redundant and unnecessary under the constitutional provisions that governed the compact negotiations and approval process.[42] The FSM Congress thought otherwise given the extensive amendments made to the compact.

As the stalemate continued in Washington and on Pohnpei, Nakayama turned to personal diplomacy. He traveled to Saipan in mid-October to meet with Vice President George Bush during his two-day visit en route to the People's Republic of China.[43] A welcoming reception for the vice president was interrupted by the emergence from the nearby bushes of a drunken and disheveled Larry Hillblom, the head of DHL Worldwide Express, Inc.[44] Security personnel were in the process of removing Hillblom when Nakayama stepped forward to vouch for his identity. Nakayama had visited Hillblom's Saipan resort, Cowtown, a day or two earlier and observed firsthand the owner's wealth and eccentricity. The incident had no effect on the meeting. Before departing Saipan, Bush issued a strong statement of support for the compact and added that the Reagan administration was also frustrated with the delays in Congress.

The congressional stalemate was finally broken when the U.S. Senate voted on 15 November to adopt the compact and its enabling legislation.[45] The two senators from South Carolina, Strom Thurmond and Ernest Hollings, withdrew their tax and textile amendments with the understanding that a final determination on them would be made by the House of Representatives. An amendment dealing with the use of compact funds for marine surveillance purposes was also left to the House to resolve. By placing final determination of these issues with the House, the legislative maneuver in the Senate avoided the need to hold a conference on the differences in the two compact bills. While Thanksgiving 1985 was thought to be a realistic deadline for congressional approval of the compact, American Samoa's congressional delegate Fofo I. F. Sunia attempted to protect his islands' tuna canneries by requesting the House Interior Committee place a quota on the amount of tuna that could be imported duty-free into the United States from the FSM and the Marshalls.[46] The measure was defeated but added to the delay.

Final congressional approval came on 13 December 1985 when the United States approved by unanimous vote a version of the compact that had been agreed upon by the various House and Senate committees involved in the review process.[47] The compact was then sent on to President Reagan who signed it into law as U.S. Public Law 99–239 in early January 1986.[48] The amount of funding and its three five-year periods of distribution remained as previously agreed upon. As compensation for the reduction in tax and trade incentives, the resolution approving the compact created an Investment Development Fund that could be used to make loans to private companies to set up businesses in the FSM, and for other development purposes. Several federal programs were extended including those of the Federal Deposit Insurance Corporation, the Small Business Administration, the Economic Development Administration, and the Rural Electrification Administration. Assistance provided under the Job Training Partnership Act and through several U.S. Commerce Department development programs in the areas of tourism and marine resources was also continued.

There followed a local review and approval process of U.S. Public Law 99–239. Nakayama would have preferred to do without this second review process but the FSM Congress had decided otherwise. The FSM status commission prepared a review of the compact at the request of the four state governors.[49] There were also reviews by each of the state legislatures, the FSM Legislators Conference, and the FSM Congress. The approval process was completed on 26 March when the FSM Congress adopted a resolution ratifying the Compact of Free Association and its related agreements as contained in U.S. Public Law 99–239.[50] As difficult as the review and approval process of the compact had been, the situation in the Federated States of Micronesia contrasted favorably with what took place in the Republic of Palau. The incompatibility between that nation's constitutional ban on the use, storage, and transfer of nuclear materials conflicted with American security interests. There followed a seven-year stalemate that included violence, public protests, and eight separate, hotly contested referendums on changes to the Palauan constitution before the Compact of Free Association was finally approved in 1993.[51]

Speaking at the opening of the 53rd session of the UN Trusteeship Council on 12 May 1986, Tosiwo Nakayama, as much relieved as elated at the end of a nearly twenty-year negotiating and approval period, called for the immediate termination of the Trusteeship Agreement.[52] He noted that the FSM had an already fully functioning government under a popularly mandated constitution and that there existed no reason for the trusteeship to be continued. The Trusteeship Council passed and transmitted to the Security Council a resolution on 28 May calling for the termination of the trusteeship.[53] Reassured by the Trusteeship Council's decision and aware that a formal vote by the UN Security Council would be considerably delayed by the objections of the Soviet Union, the Reagan administration unilaterally declared the termination of the Trusteeship Agreement over the Marshalls and the FSM on 3 November 1986. With less than a year left in his second and final term as president, Tosiwo

Nakayama now headed an autonomous, self-governing nation that had come into being as the result of his efforts and visions, as well as those of others.

## Seeking International Recognition

In preparation for the eventual termination of the trusteeship agreement, Nakayama sought to earn international recognition for the fledgling FSM government. To this end, Nakayama traveled extensively to make the FSM's case before foreign governments, regional bodies, the United Nations, and the executive and legislative branches of the United States government. He also entertained a steady stream of foreign visitors who discussed the possibilities of future cooperation and assistance. Japan provided steady technical and grant assistance during the transition period. The first Japanese assistance to the FSM came in May 1981 when the new nation received $1.4 million for the purchase of heavy equipment for secondary road construction. This was also the first international agreement signed by the FSM with any foreign government other than the United States, and was hailed as a significant step in the recognition of the FSM as a new member of the international community.[54] Over the next three years, there followed additional grants from Japan, primarily in the area of fisheries development; these grants were heralded by visits from Japanese government officials. Most notably, the FSM and Japan signed a new $2.5 million fishing agreement on Guam that allowed Japanese fishing vessels to fish within the FSM's 200-mile extended fishery zone for one year.[55]

Nakayama journeyed on numerous occasions to Japan. His paternal lineage made those trips personally comfortable and diplomatically successful. On 15 May 1984, President and Mrs. Nakayama attended a reception for Crown Prince Akihito and Princess Michiko hosted by the Japan-Micronesia Association at the Ginza Hotel in Tokyo.[56] The imperial couple had been informed of Nakayama's presence and, as a matter of protocol, made it a point to greet him personally and inquire about his family. Two days later, the Nakayamas visited Yokohama to attend the annual gathering of the Nan'yō Guntō Kai, a nationwide association of Japanese citizens who had lived and worked in Micronesia during the Mandate days. Nakayama thanked his Japanese hosts for their support, and recalled that his father was from Yokohama and had been a member of the association.[57] While in Yokohama, the Nakayamas visited the home of one of his uncles in the Tsurumi section and paid their respects at the grave of his paternal grandfather.

In early September 1984, Nakayama returned to Japan to attend the Green Summit at Kumamoto on the southern island of Kyushu. The invita-

**Fig. 7.2.** Tosiwo Nakayama meets with Prime Minister Nakasone Yasuhiro of Japan in 1984. Amata Kabua, president of the Republic of the Marshall Islands, shakes the prime minister's hand. Haruo Remeliik, president of the Republic of Palau, stands to Nakayama's left (Micronesian Seminar).

tion came from the conference organizers; Crown Prince Akihito and Princess Michiko were in attendance and again made it a point to acknowledge Nakayama.[58] While in Japan, Nakayama, along with the presidents from the Marshalls and Palau, attended a gathering of the Asia Pacific Parliamentarians Union, and met with Japanese prime minister Nakasone Yasuhiro.[59] It was the first formal diplomatic meeting with a Japanese prime minister for the three Micronesian leaders. In a December 1984 interview with the *Yomiuri Shimbun,* Nakayama called for more assistance from Japan and anticipated even closer ties between the two countries in the years to come. He also took the opportunity to explain the compact and its defense provisions, and to express the hope that outstanding war claims between Japan and the FSM would be settled "with some kind of formula to pay people what is due them."[60] These approaches, limited though they were, enhanced the regional profile of Nakayama and the FSM.

Nakayama, along with his secretary of external affairs, Andon Amaraich, also worked to raise the standing of the FSM among its more immediate neighbors. In 1982, the FSM had been awarded inclusion in the South

Pacific Commission.[61] Nakayama invested considerable time and effort to win membership in the South Pacific Forum, an association of independent Pacific Island nation-states that had separated from the older, metropolitan dominated South Pacific Commission. His diplomatic initiatives helped win formal observer status for the FSM in 1981. The following year came membership in the South Pacific Forum Fisheries Agency.[62] At the Forum meeting in August 1981 on Vanuatu, the FSM delegation, led by Nakayama, backed a resolution in support of independence for New Caledonia and voted against measures endorsing Japanese nuclear dumping in the region and a marine research proposal by the Soviet Union.[63] Nakayama attended two of the next three Forum meetings and lobbied for FSM interests with other heads of state, including Bob Hawke of Australia, Ratu Sir Kamasese Mara of Fiji, and Michael Somare of Papua New Guinea.[64] The FSM's persistent engagement with the Forum eventually won it full membership in 1987.

Nakayama's regional commitment was real, and drew on moral principle as well as practical politics. As he had during his days in the Congress of Micronesia, Nakayama consistently opposed any and all plans to dump nuclear waste into Pacific waters. The FSM's need for Japanese assistance did not prevent Nakayama from speaking out against the degradation of the region's marine environment. In September 1980, he joined with chief executives from other parts of the Micronesian region in asking Japan not to dump 10,000 barrels of low-grade nuclear waste into international waters 540 miles north of the Mariana Islands.[65] That position was reiterated by the FSM on 18 November 1980 when Masao Nakayama, the president's brother and head of the International Affairs Division of the Department of External Affairs, officially delivered the FSM government's position to a visiting Japanese delegation seeking support for the dumping proposal.[66]

In late June 1984, Nakayama spoke to the crew of the visiting *Pacific Peacemaker* on Pohnpei and assured them of the FSM's opposition to all nuclear testing and dumping in the region. He voiced his intention to support all anti-nuclear testing and anti-dumping resolutions at the South Pacific Forum meeting on Tuvalu later that year. Nakayama also reassured the group that the FSM had not compromised its sovereignty by agreeing to the Compact of Free Association and its accompanying Mutual Security Pact. He called attention to the prohibitions against nuclear testing, storage, and dumping in the FSM Constitution. He pointed to the uniqueness of the compact and added, "We only give the U.S. defense rights, and we do that because we do not have an armed force."[67] Nakayama went on to say that the memories of World War II were still fresh in islanders' minds, and that the security needs of the young nation necessitated entrusting its defense to the United States.

As noted earlier, war claims had been a long and lingering issue of discontent within the islands.[68] As in other areas of foreign policy, Nakayama and his government were both diplomatic and persistent in the satisfaction of Micronesian interests. The United States government had reached a bilateral settlement with Japan in 1969 that in essence allowed that country to avoid any financial liability for the loss of life or property during the war. The Congress of Micronesia had sought unsuccessfully to seek a fairer settlement that provided compensation from Japan for Micronesian losses while waiting for the United States to make good on promised compensation for the loss of life and property during the war. Appeals to the United States government to pressure Japan had proved futile; the United States responded that its 1969 agreement with Japan had settled the issue. Dissatisfied with the lack of progress, Nakayama opted in 1980 to appoint a task force on war claims made up of members from the executive and legislative branches of the FSM government. He felt such an approach a more appropriate first step than yet another direct appeal to the two metropolitan governments. As he often did, Nakayama turned to his brother Masao in the Department of External Affairs, to chair the task force. The group was charged with reviewing the current status of the war claims issue and making recommendations on ways to bring about a settlement.[69] The task force quickly came to the conclusion that efforts at recovery from Japan would have a better chance of success if framed in terms of "foreign aid" rather than "war claims."[70] This is in effect what happened, though not to the satisfaction of privately organized groups of citizens who sought direct personal compensation for loss of life and property during the war.

One of the more significant international achievements in the transition period was the FSM signing of the Law of the Sea Treaty and its acceptance as a signatory of the international Law of the Sea Convention. The FSM wanted to secure and protect the resources of its surrounding seas through the formal signing of the convention. The Micronesian Maritime Authority (MMA), created by the Congress of Micronesia in 1976 with the strong involvement and support of Tosiwo Nakayama, was charged with the management of the islands' 200-mile extended economic zone. With the establishment of the FSM government, the MMA provided a revenue stream, albeit modest, through the licensing fees charged foreign fishing vessels wanting to operate in FSM waters. Further enhancing its credibility and that of the MMA, the FSM, signed in 1982 the Final Act of the Law of the Sea Conference as a full participating member.[71] This was done over the initial opposition of the United States. The FSM's signing of the actual convention took place later. To be sure, the licensing of foreign fishing vessels was less than perfect as the FSM had limited capability to police, seize, and prosecute offending vessels. The MMA was forced to

**Fig. 7.3.** The first official FSM delegation to the People's Republic of China, 1987 (Micronesian Seminar). Front row from left to right: Petrus Tun of Yap, Ambros Senda of Pohnpei, Robert Mori of Chuuk, Ieske Iehsi of Pingelap. Along the back row: Resio Moses of Pohnpei (far left), Tosiwo Nakayama (fourth from left), Hans Williander of Chuuk (third from right), Asterio Takesy of Chuuk (second from right), Moses Mackwelung of Kosrae (far right).

use its resources, including patrol boats and on-ship observers, selectively, but to good effect as a number of foreign fishing vessels violating FSM waters were seized and fined.[72] The MMA also took a firm stand in licensing talks with the American Tuna Boat Association and various Japanese fishing associations that resulted in increased licensing fees for the FSM.[73]

In late 1986, there began a string of diplomatic developments that enhanced the FSM's standing as a member of the international community. On 3 November, the same day that Reagan proclaimed the implementation of the Compact of Free Association, the FSM announced it would begin issuing its own passports.[74] In March 1987, the FSM and the Republic of the Marshall Islands exchanged diplomatic notes affirming their intention to establish full diplomatic relations with each other.[75] In early April 1987, FSM representatives signed the Multilateral Fisheries Treaty with the United States during a special ceremony in Papua New Guinea.[76] In the years immediately following the conclusion of Nakayama's second term as president, the FSM established formal diplomatic relations with a host of nations that included New Zealand, Papua New Guinea, Israel, Kiribati, the Philippines, Fiji, Japan, Tonga, the People's Republic of China, and Indonesia. Diplomatic relations with the People's Republic of China were made possible by an earlier 1987 visit of an FSM delegation led by Nakayama that resulted in an initial agreement of economic cooperation between the two nations.[77] In 1991, came admission to full membership in the United Nations, a singular feat in the eyes of many, and a direct result of the initiatives begun by Tosiwo Nakayama, Andon Amaraich, and the staff of the Department of External Affairs' Division of International Affairs.

## Local Skyways

Physically linking the islands to the larger world was another of Nakayama's priorities. Descended from a line of navigators, he understood the importance of the skies as well as the seas. During his congressional career, Nakayama had concerned himself with the development of air and sea services in the islands. He sought to foster a supportive system of transportation in which the cost of freight and passenger services would be kept reasonable and thus aid the development of the region's economy. A 1980 dispute between Continental Airlines and Japan had caused a reduction in service to the FSM. After extensive negotiations, Japan agreed to allow Continental Air Micronesia to increase both its flights and the number of Japanese cities serviced.[78] With these increased routes, Continental Air Micronesia agreed to restore the third weekly flight to the Federated States of Micronesia that had been cut earlier due ostensibly to rising fuel costs. To Nakayama's way of thinking, the whole situation revealed yet again how economic development was held hostage by the monopoly power that Continental enjoyed in the Micronesian region.

A supporter of Continental Airlines back in 1966 when it successfully competed to supplant Pan American, Nakayama had hoped that the airline company would prove a loyal and dependable partner in the development of the islands.[79] Such proved not to be the case. Frustrated, Nakayama now sought to have the FSM government gain control of Air Micronesia through the government-arranged purchase of stock then held by the United Micronesia Development Authority (UMDA), a group of foreign investors and local businessmen whose most prominent and active member was Larry Hillblom, the founder and CEO of DHL. Nakayama's efforts were thwarted by UMDA majority shareholders, led by Hillblom, who blocked the agreement of sale that the FSM had worked out with Continental Airlines, the parent company of Air Micronesia.[80]

While Nakayama never achieved the goal of a locally owned airline to provide less expensive and more effective air service to the FSM, he did enjoy the satisfaction of seeing a 3,500-foot runway and airport built on his home island of Onoun in Namonuito Atoll. Four years after completing his second term as president of the FSM, Nakayama journeyed to Onoun for the 2 August 1991 dedication ceremony.[81] Nakayama spoke first and in place of his older brother Minoru who was the chief of Onoun. He noted with satisfaction that the completion of the airport and runway made good on a promise he had given to the people of Onoun when he became president. Ta in the Mortlocks would be next, he said. Other speakers followed praising the efforts of the people, the improvement of such basic infrastructure that would better link Onoun to the rest of Chuuk, the FSM, and the larger Pacific, and the development opportunities that the new airstrip now made possible. Though air service to the island would later be discontinued, the ceremonies on Onoun offered an allegory of sorts for the work of Tosiwo Nakayama. His vision for the FSM was bold, broad, and inclusive. Atolls such as Onoun or Ta were not to be considered too small or distant; they were to be included in development plans as a way to better integrate them into the fabric of the nation, and provide more opportunities and a better quality of life for their citizens.

## Atoll Hopping

Nakayama, throughout his presidency, demonstrated an acute awareness of the need to create a nation out of a disparate collection of islands whose limited contact and association with one another since the late nineteenth century had been largely through four shared colonial regimes. Nakayama understood that speeches were not sufficient. Words spoken about lofty political principles could not by themselves bring people together. The building of a national community required contact, communication, sharing, exchange, and interaction among its prospective members. Nakayama participated in numerous community celebrations, feasts, and funerals on Pohnpei, welcomed to his office visiting officials and everyday citizens from all four states, and traveled extensively throughout the FSM. He made himself accessible, and took the opportunity to nourish a sense of commitment and belonging to the fledgling, still tenuous nation.

Nakayama was as much concerned with nation building at home as he was with winning international recognition and support abroad. This was necessary given the fragility of the new national union called the Federated States of Micronesia. Ships, not planes, were the vessels used to connect with the populations of the country's more distant islands and atolls. Nakayama was perhaps at his diplomatic, political, and personal best when visiting the islands and atolls that made up the Federated States of Micronesia. He showed himself to be comfortable, at ease, caring, and concerned. He was an atoll dweller himself, and understood intuitively the beaches he crossed, the people he met, and the lifestyle he encountered. His July 1981 trip through the typhoon-ravaged Mortlocks is a case in point.[82] On 26 July, Nakayama left Weno in Chuuk to visit the Mortlock Islands, including Kutu, Satawan, Ta, Lukunor, and Oneop in the Lower Mortlocks and Nama in the Upper Mortlocks. Accompanying Nakayama was a large group of national, congressional, and state officials that included Speaker of the Congress Bethwel Henry, Secretary of External Affairs Andon Amaraich, Senator Raymond Setik of Chuuk, and Chuuk State governor Erhart Aten. At Kutu, Satawan, and Ta, the delegation received warm welcomes and tours of the storm-damaged areas. The group was also shown the deteriorating public facilities and abandoned or unfinished public projects for which the people were now requesting assistance.

The stop at Lukunor held special significance for Nakayama because he had lived there as a child before the war; he visited a concrete well on the island that had been built by his father. At Oneop, the welcoming ceremonies proved the longest and liveliest on the trip as there were singing groups and stick dancers from nearby Etal. There were also signs in English that spoke of both initiative and need: "We Can Do More With Very Little," "Let the People Rule," "Times Are Hard, But Victory Is Certain, and "Mr. President, Light Your Torch To See Our Fellow People." At each stop, Nakayama promised assistance but also underscored the need for initiative, self-reliance, and responsibility. At Oneop, he pointed to the new dock as a symbol of cooperation, and reminded people that future requests for funds would be measured against the outcome of previous projects; "Did you abuse it? Did you complete it? If the answer is yes, you abuse [*sic*] it, I have no recourse but to disapprove it."[83] The tour of the Mortlocks was his first outer island trip as president; Nakayama pledged to return, which he did on three separate occasions before completing his second term in mid-1987. By the end of his presidency, he had visited every inhabited island in the Federated States of Micronesia except for two in Yap State where inclement weather had intervened to cancel his planned visits.

The 1982 trip to Yap was particularly impressive.[84] Among the four FSM states, support for Nakayama was strongest in Yap, a function in part of his clan membership. Through his mother, he belonged to the Pike clan, some of whose members resided on islands and atolls in Yap State. Nakayama began his trip on 15 June 1982 when he flew to Weno and then boarded the field trip ship, *Micro Dawn*. Accompanied by Chuuk lieutenant governor Robert Mori, Nakayama's party made stops at Nomwin, the Hall Islands, and his home island of Onoun in Namonuito Atoll, before heading to Satawal, the atoll that lay along

Fig. 74. Tosiwo Nakayama being ferried ashore during his 1982 visit to Yap State (Micronesian Seminar).

the southeastern border of Yap State. The presidential party arrived on 18 June in Satawal where they joined Yap senator John Mangefel and transferred to the *Micro Spirit*. Bad weather plagued the fifteen-day trip through Yap, but it did not dampen the enthusiasm with which the visitors were greeted. At each island, the presidential party was met by welcoming parties of women who gave them flowered head wreaths and leis of welcome. Passing through long receiving lines, the visitors then proceeded to men's houses where they were greeted by chiefs, presented with gifts of food, and entertained with singing, dancing, and chanting. As in the Mortlocks, Nakayama and his party toured the islands, observed those public facilities in need of repair or replacement, listened to requests and petitions, and responded with promises of assistance as best they could. At Faraulep, Nakayama visited with an elderly clan relative who reminded him of his ancestral connection to the atoll.

Dressed on occasion in a traditional loincloth with a flower head wreath and body lei, Nakayama spoke to his audiences about the compact negotiations and transition issues with which the FSM government was then engaged. Addressing the council of chiefs from the outer islands of Yap at Mogmog Atoll, Nakayama reminded his audience, "We have been victims of foreign powers."[85] Those outside groups, he said, had deprived the people of the right to rule themselves. Micronesians were now doing what those foreign groups said they couldn't. Nakayama also took the opportunity at several stops to speak about self-reliance and the need for state and national development plans. Nakayama's last outer island trip came in April 1987 when he visited Mokil and Pingelap.[86] Less than two months remained in his presidency. He looked tired but happy to be back in the outer islands and among people with whom he felt a kinship. He had relied heavily on Pingelap during his two administrations, and benefited from the efforts of Ambilos Iehsi, Kikuo Apis, and Ieske Iehsi who had served in different capacities over the course of his two administrations. He flew into Pingelap and was welcomed warmly. There were speeches, a luncheon, entertainment, and a boat tour of the lagoon that included a visit to some of the island's more fabled and mythic locations. Then, it was time for the flight home. All of his visits had proven an incredibly important and successful strategy in the ongoing process of building a Federated States of Micronesia government that people could relate to and identify with. The trips had facilitated communication, allowed for dialogue, and given a face to the new government.

## Nation Building

Tosiwo Nakayama had a very clear understanding of the relationship between the national government and the states. He described the FSM as a loose federation, and pointed to the constitution that gave specific powers to the federal government and the rest to the states. Nakayama regarded the national government as the arm of the states in that it acted in their interests. In fact, he argued, in the loose federation that was and is the Federated States of Micronesia, the states are "more powerful" than the national government.[87] Nakayama also made it a point to distinguish between the Federated States of Micronesia and the national government. In a November 1980 memo, he reminded all employees that the national government was not the nation but rather an integral part of a federal system created by the constitution to serve the people.[88] To further underscore the message, Nakayama had the *National Union,* the official publication of the national government, print the Preamble and different articles of the FSM Constitution in sequential order beginning with the 15 January 1981 issue. Nakayama also employed a host of other, more immediately popular strategies to promote nationhood in the FSM. He sponsored legislation to create Constitution Day, a national holiday established to mark the inauguration of the FSM Constitution on 10 May 1979; he used the occasion to give speeches on the importance of nation building and the need for unity.[89] Early in his presidency, he appointed a special committee to plan for a Micronesian Olympic Games that came into being several years later.[90]

His commitment to the nation also led him to participate in state celebrations. On his return from Guam where he had traveled to meet the pope, Nakayama stopped in Chuuk and took part in ceremonies to mark the first raising of the state's new flag on 27 February 1981.[91] Speaking in Chuukese, Nakayama told those assembled that they were fortunate to have their own flag. Their flag, he went on, signified that Chuuk was a sovereign state and also one of the four main pillars of the Federated States of Micronesia. He regarded it as a symbol of integrity, pride, and accomplishment. He added that while on Guam to visit the pope, he had seen many flags, some with one star, others with two or three. It pleased him that the FSM flag showed four stars in its light blue field.

The State National Leadership Councils also proved on balance to be effective vehicles to promote national unity, facilitate communication between the state and national governments, and coordinate policies, laws, and directives among those responsible for the administration of the new government. The conferences were Nakayama's idea, and were born of his experiences in helping to create the Federated States of Micronesia. The states took turns hosting the conferences; on average, there were two a year during Nakayama's first term as president. Their agendas were full and touched upon almost every aspect of government, administration, and legislation. There were also state and national planning conferences such as the one held on Pohnpei in

**Fig. 7.5.** Tosiwo Nakayama and the four state governors of the FSM. From left to right: Gideon Doone of Chuuk, Yosiwo George of Kosrae, Nakayama, Resio Moses of Pohnpei, Petrus Tun of Yap (Micronesian Seminar).

January 1983 to draft a National Development Plan.[92] The FSM Chief Executives Conferences were yet another medium used by Nakayama to facilitate administrative communication, coordination, and policy input between the national government and the four states. The conference membership consisted of Nakayama and the four state governors. There were a total of eleven chief executives' conferences held during Nakayama's eight years as president. The conferences allowed the president and the four governors to consult on national and state relations, and over a host of issues that included tax reform, national and state development plans, the Compact of Free Association, capital improvement funding, and air service.

Nakayama realized that a new nation required the creation of national services and facilities that would allow it to function within its borders and to interact with the larger world. These services included a national banking system, a communications network, and a postal service. Institutions of higher learning also served the cause of nation making as well. The College of Micronesia was no different in that respect. An amalgamation of the Community College of Micronesia on Pohnpei, the Nursing School on Saipan, and the Micronesian Occupational College in Palau, the college showed itself to be deeply affected by the same divisions that had frustrated the emergence of a unified Micronesian state. With the separation of the Marianas, the Marshalls, and Palau, the College of Micronesia looked fragile and its future appeared uncertain. In March 1982, Nakayama attended a summit on the future of the College of Micronesia with leaders from the Marshalls and Palau.[93] The meeting produced what came to be known as the "Saipan Accords" that addressed issues of mutual concern, including higher education. Nakayama announced that the FSM national government would support a regional College of Micronesia. As part of the capital improvement projects to be completed prior to the implementation of the Compact of Free Association, the FSM government was asking the United States to provide funds for a new college campus to be built near the capitol site at Palikir. Nakayama underscored the importance of the college as a national institution when speaking at the 7 June 1982 commencement of the Community College of Micronesia. He noted the need for an institution within the FSM that could train professional people "in our environment and relative to our needs."[94] An agreement among the three nations on adequate and stable funding for the college was imperative. Ultimately, regional support for the College of Micronesia never developed as the Marshalls and Palau opted to develop their own postsecondary systems of education. The two-year College of Micronesia was eventually built at Palikir as a postsecondary institution of higher learning for the FSM with satellite or extension campuses in each of the four states.

## The Judiciary

In creating a three-tiered system of government, the FSM government modeled itself after the United States. Among the three branches of the FSM government, the judiciary showed itself to be especially assertive in its efforts to separate from the Trust Territory. Tosiwo Nakayama chose Ed King to be his chief justice. King had worked in Micronesia previously as the head of the Micronesian Legal Services Corporation and had earned a reputation as an effective and passionate defender of Micronesian rights. King was confirmed as chief justice of the FSM Supreme Court on 24 October 1980 after his confirmation hearings went smoothly.[95] King saw his mission as twofold: to set up a functioning, independent court system, and to educate people on a legal system that was alien to most citizens of the FSM.

The most immediate concern surrounding the establishment of a national judiciary was its relationship to and compatibility with local traditional systems of justice and dispute resolution. The mayor of Weno, Fujita Bossy, saw the traditional justice system in the islands as still relevant, applicable, and not necessarily incompatible with the national legal system being established in the FSM. Fujita Bossy, the uncle of Nakayama's most prominent opponent Nick Bossy, publicly articulated this view at ceremonies marking the first hearing held by the FSM Supreme Court. An effective delegate to the 1975 Micronesian Constitutional Convention, Bossy spoke of the need for unity and togetherness, values that were essential to the success of the new government.[96] Bossy noted that, like the FSM government, ancient practices that once guided Chuuk revolved around three branches of government. Speaking to a large audience in the Chuuk High School gymnasium on the evening of 12 July 1981 with Chief Justice King present, Bossy recited an *itang* that spoke of those chiefly leaders who sought consensus, those who were responsible for justice, and those who decided. The similarities between the old and new forms of government reassured Bossy; he saw the foundations of the FSM judicial system as quite compatible with the practices of old. King himself seemed to agree; a year later, at a judicial conference, he acknowledged the need to include custom in sentencing and other aspects of litigation.[97] More difficult for the FSM's new judicial system was the recognition that clans and lineages claimed legal rights along with individuals and governments. This was a point that Bossy felt quite strongly about.

King concerned himself in his first months with setting new guidelines and requirements for those practicing law in the FSM, running legal training programs for local judges and court officials, and ensuring that court facilities and legal resources in the four states came under the management and control of the FSM. As would soon become clear, the FSM judiciary found the most serious challenge to its authority coming not from traditional values and practices or the lack of trained personnel, but from the Trust Territory High Court, which, in a number of contentious and controversial issues, insisted on continuing jurisdiction in what was now the Federated States of Micronesia.[98] As important as they were to the integrity of an independent judiciary, the conflicts created a distance between Nakayama, the quiet consensus seeker, and his more assertive chief justice. King also clashed with Congress over a separate salary plan and benefits package for judges and judiciary staffers, and over support for the educational needs of his children. This further complicated his relationship with Nakayama. Toward the end of his first administration, Nakayama used Attorney General Fred Ramp as a go-between rather than meet with King directly. Despite the distance between them, King remained a strong admirer of Nakayama. Nakayama would not be invited to the dedication of the new capitol complex at Palikir in 1989. It was King, in a speech for that occasion, who reminded those present of the former president's absence and his enormous contributions to the creation of the FSM.

## Faichuk

Despite Nakayama's best efforts to foster national unity, there were direct challenges to unity and nationhood from within. The most serious of these came
from Nakayama's home state of Chuuk. A group of four main islands cover-
ing 41.9 square kilometers in the western part of the Chuuk Lagoon, Faichuk
lagged in facilities and infrastructure development despite the prominence of
some of its residents in business and state government. Leaders from the area
saw statehood as the solution to the area's problems. In 1977, there emerged
from Faichuk a petition for statehood in the new FSM government. The movement gained greater impetus in 1979 when a group of representatives from
the area gathered at the Chuuk Airport on Weno to meet the plane of High
Commissioner Adrian Winkel and present him with the petition. The recently
inaugurated Tosiwo Nakayama was also on that plane and expressed surprise
and displeasure at the boldness of the Faichuk people. He had come to Chuuk
to be honored by state and traditional leaders on his inauguration as president
and, as it turned out, to bury his father. Highly displeased, Nakayama unchar-
acteristically confronted the Faichuk delegation at the airport and asked them
pointedly if it was their intention to embarrass him. A spokesman for the
group responded that they had no idea that Nakayama would be traveling on
the same plane with the high commissioner.[99]

The prospect of a second Chuukese state was cause for great concern
in the other areas of the FSM. The balance of legislative power and the distribution of financial resources worried the smaller states of Kosrae and Yap.
Chuuk's growing reputation for waste, corruption, and mismanagement only
heightened tensions. Tosiwo Nakayama's relationship with the region was
complicated. A close family friend from childhood days, Susumu Aizawa, held
the title of paramount chief for Tol, the largest of the Faichuk islands. Unlike
the Nakayama brothers, Aizawa had been repatriated with his father following
the conclusion of the war. He became a successful businessman on Weno after
returning from Japan in 1958. Aizawa had supported Nakayama in each of his
congressional elections, and had resisted the alleged invitation of an American
official to run against Nakayama in the 1979 congressional elections. More
problematic was Nakayama's relationship with Kalisto Refalopei, Faichuk's
representative in the FSM Congress and an outspoken advocate of statehood.
The two had a direct confrontation on election day in 1979 when Nakayama
traveled to Tol to counter accusations of corruption and to witness firsthand
Refalopei's intimidation of voters.

Death was also a part of the Faichuk statehood story.[100] In early October
1981, a group from Wonei in the Faichuk area had assaulted several young men

from Toloas on Weno in front of the Truk Trading Company. The Wonei men included members of the Engichy and Otokichy families. Kalisto Refalopei was closely related to the two families; in fact, his father had been implicated in the incident, and had fled to Guam on a plane a day after the assault, where he was arrested and returned to Chuuk. One of the young men died, and charges were brought against several of the attackers. In a letter to Nakayama, Refalopei criticized the government's prosecution of the case, and claimed it was directly tied to efforts to discredit the Faichuk statehood movement.[101] Nonetheless, at a special session in Chuuk, members of the Congress of the Federated States of Micronesia passed without dissent a bill to award statehood to the Faichuk islands. On 24 September, two months after its passage by the FSM Congress, the bill went to Nakayama's desk for his signature. Nakayama had asked Speaker of the Congress Bethwel Henry to delay transmission as a way to secure more time for a review of the bill and an investigation of its impact and consequences.[102]

Reaction was predictably strong on Pohnpei. At an earlier conference of elders that included the island's paramount chiefs, elected representatives, appointed officials, and community leaders, Governor Leo Falcam gave an address in which he identified the many serious problems that Faichuk statehood posed for Pohnpei and the rest of the FSM. Edwel Santos, the Speaker of the state legislature, seconded Falcam's assessment. Some traditional leaders present spoke cryptically about the need for difficult decisions to ensure the welfare of the people of Pohnpei.[103] In a later interview, Falcam was more direct in his assessment that passage of the bill would cause Pohnpei to consider leaving the FSM.[104] He hoped that unity could be maintained and expressed displeasure with the FSM Congress for acting recklessly and without public input. Yap's leaders came out in direct opposition to the bill on constitutional grounds, while Kosrae's representatives made no comment.[105] Chuuk State's elected leaders backed the bill. The Speaker of the Chuuk State Legislature, Tadasy C. Wainit, himself from Faichuk, expressed full support for the bill as it met the economic needs and political aspirations of the people of Faichuk.[106]

It became clear early on that the fate of the FSM was at stake. Nakayama sought input from state leaders in Chuuk on the Faichuk statehood bill, and dispatched a three-member task force led by his brother Masao to meet with leaders on Tol and in the larger state.[107] In a courageous act, Nakayama ended up vetoing the bill.[108] Before doing so, he flew to Chuuk and held meetings with leaders there on 19 and 20 October. He ended up being stranded on Weno when bad weather forced the Air Micronesia flight from Guam to overfly the state and proceed directly to Pohnpei. From Chuuk, Nakayama phoned Vice President Petrus Tun on 23 October and ordered him to sign the veto mes-

sage disapproving the bill and transmit it to the Speaker of the Congress. This
was one day before the bill was scheduled to take effect without his signature.
Nakayama called the veto "the most difficult decision of my period as chief
executive of this nation."[109]

In his veto message to Speaker Bethwel Henry, Nakayama gave several
reasons for his decision.[110] He cited the lack of any procedure set by Congress
for creating a new state. He also pointed to the lack of political institutions
and physical infrastructure in Faichuk as impediments to forming a truly
viable, functioning state government. Rather than make things better, the passage of the bill, he argued, would only lead to further economic hardship and
regression. He added that he had been informed that the United States would
not fund any new physical facilities for the would-be state or the operating
expenses of its government. If Faichuk were to become a separate state, medical, police, and other services for Chuuk State would have to be significantly
reduced. Nakayama also cited technical errors in the language of the bill, and
its failure to include the reef area as part of the new state's territory. Nakayama
proposed instead a new governmental structure for Faichuk that would function as a part of Chuuk State with a mayor as its chief executive and a council
as its legislative body. In his letter, Nakayama informed Speaker Henry that he
would seek more development funds for Faichuk, and proposed a task force
drawn from his office, the state governor's office, and the Faichuk area to prepare for greater home rule and development in Faichuk. He also indicated his
intention to invite Susumu Aizawa, the chief magistrate for Tol, to Pohnpei for
discussion on Faichuk's future.[111]

Political calculations were very much a part of this process. In an interview with *Pacific Magazine*, Nakayama described the meetings on Chuuk that
had preceded his veto:

> It's a scary thing. I knew very well that if I vetoed Faichuk statehood at
> that time it would mean losing whatever support I had from that area,
> but Faichuk has been the section of Truk State that perhaps has never
> been on my side. I have the feeling that after I vetoed the bill, I gained
> some support from that particular region; just the opposite of what I
> thought in the beginning.
>
> I had a two-day meeting with the Faichuk leaders in which I
> said to them "The simplest thing I can do for you is to sign this bill and
> appease you because then you would vote for me, even if you never
> did before. And if you become a state, you will have senators in the
> Congress and naturally they will vote for me and I can be re-elected
> president. But I tell you 'No.' I do not want you to be a paper state

because I don't think that in that role you can resolve your concerns, which I understand to be economic development. By declaring that you are a state, that's it—just on paper. There is no provision for electing the government. Nothing. And so I will veto it."

They said "No, don't veto it. Because if you agree (to statehood), we will support you." I went back, picked up the phone and called the vice president, and I said "veto." I told some of the Faichuk leaders on the way out to the airport. They kind of laughed at me; they thought I was kidding. I told them, "No truth [*sic*], I am not kidding. I vetoed the bill." They said, "Really, you did?" I said, "Really, I did." A few of them said "Yes, you did the right thing."[112]

As promised, Nakayama invited Tol chief magistrate and traditional leader Susumu Aizawa to Pohnpei to discuss the veto. Tosiwo Songeni, another Faichuk official from Fanapenges Island, accompanied Aizawa as did Chuuk governor Erhart Aten. Nakayama described the meeting that took place in early November as amicable and cordial. He publicly acknowledged that Aizawa and Songeni were disappointed by his veto. Privately, Aizawa supported the veto and the reasons for it.[113] With Aten pledging his support, Nakayama indicated his intention to make Faichuk an "economic showcase." The meeting included promises of support for a fisheries project on Toloas, improved medical services for the region, the formation of a local youth corps, and the use of Japanese Overseas Volunteers. The four also agreed to further investigate the possible designation of certain compact monies for Faichuk from the Chuuk allotment, and the possibility of direct aid requests from Faichuk through Chuuk State to the United States government.[114] Things quieted down, but only for a while. The Faichuk issue did not cost Nakayama a second term as president; neither did it go away. Throughout the balance of Nakayama's presidency, proponents sought to speed the developmental process along with special funding appropriations that flaunted congressional procedures, taxed already strained resources, and provided little in the way of monitoring mechanisms on the use of funds.

Adding to the tensions around the Faichuk statehood issue was an outbreak of cholera in Chuuk in the latter half of 1982. The first cases occurred in the western islands, but disappeared quickly. The quick end to cholera in the western islands led some to believe the worst was over, but such proved not to be the case. The disease soon showed itself in the Lagoon area. On 29 September 1982, the Nakayama administration reported that there were 71 confirmed cases, another 755 suspected cases, and 9 suspected cholera deaths.[115] Governor Erhart Aten aggressively lobbied the FSM and the Trust

Territory governments as well as the U.S. Congress for assistance. Technical help was also sought from the World Health Organization and the Centers for Disease Control in Atlanta, Georgia. A second report issued on 8 October by Nakayama's office listed 989 suspected cases, 148 confirmed cases, 2 confirmed cholera deaths, and 11 suspected ones.[116] A mid-December report put the total number of suspected cases at 2,165; there were 759 confirmed cases, 17 suspected cholera deaths, and 4 confirmed cholera-caused deaths.[117]

The cholera epidemic posed a real political threat. FSM secretary of external affairs Andon Amaraich told a visiting delegation from Washington that the epidemic could slow or delay the public information program on the Compact of Free Association in the affected areas because of the restriction on travel.[118] FSM national planner Dan Perrin added that the cholera epidemic was affecting a number of newly developed enterprises in the FSM such as the cultivation and export of marine products to Guam and the Northern Marianas. Given the negative associations that accompany a disease such as cholera, Perin also expected a decline in tourism to Chuuk and the FSM.

Aware that the nation as a whole, not just Chuuk, was vulnerable to a cholera outbreak, the FSM government put together a multi-million dollar proposal to the U.S. Department of Interior to upgrade sanitation facilities, improve the quality of drinking water, and create a health education program. Saying that the FSM was sitting on a powder keg of unsanitary conditions, Nakayama personally traveled to Saipan in December 1982 to make a direct appeal to the high commissioner.[119] The U.S. Congress responded with an additional $1,699,000 appropriation to the FSM fiscal 1983 budget to fight the cholera epidemic. The funds were to be used for water purification, laboratory supplies, and medicine.[120] Reports from early January 1983, indicated that the epidemic was beginning to slow.[121] Nakayama presided over a meeting to finalize government plans for an eradication program, and then visited the Faichuk area on 3 March with Governor Erhart Aten and Lieutenant Governor Bob Mori.[122] A tour of local villages led him to claim progress in the efforts to eradicate the disease; he noted that the areas of Faichuk devastated earlier by cholera had not reported any new cases in the latest three-week report period.

Chuuk was declared cholera-free in June 1983, but a second outbreak occurred in the report period between 18 July and 6 September when 84 new cases were confirmed. In consultation with Aten, Nakayama issued a 14 September emergency order to limit this latest outbreak; the order included a ban on food shipments from the state as well as the screening of travelers, shipments, and packages in and out of Chuuk.[123] Despite these efforts, cholera spread to the Lower Mortlocks. In a dispatch to Nakayama, Aten reported 2 cases in Satawan among the 133 new and confirmed cases in Chuuk for the report period ending 7 October.[124] Another 47 cases along with 3 cholera-caused deaths were reported on 5 December before the disease finally abated and disappeared.[125]

A related problem was the alleged misuse of government funds to combat cholera. An auditor's report on these funds commissioned by Nakayama revealed excessive overtime charges. Public Auditor John Dye found that of the $800,000 released by the high commissioner from the nearly $1.7 million provided by the U.S. Congress, there were $273,868 in overtime charges by Chuuk State employees that were questionable and undocumented.[126] Two extreme cases involved individuals who submitted requests for 225 and 229 hours of overtime compensation respectively in a single two-week pay period. The public auditor also questioned the charging of exceptionally high rental rates for the use of local equipment and facilities. Dye stated that costs not allowable in the cholera account would have to be born by Chuuk State.

The financial strain placed upon Chuuk State by the cholera epidemic was compounded by state legislators' decision in June 1983 to approve cost-of-living adjustments for all salaried officers and employees of the state government.[127] The following June, the state legislature in Chuuk approved an increase in its members' salaries and office allowances.[128] These instances during the Nakayama years foreshadowed a larger problem to come with indiscriminate hiring and a radically inflated government payroll that crippled the state financially. Problems in Chuuk spilled into the FSM Congress. Soon after Nakayama left office, Leo Falcam, then a senator from Pohnpei, gave a strong, only slightly veiled rebuke of the Chuukese congressional delegation when he called spending on local patronage projects "a national disgrace."[129] He charged that cronyism was taking over and warned against the abuses of power being concentrated in the hands of a few. Nakayama's problems with the congressional delegation from his home islands had been a significant part of his larger struggles with the Congress of the Federated States of Micronesia that began soon after his inauguration and intensified over the course of his two administrations.

# CHAPTER 8

# Rough Seas and Later Years

TRYING TO CREATE A NATION out of islands and island
groups whose residents did not see themselves as citizens of a larger political
entity posed a daunting task for the Nakayama administration. Compounding the difficulties were the alien governing structures and procedures and an
understandable insistence on the privileging of local interests and needs. The
creation of a national government involved intense contestations at more local
levels over identity, belonging, obligation, and allegiance. Nakayama tried to
minimize the conflicting interests by describing the national government as
the agent of the states. He said in 1982:

> We regard ourselves in the national government as an arm of the states
> in that we act in their interests. We assist in their programs; we testify
> and present state budgets in Washington, D.C.; we represent them in
> foreign countries. That's all. We don't run the federal programs. We
> have no control or power over the states because we are a loose federa-
> tion and the states are more powerful than the national government.[1]

Nakayama was right. The FSM Constitution did mandate a loose federation
that privileged states' rights and powers. Despite this fact, there were real
clashes between the national and state governments over jurisdiction, allo-
cation formulas, budgets, and the initial priority given to the establishment
of a functioning executive branch. The national and state leadership conferences had helped to facilitate communication and to negotiate the differences

among the competing parties, but only to a point, as the national government aspired to be just that, a national government.

The Congress of the Federated States of Micronesia, however, proved a much more aggressive and persistent source of opposition to Nakayama throughout his eight years as president. The problem resulted, in part, from the very nature of the FSM presidency. The president's most immediate and demanding constituency was the Congress that elected him. To avoid the partisan divisions that a popular election for president might cause in a still fragile collection of different island groups, the framers of the FSM Constitution had entrusted the selection of the president to the Congress from among the holders of the four at-large seats from each of the four states. The arrangement placed severe constraints on the exercise of executive authority and blurred the separation of powers between the two branches of government. A generational shift also exacerbated tensions. The distance between the executive and legislative branches of the FSM steadily worsened over the course of Nakayama's presidency, and around money, power, politics, and local rivalries that showed themselves in more subtle, somewhat disguised forms at the national level. Much of the opposition came from the Chuukese congressional delegation that became increasingly aggressive in demanding of the national government a greater share of national resources, and by means that were markedly partisan and at times unconstitutional. Nakayama's frustrations with Congress stayed with him in his later years. He felt disrespected and largely forgotten by a younger generation of legislators whose immediate loyalties were local, self-serving, and who had little commitment to the concepts of unity and nationhood that he so deeply believed in.

## Money Matters

The costs of establishing and sustaining the executive branch proved an immediate area of contention. Congress and Nakayama quickly clashed over salaries and recruitment expenses, funds for office rentals and renovations, and supplies. In an early test of wills, Nakayama insisted on the remodeling and furnishing of an executive conference room despite congressional concerns over the costs and necessity of such a project.[2] Hiroshi Ismael's efforts to broker a compromise between the two branches of government failed.[3] On 31 January 1980, Senator Peter Christian of Pohnpei made remarks on the Congress floor that revealed the growing distance between the legislative and executive branches of government. Christian, as he would do so often during Nakayama's presidency, expressed reservations about the costs and conduct of the executive branch. He was concerned about the recruitment of executive branch employees, the criteria for their selection, the costs of their contracts, and the use of government property by employees of the executive branch for personal reasons.[4] The Department of External Affairs was a frequent target of congressional criticism during the Nakayama years. Members of the legislative branch often criticized the costs of diplomacy and international initiatives, complained about the confusion over the department's policies, procedures, and responsibilities, and resisted or reduced the budget requests made by the Nakayama administration to open embassies and consular offices in the Pacific region or in support of regional and international commitments.[5] Informing this criticism was the Congress' desire to involve itself in negotiations over the terms and distribution of foreign assistance. A bill first introduced in the Second FSM Congress to alter the structure and functions of the department reappeared during later sessions in various revised forms; it was vetoed a third and final time by Nakayama in the last full year of his presidency.[6]

Nakayama assured Congress that the FSM was well within its overall budget for the first eight months of fiscal 1981, though he admitted the executive branch had exceeded the authorizations set by the FSM Congress in certain areas related to the housing, staffing, and supplying of the national government.[7] Nakayama justified the extra spending as necessary; he requested re-authorization in these areas to further expedite the establishment of a functioning national government. Nakayama did share Congress' concern with the cost of government and placed a temporary freeze on recruitment and the purchase of supplies while he waited for congressional approval of the additional funds being requested.

Others in Congress, including old friends and allies of Nakayama, echoed Christian's concerns. Luke Tman, the chairman of the Ways and Means Committee, criticized the government for its failure to submit on time and in a clear manner a budget for the executive branch. Moreover, he was shocked by the size of the request that his committee ultimately did receive. Tman, a strong supporter of Nakayama from Congress of Micronesia days, stated:

> We had hoped to create this National Government for the FSM predicated upon the principle that it was going to be a small government because we are a small people, we are a real people. Perhaps, the president intends to do that, but he has a staff who have surrounded him that carry the mentality in the old headquarters fashion.[8]

Tman also complained about members of the executive branch who disregarded the requests, recommendations, and cautions of his committee. Another ally and friend, Senator Raymond Setik of Chuuk, spoke in late 1982 about the relationship between the state and national governments.[9] Setik noted that during the transition period the revenues generated by the Micronesian Maritime Authority, coupled with the allotments provided by the Department of the Interior for transition purposes, gave the executive branch a considerable pool of discretionary funds. The states, meanwhile, had little money beyond what was available to them through annually appropriated congressional funds and tightly controlled federal grants. With the implementation of the compact, the resource imbalance would shift in favor of the states, and the national government would have a difficult time sustaining its operation. Setik thought it was time for his friend, the president, and other members of the executive branch to recognize that fact and to begin streamlining operations.

The second regular session of the Second FSM Congress, held in late 1981, proved particularly contentious. Members of Congress took strong exception to the coverage of housing costs and the annual home leave given to employees of the national government who were hired from areas outside of Pohnpei. The Congress passed two pieces of legislation; the first replaced the full reimbursement of rental payments with a smaller, set housing allowance, while the second eliminated the in-service home leaves for those employees coming from other states and areas to work for the national government on Pohnpei. Nakayama objected to the legislation. In his veto messages, he argued that the housing inducements were essential to attract quality personnel to the national government; the elimination of home leave would hurt those who had come to Pohnpei with this provision in their contract, especially lower paid employees from within the FSM.[10] Nakayama's veto of the bill to reduce the housing allowance for government employees stood; Congress, however, overrode his veto of the bill eliminating in-service home leave for employees of the national government.[11]

There was more at stake than the costs of government in the struggle between president and Congress. Some members of the national legislative body openly challenged the powers delegated to the executive branch by the FSM Constitution, and in ways that were at odds with the constitution. Speaking on 17 May 1981, Senator Jack Fritz, from Kutu in the Mortlocks and a graduate of the University of Hawai'i's William S. Richardson School of Law, noted that the FSM Constitution gave the national government the power to regulate banking and foreign and interstate commerce. He felt, however, that the states were in a better position to decide on the types of foreign investment and banking institutions that best suited their needs. He proposed that the executive branch simply designate these powers to the states as a way to avoid the lengthy process of amending the constitution.[12] Peter Christian thought the constitutional procedures for amending the FSM Constitution were them-

selves in need of amendment; he took the opportunity on 8 June 1981 to criticize Nakayama's earlier veto of a bill sponsored by John Haglelgam of Yap to
revise procedures for constitutional amendments.[13] Christian characterized
the veto as a betrayal of promises made earlier to Pohnpeians that their reservations about the power of the national government would be addressed by
the possible amending of the constitution. Nakayama viewed Haglelgam's bill
as unconstitutional; in his veto message, he had characterized the legislation
as inappropriate, confusing, and threatening to the ongoing negotiations over
the Compact of Free Association.[14]

Fritz proved a persistent, aggressive, and outspoken critic of Nakayama.
His career trajectory resembled that of Nakayama. Like Nakayama, he hailed
from one of Chuuk's outer island areas; he had moved to Toloas early in his
life and married into the Sópwunupi, the most prominent and powerful of the
Lagoon area's clans. There were those who thought his ultimate political ambition was to simply bring down Nakayama.[15] Fritz delivered a pointed speech
before the Congress on 9 November 1981 that heavily criticized Nakayama and
the executive branch.[16] Fritz complained about the lack of leadership. Using
Nakayama's own metaphor, he characterized the FSM canoe as directionless.
He pointed to the failure of the executive branch to produce a national plan, and
called much of the proposed legislation submitted to Congress by the executive
branch confusing and uncoordinated. Fritz worried about the Department of
External Affairs' management of foreign aid, especially the aid coming from
Japan. He accused the executive branch of acting in bad faith and of refusing
to cooperate with the Congress. The Chuukese congressman noted that more
than 50 percent of the national government's revenue went to cover personnel
costs. He also cited the FSM attorney general's failure to appear before the Congress to testify on legislation, and the failure of other executive departments to
offer opinions on legislation relevant to their interests. Fritz bemoaned what he
understood as a general feeling of inferiority among Micronesian employees
of the government, and the reliance on expensive, short-term expatriate and
foreign expertise. He blamed all of this on Nakayama and those around him:

> We must wake up our navigator and helmsman, make them realize
> we have limited energy to sail this canoe ashore and will not tolerate
> any inaction on their part. Remind them of our forefathers rule when
> a sailing canoe is negligently lost at sea. We must help them find a
> destination.[17]

The sparring between the executive and legislative branches intensified
over subsequent congressional sessions, and over questions of jurisdiction and

authority. Members of Congress continued to seek a role in the negotiations over foreign aid, an area of responsibility delegated specifically to the executive branch. Congress passed a bill giving it the power to distribute goods and services received through foreign aid grants. Nakayama vetoed the measure, citing Congress' intrusion into areas where the president had constitutionally mandated powers.[18] The Congress then passed a second, related bill calling for a constitutional amendment that gave it greater involvement in negotiations over development aid and other forms of foreign assistance. Congress' position was based on a reading of foreign aid agreements as treaties that required congressional ratification. Nakayama objected to the bill on the grounds that foreign aid agreements were not treaties, and therefore did not require congressional review and approval. In his veto message, Nakayama argued further that such congressional involvement in foreign aid agreements would slow down the negotiating process, expose negotiating strategy to public debate, and give the Congress power to dictate negotiating instructions.[19] Congress, however, would prove unrelenting in its challenge to the executive branch's authority in foreign affairs throughout the Nakayama presidency.

## No Respite

Following elections in March, the first regular session of the Third FSM Congress convened on 9 May 1983. The first order of business was the selection of a new president and vice president. Nakayama was the obvious choice. He had run virtually unopposed for the four-year, at-large seat from Chuuk, victory in that race being a prerequisite of his candidacy for the office of president. Kalisto Refalopei placed Nakayama's name in nomination. Though surprising, Refalopei's action was not without purpose. His nominating speech served at once as a gesture of reconciliation and a reminder to Nakayama of his earlier pledge to develop the Faichuk area economically following the veto of the statehood bill. Bailey Olter was chosen as vice president. Olter's selection resulted from the decision of Petrus Tun not to seek re-election to the four-year, at-large seat from Yap and hence the vice presidency. Aside from his stated desire to return home, there were two major motivations behind Tun's decision. The first was to create an opening in the vice presidency that, by most observers' calculations, would go to the holder of the four-year, at-large seat from Pohnpei. Tun and others thought the slotting of the vice presidency to Pohnpei would be a way to solidify that island's ambivalent, sometimes oppositional relationship to the Federated States of Micronesia. A chance to address publicly the increasing tensions between the executive and legislative branches provided a second reason behind Tun's decision to leave the national government.

**Fig. 8.1.** Chief Justice Edward King swears in Tosiwo Nakayama for a second term as president in 1983. Miter Nakayama holds the bible on which her husband's hand rests (Micronesian Seminar).

Following the announcement of his decision, Tun was invited to address a joint session of Congress. Though the Congress had passed a resolution thanking him for his many years of service, Tun was in no mood to return the gesture.[20] In a special address to the Congress delivered on 26 May, Tun noted the FSM's significant achievements in the area of political development, especially political institutions. He strongly endorsed Nakayama's re-election as being in the best interests of the nation for the continuity and stability it provided. Much work needed to be done, however. Avowals to the contrary, the FSM was continuing to become more and more economically dependent. Most discouraging, however, was the lack of cooperation and trust between the executive and legislative branches of the national government. The disharmony threatened the future of the young nation.

Reflecting back over the first four years of the FSM government, Tun pointed to the obsession with checks and balances "at the expense of equally or more important things such as common sense and teamwork."[21] He thought there was much to learn from a more parliamentary form of government that stressed consultation rather than confrontation, which seemed to be a hall-mark of American-style democracy. He criticized those who made decisions based solely on the needs of the state and not the national government. By thinking of national needs and working with the national government, there would be less fighting in Congress over the distribution of resources, and more time to devote to the important work of nation building. Tun called for a stronger commitment to the nation as a way to deal more effectively with the needs of the state. He took the opportunity to denounce those rumors that had him going back to Yap to help it secede from the FSM. He would not tear down, he said, what he had helped build up. Tun closed by saying he had chosen to go back to Yap to assist in the development of the national economy from the state level.

Tun's admonishment did little to calm the tensions between the executive and legislative branches of the FSM government. The Congress persisted in its efforts to counter the costs and powers of the executive branch. During the first regular session of the Third Congress in mid-1983, members passed a bill that sought to reduce the maximum base salary of public service employees. In his veto message, Nakayama explained that he supported a freeze but not a reduction on current salaries being earned in excess of the maximum rate. He felt a reduction would be unfair to employees currently under contract and might lead to litigation.[22] Nakayama also vetoed a bill requiring public officials whose appointments were subject to the advice and consent of the Congress to submit their resignations to the president within thirty days of inauguration if their nominations had not yet been acted upon. The administration had ear-lier proposed a ninety-day resignation requirement but the Congress rejected the compromise. Nakayama ended up vetoing the bill on the grounds that the thirty-day limit would effectively kill a nomination if Congress were slow to act; this, in turn, would disrupt the business of the national government as well as impose hardships on the nominee and his family.[23] Nonetheless, the Congress persisted and countered Nakayama's veto.[24]

The Micronesian Maritime Authority (MMA), now under the very capa-ble direction of Mike McCoy, was another target of Congress. A former Peace Corps volunteer in Yap, McCoy had married a local woman, developed close ties with famed Satawal navigator Mau Piailug, and earned a reputation for his expertise in marine fisheries. Nakayama had been a strong advocate and supporter of the MMA in the Congress of Micronesia. The MMA's licensing of foreign fishing vessels and the revenues that licensing generated fell under the control of the executive branch, a fact that irritated some in Congress who sought to put limits on the MMA by requiring that all fisheries' agreements involving six or more boats be subject to congressional review and approval.

Its existing charter gave the MMA the power to conclude foreign fishing agreements with groups of fewer than ten boats. Moreover, the FSM Department of Resources and Development had the power to approve agreements with larger entities when Congress was not in session. In Nakayama's mind, the bill limiting the powers of the MMA would effectively eliminate the capacity of the government to approve foreign fishing agreements in a prompt and timely fashion, and throw into disarray the regulation of the 200-mile economic zone. These arguments formed the basis of his veto message.[25]

Despite his fears, Nakayama's cabinet nominations for his second term moved quickly through the Congress. The quality of the nominees, coupled with the relatively equitable distribution of cabinet seats among the four states, made for a smooth process. Andon Amaraich and Aloysius Tuuth returned to their positions as secretary of external affairs and secretary of finance, respectively. Bernard Helgenberger of Pohnpei, who had become secretary of resources and development following the premature death of Ambilos Iehsi in 1981, continued in his position. Del Pangelinan, also of Pohnpei, was confirmed for a second term as budget officer. David Nevitt of Seattle, Washington, replaced Fred Ramp as attorney general while John Brackett of New York remained public defender. Asterio Takesy was confirmed as deputy secretary of external affairs and Epel Ilon of Chuuk won congressional endorsement as the FSM's representative to Washington, D.C.[26] Kohne Ramon of Pingelap succeeded Kasio Mida of Chuuk as personnel officer. Mida had angered a number of congressmen who refused to support his renomination to the position. Nakayama, however, found him both loyal and competent. Mida, along with Ieske Iehsi of Pingelap, were chosen to be special assistants to the president. Nakayama's nomination of Dan Perrin for a second term as FSM national planner, however, was a victim of the tensions between the executive and legislative branches over money and power. Perrin's nomination was brought to a vote during the first special session of the Third Congress that met from 22 August to 3 September 1983. While the Committee on Resources and Development had endorsed Perrin's nomination, a minority report criticized his failure to consult Congress, his unilateral actions, his misrepresentations to Congress, and his failure to complete and submit a national development plan to Congress. It was the minority report that was adopted by Congress.[27]

Confusion, contention, and delays had certainly hindered efforts to draft a national development plan for the FSM as required by the Compact of Free Association with the United States. The Nakayama administration submitted a formal plan to Congress in early 1984. It drew immediate criticism from the four state governors. A United Nations Development Programme team also reviewed the plan and recommended substantive changes.[28] Consequently, the

Congress voted down a resolution calling for adoption of the plan.[29] A year later, the Congress did approve a resolution that endorsed the "First National Development Plan, 1985–1989." This revised plan was the product of a task force mandated by the Congress and drawn from all areas of the national government. The task force made substantive changes to the administration's earlier plan.[30]

The 1985 election for the ten two-year congressional seats led to a further deterioration in the administration's relationship with Congress as the results were less than favorable for Tosiwo Nakayama. Two of his most formidable critics, Jack Fritz and Kalisto Refalopei, won re-election. The loss of Nakayama's brother-in-law Sasauo Gouland to longtime rival Nick Bossy was even more discouraging. Gouland had been the chair of the resources and development committee at the time of his defeat; his loss deprived Nakayama of a strategic political ally.[31] A year later, Gouland lost to Gideon Doone in an election for the Chuuk governorship. Nakayama received heavy criticism on Pohnpei for his public efforts in behalf of his brother-in-law during the gubernatorial campaign, something expected of him by Chuukese cultural standards.[32] Nakayama found himself in an even more awkward situation when he attended the inauguration of Gideon Doone later that year and had to give a speech assuring the gathering of the national government's full cooperation with the new state administration.[33]

The 1985 elections further emboldened an already aggressive and critical Congress that now insisted on the right to review and approve any amendments made to the Compact of Free Association by the U.S. Congress. Congress' position in the matter was not unreasonable given the changes made to the compact by the U.S. Congress. Nakayama, however, worried about further delays and complications to a negotiating process that had been going on for more than sixteen years. During the first special session of the Fourth FSM Congress, members passed a resolution that requested the U.S. Congress to carefully consider the freely expressed wishes of the people of the FSM, and disapprove any changes that materially revised the compact approved by FSM voters in the 1983 plebiscite.[34] Nakayama was quite comfortable with the resolution, but balked at a bill introduced by Senator Isaac Figir of Yap that required the review and approval of a changed compact by the FSM Congress and the four state legislatures before its implementation.

Nakayama countered with the argument that the constitutional mandates for approval of the compact had been met in 1983.[35] He expressed the fear that any additional reviews by the Congress and state legislatures would cost time and money, and cause divisiveness. He noted that no public hearings had been held on the bill, and that it was of "questionable constitutional valid-

ity" because it infringed upon the power of the executive branch as defined by
the FSM Constitution. Nakayama pledged that he would make no decision on
the implementation of the compact without consulting the Congress and the
states. The Congress, however, rejected Nakayama's assessment and overrode
his veto on 28 October 1985.[36] During that same session, Senator Nick Bossy of
Truk, Nakayama's longtime political rival, criticized the executive branch and
appropriate offices and departments for not keeping Congress better informed
on the progress of the compact in the U.S. Congress.[37] He gave a tangible edge
to his criticism by introducing a resolution that requested the president of the
Federated States of Micronesia and the executive director of the Commission
on Future Political Status and Transition report to the Congress their views on
whether or not the commission should be abolished.[38]

The increasing proclivity of the Congress of the Federated States of
Micronesia to allocate project monies to the states that bypassed or ignored
the national and state development plans exacerbated tensions between the
executive and legislative branches. Nakayama had sought in previous years to
limit congressional appropriations for local projects that were ill-conceived,
poorly defined, and more about enhancing the re-election chances of the
sponsoring congressmen than addressing real community needs. The problem became particularly acute when Kalisto Refalopei and other members of
the Chuukese delegation sought to expedite congressional funding to Faichuk
as a way to mitigate Nakayama's veto of the statehood bill. There resulted a
prolonged battle between Nakayama and Congress that resulted in the passage
of a bill over the president's veto. A legal review of the bill found it constitutionally flawed in its appropriation of federal funds to public projects that
bypassed the oversight of the state governor's office. Congress then passed a
second bill that authorized the direct appropriation of funds to Faichuk and
designated Senator Kalisto Refalopei, the congressional representative from
the area, as the allottee. In his veto message, Nakayama termed the designation
of a member of Congress as an allottee for public funds a wrongful practice.[39]
He argued that monies for public projects should have nothing to do with
congressional operations or congressmen personally. He noted that the state
governors had recently criticized the practice of changed allottees as serving
the political aspirations of congressmen rather than the developmental needs
of the state. Nakayama termed the law as amended "unenforceable." Jack Fritz
responded to the presidential veto by declaring that the executive branch had
no choice in the matter but to enforce the law; he termed Nakayama's characterization of the law as "unenforceable" a form of lawlessness.[40]

The issue carried over into the next session of Congress where supporters of Faichuk tried yet again to pass a bill that amended the appropriations

process. Nakayama did not waver. In his veto message, Nakayama noted that funds for several designated projects had already been allotted through proper channels and spent.[41] The bill, in effect, would fund these projects a second time. Nakayama found particularly objectionable the allotment of money for the construction of fourteen meeting halls in communities that already had them. He argued that the new meeting halls, all slated for Faichuk, were not needed and did nothing to advance economic development. He noted further that they were to be built not on community property but on the lands of individual families, and that some villages were to receive as many as four community halls. "This practice," he wrote, "leaves the Government open to charges that elected Government officials are rewarding the loyalty of their friends and families by construction of projects that only benefit individual families."[42] Moreover, one of the community meeting halls was to be built upon a parcel of land that belonged to Kalisto Refalopei, a sponsor of the bill and the designated allottee for the funds.

Nakayama mentioned the problem in his Sixth State of the Nation Address; he argued that the appropriation of limited national resources for local conferences, redundant meeting halls, and useless seawalls to be of no value whatsoever.[43] Such an approach was a real disservice to future generations forced to deal with the consequences of misspent monies at a time when funds from the Compact of Free Association would be declining as a result of provisions that specified reductions in financial assistance at five-year intervals. Jack Fritz termed the president's criticisms unfair, and blamed those charged with educating people on the economic assistance terms of the Compact of Free Association with doing a poor job.[44] In the end, the Congress made minor adjustments to the bill in question, including the deletion of funds for a meeting hall on land owned by one of the congressional sponsors, and passed it and an accompanying series of related measures over Nakayama's veto.[45]

Nakayama's supplemental budget requests remained a continual source of contention with the Congress throughout the course of his administration. Nick Bossy accused Nakayama of ignoring the financial facts when he submitted a supplemental budget request to Congress during its March 1986 special session. In a sharply worded statement, Bossy criticized Nakayama for submitting supplemental appropriation requests "that would immediately appropriate every nickel that Congress might have left in the public purse."[46] Bossy accused the president of poor management skills, stating the he "objected to having the Congress forced to fill a leadership vacuum created when the Chief Executive doesn't execute his management responsibility."[47] Bossy complained that Nakayama could not say "no" and that he was abdicating his fiscal responsibilities by leaving it to the Congress to prioritize funding requests from his departments. Peter Christian of Pohnpei, the chair of the Ways and Means Committee, seconded Bossy's criticisms. The supplemental budget request sought funds to cover budget shortfalls in travel, personnel costs, international obligations and memberships, and the repair of embassy and local postal facilities. Nakayama worried that the failure to fund this supplemental request would result in the critical loss of important social services and the failure of the government to meet its international responsibilities. Expressing surprise at Bossy's criticisms, Nakayama acknowledged a difference in priorities, but asserted that the executive branch could not always compromise with the Congress on the funding of items it considered essential.[48]

As his second term wound down, Nakayama called a special session of the FSM Congress to deal with a number of important matters that he believed needed action before the convocation of the next Congress and the selection of a new president and vice president. Nakayama identified thirteen measures for congressional consideration that included revising the Foreign Permit Investment law, amending the distribution formula for compact funds, and ratifying the multilateral fisheries treaty between the South Pacific Forum countries and the United States. He conceded it was an ambitious agenda but contended that this important work needed to be completed before the beginning of the Fifth Regular Congress. He added that, "This will be our last opportunity to work together in our respective positions."[49] The Fourth Congress in its final ten-day session chose instead to focus on its own agenda that included the approval of nine bills, the majority of which dealt with public works appropriations to the states.[50]

## Trying Times

Nakayama found the presidency to be a very difficult and stressful job. He described it as a twenty-four-hour-a-day job: "you go home with problems and sleep with problems and things... and wake up with problems."[51] It was a lonely job too as he wrote in a letter of appreciation to David Nevitt upon the occasion of Nevitt's resignation as FSM attorney general.[52] The meetings were endless, and the travel over long distances frequent and exhausting. There was too the ever-growing backlog of correspondence, reports, and legislation piled high on his desk and the surrounding floor. When he wasn't traveling, he spent long days in his office before returning at night with a briefcase full of papers to his rented home outside Kolonia in Nett municipality on land owned by the Etscheit family. For someone who did not enjoy reading, he was required to read a lot. His family suffered too from his many travels, long absences, and the demanding work of nation building. Miter and the younger children resided with him on Pohnpei; his older children and their families remained in Chuuk and saw him infrequently. Miter herself returned to Chuuk after the containment of the cholera epidemic while Tosiwo finished out his last year as president in Pohnpei. Fishing was his primary form of recreation. When he could, he went by boat to nearby Ant Atoll with a small party of friends and colleagues where he would spend the night sitting quietly on deck with a fishing pole in hand and a can of beer by his side.[53]

Over the course of the presidency, there were two threats against his life. One was delivered indirectly from a man already in prison who claimed to have heard U.S. Secret Service agents talking about a plot to assassinate Nakayama and Quirino Mendiola, his director of immigration. The FBI investigated the report and concluded there was no danger to Nakayama.[54] The second incident involved a May 1986 threat from Seferein Ysam, the husband of family friend Nessa who had sold the Nakayamas a piece of land above Nantaku in Weno where they built a second home. Under interrogation, Ysam claimed that his threat to shoot Nakayama was only a figure of speech intended to underline his disagreement with some of the president's policies.[55] The 1985 assassination of Palauan president Haruo Remelik had intensified security around Nakayama and resulted in a temporary increase in the number of federal policemen assigned to guard his house. There were also concerns about visits to his office by unscrupulous businessmen and underworld figures from Japan seeking opportunities in Pohnpei and the FSM.[56] One of Nakayama's assistant attorney generals, Fred Canover, had a fascination with guns. To the dismay of Nakayama and his immediate staff, Canover sometimes brought his latest acquisitions into the executive office to show the president.[57] There were lighter moments too. On one occasion, Nakayama thought he had lost an important folder full of confidential documents only to discover some days later that his personal driver Kuhpas Ikosaia, a short man from Pingelap, had taken the folder to use as a seat cushion that allowed him a better view of the road.[58]

There were certainly honors and privileges accorded Nakayama during his eight years as president. He met with world leaders, including Jimmy Carter, Ronald Reagan, and George Bush, as well as the prime ministers of Australia, Japan, and numerous Pacific nations. On 29 March 1982 he was publicly recognized by the University of Hawai'i for his accomplishments.[59] The East-West Center in Honolulu recognized Nakayama as one of its two distinguished alumni for 1984.[60] In making its award, the center cited his stature as a regional and international statesman. At the time of the award, Nakayama was serving as a member of the Pacific Islands Conference Standing Committee charged with overseeing the East-Wester Center's Pacific Islands Development Program. Travel brought perks and other forms of recognition such as the invitation to throw out the ceremonial first pitch at a Chicago White Sox baseball game on 17 May 1985.[61] Nakayama had traveled to Chicago after addressing the 52nd annual meeting of the UN Trusteeship Council on 13 May in New York City. The day following the baseball game, he attended a reception in his honor on board the *Star of Chicago* cruise ship on Lake Michigan. Intended to introduce the president to midwestern political and business leaders, the event was billed as a "Chicago Tribute to Micronesia and the Marshall Islands." Donald Hannah, president of Hannah Marine Corporation that ran a barge and tugboat operation connecting Honolulu, Johnston Island, Wake Island, Midway Island, and Kwajalein Atoll, hosted the reception.

Despite the incredible pressure of his job, Tosiwo Nakayama never lost his ability to make people feel comfortable and at ease. Joan King, the editor of the *JK Report* and the spouse of FSM chief justice Ed King, remembered Nakayama taking the time amidst a public meeting to help her locate and then refasten a lost earring.[62] Nakayama did not hold grudges and often showed himself to be forgiving and generous in spirit. He delivered the eulogy for his longtime congressional colleague and first FSM director of resources and development Ambilos Iehsi on 14 March 1981.[63] The two had been close allies, though it was rumored that Iehsi had cast the deciding vote back in 1974 that accepted the minority report on the contested election between Nick Bossy and Andon Amaraich; the vote cost Nakayama's closest congressional colleague his seat in the Congress of Micronesia. The rumor did not damage the relationship between Nakayama and Iehsi as time later proved. Nakayama was also caring and courageous. In early 1987, he intervened to prevent further violence after the murder of Chuukese student Everly Lippwe by Bernard Mengebuch, a Yapese student studying at the Ponape Agricultural and Trade School in Madolenihmw.[64] Nakayama recruited Secretary of Finance Aloysius Tuuth to calm members of the Yapese community on Pohnpei while he stood with the Chuukese in a reconciliation ceremony with armed police at the ready.[65] Two years after leaving the presidency, Nakayama sat all night beside the body of Kalisto Refalopei, one of his strongest opponents in Congress, who passed away suddenly in 1989.[66]

## Stepping Down

The year 1987 brought the end of the Nakayama presidency, and also the loss of key allies, colleagues, and friends in that year's congressional elections.[67] Bailey Olter, Nakayama's vice president, lost to Leo Falcam by fifteen votes in the race for the four-year, at-large seat from Pohnpei. Bethwel Henry, the longtime Speaker of the Congress and one of the architects of the Federated

States of Micronesia, ran in that same race and lost. Raymond Setik was also defeated. Nick Bossy, Jack Fritz, and Kalisto Refalopei, all strong opponents of Nakayama, now headed Chuuk's congressional delegation. The generation that had served in the Congress of Micronesia, helped create the FSM and the constitution it rested upon, and negotiated the Compact of Free Association was largely gone. The first order of business for the new Congress that convened on 11 May 1987 was the selection of a new president and vice president.

John Haglelgam of Eauripik Island in Yap State succeeded Tosiwo Nakayama and became the second president of the Federated States of Micronesia. His election surprised many, and was made possible by Leo Falcam's aforementioned defeat of Bailey Olter in the congressional elections. Prior to his defeat, Olter was thought to be the odds-on favorite because of his long association with the Congress, the national government, and the belief in the eyes of most that it was Pohnpei's turn to hold the presidency. Hiroshi Ismael, who had bounced back from his 1983 loss to Joab Sigrah, won Kosrae's four-year seat and was chosen to be Haglelgam's vice president. The Chuukese congressional delegation had been instrumental in getting Haglelgam elected president. Their enthusiasm for Haglelgam stemmed in part from his marriage to a woman from Uman, his criticism of the Nakayama administration, and his general sympathy and support for Chuukese legislative interests. Haglelgam's candidacy was also aided by the deep dislike that many members of Congress felt toward the Pohnpeian candidate Leo Falcam whom they regarded as outspoken, abrasive, and self-serving.

Nakayama considered Haglelgam young and inexperienced. In a meeting with Haglelgam and his vice president Hiroshi Ismael before their inauguration, Nakayama urged Haglelgam to be patient and seek the counsel of others; he complimented Ismael on his record of distinguished public service, urged him to limit his drinking, and asked the new vice president to be more of an executive for the sake of the nation.[68] Smart, capable, and well intentioned though he was, Haglelgam did prove impatient. In his inaugural address, Haglelgam rightly called for controlling the size and costs of government, and reorganizing the executive branch.[69] Haglelgam's first executive decision was to put a freeze on hiring, purchases, and travel, and to severely restrict the use of government vehicles for anything other than official business.[70] Nakayama was aware of these problems and had attempted to address them late in his presidency but to no avail.[71] Haglelgam's efforts caused considerable anger and resentment. He received strong resistance from national government employees who questioned his authority and challenged his right to make such decisions. The opposition to his cost-cutting plans was so intense that Haglelgam found himself forced to lift the freeze by the end of the year.[72]

The election of Haglelgam created hard feelings on Pohnpei. Kalisto
Refalopei received an anonymous and threatening letter that he entered into the
congressional record.[73] The letter, dated 1 May 1987, expressed disappointment
over rumors that the presidency was not going to Pohnpei as the gentleman's
agreement from the 1975 Micronesian Constitutional Convention stipulated.
The author, who identified himself only as a concerned citizen of Pohnpei,
threatened violence and predicted dire consequences for the unity of the FSM if
Pohnpei were denied the presidency in favor of Chuukese and Yapese interests.
After the election, Leo Falcam gave an address in which he spoke of Pohnpei's
disappointment at being denied both the presidency and key leadership positions in the Congress.[74] Falcam's congressional address was more moderate in
tone than a radio interview he had given earlier in which he predicted somewhat cryptically that people on Pohnpei would *alu nan nta* or "walk in blood"
if the next president were not Pohnpeian.[75] He complained now about the small
clique that had developed within the Congress. That clique, he claimed, had
come to dominate the Congress and to undermine much of the authority of
the executive branch. Falcam commented on how the Congress had denied
the national government the resources needed to serve the people in favor of
wasteful appropriations designed to ensure the re-election of incumbents. He
called it a national disgrace, adding that he had watched Nakayama struggle
with Congress over this issue for eight years only to fail. Falcam described an
environment in which cronyism had taken over and greed was rampant. He
criticized members of Congress for being concerned with collecting their salaries and office allowances to the neglect of far more important issues. With the
election of Haglelgam, the core leadership from the last Congress now seemed
to control both branches of government. Falcam was fearful of what was to
come. He acknowledged that the candid expression of his views was possibly
un-Micronesian but thought that it was now a time for candor and openness.

Nakayama was not particularly close to Falcam but agreed with much
of what the Pohnpeian had said. Nakayama's disappointment showed clearly
in the farewell address that he delivered at the invitation of Congress on 6
June 1987, about a month after stepping down as president.[76] Reflecting back
on his eight years as president, Nakayama felt his proposals deserved better
treatment than they had received. "Perhaps, I was wrong in feeling that executive initiatives were oftentimes put aside as secondary to community halls and
sea walls."[77] He cautioned Congress against infringement on the duties and
responsibilities of the executive branch, and urged its members "to focus more
on the formulation of laws and policies, and let the executive branch spend
time enforcing and carrying them out as is mandated by our Constitution."[78]
In an oblique reference to those within the Chuukese congressional delegation

who had opposed him so vigorously, Nakayama warned against any group trying to dominate others, a process he described as "cultural imperialism." He had little enthusiasm for reorganization plans and criticized change for change's sake. Any streamlining of government, he insisted, "must be done in the interest and the atmosphere of trust, of belief in our growth as a common entity, in solidarity with our commonality and not out of malice, avarice or out of the 'show of power.' "[79]

Despite the hurt and disappointment that he felt, Nakayama remained diplomatic throughout the transition period. Soon after his inauguration, Haglelgam traveled to the islands of Uman and Toloas in Chuuk State.[80] The trip was Haglelgam's first as president; Jack Fritz, now the Speaker of the FSM Congress, accompanied him. After leaving Pohnpei, the presidential party first touched down in Weno and was greeted by Governor Gideon Doone and other local government officials. Tosiwo Nakayama, who had by this time returned to Chuuk from Pohnpei, was a part of the Weno greeting party. The next day, the entourage, minus Tosiwo Nakayama, headed by boat for Uman. In Uman, Haglelgam took part in a traditional investiture ritual, the *nuun afaramau*. At the conclusion of investiture, Haglelgam returned to Weno, spent the night, and headed for Toloas the next day for a similar investiture. Accompanying

**Fig. 8.2.** Tosiwo Nakayama and John Haglelgam, Chuuk, 1987 (Micronesian Seminar).

him now was Tosiwo Nakayama who found it hard to be among those who had criticized him so harshly and frequently, and whose machinations had helped bring Haglelgam to the presidency.

In his address to the gathering on Toloas, Haglelgam acknowledged Nakayama for all that he had done in helping to bring the FSM into being "during our difficult days of nation building."[81] Nakayama, in his own speech, responded by thanking the people assembled for the guidance and support they had given him as president, and apologized to the presidential party for not being able to accompany them to Uman. He assured everyone that he had great hopes for the new president. Addressing Haglelgam directly, Nakayama advised him to be professional in working for the nation, and not take things personally lest the job become too emotionally burdensome. "In my eight years as president, I learned to accept chides, indignities, and strong letters from the Congress because it was the job given to me by them—and it was my job."[82] He acknowledged it was hard being out of office and not having anything to do. Looking around him, he mused that most of the children in attendance were probably born during his administration.

Tosiwo Nakayama regretted the lack of transition between the FSM national government's first two administrations. He thought the lack of consultation severely limited the incoming Haglelgam administration.[83] Compounding the lack of communication were the ill feelings and distrust that many FSM workers had developed toward the new vice president, Hiroshi Ismael, over the course of the years.[84] There was also less money available during the Haglelgam years as the first step-down in compact funds took effect during his administration. Haglelgam ended up serving only one term in office with one of his most impressive contributions being the FSM's successful campaign to win membership in the United Nations. Any chance Haglelgam had for a second term disappeared when he lost the 1991 election for Yap's four-year at-large seat in the FSM Congress. Prior to the election, Haglelgam as FSM president had ordered the sailing of the government field trip ship from Yap for the outer islands before one of the senior Yapese ships scheduled to make the voyage reached the dock. The failure to wait angered the outer islands' chiefs who saw it as a sign of disrespect by one of their own people toward the paramount chiefs of Yap. The subsequent refusal of the outer island chiefs to support Haglelgam cost him the election.

## After the Presidency

Tosiwo Nakayama's most immediate concern upon leaving the presidency was employment that would provide income for him and his family. It was painfully clear that there would be no place for him in the national government. In addition, the fledgling FSM nation had no pension or support fund for its chief executives. While consideration had been given to the issue in light of Nakayama's pending retirement, the consensus in Congress was that there existed too many other pressing priorities for the limited funds available.[85] Fortunately it did not take long for Nakayama to find employment. Soon after leaving office Nakayama traveled to Guam to receive an honorary doctorate from the University of Guam, his first degree of any kind. Before the graduation ceremony, Nakayama met with a representative of the Bank of Guam who inquired about Nakayama's interest in working for the bank.[86] This man told the former president that he and others thought Nakayama would be an excellent representative of the bank in the larger Micronesian region. Soon after, Anthony A. Leon Guerrero, the chairman of the bank's Board of Governors, journeyed to Chuuk to actively recruit the former president.

Nakayama, Leon Guerrero, and their wives had dinner at the Blue Lagoon Hotel. There, Leon Guerrero gave Nakayama an envelope. When Nakayama inquired about its contents, Leon Guerrero replied that it held a draft contract for his appointment as a vice president of governmental affairs. Leon Guerrero asked Nakayama to review the draft, make any changes he thought appropriate, and fill in the salary line with a figure he thought fair. Nakayama was taken aback by the offer. The next morning, he returned the contract to Leon Guerrero. He had made some changes and signed the document but left the salary line blank. He asked Leon Guerrero to decide on a figure for his compensation. The chairman asked what Nakayama received as president of the FSM; US$32,000 per annum was the reply. Leon Guerrero then announced that the bank would pay him an annual salary of $35,000; Nakayama thought this amount too generous. They then agreed on compensation that matched Nakayama's presidential salary. A year later, during a trip to Guam for a meeting of the bank's Board of Directors, Nakayama received a new contract that included an immediate $10,000 raise and a clause that stipulated an additional $8,000 raise for the following year.

Nakayama's chief responsibility as a vice president for governmental affairs was to provide general consulting services and to assist in the expansion of its regional operations in the Caroline and Marshall Islands.[87] Nakayama accompanied Leon Guerrero and other bank officials on their trips to meet with local officials about chartering branch banks in their respective island nations. His presence added credibility to the Bank of Guam's efforts, but also revived memories of former political differences and rivalries in what was now the Republic of the Marshall Islands and the Republic of Palau. Amata Kabua, the Marshalls' leader, was not particularly pleased or persuaded by Nakayama's presence on the Bank of Guam delegation that visited the Marshalls.[88] He declined to support the bank's application to expand its services in the Marshalls.

In Palau, Roman Tmetuchl showed himself more welcoming of the delegation's visit even though he was running a bank of his own. At a meeting Leon Guerrero asked how Tmetuchl's bank was doing.[89] Not well, replied the Palauan; people were repaying their loans. The members of the bank's delegation found Tmetuchl's response odd and asked him why the timely repayment of loans distressed him. Tmetuchl joked, tellingly perhaps, that he did not want his money back but rather the land that had been offered as collateral in support of the loan. Nakayama proved an asset to the Bank of Guam in the region, though financial irregularities at the Chuuk branch later led to its temporary closing and to the firing of most of its managerial staff.[90] By all accounts, Nakayama had nothing to do with the branch office's problems or the corrective measures taken to remedy them. Nakayama remained with the Bank of Guam until 2003 when his rapidly failing health forced him to resign.

Back in Chuuk, Nakayama, as he had during his time as president, remained largely apart from the swirling vortex of local Chuukese politics. He did receive visits from candidates for elective office who sought his support. Nakayama met with them, offered counsel and advice, but rarely campaigned or made public endorsements. He didn't think it right. Out of office, Nakayama did not have much contact with the FSM government, and felt largely ignored or forgotten by both the executive and legislative branches. He was not even invited to the opening of the FSM capitol complex at Palikir on Pohnpei in 1991. At the request of President John Haglelgam, Nakayama did travel to Japan in 1989 to represent the national government at the coronation of the new Japanese emperor, Akihito.[91] Nakayama had made numerous trips to Japan over the course of his public career and had met with prime ministers, high government officials, and even Akihito himself when he held the rank of crown prince. The now former president had no doubts that his Japanese ancestry gave him and the FSM access to leaders in Japan. His connections with Japan continued after his presidency. Nakayama served as the president of the Japan–Federated States of Micronesia Parliamentarian Friendship League from its founding in 1991 until 2003.[92] Nakayama's successor as head of the league was Mori Yoshiro, the former prime minister of Japan whose father had served in the army on Chuuk. During the war, the Aizawa family had befriended the older Mori.[93] Years later, Mori Yoshiro met the Aizawa family, kept in regular communication with them thereafter, and came to consider Susumu Aizawa "like a brother in Chuuk."[94]

Nakayama continued to be an avid defender of the FSM's constitution after he left office. The constitution authorizes the calling of a constitutional convention every ten years to consider those areas of constitutional government in need of amendment or change. Convened on Pohnpei, the 1990 convention revisited those issues that had been the most contentious on Saipan.[95] Delegates to the 1990 constitutional convention debated the role of traditional chiefs in the national government; states' rights and powers in relation to the national government as they pertained to taxation, the distribution of revenues, and jurisdiction and control over land and other natural resources; and the right of secession. Tosiwo Nakayama served as a member of the delegation from Chuuk, and brought historical perspective and legislative and executive experience to the deliberations. He intervened during the course of the discussions on the right of secession in defense of the national union. When queried about the continuing need for a chamber of chiefs, an entity acknowledged by the constitution but not yet authorized by the Congress, Nakayama replied, "During my administration, I felt the need for it. I put a request for funding in my budget, but the Congress did not supply the money."[96]

Nakayama's answer overcame the reluctance of skeptics who sought to remove the provision for a chamber of chiefs from the constitution. The convention went on to approve a resolution affirming the importance of the chamber of chiefs to the maintenance of customs and traditions, and calling upon the Congress to enable its functioning. Nakayama had relied heavily on chiefs throughout his political career; they had proven supportive of the FSM Constitution and the Compact of Free Association with the United States, and had backed him during his struggles with the FSM Congress and the Pohnpei State elected leadership. His endorsement of the chamber of chiefs at the 1990 constitutional convention affirmed that relationship. Majorities in the four states remained, however, reluctant to assign their traditional leaders a formal place in the national government. In the end, none of the proposed amendments to the FSM Constitution earned the 75 percent voter approval required for ratification in the popular referendum that followed. The results, in part, reaffirmed the wisdom and compromise that had combined to forge the original draft constitution; the high voter endorsement required for the approval of any constitutional amendment, coupled with the divisions and differences over the issues in question, also explained the failure of any of the proposed amendments to pass.

A second constitutional convention in 2001 proposed a sweeping series of amendments that centered largely on state versus national jurisdiction, the powers of Congress, and election reforms at the national level.[97] As with the amendments proposed at the 1990 constitutional convention, none of the amendments from the 2001 gathering won ratification.[98] With his health already failing, Nakayama did not participate in the 2001 convention. He took satisfaction in its outcome, however. Tosiwo Nakayama did not believe the 1975 constitutional convention had produced a perfect document. He felt time would show what adjustments and changes would be needed, and there were in place procedures for that review and ratification process. Nakayama believed too that with each passing decade the nation would mature, develop a clearer sense of itself, and become stronger and more unified. The fates of the different amendments mattered less than the process. What satisfied him most was the care and consideration that had characterized the whole undertaking; he found reassurance in the selecting of delegates, the convening of the conventions, the deliberations over proposed amendments, and the decision of the people of the Federated States of Micronesia as evidenced in the results of the referendums.

## Pain and Loss

At 56, Nakayama was certainly not an old man when he stepped down from the presidency. The physical toll his public career had taken on his health began to show all too quickly, however.[99] In 1992, he suffered his first stroke from which he eventually recovered. He was taken by stretcher to the Chuuk Airport and put on board a flight to Honolulu. There, he spent a week in Straub Hospital and then another two months as an outpatient relearning how to speak, walk, and regain the use of other motor skills. He made a significant recovery, though the stroke slowed his speech, affected his memory, and weakened his left side. In 1998, he experienced chest pains and shortness of breath, and was advised to seek medical treatment outside of Chuuk. He requested travel assistance to Guam from the FSM national government, but never received a reply.[100] With daughters Rosemary and Sydnina, he traveled at his own expense to Guam where doctors referred him to Hawai'i. At Queen's Hospital in Honolulu, he underwent quadruple bypass surgery.[101] During recovery, he declined painkillers, insisting to shocked nurses that he did not need or want the medicine.[102] Nakayama was discharged from the hospital three days after surgery and moved to an apartment building near the hospital. He covered the considerable costs of surgery and convalescence in Honolulu with his own funds. What medical coverage he had through the Bank of Guam ended earlier when the bank's health insurance provider went bankrupt. A third trip to Honolulu for laser eye surgery at Queen's Hospital left him partially blind in one eye, a consequence that Nakayama himself thought grounds for a malpractice suit. He could not find anyone willing to take his case, however.

Nakayama's health problems were compounded by the loss of his wife.

Miter passed away on 11 September 1999. Her health had been a subject of concern throughout much of her adult life. Hiroshi Ismael had served as her attending physician at times when congressional business brought the Nakayamas and Ismaels together.[103] Raised a Protestant, Miter had converted to Catholicism as a condition of her marriage to Tosiwo. Over the course of her adult life, she became a devout Catholic. Miter was returning from a trip to Rome and an audience with the Pope when she learned of the death of her adopted daughter Soncy.[104] Upon landing at Chuuk, she went straight to the funeral, having slept or eaten little since learning of Soncy's passing. The shock of her daughter's death and the strain of the funeral took their toll on a body already weakened by diabetes. A scan at the Chuuk State hospital showed her kidneys to be swollen. The absence of the hospital's resident physician due to a family crisis precluded any immediate medical treatment. With her own family gathering in support, Miter was returned to the family compound above Nantaku. Around 6:00 a.m. on the morning of 11 September, Rosemary, now the Nakayamas' eldest child, woke her father to tell him that Miter's breathing had become shallow. A priest was called—the one who had accompanied Miter and others to Rome—to administer last rites. Miter died shortly after the administration of the sacrament. Thousands of people attended her funeral in the village of Mwan at the communal house of the Sópwunupi clan. It was one of the largest gatherings seen on the island in years. A funeral mass followed at Holy Family Church in Nepukos after which Miter was laid to rest outside of the Nakayama family home in Mwan near the grave of Tosiwo's father, Masami.

Tosiwo Nakayama also confronted a number of personal and painful problems resulting from the activities or conduct of family members. Sasauo Gouland, Nakayama's brother-in-law, faced impeachment over the misuse of government funds and was forced to resign the governorship in 1991. This was not the first time that Gouland had run afoul of the law. In 1986, during an earlier and unsuccessful run for the Chuuk governorship, Gouland was charged by the FSM attorney general's office with receiving reimbursements between October 1982 and June 1984 for the use of a car rented from a local car rental agency owned by Nakayama's oldest son Rodney.[105] The car in question actually belonged to Gouland. Under threat of prosecution, Gouland agreed to repay the government the money he had falsely claimed. Nakayama refrained from interfering and gave his attorney general's office free rein in pursuing the charges. Nakayama was an exceptionally honest leader; he was not involved in any questionable dealing or transaction during his public career. Unlike many of his colleagues, he refused to use public office for financial gain or commercial advantage. The later indictment of his daughter Rosemary and his son-in-law John Engichy proved even more personal and painful.

The eldest surviving child after the passing of Soncy, Rosemary, had first been married to Sammy Mori who died of liver disease while still a young man. Sammy's death left Rosemary with five children. Against the particularly strong objections of her mother, Rosemary then married John Engichy, the younger half brother of Kalisto Refalopei. Miter's objections resulted not from the fact that Engichy was the half brother of one of her husband's opponents, but rather that Engichy was not a Catholic.[106] Despite the objection, John and Mary entered into a common-law marriage, raised a family, and managed several business enterprises on Weno, including Island Import and the Merry Sand Mining Company. On 11 November 2003, John and Rosemary Engichy were indicted in the FSM Supreme Court along with thirteen other people in the theft of more than $1.2 million in government funds.[107]

Among those indicted were three sitting Chuukese congressmen, several state officials, and a number of local businessmen. Criminal charges included money laundering, bribery, theft, corruption, conflict of interest, conspiracy, and the obligating of government funds for purposes other than allotted. The indictment alleged that the defendants collaborated in an elaborate scheme to defraud the government. A year earlier, Jack Fritz, a long-standing opponent of Nakayama, had been indicted on charges of fraud, criminal solicitation, and the theft of government funds.[108] Fritz was found guilty; in August of 2004, he was sentenced to a one-year suspended prison term, required to pay a $4,000 fine, and forced to resign his seat in the Congress.[109] The trials of John and Rosemary and their codefendants would drag on for several years before all were eventually found guilty.[110] In the interim, tensions ran high and the political environment became highly charged in the Federated States of Micronesia.

Some partisan observers saw in the legal filings against Jack Fritz, the three FSM congressmen, and the eleven other defendants a strong prejudice against Chuukese. Henry Asugar of Chuuk, the floor leader for the FSM Congress, had introduced a bill that granted amnesty "to certain classes of people who are now being accused, or yet to be accused, or who have been prosecuted of certain types of crimes against the sovereignty of the Federated States of Micronesia, but not yet convicted, and for other purposes."[111] There resulted a prolonged series of legal maneuverings as members of the Chuuk congressional delegation sought to disqualify the presiding judge in the case involving the three congressmen, the Engichys, and others, and to have the prosecuting attorneys in the government's case against Jack Fritz declared persona non grata.[112] The divisions within Micronesia that Tosiwo Nakayama had so skillfully negotiated were once again showing themselves and threatening to dissolve the union. Moreover, two of his family members were principals in the crisis.

General criticism of the amnesty bill focused on the abuse of power and privilege by a Chuukese-dominated Congress whose members had already compromised the appropriations process to serve their political purposes.[113] Critics charged that the bill, in its efforts to place members of Congress beyond the reach of the law for any past, present, or future wrongdoings, threatened to undermine the constitution. Others saw yet the most recent visible manifestation of long-standing problems in Chuuk involving corruption and the misuse of public funds. One of the most upsetting features of the amnesty bill was the implication that the misuse of public funds was rampant throughout the FSM and that to call attention to Chuuk was to miss the ocean for the island.[114] In short, the authors of the bill were arguing that a large percentage of high officials would be implicated if the government decided to prosecute all the wrongdoers. To prosecute only Chuukese was patently discriminatory.

To further their argument, Chuukese legislators in January 2004 proposed two other resolutions; one, CR 13–80, would have created a special congressional committee to investigate corruption in the executive branch of the government, presumably starting with the president and vice president.[115] CR 13–73 requested the president conduct an investigation into the purchase of land for the College of Micronesia's Chuuk campus. The intended target of this inquiry was Vice President Redley Killion of Chuuk who had sold the land to the college and who some members of the Chuukese congressional delegation believed to be actively encouraging the indictments and prosecutions to his own political advantage. For many outside analysts, the issues surrounding the misuse of public funds and the local political tensions that they engendered only served to underscore the necessity for the strict monitoring of federal funding that the United States government had written into the 2003 extension of the Compact of Free Association with the Federated States of Micronesia.

The threat posed to national unity from the amnesty bill was even more ominous. The Yap State government let it be known that approval of the bill jeopardized Yap's continued participation in the Federated States of Micronesia.[116] Members of the Pohnpei State Legislature expressed their strong concerns, and the governor contemplated a special meeting with the island's traditional leaders to consider a number of possible responses.[117] Testimony against the bill at public hearings proved particularly strong. In the end, the bill was defeated and tensions subsided. The amnesty bill brought to the floor concerns about Chuuk and its relationship to the national polity. In the eyes of more than a few observers both within and beyond these islands called Micronesia, Chuuk offered the ultimate irony; it was at once the home to several of the earliest and most capable FSM leaders, including Tosiwo Nakayama and Andon Amaraich, and also the source of decisive tensions that threatened the unity of the country. The congressional chambers in Palikir had served as a stage for the playing out of intense political rivalries within Chuuk, and between Chuuk and the rest of the FSM.

Deteriorating health had prevented Tosiwo Nakayama from weighing in on a problem with which he was all too familiar. Had he been able, his intervention would have come down decidedly in defense of the FSM, and against the partisan and local politics that were once again threatening to cripple it. A weakened heart necessitated yet another medical trip to Honolulu and surgery to have a pacemaker implanted. This was in 2005. Three days after the surgery, he suffered a stroke that left him paralyzed and unable to speak but fully cognizant.[118] He spent the last two years of his life under the watchful care of family at an apartment in Waipahu, a former plantation town on the island of Oʻahu. Tosiwo Nakayama passed away on 29 March 2007 at the Hawaii Medical Center–West in Waipahu. His passing attracted international comment and resulted in numerous expressions of condolence across the Pacific region. The outpouring of grief was especially strong among those who knew him personally and worked for him professionally. Ieske Iehsi, a special assistant to Nakayama during his second administration, called him "a statesman like I've never seen…so humble and yet a great leader…I am at a loss to explain how deeply I felt about the man." In response to a question about Nakayama's greatest accomplishment, Iehsi answered, "It was his steadfast determination to bring [the] FSM to self-government in spite of the odds."[119]

A memorial mass was held at Our Lady of Good Counsel Church in Pearl City, Hawaiʻi on 11 April. Members of the Chuukese community on Oʻahu filled the pews. A local choir sang hymns, while family members, friends, and former colleagues read appropriately themed selections from Isaiah, Corinthians, and the Gospel of John. There had been initial talk of a state funeral on Pohnpei, but logistical concerns and the preferences of the family resulted in the selection of Chuuk. Nakayama's body was flown from Honolulu to Chuuk on 14 April. The Continental Airlines flight extended its stopovers on Majuro and Pohnpei so that people on those islands could pay their respects and meet with members of the Nakayama family who were accompanying the former president back to Chuuk.[120]

Upon reaching Chuuk on 14 April, the body of Tosiwo Nakayama lay in repose at the family compound above Nantaku where mourners came to offer their condolences to the family. On the morning of the 17th, a procession took Tosiwo Nakayama's body to the Sarem en Chuuk Hall near his first family home in Mwan Village. A service of tributes and remembrances followed. FSM president Joseph Urusemal and Chuuk governor Wesley Simina gave welcoming remarks. Former FSM president Leo Falcam, FSM Congress Speaker Peter

Christian, and James Stovall of the FSM Embassy in Washington, D.C., all spoke. Masao Nakayama, Tosiwo's younger brother and the FSM ambassador to Japan, concluded the tributes and remembrances with words of appreciation and gratitude from the family to those gathered. Bethwel Henry delivered the eulogy. The body was then taken to the Holy Family Catholic Church in Nepukos for a funeral mass. Internment followed at Mwan where Tosiwo Nakayama was laid to rest near his wife Miter and his father Masami. In a sense, things had come full circle. Nakayama had returned to the island that had adopted, elected, and then resisted him. The tributes would have made this quiet, humble, self-effacing man uncomfortable. An island nation still very much in the process of becoming had stopped to honor the individual most responsible for its founding. Though many from beyond still struggle to understand the area called "Micronesia" as anything more than a collection of small, seemingly insignificant islands, there was nothing small or insignificant about Tosiwo Nakayama, what he did, and how he viewed the world.

Nakayama was certainly not without his critics. There were those cynics who regarded the move toward independent self-government as nothing more than Micronesians playing at decision making. Others wrongfully described him as more a politician than a leader. Somewhat more sympathetic observers viewed Nakayama as well-intentioned, but ultimately rendered ineffective as a chief executive by the internally flawed distribution of governing power in the FSM that favored the states over the national government, and by the fact that any president's most immediate and most difficult constituency is the Congress that elects him. Critics also regarded Nakayama as having been naïve about the problems of creating a national government out of a disparate collection of islands and through negotiations with a world power that was always intent on "staying while leaving."[121] Perhaps, but then people with vision are often seen as naïve. Had Nakayama listened to his detractors, there would be no Federated States of Micronesia.

## A Yet-to-Be-Written Postscript

There is a yet-to-be written postscript to Nakayama's life, his commitment to modernity, and his efforts in behalf of the creation of the Federated States of Micronesia. The political entity that Tosiwo Nakayama helped create persists, but not without its problems. The FSM has certainly had its successes. Since its beginnings in 1979, the island nation has secured diplomatic relationships with key nations in the Asia and Pacific region. It is a member of the United Nations and the South Pacific Forum, and a signee to the Law of the Sea Treaty. It has also made its voice heard on key environmental concerns. There are, however, gross disparities that are perpetuated by the Compact of Free Association. The first compact between the two governments contained provisions that allowed the United States government to audit FSM government expenditures of compact funds. These provisions have been strengthened by the terms of the revised compact agreed to by the two governments in 2003. The revised compact establishes a Joint Economic Management Committee (JEMCO) made up of five members—three Americans and two Micronesians. The committee is based in Honolulu and has the right of final review, approval, and authorization of all compact funds appropriated by the U.S. Congress. Many, including former FSM president John Haglelgam, Tosiwo Nakayama's immediate successor, have termed this arrangement a serious infringement on the sovereignty of the nation.[122] The added oversight came at the insistence of the United States government representatives who had expressed dismay at what they understood as the waste, inefficiency, mismanagement, and corruption that had characterized the use of funds from the first compact.

Critics also note that the infusion of monies through compacts I and II brought little in the way of economic development; the FSM remains heavily dependent on American congressional appropriations and on other forms of foreign aid. The migration of Micronesians from the islands to Guam, Hawai'i, and the North American continent appears to some as testament to the failure of the nation-state experiment that is the FSM. Equally ominous is the Mutual Security Pact, one of several appendices that were a part of the first compact signed by the United States and the FSM; it gives to the United States in perpetuity defense rights and responsibilities over the islands, and access to the lands and seas of the islands in times of emergency as determined by the United States.

There are other, more internal barriers to the long-term sustainability of the Federated States of Micronesia. Over time, the Congress of the Federated States of Micronesia has established itself as the arbiter and dispenser of local development funds to the states, and in a way that promotes the power and incumbency of congressmen. Chuuk State's bankruptcy, its mismanagement of both development and aid monies, its chronic political in-fighting, and the failings of many of its elected and appointed officials have intensified tensions, prompted talk of dissolution, and led the other three states to project alternative political futures. The aforementioned auditing and oversight requirements of the revised Compact of Free Association between the United States and the FSM have led to the further bureaucratization of government and reliance on an expanded list of aid donors that include foreign governments, regional organizations, and international agencies and banks. Some argue that Nakayama's FSM compromised itself from the very beginning by adopting uncritically the organization, structures, and functions of the old Trust Territory government.

How, then to assess, the life and career of Tosiwo Nakayama? By all accounts, he was a fine, humble, honest, and extremely patient man with a marked talent for bringing people together and building consensus toward a common cause. It is no stretch of the imagination to say that were it not for Tosiwo Nakayama, the Federated States of Micronesia would never have come into being. He had done everything possible to promote national unity and self-government for island peoples who had long lived under a succession of colonial administrations. In his final address before the FSM Congress, Nakayama identified patience, endurance, confidence, and resiliency as Micronesian virtues.[123] They were certainly among his. A final assessment of his public career awaits the still-to-be-determined fate of the nation he helped make. What then is the state of the Federated States of Micronesia in the early decades of the twenty-first century?

Josh Levy writes of the FSM as a profoundly different entity from the sort of political and cultural grouping once desired by the American colonial administration.[124] It is not recognizable solely in terms of Western nationalism but should be understood rather against a broader Hauʻofian process of enlargement—a contemporary network of interdependency that includes the Compact of Free Association, a large and growing Micronesian expatriate population, and the remittances they send home. While the boundaries are fluid, local autonomies and identities have persisted in areas beyond the territorial borders of the FSM, and in ways that have proven flexible, adaptive, and viable. Still, another way to assess the FSM, outside of an exclusively nation-state model, is to think of it as the product of deeper historical patterns and forces that predate colonialism. The issues of navigation and voyaging, and Tosiwo Nakayama's relationship to them, come into play here. As noted at the start of this life history, the term "navigator" certainly applies to the life of Tosiwo Nakayama. Nakayama himself came from a family of navigators and at a critical juncture in his adult life seriously considered abandoning his public career to study traditional navigation techniques. His uncle Raatior and granduncle Opich were highly regarded *palu* or navigators who belonged to the same school of navigation—*weriyeng*—as Mau Piailug of Satawal and Hipour of Polowat. Voyaging had enabled the settlement of the islands and allowed for communication and exchange thereafter. The *sawei* exchange system, with its center on Yap, had stretched to islands as far east as Namonuito Atoll, Nakayama's birthplace. Indeed, there is the larger, centuries-old Carolinian or Chuukic continuum of languages and dialects that stretches from Tobi in the west to the Lower Mortlocks in the east, is inclusive of the former *sawei*, and rests at the geographical core of the Federated States of Micronesia.

The canoe was Nakayama's oft-used metaphor for the FSM. We might then regard the FSM as not only the product of a navigational tradition but as itself a voyaging canoe that should be understood in terms of larger circumstances and conditions that necessitate decisions regarding routes, timing, tacking, respites, repairs, and re-provisioning needed to ensure the success of a long, arduous, and ongoing voyage of survival and possibility. In any event, a postscript to the life of Tosiwo Nakayama involves the future of the FSM that, in turn, may require us to see the FSM as something other than a nation-state within the limiting framework of Euro-American understandings of nationalism. Despite the predictions of its disintegration, the FSM persists. Whether or not it survives as a viable political entity, only time will tell. If it falters and fails, it will be in spite of the prodigious efforts of one of its founders. What is remarkable about the life of Tosiwo Nakayama was the reach and range of his efforts, and the expansiveness of his vision. "Macronesia," not "Micronesia," seems a more appropriate term for the world he inhabited and tried to make accessible to others.

# Notes

Introduction: Writing a Biography of Tosiwo Nakayama

1   I draw here on Epeli Hau'ofa's *We Are the Ocean: Selected Works* (Honolulu: University of Hawai'i Press, 2008), and Paul D'Arcy's *The People of the Sea: Environment, Identity, and History* (Honolulu: University of Hawai'i Press, 2006).

2   I authored an earlier book, *Remaking Micronesia: Discourses over Development in a Pacific Territory, 1944–1982* (Honolulu: University of Hawai'i Press, 1998), in which I sought to chart these colonial constructions. Responsibility for any confusion between the titles of this book and that earlier volume is mine.

3   P. F. Kluge, *The Edge of Paradise: America in Micronesia* (New York: Random House, 1991), p. 105.

4   Ibid.

5   Congress of Micronesia, Joint Committee on Future Status, *Hearings of the Eastern Districts Subcommittee (Truk, Ponape, and the Marshalls)*. Fifth Congress (Saipan, Mariana Islands: Trust Territory Government Press, November 1973), p. 121.

6   Antonio Gramsci, *Selections from the Prison Notebooks,* edited and translated by Quentin Hoare and Nowell Smith (London; Lawrence and Wishart, 1971), p. 12.

7   I am making reference here to V. S. Naipaul's *The Mimic Men* (London: Deutsch, 1967).

8   Ranajit Guha, *Elementary Aspects of Peasant Insurgency in Colonial India* (Delhi: Oxford University Press, 1983), pp. 333–334.

9   Francis X. Hezel, S.J., *The First Taint of Civilization: A History of the Caroline and Marshall Islands in Pre-Colonial Days, 1521–1885,* Pacific Islands Monograph Series no. 1 (Honolulu: University of Hawai'i Press, 1983), p. 197.

10  Congress of Micronesia, *Journal of the Senate,* Third Congress, third special session, 12 January to 30 January 1970 (Saipan: Trust Territory Government Press 1970), p. 101.

11  Interview, Andon Amaraich, Kolonia, Pohnpei, 29 May 2003.

12  For more on the concept of mósónósón, see Ward H. Goodenough, *Property, Kin, and Community on Truk,* second edition (Hamden, CT: Archon Books, 1978), pp. 142–145.

13  Frank Rosario and John M. Simpson, "U.S. Bribe Attempt in Truk Hotly Debated," *Micronesian Support Committee Bulletin* 5:3–4 (Fall/Winter 1980): 16.

14  Mark R. Peattie, *Nan'yō: The Rise and Fall of the Japanese in Micronesia, 1885–1945.* Pacific Islands Monograph, no. 4 (Honolulu: University of Hawai'i Press, 1988), p. 189.


Chapter 1: A World of Islands

1   These introductory paragraphs borrow from my earlier work; see Hanlon, *Remaking Micronesia* (Honolulu: University of Hawai'i Press, 1998), pp. 1–2.

2   For a consideration of the colonial politics that informed the naming of these islands, see David Hanlon, "The 'Sea of Little Lands': Examining Micronesia's Place in 'Our Sea of Islands,'" *The Contemporary Pacific* 21:1 (2009): 91–110. The most recent argument for Micronesia as a coherent and unified cultural entity can be found in Glenn Petersen, *Traditional Micronesian Societies: Adaptation, Integration, and Political Organization* (Honolulu: University of Hawai'i Press, 2009).

3   Hezel, *The First Taint of Civilization* (Honolulu: University of Hawai'i Press, 1983), p. xi.

4   Greg Dening, Review of *Marists and Melanesians* by Hugh Laracy, *New Zealand Journal of History* 12 (1978): 82.

5   John Byron Thomas, "Adoption, Filiation, and Matrilineal Descent on Namonuito Atoll, Caroline Islands" (PhD dissertation, University of Hawai'i at Mānoa, 1978), p. 18.

6   Epeli Hau'ofa, "Our Sea of Islands," in his *We Are the Ocean: Selected Works* (Honolulu, University of Hawai'i Press, 2008), p. 32.

7   Willard C. Muller, *Faces of the Islands: When Pacific Islander and American*

*Ways Meet* (Port Angeles, WA: Lincoln Square Publishing Company, 2002), p. 189.

8 Cited in Thomas, 1978, p. 28.

9 Thomas Gladwin, *East Is a Big Bird: Navigation & Logic on Puluwat Atoll* (Cambridge, MA: Harvard University Press, 1970), pp. 34–35.

10 Thomas Gladwin and Seymour B. Sarason, *Truk: Man in Paradise,* Viking Fund Publication in Anthropology no. 20 (New York: Wenner-Gren Foundation for Anthropological Research, Inc., 1950), p. 36.

11 Hanlon, 2009, p. 103.

12 This description and analysis of the *sawei* exchange system draws from William Akire, *An Introduction to the Peoples and Cultures of Micronesia* (Menlo Park, CA: Cummings Publishing Company, 1977), pp. 49–53; and "Technical Knowledge and the Evolution of Political Systems in the Central and Western Caroline Islands of Micronesia," *Canadian Journal of Anthropology* 1:2 (1980): 229–237. See also Paul D'Arcy, *The People of the Sea* (Honolulu: University of Hawai'i Press, 2006), pp. 146–147; Rosalind Hunter-Anderson and Yigal Zan, "Demystifying the *Sawei,* a Traditional Interisland Exchange System," *Isla* 4 (1996): 1–45; Patrick Vinton Kirch, *On the Road of the Winds: An Archaeological History of the Pacific Islands before European Contact* (Berkeley: University of California Press, 2000), pp. 191–193; Sherwood Lingenfelter, *Yap: Political Leadership and Culture Change in an Island Society* (Honolulu: University Press of Hawai'i, 1975), pp. 147–155; Eric Metzger, "Carolinian Voyaging in the New Millennium," *Micronesian Journal of the Humanities and Social Sciences* 5:1&2 (2006): 294–295; and Petersen, 2009, pp. 34–35.

13 D'Arcy, 2006, p. 152.

14 Julianna Flinn, *Diplomas and Thatch Houses: Asserting Tradition in a Changing Micronesia* (Ann Arbor: University of Michigan Press, 1995), p. 153.

15 Ibid., pp. 153–154; see also D'Arcy, 2006, p. 156.

16 Thomas, 1978, p. 29.

17 Ibid., p. 29.

18 D'Arcy, 2006, pp. 156–163.

19 Thomas, 1978, p. 28; D'Arcy, 2006, p. 162, puts the number of people recruited from Namonuito at 1,234.

20 Jeff Marck, "Some Clan Names of the Chuukic-Speaking Peoples of Micronesia," 2008, p. 29, www.jeffmarck.net/publications/MarckClansChk.pdf.

21 Interview, Tosiwo Nakayama, Weno, Chuuk, 29 December 2000. See also Marck, 2008, p. 6.

22 Interview, Tosiwo Nakayama, Weno, Chuuk, 29 December 2000.

23 Petersen, 2009, p. 22.

24  Interview, Joseph Urusemal, Palikir, Pohnpei, 23 May 2003.

25  Interview, Tosiwo Nakayama, Weno, Chuuk, 29 December 2000.

26  Muller, 2002, pp. 174–175.

27  Ibid., p. 175.

28  Interview, Polycarp Basilius, Koror, Palau, 17 July 2002. See also "Congress Shipping Committee Ends Tour," *Highlights*, 1 March 1970, p. 11.

29  Interview, Tosiwo Nakayama, Weno, Chuuk, 29 December 2000. See also "Faichuk Slows Cholera by Cleaning Up Environment," *The National Union*, 15 March 1983, p. 4.

30  Kirch, 2000, p. 167.

31  Marck, 2008, p. 1.

32  Masao Nakayama and Frederick L. Ramp, *Micronesian Navigation, Island Empires and Traditional Concepts of Ownership of the Sea* (Saipan: Study for the Joint Committee of the Law of the Sea Conference, Fifth Congress of Micronesia, 14 January 1974).

33  Manuel Rauchholz, "Notes on Clan Histories and Migration in Micronesia," *Pacific-Asia Inquiry* 2:1 (2011): 62–63.

34  For a description of the physical and political geography of greater Chuuk, see Michael Cain, *A Survey of Historical Sites and Their Association with Oral Histories in Eastern Weno, Chuuk State, Federated States of Micronesia* (Weno: Chuuk State Historic Preservation Office, September 1996).

35  Ibid., p. 4.

36  This account of first contacts between the peoples of the Chuuk Lagoon and those from European shores borrows from Hezel, 1983, pp. 23–25, 82–83, 90–91, 97–101, 248–249, 256–262.

37  Ibid., p. 101.

38  Ibid., p. 257.

39  Ibid., p. 197.

40  Francis X. Hezel, S.J., *Strangers in Their Own Land: A Century of Colonial Rule in the Caroline and Marshall Islands*, Pacific Islands Monograph Series no. 13 (Honolulu: University of Hawai'i Press, 1995), p. 63.

41  Interview, Tosiwo Nakayama, Weno, Chuuk, 29 December 2000. See also Peattie, *Nan'yō: The Rise and Fall of the Japanese in Micronesia, 1885–1945* (Honolulu: University of Hawai'i Press, 1988), p. 316.

42  This account of Mori Koben's life comes from Peattie, 1988, pp. 26–33, and Hezel, 1995, 77–79.

43  For a review of the German colonial period in Chuuk and the larger Micronesian geographical area, see Hezel, 1995, pp. 94–145.

44  Ibid., p. 101.

45 Thomas, 1998, p. 30.

46 For a study of the Japanese colonial period in the Caroline, Mariana, and Marshall Islands, see Peattie, 1998; also Hezel, 1995, pp. 146–241.

47 "In Memoriam: Masami Nakayama," *Truk Chronicle* 1:11 (24 August 1979), p. 7.

48 The *Truk Chronicle*'s obituary for Nakayama Masami reported that he had four brothers and one sister. In an interview on 29 December 2000, Tosiwo Nakayama spoke of his father as having three brothers and one sister, but named only two of the male siblings. Later, in that interview, he mentioned the visit of his father's "brother or cousin" to Chuuk after the war started. At this time, the family was living on Tol. This individual, said Nakayama, perished when the ship carrying him back to Japan was attacked and sunk by an American naval vessel. Peattie, 1988, pp. 277–278, describes the disruption to Japanese shipping caused by American air and sea attacks; his account includes a number of specific sinkings, though with no information that helps identify the lost ship carrying the possible Nakayama relative.

49 This reconstruction of Nakayama Masami's life derives from interviews with Tosiwo Nakayama at Weno, Chuuk, on 29 December 2000.

50 "In Memoriam: Masami Nakayama," p. 7.

51 Interviews, Tosiwo Nakayama, Weno, Chuuk, 29 December 2000 and 3 January 2001.

52 On education under the Japanese, see Peattie, 1988, pp. 90–96.

53 Interview, Tosiwo Nakayama, Weno, Chuuk, 3 January 2001.

54 "President Gets Message on Mortlocks Trip," *The National Union,* 15 August 1981, p. 5.

55 Interview, Tosiwo Nakayama, Weno, Chuuk, 29 December 2000.

56 For a history of the Catholic mission on Lukunor and in the greater Micronesian geographical region, see Francis X. Hezel, S.J., *The Catholic Church in Micronesia: Historical Essays on the Catholic Church in the Caroline-Marshall Islands,* Micronesian Seminar (Chicago: Loyola University Press, 1991), pp. 123–139.

57 In an interview on 29 December 2000, Nakayama identified the Capuchin brother as Herswick. Hezel, 1991, pp. 134 and 185, lists Aniceto Arizaleta as the only Capuchin brother working on Lukunor during the period that the Nakayamas were resident there.

58 Interview, Tosiwo Nakayama, Weno, Chuuk, 3 January 2001.

59 Interview, Tosiwo Nakayama, Weno, Chuuk, 29 December 2000.

60 Interview, Joakim Peter, Weno, Chuuk, 1 August 2002.

Chapter 2: Japanese Times

1    This section draws heavily from Peattie, 1988, pp. 34–36, and Hezel, 1995, pp. 146–149.

2    On early U.S. relations with Japan, see Akira Iriye, *Pacific Estrangement: Japanese and American Expansion, 1897–1911* (Cambridge, MA: Harvard University Press, 1972); also *Across the Pacific: An Inner History of American-East Asian Relations,* revised edition (Chicago: Imprint Publications, 1992).

3    For the American position on Japan's formal acquisition of the Caroline, Mariana, and Marshall Islands from Germany at the 1919 Paris Peace Conference, see George Blakeslee, "Japan's New Island Possessions in the Pacific: History and Present," *Journal of International Relations* 12:2 (1921): 98–115; Russell H. Fifield, "Disposal of the Carolines, Marshalls, and Marianas at the Paris Peace Conference," *American Historical Review* 51 (April 1946): 472–479; Frank Ikle, "Japanese-German Peace Negotiations During World War I," *American Historical Review* 71 (October 1966): 62–76; Werner Levi, "American Attitudes Toward Pacific Islands, 1914–1919," *Pacific Historical Review* 17:1 (February 1948): 55–64; Earl Pomeroy, "American Policy Respecting the Marshalls, Carolines, and Marianas 1898–1941," *Pacific Historical Review* 17:1 (February 1948): 43–53; and Charles Schencking, "Bureaucratic Politics, Military Budgets, and Japan's Southern Advance: The Imperial Navy's Seizure of German Micronesia in the First World War," *War in History* 5:3 (1998): 308–326.

4    On the Japanese Navy's administration of the Caroline, Mariana, and Marshall Islands, see Peattie, 1988, pp. 64–68, and Hezel, 1995, pp. 149–156.

5    Japan's civilian administration of its Mandate Islands is described in Hezel, 1995, pp. 166–180, and Peattie, 1988, pp. 68–80. See also Paul H. Clyde, *Japan's Mandate Islands* (New York: Macmillan Company, 1935); Willard Price, *Japan's Islands of Mystery* (New York: John Day, 1944); and Tadao Yanaihara, *Pacific Islands Under Japanese Mandate* (London: Oxford University Press, 1938).

6    Japan's efforts at development in its Mandate Islands is described by Peattie, 1988, pp. 118–152, and Hezel, 1995, pp. 180–185, 194–206.

7    Japanese immigration to the islands is addressed by Peattie, 1988, pp. 153–197, and Hezel, 1995, pp. 186–194.

8    On Japanese policy and attitudes toward the native peoples of the Mandate Islands, see Peattie, 1988, pp. 111–112. Race relations are covered on pp. 216–221. See also Hezel, 1995, pp. 206–214.

9    Both Peattie, 1988, pp. 90–96, and Hezel, 1995, pp. 172–174, provide a summary and critique of Japanese educational policies in the Mandate Islands.

10   Hezel, 1995, p. 172.

11   Ibid., pp. 186–188, describes economic activity in Chuuk, both before and after the arrival of Okinawan immigrants. See also Peattie, 1988, pp. 180–184.

12   Cited in Peattie, 1988, p. 211; also Hezel, 1995, p. 201.

13   "In Memoriam: Masami Nakayama," *Truk Chronicle,* 24 August 1979, p. 7. A chronological outline of Tosiwo Nakayama's life prepared by the FSM government lists his residence on Toloas as being from 1939 to 1942. A copy of this document is in the possession of the author.

14   Interview, Tosiwo Nakayama, Weno, Chuuk, 29 December 2000, and 3 January 2001.

15   Interview, Tosiwo Nakayama, Weno, Chuuk, 3 January 2001.

16   Ibid.

17   The militarization of the islands and the debate about when preparations for war actually began are addressed extensively in Peattie, 1988, pp. 220–256, and Hezel, 1995, pp. 214–224.

18   This account of the fortification of Chuuk borrows from Hezel, 1995, pp. 218–222. See also Peattie, 1988, pp. 251–253, and Lin Poyer, Suzanne Falgout, and Laurence Marshall Carucci, *The Typhoon of War: Micronesian Experiences of the Pacific War* (Honolulu: University of Hawai'i Press, 2001), pp. 48–50.

19   P. F. Kluge, a Peace Corps volunteer who worked with Nakayama as a public relations officer in the Congress of Micronesia and later wrote the preamble to what became the constitution of the Federated States of Micronesia, describes Nakayama as having sailed as a young boy around the *Yamato* and the *Musashi* when they were at anchor in the Chuuk Lagoon. See Kluge, 1991, p. 91.

20   Hezel, 1995, p. 226.

21   Peattie, 1988, pp. 263–265, details the intensification of military preparations on Chuuk and the effects on its people following the outbreak of war between Japan and the United States. See also Poyer, Falgout, and Carucci, 2001, pp. 81–84.

22   Hezel, 1995, pp. 226–227, 239–240.

23   Interview, Tosiwo Nakayama, Weno, Chuuk, 3 January 2001.

24   Peattie, 1988, p. 240.

25   Accounts of Operation Hailstone can be found in Peattie, 1988, pp. 274–275, and Hezel, 1995, pp. 232–234. For an account of Chuukese experiences during Operation Hailstone and the bombing that followed, see Poyer, Falgout, and Carucci, 2001, pp. 138–145.

26   Peattie, 1988, p. 277.

27  Interview, Tosiwo Nakayama, Weno, Chuuk, 29 December 2000.

28  Ibid. Nakayama's account is similar to that of another Chuukese boy, Kimiuo Aisek, described in Hezel, 1995, pp. 232–233. In an interview on 30 December 2000, Nakayama said he did not know Aisek.

29  For an account of the terror and hardships experienced by Chuukese and other islanders during American bombing raids, see Poyer, Falgout, and Carucci, 2001, pp. 144–154.

30  Ibid., p. 147.

31  Quoted in ibid., p. 153.

32  Ibid.

33  Hezel, 1995, p. 240.

34  Ibid.

35  Poyer, Falgout, and Carucci, 2001, p. 179.

36  Ibid., p. 179.

37  Ibid., p. 211.

38  Ibid., p. 33.

39  Ibid., p. 210; see also Peattie, 1988, pp. 218–219.

40  Interview, Tosiwo Nakayama, Weno, Chuuk, 30 December 2000.

41  Poyer, Falgout, and Carucci, 2001, p. 207.

42  Ibid., p. 185.

43  Ibid., p. 220.

44  Ibid., p. 225.

45  Ibid., p. 224.

46  Ibid., p. 234; also Hezel, 1995, p. 240.

47  Interview, Tosiwo Nakayama, Weno, Chuuk, 29 December 2000. There is also an account of this encounter in Kluge, 1991, p. 91.

48  Peattie, 1988, pp. 299–300.

49  For an account of the Japanese surrender at Chuuk see Hezel, 1995, pp. 242–244, and Peattie, 1987, pp. 307–308.

50  Poyer, Falgout, and Carucci, 2001, p. 254.

51  Dorothy E. Richard, *United States Naval Administration of the Trust Territory of the Pacific Islands,* vol. 2 (Washington, D.C.: Office of the Chief of Naval Operations, 1957), p. 44.

52  Ibid., p. 38.

53  For accounts of the repatriations of Japanese nationals, see Hezel, 1995, pp. 249–250, and Peattie, 1988, pp. 309–311.

54  Gregory Dvorak has explored the strong social ties that developed between Japanese nationals and the Marshallese over the course of Japan's colonial

administration there, including the war. His important work seeks to displace the master narratives of war with histories of the complex and personal relationships among Marshallese, Japanese, and Americans that are so often elided or suppressed by strictly military accounts of combat and conquest. His research is relevant to other areas of the Mandate, including Chuuk. See his "seeds from afar, flowers from the reef: re-membering the coral and concrete of kwajalein atoll" (PhD dissertation, Australian National University, 2008).

55  Hezel, 1995, pp. 249–250; also Poyer, Falgout, and Carucci, p. 267.

56  Interview, Tosiwo Nakayama, Weno, Chuuk, 29 December 2000. Nakayama guessed the year of his father's repatriation to be 1948 or 1949. In all likelihood, it was 1946.

57  Interview, Tosiwo Nakayama, Weno, Chuuk, 29 December 2000.

58  Poyer, Falgout, and Carucci, 2001, pp. 256–257.

59  Ibid., pp. 273–274.

60  Ibid., p. 321.

61  Ibid., p. 298.

62  Hezel, 1995, pp. 264–270, provides a summary of the U.S. Navy's efforts at governance and economic development in the postwar period to 1947. See also Hanlon, 1998, pp. 26–43.

63  Poyer, Falgout, and Carucci, 2001, pp. 309–311.

64  Ibid., pp. 340–347.

65  Interview, Tosiwo Nakayama, Weno, Chuuk, 29 December 2000.

66  Interview, Tosiwo Nakayama, Weno, Chuuk, 3 January 2001.

67  Quoted in Hanlon, 1988, p. 26.

68  Quoted in Poyer, Falgout, and Carucci, 2001, p. 351.

69  Kluge, 1991, p. 108.

70  Nakayama was quite emphatic about this point in an interview on 29 December 2000 at Weno, Chuuk.

## Chapter 3: An Education

1  For summary histories of the postwar period and the naval administration of the Trust Territory of the Pacific Islands, see Hanlon, 1998, pp. 21–86; Hezel, 1995, pp. 242–270; and Richard, 1957.

2  Quoted in Hanlon, 1998, pp. 34–35.

3  Hezel, 1995, p. 258.

4  Ibid.

5  Ibid., p. 257. For an extremely insightful, sophisticated, and much needed

critique of schooling during the American administration of Micronesia, see David Kupferman, *Disassembling and Decolonizing School in the Pacific: A Genealogy from Micronesia,* Contemporary Philosophies and Theories in Education, vol. 5 (Dordrecht, Netherlands: Springer, 2012).

6 Hezel, 1995, p. 172.

7 Interview, Tosiwo Nakayama, Weno, Chuuk, 29 December 2000.

8 Ibid., 3 January 2001.

9 Ibid., 30 December 2000.

10 Ibid., 29 December 2000.

11 For more on Gladwin's views concerning political development in Chuuk and elsewhere in the Trust Territory, see Glenn Petersen, "Politics in Postwar Micronesia," in Robert C. Kiste and Mac Marshall, eds., *American Anthropology in Micronesia: An Assessment* (Honolulu: University of Hawai‘i Press, 1999), pp. 152–153, 170.

12 Interview, Willard Muller, Honolulu, Hawai‘i, 15 February 2001. Interview, Tosiwo Nakayama, Weno, Chuuk, 29 December 2000.

13 Hezel, 1995, p. 291.

14 Robert Trumbull, *Paradise in Trust: A Report on Americans in Micronesia* (New York: William Sloane, 1959), p. 112.

15 Interview, Tosiwo Nakayama, Weno, Chuuk, 29 December 2000, and 3 January 2001.

16 Ibid., 3 January 2001.

17 Ibid.

18 Ibid., 29 December 2000.

19 Ibid.

20 Ibid., 3 January 2001.

21 This description of Nakayama's responsibilities with the Island Affairs section is found in The Federated States of Micronesia National Archives, Office of Administrative Services (OAS), roll no. 257, item no. 028. A copy of this microfilmed archive is housed with the FSM Office of National Records and Cultural Properties, Palikir, Pohnpei, Federated States of Micronesia.

22 FSM National Archives, Russ Curtis, "Performance Ranking for Micronesians: Tosiwo Nakayama," 6 April 1954, Office of the President (PRES), roll no. 237, item number not listed.

23 Muller, 2002, p. 224.

24 "Scholarship Competition Open," *Micronesian Monthly* 2:1 (November 1952): 6.

25 Interview, Susumu Aizawa, Weno, Chuuk, 30 July 2002.

26 Interview, Daiziro Nakamura, Koror, Palau, 15 July 2002.

27 Material for this section on Nakayama's student days in Hawai'i is drawn from the Micronesian student files maintained by Mrs. Marion Saunders and other members of the University of Hawai'i at Mānoa's International Student office. These files have not been processed or catalogued; they are currently housed in Hamilton Library's Pacific Collection located on the Mānoa campus in Honolulu, Hawai'i, and are used with the permission of the Nakayama family. They can be found in a small gray filing cabinet at the back of the Pacific Collection's private stacks, and consist of 3" × 5" cards and sheets of paper arranged by general subjects and student names.

28 "Tosiwo Nakayama," Micronesian Student Files, University of Hawai'i at Mānoa, 27 September 1957.

29 Interview, Tosiwo Nakayama, Weno, Chuuk, 29 December 2000.

30 University of Hawai'i at Mānoa, "100 Contributions," *The 100th Annual Commencement Exercises Program* (Honolulu: University of Hawai'i at Mānoa, 2011), p. 33.

31 A. R. King, ed. admin. to M. Saunders, "Tosiwo Nakayama," Micronesian Student Files, 23 June 1955.

32 Ibid.

33 "Tosiwo Nakayama," Micronesian Student Files, University of Hawai'i at Mānoa, November 1956.

34 Interview, Soukichy Fritz, Weno, Chuuk, 1 August 2002.

35 "Tosiwo Nakayama," Micronesian Student Files, University of Hawai'i at Mānoa, 8 May 1957; also, interview, Tosiwo Nakayama, Weno, Chuuk, 29 December 2000.

36 Interview, Tosiwo Nakayama, Weno, Chuuk, 29 December 2000.

37 "Tosiwo Nakayama," Micronesian Student Files, University of Hawai'i at Mānoa, 8 May 1957.

38 Interview, Tosiwo Nakayama, Weno, Chuuk, 29 December 2000.

39 Ibid.

40 For a history of the University of Hawai'i, see Robert M. Kamins, Robert E. Potter, and Members of the University Community, *Mālamalama: A History of the University of Hawai'i* (Honolulu: University of Hawai'i Press, 1998).

41 "Personnel File: Tosiwo Nakayama," Federated States of Micronesia, Microfilmed Archives, OAS, reel no. 257, item no. 28.

42 Interview, Daiziro Nakamura, Koror, Palau, 15 July 2002.

43 Interview, Victorio Uherbelau, Koror, Palau, 17 July 2002.

44 See Norman Meller, with the assistance of Terza Meller, *The Congress of Micronesia: Development of the Legislative Process in the Trust Territory of the Pacific Islands* (Honolulu: University of Hawai'i Press, 1969), pp. 22–91,

for a history of American efforts at developing local government in the Trust
Territory of the Pacific Islands; also Hezel, 1995, pp. 276–282.

45  Hanlon, 1998, p. 53.

46  On the development of municipal government in Chuuk, see Meller, 1969,
pp. 47–50.

47  Copies of the proceedings of the Third (29 November to 3 December 1954),
Fourth (17 January to 24 January 1956), Sixth (23 July to 25 July 1957), and
Seventh (11 September to 12 September 1958) Annual Conferences of the
Truk District Council of Magistrates are located in the Hamilton Library's
Pacific Collection on the University of Hawai'i at Mānoa campus, Honolulu,
Hawai'i.

48  Job descriptions for Nakayama's two tours of duty with the Island Affairs
section and his work as a political and economic affairs officer under Russ
Curtis can be found in the FSM National Archives, OAS, reel no. 257, item
no. 028.

49  Muller, 2002, p. 223.

50  Trumbull, 1959, p. 102, notes this practice.

51  "Personnel File: Tosiwo Nakayama," Federated States of Micronesia Microfilmed Archive, OAS, reel no. 258, item no. 028.

52  "Book of Parliamentary Procedures by Education Department," *Truk Review*
II:1 (February/March 1959): 11. See also Thorwald Esbensen, *Puken Nap-
anapan Mwich: A Handbook of Parliamentary Procedure for Truk District
Municipalities and Congress,* translated by Napoleon DeFang (and) Tosiwo
Nakayama, Education Department (Truk District: Literature Production
Center, 1959).

53  Ibid., p. 2.

54  Meller, 1969, p. 56.

55  Information on the agenda, deliberations, and membership of the Truk District Congress can be found in the concurrent issues of the *Truk Review* for
the time period under study. See also the pertinent volumes of the Office
of the High Commissioner, Trust Territory of the Pacific Islands, *Annual
Report of the High Commissioner of the Trust Territory of the Pacific Islands
to the Secretary of the Interior* (Washington, D.C.: United States Government Printing Office, 1950–1979), for additional information on meetings
of the Truk District Congress. The Truk District Congress ends in 1969, and
becomes the Truk District Legislature in 1970.

56  United States Department of State, *12th Annual Report to the United Nations
on the Administration of the Trust Territory of the Pacific Islands, July 1, 1958
to June 30, 1959,* p. 176.

57  Truk District Congress, *Proceedings of the Second Trukese Congress,* 15
September to 19 September 1958, Pacific Collection, Hamilton Library,

University of Hawaiʻi at Mānoa, Honolulu, Hawaiʻi. Also, "Truk Congress Holds Third Session," *Truk Review* II:5 (November 1959): 3; and United States Department of State, 13th *Annual Report to the United Nations on the Administration of the Trust Territory of the Pacific Islands, July 1, 1959 to June 30, 1960,* p. 174.

58 United States Department of the State, *14th Annual Report to the United Nations on the Administration of the Trust Territory of the Pacific Islands, July 1, 1960 to June 30, 1961,* p. 160. See also "The Fourth Truk Dist. Congress," *Truk Review* II:12 (October/November 1960), p. 1.

59 Trumbull, 1959, pp. 117–125.

60 Quoted in Hezel, 1995, p. 290.

61 Interview, Tosiwo Nakayama, Weno, Chuuk, 3 January 2001.

62 Ibid.

63 "Tosiwo Nakayama," Micronesian Student Files, University of Hawaiʻi at Mānoa, 8 May 1957.

64 This account of Petrus Mailo draws heavily from Gladwin, "Chief Petrus Mailo," in *In The Company of Men,* edited by Joseph Casagrande (New York: Harper, 1960), pp. 41–62; see also "Interview: Chief Petrus Mailo," *Micronesian Reporter* 17:4 (1969): 2–5, and 18:1 (1970): 3–7; see also E. J. Kahn, *A Reporter in Micronesia* (New York: Norton, 1966), pp. 114–115; Trumbull, 1959, pp, 90–93; and "Micronesia Mourns Chief Petrus Mailo," *Met Poraus* III:41 (17 September 1971), pp 1–2, and 4.

65 Hanlon, 1998, pp. 73–80. See also Frank J. Mahony, "The Innovation of a Savings System in Truk," *American Anthropologist* 62:3 (June 1960): 465–482.

66 Gladwin, 1960, p. 42.

67 Quoted in Kahn, 1965, p. 114.

68 Hezel, 1995, p. 298.

69 "A Supplication from Chief Petrus," *Met Poraus,* III:15 (13 Feburary 1970): 2, 9.

70 Interview, Susumu Aizawa, Weno Chuuk, 30 July 2002.

71 Gladwin, 1960, p. 48.

72 This assessment of Petrus Mailo was strongly seconded by Andon Amaraich in an interview at Palikir, Pohnpei on 21 May 2003.

73 This biography of Miter Haruo draws from Nick Bossy, "Trukese Women Sweep Election," *Micronesian Reporter* 13:3 (1965): 4–5.

74 Interview, Tosiwo Nakayama, Weno, Chuuk, 3 January 2001.

75 Ibid., 30 December 2000.

76 Interview, Susumu Aizawa, Weno, Chuuk, 30 July 2002.

77 See, for example, The Supreme Court of the Federated States of Microne-

sia, *Chipuelong v. Chuuk,* 6 FSM Intrm. 188 (Chk. S.Ct. Tr. 1993); *Sellem v. Maras,* 7 FSM Intrm. 1 (Chuuk S.Ct. Tr. 1995); and *Sellem v. Maras,* 9 FSM Intrm. 36 (Chuuk S.Ct. App. 1999). Transcripts of these decisions have been collected by the Legal Information System of the Federated States of Micronesia and can be found on line at http://www.fsmlaw.org/fsm/decisions.

78   Statement by Bob Savage, Principal, Intermediate School, Truk, in "Tosiwo Nakayama," Micronesian Student Files, University of Hawai'i at Mānoa, 22 May 1956. Muller learned of the petition and Nakayama's endorsement of it. Muller apparently did not hold a grudge as evidenced by his highly favorable portrayal of Nakayama in his book, *Faces of the Islands.*

79   "Tosiwo Nakayama," Micronesian Student Files, University of Hawai'i at Mānoa, 8 May 1957.

80   Trumbull, 1959, pp. 99–102.

81   Griffin provides this assessment in a foreword to Douglas L. Oliver, ed., *Planning Micronesia's Future: A Summary of the United States Commercial Company's Economic Survey or Micronesia 1946,* rev. ed. (Honolulu: University of Hawai'i Press, 1971), p. ix.

## Chapter 4: Representing Micronesia, 1961–1975

1   For an overview of the first efforts at representative government involving the civilian administrator conferences, the district administrator conferences, and the Inter-District Advisory Committee meetings, see Meller, 1969, pp. 181–196; also Hezel, 1995, pp. 294–296.

2   L.M.T., "Council of Micronesia," *Micronesian Reporter* 9:6 (1961): 1.

3   L.M.T., "Sixth Inter-District Conference Convenes," *Micronesian Reporter* 9:6 (1961): 6–8.

4   "Delegates Welcomed," *Micronesian Reporter* 9:6 (1961): 4.

5   Interview, Tosiwo Nakayama, Weno, Chuuk, 30 December 2000.

6   Elizabeth Udui, "Origin of the Congress of Micronesia," *Micronesian Reporter* 13:2 (1965): 16.

7   "Council of Micronesia Deliberates at Home," *Micronesian Reporter* 10:5 (1962): 6–8.

8   United States Department of State,*16th Annual Report to the United Nations on the Administration of the Trust Territory of the Pacific Islands, July 1, 1962 to June 30, 1963* (Washington, D.C.: United States Government Printing Office, 1963), pp. 150–152.

9   "Council of Micronesia's Special Session," *Micronesian Reporter* 11:1 (1963): 8–10. See also "Proceedings of the Special Session of the Council of Micronesia," Saipan, Mariana Islands, 19 March to 26 March 1963. A copy of the

proceedings that includes the report of the Legislative Drafting Committee is housed in the Pacific Collection, Hamilton Library, University of Hawai'i at Mānoa, Honolulu, Hawai'i. A summary of the debate between unicameralism and bicameralism can be found in Meller, 1969, pp. 201–204.

10  A copy of this speech is also recorded in Kahn, 1966, p. 12.

11  "Fourth Session, Council of Micronesia, November 12, 1963, Saipan, M.I.," *Micronesian Reporter* 11:4 (1963): 5.

12  Ibid.

13  For an extensive review of the secretarial order chartering the Congress of Micronesia, see Meller, 1969, pp. 197–221; also Hanlon, 1998, pp. 131–132; Hezel, 1995, pp. 305–306; and Udui, 1965, pp. 16–18.

14  Meller, 1969, pp. 244–274, provides a summary of the first elections for the Congress of Micronesia, including district administrative measures, registration of voters, balloting, nominations and candidacy, campaigning, the conduct of elections, and results.

15  Ibid., p. 256.

16  Ibid., p. 269.

17  Ibid., pp. 275–290.

18  "About the Buildings," *Highlights*, 22 February 1971, p. 8.

19  For an account of the training workshop, see Meller, 1969, pp. 291–305.

20  Ibid., pp. 306–312.

21  An account of the political dynamics that surrounded the election of Tosiwo Nakayama as the president of the House of Delegates can be found in Meller, 1969, pp. 317–319. Also, interview with Tosiwo Nakayama, Weno, Chuuk, 30 December 2000.

22  Interview, Tosiwo Nakayama, Weno, Chuuk, 30 December 2000.

23  Meller, 1969, pp. 325–329, summarizes the procedural difficulties of the first Congress.

24  "HICOM Vetoes Eminent Domain Bill," *Highlights*, 5 August 1968, p. 1.

25  "15 Bills Passed During Special Session," *Highlights*, 1 June 1971, p. 1.

26  Meller, 1969, pp. 353–354.

27  Homi Bhabha, "Of Mimicry and Man: The Ambivalence of Colonial Discourse," in *October: The First Decade,* edited by Annette Michelsen, Rosalind Krauss, Doug Crimp, and Joan Copjec (Cambridge, MA: MIT Press), pp. 318–322.

28  These American Peace Corps lawyers included Brad Coates, Adrien de Graffenried, Daniel Foley, Don Parkinson, Fred Ramp, Dana Smith, Scott Stege, Tom Sterling, and Michael White. Fred Ramp, personal communication, 4 April 2012.

29  " Secretary Notes," *Highlights,* 7 February 1967, p. 2.

30  Bill Jaynes, "P.F. Kluge, Not Just Another 'Dog Day Afternoon' on the 'Edge of Paradise,'" *The Kaselehlie Press,* 9 January 2008, p. 2, http://www.stpns .net/view_article.html?articleId=758453810454.

31  Pierre Bourdieu, *Outline of a Theory of Practice,* translated by Richard Nice (Cambridge: Cambridge University Press, 1977), pp. 37–38.

32  "15 Bills Passed During Special Session," 1971.

33  United States Department of State, *22nd Annual Report to the United Nations on the Administration of the Trust Territory of the Pacific Islands, July 1, 1968 to June 30, 1969,* p. 5.

34  United States Department of State, *26th Annual Report to the United Nations on the Administration of the Trust Territory, July 1, 1972 to June 30, 1973,* p. 20.

35  United States Department of State, *24th Annual Report to the United Nations on the Administration of the Trust Territory of the Pacific Islands, July 1, 1970 to June 30, 1971,* p. 25.

36  Quoted in Meller, 1969, p. 290.

37  Congress of Micronesia, *Journal of the Senate,* Second Congress, third regular session, 10 July to 8 August 1970, p. 345.

38  Congress of Micronesia, *Journal of the Senate,* First Congress, second regular session, 11 July to 9 August 1966, pp. 223, 265.

39  Ibid., p. 285.

40  Congress of Micronesia, *Journal of the Senate,* Second Congress, fourth regular session, 10 July to 8 August 1968, Appendix I, "Meeting of Conference Committees, Senate Bill No. 40, S.D. 2, H.D. 1," pp. 360–376.

41  Congress of Micronesia, *Journal of the Senate,* Third Congress, first regular session, 13 January to 27 January 1969, p. 126.

42  Congress of Micronesia, *Journal of the Senate,* Fifth Congress, first regular session, 8 January to 26 February 1973. The full text of the speech is found on pp. 94–97. Nakayama gave an earlier and similar speech to the graduating class of Truk High School on 28 May 1971; see Congress of Micronesia, Office of the Legislative Counsel, *Public Speeches, The Congress of Micronesia, 1970–1971* (Saipan, Mariana Islands: Trust Territory Government Printing Office). A copy of this collection can be found in the Pacific Collection, University of Hawai'i at Mānoa, Honoulu, Hawai'i.

43  Ibid., p. 97

44  "Interview with Tosiwo Nakayama," *Micronesian Reporter* 22:4 (1974): 9.

45  Quoted in Hanlon, 1998, p. 138.

46  Trust Territory of the Pacific Islands, *General Elections to the Congress of Micronesia,* Saipan, Mariana Islands, 19 January 1965, p. 4. A copy of this

document can be found in the Pacific Collection, Hamilton Library, University of Hawai'i at Mānoa, Honolulu, Hawai'i.

47 "1968 General Election Results to the Congress of Micronesia," *Highlights*, 1 January to 15 January 1969, p. 6.

48 "Congress of Micronesia Election Results," *Highlights*, 15 November 1972, p. 3.

49 Assistant Commissioner for Public Affairs, Trust Territory of the Pacific Islands, "Amaraich Andon L.," *Micronesian Biographies* (Saipan, Mariana Islands: Literature Production Center), 1965, p. 2.

50 Congress of Micronesia, *Journal of the Senate*, Second Congress, fourth regular session, 10 July to 8 August 1968, p. 455.

51 Fred Ramp to Barry J. Israel, 25 January 1983, Microfilmed Archives of the Federated States of Micronesia, Attorney General (AG), reel no. 148, item no. 20.

52 Trust Territory of the Pacific Islands, "General Elections to the Congress of Micronesia, 8 November 1966," *Headquarters Highlights*, p. 6.

53 "Congress of Micronesia Election Results," *Highlights*, 15 November 1970, p. 3.

54 Congress of Micronesia, *Journal of the Senate*, Fourth Congress, first regular session, 11 January to 20 February 1971, p. 33.

55 Congress of Micronesia, *Journal of the Senate*, Fourth Congress, second regular session, 10 January to 28 February 1972, pp. 188–189.

56 "Revised Foreign Investment Bill Becomes Law," *Highlights*, 1 March 1970, p. 1.

57 "Statement by Senator Amaraich," *Highlights*, 9 June 1972, pp. 8–13.

58 For a copy of Amaraich's 1973 address to the UN Trusteeship Council, see "Statement by Senator Amaraich," 1 July 1973.

59 Congress of Micronesia, *Journal of the Senate*, Fifth Congress, first special session, 23 July to 9 August 1974, pp. 137–138.

60 Richard F. Kanost, "Administrative Development in Micronesia: The Senatorial Election in Truk District, 1974," *Journal of Pacific History* 17:3 (July 1982): 161; also, interview with Tosiwo Nakayama, Weno, Chuuk, 30 December 2000.

61 The Senate's deliberation over the majority and minority reports on the election dispute, as well as the reports themselves, can be found in the Congress of Micronesia, *Journal of the Senate*, Sixth Congress, first regular session, 13 January to 3 March 1975, pp. 58–69, 71–74. See also Kanost, 1982, pp. 158–165.

62 Congress of Micronesia, *Journal of the Senate*, Sixth Congress, first regular session, 13 January to 3 March 1975, p. 72.

63 Interview, Tosiwo Nakayama, Weno, Chuuk, 29 December 2000. Accounts of Nakayama's search for his father can also be found in Kluge, 1991, pp. 112–113, and Ann Nakano, *Broken Canoe: Conversations & Observations in Micronesia* (St. Lucia, Queensland: University of Queensland Press, 1983), p. 280.

64 For details on Nakayama Masami's life, see "In Memoriam: Masami Nakayama," *Truk Chronicle*. A copy of this issue can be found in the Federated States of Micronesia Microfilm Archives, PIO, reel no. 4, item no. 028.

65 "Personnel File: Tosiwo Nakayama," Federated States of Micronesia Microfilmed Archives, OAS, reel no. 257, item no. 028. Information on Nakayama's travels is provided on a security clearance form in conjunction with his appointment as assistant district administrator for public affairs in Chuuk.

66 "Napoleon DeFang Dies in a Jeep Accident," *Truk Review* II:20 (February 1962): 1–2. The *Truk Review* was published in both English and Chuukese; a Chuukese language version of this article is also given on pp. 1–2.

67 On this point, see Hezel, 1995, pp. 321–325.

68 "Personnel File: Tosiwo Nakayama," Federated States of Micronesia Microfilmed Archives, OAS, reel no. 257, item no. 028.

69 Interview, Tosiwo Nakayama, Weno, Chuuk, 30 December 2000. East-West Center documents show Nakayama to have been on grant from 5 September 1967 to 9 February 1971, studying for a BA degree in political science. See East-West Center, "All Distinguished Alumni Awardees, 1980–2012," http:// eastwestcenter.org/print/32644, and "Nakayama, Mr. Tosiwo," Participant Awards System, Participant Profile #0017256, Award Services Office, East-West Center, Honolulu, Hawai'i. The end date is misleading; in addition, Nakayama did not complete a degree program at the University of Hawai'i, Mānoa.

70 "Territory Hails Establishment of New Congress of Micronesia," *Micronesian Reporter* 12:6 (1964): 1.

71 Tosiwo Nakayama to William R. Norwood, 15 January 1969, Federated States of Micronesia Microfilmed Archives, OAS, reel no. 257, item no. 028. A copy of the note to Jesse R. Quigley is also contained in this file.

72 Jeff Lane, "Andon Amaraich Leaves Administration," *Met Poraus* II:14 (3 January 1969): 14.

73 Meller, 1969, p. 402.

74 Hezel, 1995, p. 310.

75 "Nakayama Chosen by Truk Delegation to Serve on Political Status Commission," *Met Poraus* II:10 (6 December 1968): 15; also "Congress Adjourns: Names Delegates to Washington," *Highlights*, 1 September and 15 September 1969, p. 1.

76 Interview, Tosiwo Nakayama, Weno, Chuuk, 30 December 2000.

77 Hezel, 1995, pp. 310–311.

78 A lengthy, description of the regional tour and consideration of issues that preceded the release of the final report can be found in "Future Political Status Commission Reports on Study Tour," *Highlights*, 15 April 1969, pp. 1–3. Reaction to the commission's tour and preliminary findings can be found in "Political Status Commission Begins Tour of Territory," *Highlights*, 1 May 1969, pp. 4–9. The final report was submitted to the Congress of Micronesia on 21 July 1969. See, The Future Political Status Commission, *Report* (Capitol Hill, Saipan, Mariana Islands: Congress of Micronesia, Third Congress, second regular session, July 1969).

79 "Political Status Commission Begins Tour of Territory," 1 May 1969.

80 Ibid.

81 Hezel, 1995, pp. 331–332.

82 Quoted in ibid., 1995, p. 333. For more on how the historical experiences of American minorities and native peoples informed the Micronesian negotiating position, see Glenn Petersen, "Lessons Learned: The Micronesian Quest for Independence in the Context of American Imperial History," *Micronesian Journal of the Humanities and Social Sciences* 3 (2004): 45–63.

83 Hezel, 1995, p. 334.

84 Congress of Micronesia, *Journal of the Senate*, Third Congress, third special session, 12 January to 13 January 1970, p. 101.

85 Interview with Tosiwo Nakayama," *Micronesian Reporter*, 1974

86 Jim Manke, "Typhoon Amy Sweeps Across Truk, Historic Congress Session Now Underway," *Highlights*, 15 May 1971, p. 4.

87 Hezel, 1995, p. 338.

88 Hanlon, 1998, p. 93.

89 Interview, Tosiwo Nakayama, Weno, Chuuk, 30 December 2000.

90 Manke "Typhoon Amy Sweeps Across Truk, Historic Congress Session Underway," 1971, p. 4.

91 Hezel, 1995, p. 341.

92 Quoted in Roger Gale, *The Americanization of Micronesia: A Study of the Consolidation of U.S. Rule in the Pacific* (Washington, D.C.: University Press of America, 1979), p. 245.

93 Congress of Micronesia, *Journal of the Senate*, Fifth Congress, first regular session, 8 January to 26 February 1973, pp. 282–283. Mary Vance Trent explained her position in a letter to Tosiwo Nakayama dated 25 February 1973. A copy of the letter is found on p. 311 of the journal.

94 Interview, Kohsak Keller, Palikir, Pohnpei, 23 May 2003.

95 Micronesian Seminar, *Seminar on Moral Issues Related to Choice of Political Status* (Kolonia, Ponape: Catholic Mission, 3–9 June 1973).

96   Joint Committee on Future Status, *Hearings of the Eastern Districts Subcommittee.* Fifth Congress (Saipan, Mariana Islands: Congress of Micronesia, November 1973); and *Report of the Eastern District Subcommittee to the Joint Committee on Future Status.* Fifth Congress (Saipan, Mariana Islands: Congress of Micronesia, 1973).

97   This account of separatism in the Northern Marianas draws heavily from Hezel, 1995, pp. 335–337. For a history of the commonwealth movement in the Northern Marianas, see also Howard Willens and Deanne C. Siemer, *An Honorable Accord: The Covenant Between the Northern Mariana Islands and the United States,* Pacific Islands Monograph Series no. 18. Honolulu: University of Hawai'i Press, 2002.

98   Quoted in Hezel, 1995, p. 336.

99   Ibid., p. 337.

100  "Congress of Micronesia Buildings Burn, Members Adjourn First Session," *Highlights,* 22 February 1971, pp. 1–3.

101  Hezel, 1995, p. 343.

102  Quoted in ibid., p. 343.

103  "Public Land and Revenue Bills Passed," *Highlights,* 15 August 1974, p. 1

104  "Congress Resolves Palau Election Dispute," *Highlights,* 1 January 1971, pp. 1–2.

105  Manke, "Typhoon Amy Sweeps Across Truk, Historic Congress Session Now Underway," 1971, pp. 1–2.

106  Hezel, 1995, p. 344.

107  Norman Meller, with the assistance of Terza Meller, *Constitutionalism in Micronesia* (Lā'ie: Institute for Polynesian Studies, Brigham Young University—Hawai'i Campus, 1985), p. 52.


Chapter 5: Constituting a Nation

1   Micronesian Constitutional Convention, *Journal of the Micronesian Constitutional Convention: Convened on July 12, 1975, Recessed August 23, 1975, Reconvened September 15, 1975, Adjourned November 8, 1975* (Saipan, Mariana Islands: Office of the Convention President, 1975), p. 4. P. F. Kluge also makes note of Nakayama's "now or never" assessment of self-government for Micronesia in "The Micronesian Constitutional Convention: July 12–November 8, 1975," *Micronesian Reporter* 33:4 (1975): 38–44.

2   This chapter draws heavily from Meller, 1985. See his "Introduction," pp. vii–x, on the drama and uncertainty that characterized the 1975 Micronesian Constitutional Convention and the larger quest for self-government in the islands. A brief account of the convention can also be found in Hezel, 1995, pp. 347–350.

3   Meller, 1985, pp. 109–127.

4   Ibid., p. 109.

5   Ibid., p. 112.

6   Ibid., p. 109.

7   Ibid., p. 110.

8   Ibid., p. 111.

9   Ibid.

10  Ibid.

11  Ibid., p. 112.

12  Ibid.

13  Ibid., p. 114.

14  Ibid.

15  Ibid., p. 115.

16  Ibid., p. 118.

17  Task Force on Education for Self-Government, "Interview with Tosiwo Nakayama," 30 August 1974, *Dialogue for Micronesia: July 1974...December 1975* (Saipan, Mariana Islands: Department of Public Affairs, Trust Territory of the Pacific Islands). This document is a written summary of the interview with Nakayama.

18  Meller, 1985, pp. 118–119.

19  Ibid., pp. 119–121.

20  Ibid., pp. 122–123.

21  Ibid., p. 135.

22  Ibid., pp. 135–136.

23  In an extended review of Norman Meller's *Constitutionalism in Micronesia* that was part of a larger forum, Glenn Petersen addresses the question of American interference in the Micronesian Constitutional Convention, including the collusion of staff lawyers with representatives of the U.S. Department of State present on Saipan during the convention. He rejects the arguments for this collusion, but points to the likelihood of CIA surveillance in the region at this time and to convention delegates' general frustration and discomfort with the American staff lawyers. See Petersen, "Book Review Forum," *Pacific Studies* 10:3 (1987): 107–124.

24  Ibid., pp. 146–147.

25  Nakayama had words of high praise for Mihaly; see interview, Tosiwo Nakayama, Weno, Chuuk, 2 January 2001.

26  Meller, 1985, p. 148.

27  Ibid., pp. 150–151.

28  Interview, Victorio Uherbelau, Koror, Palau, 17 July 2002.

29  Meller, 1985, pp. 150–151.

30  Ibid., pp. 153–156.

31  Quoted in Meller, 1985, p. 155.

32  *Journal of the Micronesian Constitutional Convention,* 1975, pp. 3–4. The underscoring of the words is Nakayama's.

33  An account of Tosiwo Nakayama's election as president of the Micronesian Constitutional Convention can be found in Meller, 1985, pp. 157–158.

34  The members of the Yapese delegation were among the staunchest supporters of Nakayama's candidacy for the presidency of the constitutional convention. Luke Tman conveyed that support in a private meeting with Nakayama; see interview, Tosiwo Nakayama, Weno, Chuuk, 2 January 2001.

35  Ibid.

36  Meller, 1985, p. 162.

37  Ibid., p. 159.

38  Ibid., pp. 161–162.

39  Ibid., p. 161.

40  Task Force on Education for Self-Government, "Interview with Tosiwo Nakayama, Carl Heine, Leo Falcam, and Chutomo Nimwes," 22 August 1975, *Dialogue For Micronesia, July 1974…December 1975,* Program No. 45 (Saipan, Mariana Islands: Department of Public Affairs, Trust Territory Government of the Pacific Islands).

41  Meller, 1985, pp. 175–179.

42  Ibid., pp. 175–176.

43  Ibid., p. 180. Ismael was from Kosrae, which, at the time, was still administratively a part of Pohnpei.

44  Ibid., pp. 182–184.

45  Ibid., p. 205.

46  Micronesian Traditional Chiefs, *Program: Second Conference of the Micronesian Traditional Chiefs* (Moen, Truk District, Eastern Caroline Islands: Office of the Mayor, Moen Municipality, Trust Territory of the Pacific Islands, 1974), pp. 7–8. This position contrasts markedly with his comments later in life that he saw the power of chiefs as declining throughout the Micronesian geographical region; see interview, Tosiwo Nakayama, Weno, Chuuk, 2 January 2001.

47  Meller, 1985, p. 215.

48  Ibid., p. 216.

49  The dilemma posed by the scheduling of the recess is addressed in the interview with Victorio Uherbelau, Koror, Palau, 17 July 2002.

50  Quoted in Meller, 1985, p. 217.

51   Quoted in ibid., p. 218.

52   Cited in ibid., p. 220.

53   Interview, Tosiwo Nakayama, Weno, Chuuk, 2 January 2001. Victorio Uher-belau also commented on the differences that separated Nakayama and Fritz at the constitutional convention in an interview on Koror, Palau on 17 July 2002; see also the interview with Ed and Joan King, Silver Spring, Maryland, 27 September 2003.

54   Interview, Fred Ramp, Kolonia, Pohnpei, 22 April 2010.

55   Meller, 1985, p. 209.

56   Ibid., pp. 220–221.

57   Ibid., p. 221.

58   Ibid., p. 222.

59   Ibid., p. 223.

60   Quoted in ibid., p. 224.

61   Ibid., p. 225.

62   Ibid., pp. 225–226.

63   Quoted in ibid., pp. 317–318.

64   Interview, Tosiwo Nakayama, Weno, Chuuk, 2 January 2001.

65   Meller, 1985, pp. 65–67.

66   Quoted in ibid., p. 229.

67   Ibid., p. 237.

68   Ibid., pp. 248–249.

69   Ibid., p. 250.

70   Ibid., pp. 252–253.

71   Ibid., p. 254.

72   Quoted in ibid., p. 261.

73   Quoted in ibid., pp. 261–262.

74   Quoted in ibid., p. 263.

75   Ibid.

76   Ibid.

77   Ibid., p. 264.

78   Ibid., p. 267.

79   Quoted in ibid.

80   Ibid., pp. 268–269.

81   Ibid., pp. 272–273.

82   Ibid., p. 274.

83   Ibid., p. 275.

84    Quoted in ibid., p. 275.

85    Ibid., p. 276.

86    Ibid., p. 277.

87    Ibid., pp. 277–278.

88    Ibid., p. 278.

89    Ibid., p. 279.

90    Ibid., p. 280.

91    Ibid., p. 297.

92    Ibid., p. 298.

93    Ibid., p. 299.

94    Ibid., pp. 299–301.

95    Ibid., pp. 302–303.

96    Ibid., pp. 303–304.

97    Interview, Tosiwo Nakayama, Weno, Chuuk, 2 January 2001.

98    Meller, 1985, pp. 304–305.

99    Ibid., p. 249.

100   Ibid., p. 306.

101   Ibid., p. 307.

102   Ibid.

103   Interview, Tosiwo Nakayama, Weno, Chuuk, 3 January 2001.

104   Meller, 1985, p. 309.

105   Interview, Tosiwo Nakayama, Weno, Chuuk, 2 January 2001.

106   Meller, 1985, pp. 307–308.

### Chapter 6: One Canoe

1    "HiCom Presents Nakayama The ConCon Pen," *Highlights*, 1 June 1976, p. 3.

2    Nakayama used the metaphor of the canoe often in his congressional and later executive careers. The phrase "one canoe" was employed in a speech given on 11 May 1981 in Kolonia, Pohnpei, to commemorate the second anniversary of the inauguration of the FSM government. The sentiments expressed in this speech reflect Nakayama's long-standing commitment to unity and self-government. See "President Urges FSM 'to sail one canoe,'" *The National Union*, 30 May 1981, pp. 1, 3.

3    Ibid., p. 3.

4    Congress of Micronesia, *Journal of the Senate*, Sixth Congress, second regular session, 12 January to 1 March 1976, pp. 65–67.

5 Task Force on Education for Self-Government, "Summary of an Interview with Senator Tosiwo Nakayama," 29 January 1976, *Dialogue for Micronesia, Program No.* 58 (Saipan, Mariana Islands: Department of Public Affairs, 1976), pp. 1–3.

6 "Highlights of COM Special Session Based on News Reports from Ponape," *Highlights,* 1 September 1977, p. 5.

7 Congress of Micronesia, *Journal of the Senate,* Sixth Congress, second special session, 19 July to 1 August 1976, pp. 88–90.

8 Described in Congress of Micronesia, *Journal of the Senate,* Sixth Congress, second regular session, 12 January to 1 March 1976, pp. 197–198.

9 "Palau Seeks Separate Status Negotiations," *Highlights,* 1 May 1976, p. 3.

10 Congress of Micronesia, *Journal of the Senate,* Seventh Congress, first regular session, 10 January to 28 February 1977, pp. 91–100.

11 Interview, Tosiwo Nakayama, Weno, Chuuk, 1 January 2001.

12 Quoted in Meller, 1985, p. 319.

13 Quoted in ibid.

14 Ibid., pp. 319–320.

15 Ibid., p. 320.

16 Ibid.

17 Meller, 1985, p. 320.

18 Ibid., p. 323.

19 Gale, 1979, p. 295.

20 Bob Woodward, "CIA Bugging Micronesian Status Negotiations," *Washington Post,* 12 December 1976, p. A1.

21 Bob Woodward, "Kissinger Tied to CIA Surveillance, *Washington Post,* 4 May 1977, p. A1.

22 Ibid.

23 Interview, Andon Amaraich, Palikir, Pohnpei, 29 May 2003.

24 Interview, Tony DeBrum, Majuro, Republic of the Marshall Islands, 19 July 2004.

25 "COM Delegation in Washington," *Highlights,* 15 January 1977, p. 6.

26 "TT Leaders Go to Washington," *Highlights,* 15 March 1977, p. 1.

27 Meller, 1985, p. 324.

28 Office of Micronesian Status Negotiations, *The Future Political Status of the Trust Territory of the Pacific Islands: Summary Record of the U.S.-Micronesia Roundtable Conference, Guam, July 25–27, 1977.* Washington, D.C., 1977, p. 37.

29 Ibid., p. 39.

30 Meller, 1985, p. 323.

31 "Nakayama on Referendum," *Highlights,* 1 January 1978, p. 3.

32 Quoted in Meller, 1985, p. 321.

33 "Nakayama on Referendum," 1978.

34 "Statement of Principles for Free Association Signed in Hilo," *Highlights,* 1 May 1978, p. 3.

35 "Mangefel Disappointed in COM," *Highlights,* 15 March 1977, p. 3.

36 Congress of Micronesia, *Journal of the Senate,* Seventh Congress, first special session, 15 August to 29 August 1977, pp. 26–27.

37 Ibid., pp. 31–33.

38 "Trukese Demand Land Settlement," *Highlights,* 15 February 1977, p. 6.

39 "Truk Airport Expansion Near Solution," *Highlights,* 1 March 1979, pp. 1–2.

40 Congress of Micronesia, *Journal of the Senate,* Seventh Congress, second regular session, 9 January to 27 February 1978, p. 160. Nakayama responded to Bossy's use of the race issue almost a decade later when he gave his farewell address to the Congress of the Federated States of Micronesia. In that speech, Nakayama told the story of how several years before Bossy had argued with a Filipino barber on Saipan that he was Micronesian. "Sure, sure, sure, sure, I think surely you are an American," replied the barber. When Bossy insisted he was not a black American but Chuukese, the barber again replied: "Sure, sure, sure, sure." See Congress of the Federated States of Micronesia, *Journal,* Fifth Congress, first regular session, 11 May to 11 June 1987, p. 137.

41 Ibid., p. 357.

42 "Faichuk & Mortlocks Vote," *Highlights,* 15 November 1977, p. 6.

43 Congress of Micronesia, *Journal of the Senate,* Seventh Congress, second regular session, 9 January to 27 February 1978, pp. 126–127.

44 Ibid., p. 126.

45 Ibid., p. 127.

46 Ibid., pp. 484–485.

47 Kaleb Udui was a former legal counsel to the Congress of Micronesia; had attended school in Hawai'i with Nakayama; and had served as his onetime speechwriter. See interview, Tosiwo Nakayama, Weno, Chuuk, 1 January 2001.

48 Congress of Micronesia, *Journal of the Senate,* Seventh Congress, second regular session, 9 January to 27 February 1978, p. 357.

49 Interview, Tosiwo Nakayama, Weno, Chuuk, 2 January 2001.

50 Delegation of Micronesia, United Nations Law of the Sea Conference, *1975 Report,* Sixth Congress, Saipan, Mariana Islands, 1975, p. 2.

51 "Law of the Sea Convention," *Highlights,* 1 December 1976, p. 2.

52  "Andrus Upholds HiCom's Veto," *Highlights,* 1 June 1977, p. 3.

53  "Winkel Approves 200-Mile Fishery Zone for Micronesia," *Highlights,* 1 November 1977, pp. 1–2.

54  "Micronesian Maritime Authority Members," *Highlights,* 1 January 1978, p. 6.

55  "Two COM Leaders Visit Tokyo," *Highlights,* 1 December 1976, p. 3.

56  "COM to be Heard on Air Route," *Highlights,* 1 April 1977, p. 6.

57  Ibid.

58  "COM Leadership Levels Warning," *Highlights,* 1 June 1977, p. 3.

59  "Inaugural Flight a Success," *Highlights,* 15 October 1977, p. 4.

60  "COM Leaders Meet Fukuda," *Highlights,* 1 January 1978, p. 4.

61  Assistant Commissioner for Public Affairs, Trust Territory of the Pacific Islands, *Micronesian Biographies* (Saipan, Mariana Islands: Literature Production Center, 1965), pp. 7–8.

62  "Ismael Ahead in Kosrae; Killion Wins in Truk; Falcam Leads by 15 Votes," *The National Union,* 15 March 1987, pp. 1–2. Falcam won but by a narrow, highly contested margin over runner-up Resio Moses, a former Trust Territory official, Micronesian congressman, and governor of Pohnpei.

63  Meller, 1985, p. 321.

64  Ibid., pp. 327–328.

65  Ibid., p. 328.

66  Ibid., p. 329.

67  This account of the 1979 election in Chuuk is based upon an interview with Tosiwo Nakayama conducted on Weno, Chuuk, 30 December 2000.

68  Ibid.

69  Ibid.

70  Ibid., 2 January 2001.

71  HiCom to List, 30 March 1979, "Incoming and Outgoing Dispatches Regarding CIP Projects and Interim Congress Session Reporting for the Month of March," TTA, reel 1476, no document number.

72  HiCom to List, 16 April 1979, "Incoming and Outgoing Dispatches Regarding CIP Projects and Election Results for the Month of April 1979," TTA, reel no. 1476, document no. 0080.

73  Ibid.

74  Interview, Tosiwo Nakayama, Weno, Chuuk, 30 December 2000.

75  Ibid.

76  Rosario and Simpson, 1980, p. 16.

77  Ibid.

78  Ibid.; also interview, Susumu Aizawa, Weno, Chuuk, 30 July 2002.

79  Interview, Tosiwo Nakayama, Weno, Chuuk, 2 January 2001.

80  "Congress to Relocate," *Highlights,* 15 June 1977, p. 2.

81  Interview, Tosiwo Nakayama, Weno, Chuuk, 2 January 2001.

82  "Where the Offices Are," *The National Union,* 30 January 1981, p. 2.

83  "Open House of FSM Renovated Buildings," *The National Union,* 15 November 1980, pp. 4–5.

84  See for example, "Ponape Faces Severe Power Shortage," *The National Union,* 15 April 1981, p. 1; "Energy Crisis Declared for Ponape," *The National Union,* 15 May 1981, p. 3; "Moses Declares Power Crisis," *The National Union,* 15 January 1985, p. 5; and "Pohnpei Power Crisis End Seen," *The National Union,* 30 January 1986, p. 3.

85  "Santos Hits Setik on FSM Housing at Palikir Capitol," *The National Union,* 30 April 1981, pp. 1–2.

86  "Ponape Leaders Support Palikir as Capital Site," *The National Union,* 30 June 1982, pp. 1, 3.

87  "FSM Deeded Land for Capitol," *The National Union,* 30 January 1985, pp. 1, 3.

88  "Falcam Denounces Referendum on FSM," *The National Union,* 15 April 1982, p. 2.

89  "Ponapeans Dominate FSM Jobs," *The National Union,* 15 March 1982, p. 4.

90  "FSM Offered Land," *The National Union,* 15 November 1981, p. 2.

91  "Sokehs Chief Backs Unity," *The National Union,* 15 April 1982, p. 2.

92  "Joint FSM, Ponape Inauguration Set for May 12," *The National Union,* 30 April 1983, p. 3.

## Chapter 7: Governing a Rainbow

1  Tosiwo Nakayama, "Inaugural Address," *The National Union,* 1 October 1980, p. 8. See also Tosiwo Nakayama, President of the Federated States of Micronesia, "Inaugural Address," *Micronesian Reporter* 27:2 (1979): 8–9.

2  "Presidential Order Number One," *The National Union,* 30 November 1980, pp. 4–5.

3  "Where the Offices Are," *The National Union,* 30 January 1981, p. 2.

4  Interview, Aloysius Tuuth, Colonia, Yap, 22 July 2002.

5  The women with whom Nakayama worked closest in government were his executive secretaries. Lori Loughrey, an expatriate, served in that capacity during his first administration. Melody Musrasrik replaced Loughrey during Nakayama's second term; she had come to Pohnpei as the wife of Assis-

tant Attorney General Larry Bertoncini, divorced him, and married lawyer Emelio Musrasrik.

6  "Compact 'Back on Track,'" *The National Union*, 30 September 1981, pp. 1, 6.

7  "Compact Derailed by Cuts; Funds Accord Needed to Continue Talks," *The National Union*, 15 October 1981, pp. 1, 5.

8  Ibid.

9  "U.S. Told Cuts Prevent FSM Development," *The National Union*, 15 December 1981, pp. 1–3.

10  Stovall to Hezel, 22 April 1982, in Henry M. Schwalbenberg, S.J., *Memoranda on the Compact of Free Association* (Truk, Eastern Caroline Islands: Micronesian Seminar, 1981–1984). A copy of this compendium can be found in Hamilton Library's Pacific Collection on the University of Hawai'i at Mānoa campus, Honolulu, Hawai'i.

11  Hezel to Dear Friends, 2 June 1982, in ibid.

12  "Nakayama Says Cuts Fail To Meet U.S. Obligations, *The National Union*, 15 November 1981, p. 1.

13  Ibid.

14  "U.S. Told Cuts Prevent FSM Development," *The National Union*, 15 December 1981, p. 1.

15  For an extended summary of the terms of the draft Compact of Free Association agreed to in Honolulu on 1 October 1982, see Hanlon, 1998, pp. 223–224.

16  "Compact Signed; Funding Secured," *The National Union*, 15 October 1982, p. 5.

17  "Plebiscite Commission Bill Submitted," *The National Union*, 30 October 1982, pp. 1, 3.

18  "June 21 Plebiscite Recommended," *The National Union*, 28 February 1983, pp. 1, 4.

19  "President Urges Compact Study in Message," *The National Union*, 30 March 1983, p. 4.

20  "Compact Wins in Landslide," *The National Union*, 30 June 1983, p. 5. For an account of the plebiscite in the FSM as well as those in the Republic of the Marshall Islands and the Republic of Palau, see Austin Ranney and Howard R. Penniman, *Democracy in the Islands: The Micronesian Plebiscites of 1983* (Washington, D.C.; American Enterprise Institute for Public Policy Research, 1985).

21  "79% 'Yes' to Compact," *The National Union*, 15 July 1983, pp. 1, 4.

22  Ibid., p. 4.

23  "FSM Completes Ratification of Compact with U.S.," *The National Union*, 15 September 1983, pp. 1, 5.

24  Ibid., p. 5.

25  "Ponape Leaders Back Compact," *The National Union*, 15 March 1984, pp. 1, 4.

26  "All of FSM Urged to Back Compact," *The National Union*, 30 September 1983, pp. 1, 3.

27  "Compact Delegation," *The National Union*, 30 March 1984, pp. 1, 3.

28  "Reagan Sends Compact to U.S. Congress," *The National Union*, 15 April 1984, pp. 1, 3.

29  "Reagan Praised for Support," *The National Union*, 30 April 1984, pp. 1, 3.

30  "Compact Provides Dignity," *The National Union*, 30 May 1984, p. 1. See also United States Congress, Committee on Energy and Natural Resources, "Statement of the Honorable Tosiwo Nakayama, President of the Federated States of Micronesia, to the Committee on Energy and Natural Resources of the United States Senate, May 24, 1984," p. 2. In *Statements Before the Committee on Energy and Natural Resources, May 24, 1984, Regarding the Compact of Free Association*. Pacific Collection, Hamilton Library, University of Hawai'i at Mānoa, Honolulu, Hawai'i.

31  "Solarz Sees Compact Action in May," *The National Union*, 15 April 1985, pp. 1, 4, 5.

32  "Quick Compact Approval Urged," *The National Union*, 30 April 1985, p. 4.

33  Ibid.

34  "Compact Seen Implemented by Oct. 1," *The National Union*, 30 May 1985, pp. 1, 3.

35  "FSM Representative Denounces Compact Critics in UNTC," *The National Union*, 15 June 1985, p. 2.

36  "President Nakayama Expresses Concerns," *The National Union*, 30 June 1985, pp. 1, 3.

37  "Tax, Trade Changes 'Unacceptable,'" *The National Union*, 30 July 1985, pp. 1–2.

38  "Compact Strategy Meet Extended," *The National Union*, 30 August 1985, pp. 1, 3.

39  "FSM: No Compromises," *The National Union*, 15 September 1985, p. 3.

40  "President Asks Asia-Pacific Leaders to Pray for Compact," *The National Union*, 15 November 1985, p. 8.

41  "Compact Faces Filibuster in Senate," *The National Union*, 15 October 1985, pp. 1, 3.

42  "Congress Overrides Compact Review Bill Veto," *The National Union*, 30 October 1985, pp. 1, 3.

43  "Compact Faces Filibuster in Senate," 15 October 1985, pp. 1, 3.

44  Interview, Tosiwo Nakayama, Weno, Chuuk, 2 January 2001.

45  "Senate Approves Compact," *The National Union,* 15 November 1985, pp. 1, 3.

46  "Samoa Seeks Tuna Quota in Compact," *The National Union,* 30 November 1985, pp. 1, 3.

47  "Congress Okays Compact," *The National Union,* 15 December 1985, pp. 1, 3.

48  "President Reagan Signs Compact," *The National Union,* 15 January 1986, pp. 1–2.

49  "Commission to Review Compact," *The National Union,* 30 December 1985, pp. 1–2.

50  "FSM Accepts Compact Changes," *The National Union,* 30 March 1986, pp. 1, 3.

51  Hanlon, 1998, p. 221.

52  "Nakayama Calls for Immediate Termination to the T.T.," *The National Union,* 1 and 15 May 1986, pp. 1, 3.

53  "UNTC Adopted Resolution to Terminate T.T.," *The National Union,* 1 and 15 May 1986, p. 2. Procedural delays and the political rivalries among its members would keep the UN Security Council from formally dissolving the Trusteeship Agreement for another four years. The Soviet Union had opposed the termination of the trusteeship on the grounds that the different compacts fragmented the region politically, ensured the continued economic dependence of the islands on the United States, and legitimated American militarization of the area. The later disintegration of the Soviet Union removed these objections and the threat of a veto that underlay them. On 22 December 1990, the Security Council voted to officially terminate the Trusteeship Agreement. On these developments, see Ellen Boneparth and M. James Wilkinson, "Terminating Trusteeship for the Federated States of Micronesia and the Republic of the Marshall Islands: Independence and Self-Sufficiency in the Post-Cold War Pacific," *Pacific Studies* 18:2 (June 1995): 61–77.

54  "FSM Gives Japanese Mission $20 Million Aid Request Package," *The National Union,* 30 September 1981, p. 3.

55  "Japan Signs New Fishing Pact," *The National Union,* 30 April 1982, pp. 1, 6.

56  "President Thanks Japanese for Contributions," *The National Union,* 30 May 1984, p. 2.

57  Ibid.

58  "President to Meet Japanese PM," *The National Union,* 30 September 1984, p. 2.

59  "Nakasone Cites APPU Importance," *The National Union,* 15 October 1984, p. 2.

60  "FSM Looks to Japan for Technology," *The National Union,* 15 December 1984, p. 2.

61  "Reorganization Makes FSM Full-Voting Member," *The National Union,* 15 October 1983, p. 5.

62  "1982 Proved National Government Is Working, Decisions on Leadership, Compact for Voters in FSM," *The National Union,* 30 December 1982, p. 5.

63  "Speaker Says SPC Forum 'Important in Our History,'" *The National Union,* 30 August 1981, p. 5.

64  "President Goes to SP Forum," *The National Union,* 30 August 1983, p. 8; and "President Goes to Forum," *The National Union,* 30 August 1984, p. 8.

65  "Chief Executives Oppose Japanese Nuclear Dumping," *The National Union,* 1 October 1980, p. 1.

66  "FSM Opposes Nuclear Waste Dumping Plan," *The National Union,* 3 November 1980, p. 1.

67  "President Pledges Repeat of Anti-Nuclear Dumping Stand," *The National Union,* 15 July 1984, p. 3.

68  For background on the war claims issue, see Wakako Higuchi, "Japan and War Reparations in Micronesia," *Journal of Pacific History* 30:1 (1995): 87–98.

69  "Task Force on War Claims Created," *The National Union,* 30 November 1980, p. 7.

70  "Task Force Reports on Meeting," *The National Union,* 30 December 1980, p. 1.

71  "1982 Proved National Government Is Working, Decisions on Leadership, Compact for Voters in FSM, *The National Union,* 30 December 1982, p. 5.

72  "MMA Places Observers on Fishing Boats to Record Catch, Techniques," *The National Union,* 15 November 1981, p. 7.

73  See for example "Fishing Talks Suspended," *The National Union,* 30 July 1983, pp. 1, 6.

74  "FSM Passport to be Issued on Nov. 3," *The National Union,* 30 October 1986, pp. 1–2.

75  "FSM, Marshalls Exchange Diplomatic Notes," *The National Union,* 15 March 1987, p. 8.

76  "FSM to Sign Fisheries Treaty," *The National Union,* 30 March 1987, p. 5.

77  "President Returns from China, Accord Signed," *The National Union,* 15 March 1987, p. 3.

78  "FSM Attends Airline Talks in Japan," *The National Union,* 30 October 1980, p. 1.

79 For a description of the dispute, see "FSM to Gain Ownership of UMDA, Air Micronesia," *The National Union*, 30 January 1985, p. 2. See also "The Island," part II of James D. Scurlock's biography of Larry Hillbolm, *King Larry: The Life and Ruins of a Billionaire Genius* (New York: Scribner, 2012), pp. 83–192. In this account, Tosiwo Nakayama is erroneously identified as "President Nakagawa."

80 "FSM, Marshalls Plan New Airline," *The National Union*, 15 May 1985, p. 3.

81 "Onoun Dedicates 3,500 Ft. Runway Airport," *The National Union*, August 1991, p. 10.

82 Tom Bryan, "President Gets Message on Mortlocks Trip," *The National Union*, 15 August 1981, pp. 1–3, 5; also "FSM, Truk Leaders See Mortlocks Problems Solutions," *The National Union*, 15 August 1981, p. 4.

83 Bryan, "President Gets Message on Mortlocks Trip," 1981, p. 5.

84 "President Visits Yap Islands," *The National Union*, 15 July 1982, pp. 1, 4–5.

85 Ibid., p. 1.

86 "President Visits Mokil, Pingelap," *The National Union*, 15 April 1987, pp. 1, 4. See also the video of the Pingelap portion of the visit housed within the Pacific Collection of the College of Micronesia's main library at Palikir, Pohnpei, and labeled as DVD 406A.

87 "Interview: President Tosiwo Nakayama, Federated States of Micronesia," *Pacific Magazine* 7:3 (May/June 1982): 65.

88 "FSM Clarified," *The National Union*, 15 November 1980, p. 8.

89 "Unity Constitution Day Theme," *The National Union*, 15 May 1982, pp. 1–2.

90 "Ponape Team Wins FSM Tournament," *The National Union*, 28 February 1981, p. 1.

91 "Truk Flag Hoisted," *The National Union*, 30 April 1981, p. 2.

92 "Conferees Identifying Projects for National Plan," *The National Union*, 30 January 1983, p. 5.

93 "Nakayama Welcomes TT Leaders to Summit," *The National Union*, 30 January 1982, pp. 1–2.

94 "CCM to Have Expanded Role in FSM Development," *The National Union*, 15 June 1982, p. 4.

95 "King Confirmed FSM Chief Justice," *The National Union*, 15 November 1980, p. 1.

96 "Bossy Says 3 Branches in Traditional Government," *The National Union*, 30 July 1981, p. 4.

97 "Need to Consider Custom Cited in Judicial Conference," *The National Union*, 15 August 1982, p. 1, 4.

98   "'War' in the Micronesian Courts," *Pacific Magazine* 8:3 (July/August 1983): 16–17.

99   "Faichuk Citizens Meet with President," *Truk Chronicle*, 24 August 1979, p. 6. A copy of this article can also be found in the FSM National Archives, PIO, reel 4, no. 128.

100  "Truk Beating Death, Torture Charges Filed," *The National Union*, 30 October 1981, pp. 1, 6. See also Supreme Court of the Federated States of Micronesia, Engichy vs. FSM, 1 FSM Intrm. 532 (App. 1984), http://www.fsmlaw .org/fsm/decisions/vol11/1fsm532_560.htm.

101  Refalopei to Nakayama, 9 November 1981, FSM National Archives, AG, reel 213, item number not given.

102  "President Gets Faichuk Bill, Falcam Cites Funds Issue," *The National Union*, 30 September 1981, p. 3.

103  "Faichuk Bill Threatens Unity in Ponape," *The National Union*, 15 August 1981, pp. 7, 8.

104  "President Gets Faichuk Statehood Bill, Falcam Cites Funds Issue," 1981, p. 3.

105  "States' Comments Varied on Faichuk Statehood Bill," *The National Union*, 30 October 1981, p. 2.

106  Ibid.

107  "President to Consult States on Faichuk," *The National Union*, 30 August 1981, pp. 1, 3.

108  "President Vetos [*sic*] Faichuk Bill," *The National Union*, 30 October 1981, p. 1.

109  Ibid.

110  "Process, Funds Unavailable for New State, Nakayama," *The National Union*, 30 October 1981, p. 2.

111  "President Vetos [*sic*] Faichuk Bill," 1981, p. 1.

112  "Interview: President Tosiwo Nakayama, Federated States of Micronesia," 1982, pp. 66–67.

113  Interview, Susumu Aizawa, Weno Chuuk, 30 July 2002.

114  "President Wants Faichuk to be 'Showcase,'" *The National Union*, 15 November 1981, pp. 1, 3.

115  "More Cholera Cases Reported in Truk," *The National Union*, 30 September 1982, pp. 1, 2.

116  "More Suspected Cholera Cases Reported in Truk," *The National Union*, 15 October 1982, pp. 1, 7.

117  "U.S. Congress Okays Cholera Funds," *The National Union*, 30 December 1982, p. 3.

118  "Cholera Threatens Compact," *The National Union,* 15 November 1982, pp. 1, 3.

119  "FSM on Unsanitary Powder Keg," *The National Union,* 15 November 1982, p. 4; "President Takes Law to Saipan," *The National Union,* 30 November 1982, pp. 1, 3.

120  "U.S. Congress Okays Cholera Funds," 1982, p. 3.

121  "Cholera Spread Slows," *The National Union,* 15 January 1983, p. 6.

122  "Aten Takes $15.9 Million Cholera Plan to D.C.," *The National Union,* 28 February 1983, p. 3; "Faichuk Slows Cholera by Cleaning Up Environment," *The National Union,* 15 March 1983, p. 4.

123  "Truk Tackles Cholera, Emergency Procedures Set," *The National Union,* 30 September 1983, p. 2.

124  "Cholera in Mortlocks," *The National Union,* 15 October 1983, p. 5.

125  "Truk Curbs Spread of Cholera," *The National Union,* 15 December 1983, p. 8.

126  "Auditor Cites Excessive Cholera Account Overtime," *The National Union,* 30 June 1983, p. 6.

127  "Truk Cost-of-Living Bill Passed," *The National Union,* 15 July 1983, p. 2.

128  "Demonstrations Protest TSL Increases," *The National Union,* 30 June 1984, p. 6.

129  "Falcam Hits Pork Barrel Spending," *The National Union,* 30 May 1987, p. 6.


## Chapter 8: Rough Seas and Later Years

1  Quoted in David Hanlon and William Eperiam, "The Evolution and Development of the Federated States of Micronesia," in *Micronesian Politics* (Suva, Fiji: Institute of Pacific Studies, 1988), pp. 104–105. The original statement was made during an interview in *Pacific Magazine,* 1982, pp. 65–66.

2  Interview, Tosiwo Nakayama, Weno, Chuuk, 2 January 2001.

3  Interview with Hiroshi Ismael, Leluh, Kosrae, 13 July 2004. See also *Journal of the Congress of the Federated States of Micronesia,* Second Congress, third regular session, 10 May to 8 June 1982, p. 78.

4  *Journal of the Congress of the Federated States of Micronesia,* First Congress, second special session, 29 January to 7 February 1980, pp. 10–11.

5  See for example Peter Christian's speech in the *Journal of the Congress of the Federated States of Micronesia,* Third Congress, third regular session, 14 May to 12 June 1984, p. 122; also, "Congress Slashes Budget, Targets Compact Funding," *The National Union,* 15 June 1984, pp. 1, 3.

6  See "Committee on External Affairs, S.C.R. No. 4–152, September 4, 1986," in *Journal of the Congress of the Federated States of Micronesia,* Fourth Con-

gress, third special session, 25 August to 7 September 1986, pp. 167–172. Nakayama's veto message is found on pp. 216–218.

7  "President Tells Congress FSM 'Well Within' Budget," *The National Union,* 15 July 1981, p. 3.

8  *Journal of the Congress of the Federated States of Micronesia,* First Congress, fourth regular session, 13 October to 15 November 1980, p. 242.

9  *Journal of the Congress of the Federated States of Micronesia,* Second Congress, fourth regular session, 11 October to 9 November 1982, pp. 154–155.

10  "Statement of Objections to Congressional Bill No. 2–144, C.D. 1, 31 December 1981," and "Statement of Objections to Congressional Bill No. 2–143, C.D. 1, 31 December 1981," in *Journal of the Congress of the Federated States of Micronesia,* Second Congress, second regular session, 12 October to 10 November 1981, pp. 367–369.

11  *Journal of the Congress of the Federated States of Micronesia,* Second Congress, third regular session, 10 May to 8 June 1982, p. vii.

12  *Journal of the Congress of the Federated States of Micronesia,* Second Congress, first regular session, 11 May to 9 June 1981, p. 56.

13  Ibid., pp. 144–145.

14  "Statement of Objections to Congressional Bill No. 1–93, C.D. 1," in *Journal of the Congress of the Federated States of Micronesia,* First Congress, third regular session, 12 May to 15 June 1980, pp. 317–318.

15  Interview, Edward and Joan King, Silver Spring, Maryland, 27 September 2003.

16  *Journal of the Congress of the Federated States of Micronesia,* Second Congress, second regular session, 12 October to 10 November 1981, pp. 254a–254b.

17  Ibid., p. 254b.

18  *Journal of the Congress of the Federated States of Micronesia,* Second Congress, third regular session, 10 May to 8 June 1982, p. vii.

19  "President Vetoes Foreign Aid Consent Act," *The National Union,* 30 August 1982, pp. 1–2.

20  *Journal of the Congress of the Federated States of Micronesia,* Third Congress, first regular session, 9 May to 7 June 1983, pp. 85–90.

21  Ibid., p. 89.

22  "President Completes First Session Bills Action," *The National Union,* 19 August 1983, p. 5; see also "Statement of Objections to Congressional Bill No. 3–20, C.D. 1, *Journal of the Congress of the Federated States of Micronesia,* Third Congress, first regular session, 9 May to 7 June 1983, p. 269.

23  *Journal of the Congress of the Federated States of Micronesia,* Third Congress, first regular session, 9 May to 7 June 1983, pp. 269–270. See also "President Completes First Session Bills Action," 1983, p. 5. Congress had earlier

sought to enhance its oversight over nominations that required its advice and consent. Nakayama had rebuffed these; see "Statement of Objections to Congressional Bill No. 1–222, C.D. 1," *Journal of the Congress of the Federated States of Micronesia,* First Congress, third regular session, 12 May to 15 June 1980, p. 316.

24  "Congress Overrides Cabinet Resignation Act Veto," *The National Union,* 30 August 1983, p. 3.

25  "Statement of Objections to Congressional Bill No. 3–104, C.D. 1," *Journal of the Congress of the Federated States of Micronesia,* Third Congress, first special session, 22 August to 3 September 1983, p. 166.

26  "President Nakayama Cabinet Members Featured," *The National Union,* 30 June 1984, pp. 4–5.

27  See "Committee on Resources and Development, Special Committee Report No. 3–83, 29 August 1983" and "Minority Committee Report, 29 August 1983," in *Journal of the Congress of the Federated States of Micronesia,* Third Congress, first special session, 22 August to 3 September 1983, pp. 125–128.

28  "Falcam Confirmed, Plan Reviewed" *The National Union,* 15 February 1984, pp. 1, 3.

29  "Congress Sets Task Force on Plan," *The National Union,* 29 February 1984, pp. 1, 3.

30  "Congress Approves National Plan," *The National Union,* 30 January 1985, pp. 1, 3.

31  "Gouland Loses Congress Seat to Bossy," *The National Union,* 15 March 1985, pp. 1, 5.

32  Interview, Francis X. Hezel, S.J., Kolonia, Pohnpei, 29 May 2003.

33  "Gov. Doone Pledges Full Support," *The National Union,* 15 July to 15 September 1986 (combined issues), pp. 1, 4.

34  "Tax, Trade Changes 'Unacceptable,'" *The National Union,* 30 July 1985, pp. 1–2.

35  "Compact Review Bill Vetoed," *The National Union,* 30 September 1985, p. 2.

36  "Congress Overides [*sic*] Compact Review Bill Veto," *National Union,* 30 October 1985, pp. 1, 3. See also "Committee on External Affairs, S.C.R. No. 4–34, 23 October 1985," in *Journal of the Congress of the Federated States of Micronesia,* Fourth Congress, second regular session, 14 October to 12 November 1985, pp. 219–221. Jack Fritz and Kalisto Refalopei were members of the committee.

37  *Journal of the Congress of the Federated States of Micronesia,* Fourth Congress, second regular session, 14 October to 12 November 1985, pp. 6–7.

38  Ibid., p. 128.

39  "Statement of Objections to Congressional Bill No. 4–196, C.D. 1, 1 May 1986," in *Journal of the Congress of the Federated States of Micronesia*, Fourth Congress, second special session, 17 March to 26 March 1986, pp. 88–89.

40  *Journal of the Congress of the Federated States of Micronesia*, Fourth Congress, second special session, 17 March to 26 March 1986, p. 23.

41  "Statement of Objections to Congressional Bill No. 4–220, C.D. 1, 39, July 1986," in *Journal of the Congress of the Federated States of Micronesia*, Fourth Congress, third regular session, 28 May to 20 June 1986, p. 262.

42  Ibid., p. 262.

43  "Sixth Annual State of the Nation Message by the Honorable Tosiwo Nakayama, President of the Federated States of Micronesia," in *Journal of the Congress of the Federated States of Micronesia*, Fourth Congress, third special session, 25 August to 7 September 1986, p. 20.

44  *Journal of the Congress of the Federated States of Micronesia*, Fourth Congress, third special session, 25 August to 7 September 1986, pp. 33–34.

45  Ibid., pp. vi, ix.

46  "Nakayama: 'Surprised Over Accusations,'" *The National Union*, 30 March 1986, p. 6.

47  Ibid.

48  Ibid.

49  "President Calls Special Session," *The National Union*, 30 March 1987, p. 2.

50  "Congress Okays Accord with Marshalls," *The National Union*, 15 April 1987, pp. 1–2.

51  Interview, Tosiwo Nakayama, Weno, Chuuk, 3 January 2001.

52  Nakayama to Nevitt, 15 November 1985, President's Correspondence File, 1982–1986, FSM National Archives, microfilm reel no. 23, no document number.

53  Interview, Kohsak Keller, Palikir, Pohnpei, 23 May 2003.

54  "Subject: Nakayama, Tosiwo," FOIPA No. 1136835–000. Information released under a Freedom of Information Act request initiated by the author on 8 September 2009 to the U.S. Federal Bureau of Investigation. Copies of the materials released on 17 February 2010 are in the possession of the author.

55  "Police Report on the Threat Made to President Nakayama, May, 1986," FSM National Archives, AG, microfilm reel no. 213, item no. 139.

56  Nakano, 1983, p. 279.

57  Interview, Bernie Michelson, Koror, Palau, 17 July 2002.

58  Interview, Tosiwo Nakayama, Weno, Chuuk, 2 January 2001.

59  "UH to Honor Nakayama," *The National Union*, 30 March 1982, p. 7.

60 "President Named EWC Distinguished Alumni," *The National Union*, 15 January 1985, p. 7.

61 "People," *Pacific Magazine* 10:5 (September/October 1985), p. 50.

62 Interview, Ed and Joan King, Silver Spring, Maryland, 27 September 2003.

63 "Secretary Iehsi Passed Away," *The National Union*, 30 March 1981, p. 1.

64 "2 Sentenced for Manslaughter," *The National Union*, 28 February 1987, p. 6.

65 Interview, Aloysius Tuuth, Colonia, Yap, 2 July 2002.

66 Interview, Tosiwo Nakayama, Weno, Chuuk, 30 December 2000.

67 "Ismael Ahead in Kosrae; Killion Wins in Truk; Falcam Leads by 15 Votes," *The National Union*, 15 March 1987, pp. 1–3.

68 Interview, John Haglelgam, Kolonia, Pohnpei, 21 May 2003.

69 "President Unveils Reorganization Plan," *The National Union*, 30 May 1987, p. 5.

70 Interview, John Haglelgam, Kolonia, Pohnpei, 21 May 2003.

71 Nakayama to Henry, 28 April 1987, Federated States of Micronesia, National Archives, PIO, microfilm reel no. 22, no document number.

72 "Haglelgam Lifts Hiring Freeze," *The National Union*, 15 December 1987, pp. 3, 5.

73 *Journal of the Congress of the Federated States of Micronesia*, Fifth Congress, first regular session, 11 May to 11 June 1987, p. 9.

74 Ibid., pp. 55–63.

75 Hanlon and Eperiam, 1988, p. 98.

76 *Journal of the Congress of the Federated States of Micronesia*, Fifth Congress, first regular session, 11 May to 11 June 1987, pp. 135–139.

77 Ibid., p. 138.

78 Ibid., p. 136.

79 Ibid., p. 138.

80 "President Visits Southern Namoneas," *The National Union*, 30 June 1987, pp. 4–5.

81 Ibid., p. 5.

82 Ibid.

83 Interview, Tosiwo Nakayama, Weno, Chuuk, 29 December 2000.

84 Interview, John Haglelgam, Kolonia, Pohnpei, 21 May 2003.

85 Interview, Joseph Urusemal, Kolonia, Pohnpei, 23 May 2003.

86 Interview, Tosiwo Nakayama, Weno, Chuuk, 3 January 2001.

87 "Nakayama Is BOG's Veep," *The National Union*, 30 October 1987, p. 2.

88 Interview, Charles Dominik, Majuro, Republic of the Marshall Islands, 22 July 2004.

89  Interview, Tosiwo Nakayama, Weno, Chuuk, 2 January 2001.

90  Interview, Francis X. Hezel, S.J., Kolonia, Pohnpei, 29 May 2003.

91  Interview, Tosiwo Nakayama, Weno, Chuuk, 3 January 2001.

92  "Respectfully conveying the profound gratitude and sincere appreciation of the Thirteenth Congress of the Federated States of Micronesia to the Honorable Tosiwo Nakayama for his service as Chairman of the Japan-FSM Parliamentarian Friendship League and his contributions to the strengthening of ties between Japan and the Federated States of Micronesia," *Journal of the Congress of the Federated States of Micronesia,* Thirteenth Congress, third regular session, C.R. No. 13–101, 17 May 2004, www.fsmcongress.fsm/ 13congress/13THCongressionalResolutions.htm.

93  FSM Information Services, "Former Japan Leader Gets Warm Welcome in Chuuk," *Pacific Islands Report,* 19 October 2008, http://pidp.eastwestcenter .org/pireport/2008/October/10–27-re.

94  Ibid. In September of 2008, Mori paid a visit to the Federated States of Micronesia where he spoke to the FSM Congress on Pohnpei. Later, while touring Chuuk, Mori stopped to visit the graves of Susumu Aizawa at Toleisom on Tol, and Tosiwo Nakayama at Mwan on Weno.

95  Glenn Petersen, "The Federated States of Micronesia's 1990 Constitutional Convention: Calm before the Storm," *The Contemporary Pacific* 6:2 (Fall 1994): 337–369.

96  Glenn Petersen, "A Micronesian Chamber of Chiefs? The 1990 Federated States of Micronesia Constitutional Convention," in Geoffrey M. White and Lamont Lindstrom, eds., *Chiefs Today: Traditional Pacific Leadership and the Postcolonial State* (Stanford, CA: Stanford University Press, 1997), p. 193.

97  John R. Haglelgam, "The FSM Constitution and the 2001 Constitutional Convention," College of Micronesia—National Campus, n.d,, http://comfsm .fm/socscie/johnresearch.htm.

98  FSM Information Services, "FSM Voters Maintain Current Constitution," *Pacific Islands Report,* 6 September 2002, http://archives.pireport.org/ archive/2002/september/09-09-16.htm.

99  Bill Jaynes, "FSM Mourns the Loss of Its First President," *The Kaselehlie Press,* 4 April 2007, http://www.fm/news/kp/2007/april07_1.htm.

100 Nakayama did eventually receive some financial assistance from the FSM Congress in 2006 to cover his mounting medical bills; see ibid.

101 Ibid.

102 Interview, Tosiwo Nakayama, Weno, Chuuk, 3 January 2001.

103 Interview, Hiroshi Ismael, Leluh, Kosrae, 13 July 2004.

104 Interview, Tosiwo Nakayama, Weno, Chuuk, 1 January and 3 January 2001.

105    "FSM vs. Gouland," Federated States of Micronesia, National Archives, AG, microfilm reel no. 220, item no. 109.

106    Interview, Tosiwo Nakayama, Weno Chuuk, 3 January 2001.

107    "Lawmakers, Officials Indicted in Chuuk Fraud, *Pacific Islands Report*, 18 November 2003, http://pidp.eastwestcenter.org/pireport/2003/November/11-18-01.htm.

108    "Former FSM Speaker Found Guilty of Fraud," *Pacific Islands Report*, 4 August 2004, http://pidp.eastwestcenter.org/pireport/2004/August/08-04-01.htm.

109    "FSM Speaker Fritz Resigns, Gets Lighter Sentence," *Pacific Islands Report*, 31 August 2004, http://pidp.eastwestcenter.org/pireport/2004/August/08-31-01.htm.

110    Jessica Chapman, "FSM: Congressmen Court Case Suffers Blows," *Pacific Magazine*, 24 April 2006, http://www.pacificmagazine.net/pina/pinadefault2.php?urlpinaid=21590.

111    Peter Wagner, "Battle Brews Over Indicted FSM Officials," *Pacific Islands Report*, 22 January 2004, http://pidp.eastwestcenter.org/pireport/2004/January/01-22-02.htm.

112    "FSM Court Rejects Measure to Disqualify Judge," *Pacific Islands Report*, 19 August 2004, http://pidp.eastwestcenter.org/pireport/2004/August/08-19-08.htm; "FSM: Chuuk Delegation Wants AGs Out," *Pacific Magazine and Islands Business*, 8 July 2004, http://www.pacific islands.cc/pina/pinadefault.php?urlpinaid=12168.

113    See Francis X. Hezel, S.J., "FSM Amnesty Bill," *Micronesian Counselor* 49 (29 January 2004) (Kolonia, Pohnpei: Micronesian Seminar).

114    Ibid., p. 9

115    Ibid., p. 8.

116    Ibid., pp. 6–7.

117    Ibid., p. 7.

118    Jaynes, "FSM Mourns the Loss of Its First President," 2007.

119    Ibid.

120    "Tosiwo Nakayama, 1st FSM President, Laid to Rest," *Pacific Islands Report*, 18 April 2007, http://pidp.eastwestcenter.org/pireport/2007/April/04-18-10.htm.

121    Stewart Firth, *Nuclear Playground,* South Sea Books, Pacific Islands Studies Program (Honolulu: University of Hawai'i Press, 1987), p. 49.

122    John Haglelgam, "Sovereignty Undermined: The Devil Is in the Fine Print," *Pacific Magazine* 29:4 (2004): 6.

123    *Journal of the Congress of the Federated States of Micronesia,* Fifth Congress, first regular session, 11 May to 11 June 1987, p. 136.

124 Josh Levy, "Micronesian Nationalism Revisited: Reclaiming Nationalism for the Federated States of Micronesia," a paper presented to the National Imaginaries panel at the Fourth Annual Meeting of the Native American and Indigenous Studies Association, Uncasville, Connecticut, 4 June to 6 June 2012.

# Bibliography

Alkire, William H. *An Introduction to the Peoples and Cultures of Micronesia.* Menlo Park, CA: Cummings Publishing Company, 1977.

———. "Technical Knowledge and the Evolution of Political Systems in the Central and Western Caroline Islands of Micronesia." *Canadian Journal of Anthropology* 1:2 (1980): 229–237.

Bhabha, Homi. "Of Mimicry and Man: The Ambivalence of Colonial Discourse." In *October: The First Decade,* edited by Annette Michelsen, Rosalind Krauss, Doug Crimp, and Joan Copjec, 318–322. Cambridge, MA: MIT Press, 1987.

Blakeslee, George. "Japan's New Island Possessions in the Pacific: History and Present." *Journal of International Relations* 12:2 (1921): 98–115.

Boneparth, Ellen, and M. James Wilkinson. "Terminating Trusteeship for the Federated States of Micronesia and the Republic of the Marshall Islands: Independence and Self-Sufficiency in the Post-Cold War Pacific." *Pacific Studies* 18:2 (1995): 61–77.

Bourdieu, Pierre. *Outline of a Theory of Practice.* Translated by Richard Nice. Cambridge: Cambridge University Press, 1977.

Cain, Michael. *A Survey of Historical Sites and Their Association with Oral Histories in Eastern Weno, Chuuk State, Federated States of Micronesia.* Weno: Chuuk State Historic Preservation Office, 1996.

Clyde, Paul H. *Japan's Mandate Islands.* New York: Macmillan Company, 1935.

College of Micronesia, National Campus. *Nakayama's Trip to Pingelap: President Tosiwo Nakayama and His Officials Visited Pingelap Atoll.* DVD 406A. Pacific Collection, College of Micronesia Library, Palikir, Pohnpei, 1987.

Congress of the Federated States of Micronesia. *Journal.* Office of the Speaker. Honolulu: SB Printers, Inc., 1979–1980; Guam: U.S. Navy Publications and Printing Service, Branch Office, Western Division, 1981–2004.

Congress of Micronesia. *Journal of the House of Representatives.* Saipan: Trust Territory Government Press, 1965–1978.

———. *Journal of the Senate.* Saipan: Trust Territory Government Press, 1965–1978.

Congress of Micronesia, Future Political Status Commission. *Report.* Third Congress, second session. Capitol Hill, Saipan, Mariana Islands: Trust Territory of the Pacific Islands, 1969.

Congress of Micronesia, Joint Committee on Future Status. *Hearings of the Eastern Districts Subcommittee (Truk, Ponape, and the Marshalls).* Fifth Congress. Saipan, Mariana Islands: Trust Territory of the Pacific Islands, 1973.

———. *Report of the Eastern District Subcommittee to the Joint Committee on Future Status.* Fifth Congress. Saipan, Mariana Islands: Trust Territory of the Pacific Islands, 1973.

Congress of Micronesia, Law of the Sea Delegation. *United Nations Law of the Sea Conference, 1975 Report.* Saipan: Sixth Congress, 1975.

Congress of Micronesia, Office of the Legislative Council. *Public Speeches, The Congress of Micronesia, 1970–1971.* Saipan: Trust Territory Government Printing Office, 1971.

Council of Micronesia. Proceedings of the Special Session of the Council of Micronesia. Saipan, Mariana Islands, 19 to 26 March 1963. A copy of this document is housed in Hamilton Library, Pacific Collection, University of Hawai'i at Mānoa, Honolulu, Hawai'i.

D'Arcy, Paul. *The People of the Sea: Environment, Identity, and History.* Honolulu: University of Hawai'i Press, 2006.

Dening, Greg. Review of *Marists and Melanesians* by Hugh Laracy. *New Zealand Journal of History* 12 (1978): 82.

Dvorak, Gregory. "seeds from afar, flowers from the reef: re-membering the coral and concrete of Kwajalein atoll." PhD dissertation, Australian National University, 2008.

East-West Center. "All Distinguished Alumni Awardees, 1980–2012." http://www.eastwestcenter.org/print/32644.

———. "Nakayama, Mr. Tosiwo." Participant Awards System, Participant Profile, 0017256. Honolulu, Hawai'i, n.d.

Esbensen, Thorwald. *Puken Napanapan Mwich: A Handbook of Parliamentary Procedure for Truk District Municipalities and Congress.* Translated by Napoleon DeFang (and) Tosiwo Nakayama, Education Department. Truk District: Literature Production Center, 1959.

Federated States of Micronesia. Microfilmed Records of the Federated States of Micronesia National Government. Palikir, Pohnpei, FSM Office of National Records and Cultural Properties, 1979–Present.

Federated States of Micronesia, Legal Information System. *FSM Supreme Court Decisions.* 1981–2002. http://www.fsmlaw.org/fsm/decisions.

Federated States of Micronesia, Supreme Court. Engichy vs. FSM, 1 FSM Intrm. 532 (App. 1984). http://www.fsmlaw.org/fsm/decisions/vol11/1fsm532_560 .htm.

Fifield, Russell H. "Disposal of the Carolines, Marshalls, and Marianas at the Paris Peace Conference." *American Historical Review* 51 (1946): 472–479.

Firth, Stewart. *Nuclear Playground.* South Sea Books. Pacific Islands Studies Program. Honolulu: University of Hawai'i Press, 1987.

Flinn, Julianna. *Diplomas and Thatch Houses: Asserting Tradition in a Changing Micronesia.* Ann Arbor: University of Michigan Press, 1995.

Gale, Roger. *The Americanization of Micronesia: A Study of the Consolidation of U.S. Rule in the Pacific.* Washington, D.C.: University Press of America, 1979.

Gladwin, Thomas. "Chief Petrus Mailo." In *In The Company of Men,* edited by Joseph Casagrande. New York: Harper, 1960.

———. *East Is a Big Bird: Navigation & Logic on Puluwat Atoll.* Cambridge, MA: Harvard University Press, 1970.

Gladwin, Thomas, and Seymour B. Sarason. *Truk: Man in Paradise.* Viking Fund Publication in Anthropology no. 20. New York: Wenner-Gren Foundation for Anthropological Research, Inc., 1950.

Goodenough, Ward H. *Property, Kin, and Community on Truk,* 2nd ed. Hamden, CT: Archon Books, 1978.

Gramsci, Antonio. *Selections from the Prison Notebooks.* Edited and translated by Quentin Hoare and Nowell Smith. London: Lawrence and Wishart, 1971.

Guha, Ranajit. *Elementary Aspects of Peasant Insurgency in Colonial India.* Delhi: Oxford University Press, 1983.

Haglelgam, John. "The FSM Constitution and the 2001 Constitutional Convention." College of Micronesia, National Campus. n.d. http://comfsm.fm/ socscie/johnresearch.htm.

Hanlon, David. *Remaking Micronesia: Discourses over Development in a Pacific Territory, 1944–1982.* Honolulu: University of Hawai'i Press, 1998.

———. "The 'Sea of Little Lands': Examining Micronesia's Place in 'Our Sea of Islands.'" *The Contemporary Pacific* 21:1 (2009): 91–110.

Hanlon, David, and William Eperiam. "The Evolution and Development of the

Federated States of Micronesia." *Micronesian Politics,* 85–106. Suva, Fiji: Institute of Pacific Studies, 1988.

Hauʻofa, Epeli. *We Are the Ocean: Selected Works.* Honolulu: University of Hawaiʻi Press, 2008.

Hezel, Francis X., S.J. *The First Taint of Civilization: A History of the Caroline and Marshall Islands in Pre-Colonial Days, 1521–1885.* Pacific Islands Monograph Series no. 1. Honolulu: University of Hawaiʻi Press, 1983.

———. *The Catholic Church in Micronesia: Historical Essays on the Catholic Church in the Caroline-Marshall Islands.* Micronesian Seminar. Chicago: Loyola University Press, 1991.

———. *Strangers in Their Own Land: A Century of Colonial Rule in the Caroline and Marshall Islands.* Pacific Islands Monograph Series no.13. Honolulu: University of Hawaiʻi Press, 1995.

———. "FSM Amnesty Bill." *Micronesian Counselor* 49 (29 January 2004). Kolonia, Pohnpei: Micronesian Seminar.

*Highlights*

"Secretary Notes." 7 February 1967: 2.

"HICOM Vetoes Eminent Domain Bill." 5 August 1968: 1.

"1968 General Election Results to the Congress of Micronesia." 1 and 15 January 1969: 6–7.

"Future Political Status Commission Reports on Study Tour." 15 April 1969: 1–3.

"Political Status Commission Begins Tour of Territory." 1 May 1969: 4–9.

"Congress Adjourns: Names Delegates to Washington." 1 and 15 September 1969: 1

"Congress Shipping Committee Ends Tour." 1 March 1970: 11.

"Revised Foreign Investment Bill Becomes Law." 1 March 1970: 1.

"Congress of Micronesia Election Results." 15 November 1970: 3.

"Congress Resolves Palau Election Dispute." 1 January 1971: 1–2.

"About the Buildings." 22 February 1971: 8.

"Congress of Micronesia Buildings Burn, Members Adjourn First Session." 22 February 1971: 1–3.

Jim Manke, "Typhoon Amy Sweeps Across Truk, Historic Congress Session Now Underway." 15 May 1971: 4.

"15 Bills Passed During Special Session." 1 June 1971: 1.

"Statement by Senator Amaraich." 9 June 1972: 8–13.

"Congress of Micronesia Election Results." 15 November 1972: 3.

"Statement by Senator Amaraich." 1 July 1973: 10–13.

"Public Land and Revenue Bills Passed." 15 August 1974: 1.

"Palau Seeks Separate Status Negotiations." 1 May 1976: 3.

"HiCom Presents Nakayama The ConCon Pen." 1 June 1976: 3.

"Law of the Sea Convention." 1 December 1976: 2

"Two COM Leaders Visit Tokyo." 1 December 1976: 3.

"COM Delegation in Washington." 15 January 1977: 6.

"Trukese Demand Land Settlement." 15 February 1977: 6.

"Mangefel Disappointed in COM." 15 March 1977: 3.

"TT Leaders Go to Washington." 15 March 1977: 1.

"COM to be Heard on Air Route." 1 April 1977: 6.

"Andrus Upholds HiCom's Veto." 1 June 1977: 3.

"COM Leadership Levels Warning." 1 June 1977: 3.

"Congress to Relocate." 15 June 1977: 2.

"Highlights of COM Special Session Based on News Reports from Ponape." 1 September 1977: 5.

"Inaugural Flight a Success." 15 October 1977: 4.

"Winkel Approves 200-Mile Fishery Zone for Micronesia." 1 November 1977: 1–2.

"COM Leaders Meet Fukuda." 1 January 1978: 4.

"Micronesian Maritime Authority Members." 1 January 1978: 6.

"Nakayama on Referendum." 1 January 1978: 3.

"Statement of Principles of Free Association Signed in Hilo." 1 May 1978: 3.

"Faichuk & Mortlocks Vote." 15 November 1977: 6.

"Truk Airport Expansion Near Solution." 1 March 1979: 1–2.

Higuchi, Wakako. "Japan and War Reparations in Micronesia." *Journal of Pacific History* 30:1 (1995): 87–98.

Hunter-Anderson, Rosalind, and Yigal Zan. "Demystifying the *Sawei*, a Traditional Interisland Exchange System." *Isla* 4 (1996): 1–45.

Ikle, Frank. "Japanese-German Peace Negotiations During World War I." *American Historical Review* 71 (1966): 62–76.

Interim Congress of the Federated States of Micronesia. *Journal of the House of Representatives.* Guam: U.S. Navy Publications and Printing Service, Branch Office, Western Division, 1978–1979.

———. *Journal of the Senate.* Guam: U.S. Navy Publications and Printing Service, Branch Office, Western Division, 1978–1979.

Iriye, Akira. *Pacific Estrangement: Japanese and American Expansion, 1897–1911.* Cambridge, MA: Harvard University Press, 1972.

———. *Across the Pacific: An Inner History of American-East Asian Relations,* rev. ed. Chicago: Imprint Publications, 1992.

Jaynes, Bill. "FSM Mourns Loss of its First President." *The Kaselehlie Press,* 4 April 2007. http://www.fm/news/kp/2007/april07_1.htm.

———. "P.F. Kluge, Not Just Another 'Dog Day Afternoon' on the 'Edge of Para-

dise.'" *The Kaselehlie Press,* 9 January 2008: 2. http://www.stpns.net/view_
article.html?articleId=758453810454.

Kahn, E. J. *A Reporter in Micronesia.* New York: Norton, 1966.

Kamins, Robert M., Robert E. Potter, and Members of the University Community.
*Mālamalama: A History of the University of Hawai'i.* Honolulu: University of
Hawai'i Press, 1998.

Kanost, Richard F. "Administrative Development in Micronesia: The Senatorial Election in Truk District, 1974." *Journal of Pacific History* 17:3 (1982): 158–165.

Kirch, Patrick Vinton. *On the Road of the Winds: An Archaeological History of the
Pacific Islands before European Contact.* Berkeley: University of California
Press, 2000.

Kluge, P. F. *The Edge of Paradise: America in Micronesia.* New York: Random
House, 1991.

Kupferman, David. *Disassembling and Decolonizing School in the Pacific: A Genealogy from Micronesia.* Contemporary Philosophies and Theories in Education, vol. 5. Dordrecht, Netherlands: Springer, 2012.

Levi, Werner. "American Attitudes Toward Pacific Islands, 1914–1919." *Pacific
Historical Review* 17:1 (1948): 55–64.

Levy, Josh. "Micronesian Nationalism Revisited: Reclaiming Nationalism for the
Federated States of Micronesia." A paper presented to the National Imaginaries Panel at the Fourth Annual Meeting of Native American and Indigenous Studies Association, Uncasville, Connecticut, 4 to 6 June 2012.

Lingenfelter, Sherwood. *Yap: Political Leadership and Cultural Change in an Island
Society.* Honolulu: University of Hawai'i Press, 1975.

Mahony, Frank J. "The Innovation of a Savings System in Truk." *American Anthropologist* 62:3 (1960): 465–482.

Marck, Jeff. "Some Clan Names of the Chuukic-Speaking Peoples of Micronesia."
2008. *www.jeffmarck.net/publications/MarckClansChk.pdf.*

Meller, Norman, with the assistance of Terza Meller. *The Congress of Micronesia:
Development of the Legislative Process in the Trust Territory of the Pacific
Islands.* Honolulu: University of Hawai'i Press, 1969.

———, with the assistance of Terza Meller. *Constitutionalism in Micronesia.* Lā'ie:
Institute for Polynesian Studies, Brigham Young University–Hawai'i Campus, 1985.

*Met Poraus*

"Nakayama Chosen by Truk Delegation to Serve on Political Status Commission." II:10 (1968): 15.

Jeff Lane, "Andon Amaraich Leaves Administration." II:14 (1969): 14.

"A Supplication from Chief Petrus." III:15 (1970): 2, 9.

"Micronesia Mourns Chief Petrus Mailo." III:41 (1971): 1–2, 4.

Metzger, Eric. "Carolinian Voyaging in the New Millennium." *Micronesian Journal of the Humanities and Social Sciences* 5, nos. 1–2 (2006): 293–305.

Micronesian Constitutional Convention. *Journal of the Micronesian Constitutional Convention of 1975: Convened on July 12, 1975, Recessed August 23, 1975, Reconvened September 15, 1975, Adjourned November 8, 1975.* Saipan, Mariana Islands: Office of the Convention President, 1975.

*Micronesian Monthly.* "Scholarship Competition Open." 2:1 (1952): 6.

*Micronesian Reporter*

"Delegates Welcomed." 9:6 (1961): 4.

L.M.T., "Council of Micronesia." 9:6 (1961): 1.

L.M.T., "Sixth Inter-District Conference Convenes." 9:6 (1961): 6–8.

"Council of Micronesia Deliberates at Home." 10:5 (1962): 6–8.

"Council of Micronesia's Special Session." 11:1 (1963): 8–10.

"Fourth Session, Council of Micronesia, November 12, 1963, Saipan, M.I." 11:4 (1963): 5.

"Territory Hails Establishment of New Congress of Micronesia." 12:6 (1964): 1, 7.

Elizabeth Udui, "Origins of the Congress of Micronesia." 13:2 (1965): 16.

Bossy, Nick. "Trukese Women Sweep Election." 13:3 (1965): 4–5.

"Interview: Chief Petrus Mailo." 17:4 (1969): 2–5.

"Interview: Chief Petrus Mailo (continued)." 18:1 (1970): 3–7.

"Interview with Tosiwo Nakayama." 22:4 (1974): 6–10.

P. F. Kluge, "The Micronesian Constitutional Convention: July 12–November 8, 1975." 33:4 (1975): 38–44.

Tosiwo Nakayama, "Inaugural Address." 27:2 (1979): 8–9.

Micronesian Seminar. *Seminar on Moral Issues Related to Choice of Political Status.* Kolonia, Ponape: Catholic Mission, 3–9 June 1973.

Micronesian Traditional Chiefs. *Program: Second Conference of the Micronesian Traditional Chiefs.* Moen, Truk District, Eastern Caroline Islands: Office of the Mayor, Moen Municipality, Trust Territory of the Pacific Islands, 1974.

Muller, Willard C. *Faces of the Islands: When Pacific Islander and American Ways Meet.* Port Angeles, WA: Lincoln Square Publishing Company, 2002.

Naipaul, V. S. *The Mimic Men.* London: Deutsch, 1967.

Nakano, Ann. *Broken Canoe: Conversations & Observations in Micronesia.* St. Lucia: University of Queensland Press, 1983.

Nakayama, Masao, and Frederick L. Ramp. *Micronesian Navigation, Island Empires and Traditional Concepts of Ownership of the Sea.* Saipan: Study for the Joint Committee of the Law of the Sea Conference, Fifth Congress of Micronesia, 1974.

*National Union, The. An Official Publication for the People and States of the Feder-*

*ated States of Micronesia*. Kolonia, Pohnpei: Office of the President, Federated States of Micronesia, 1980–1996.

Office of the High Commissioner, Trust Territory of the Pacific Islands. *Annual
Report of the High Commissioner of the Trust Territory of the Pacific Islands
to the Secretary of the Interior*. Washington, D.C.: U.S. Government Printing
Office, 1950–1979.

Office of Micronesian Status Negotiations. *The Future Political Status of the Trust
Territory of the Pacific Islands: Summary Record of the U.S.-Micronesia
Roundtable Conference, Guam, July 25–27, 1977*. Washington, D.C.

Oliver, Douglas, ed. *Planning Micronesia's Future: A Summary of the United States
Commercial Company's Economic Survey of Micronesia, 1946*. rev. ed. Foreword by John Griffin. Honolulu: University of Hawai'i Press, 1971.

*Pacific Islands Report*

"FSM Voters Maintain Current Constitution." FSM Information Services. 6 September 2002. http://archives.pireport.org/archive/2002/
september/09%2D09.

"Lawmakers, Officials Indicted in Chuuk Fraud. 18 November 2003. http://
pidp.eastwestcenter.org/pireport/2003/November/11–18–01.htm.

Peter Wagner, "Battle Brews Over Indicted FSM Officials." 22 January 2004.
http://pidp.eastwestcenter.org/pireport/2004/January/01–22–02.htm.

"Former FSM Speaker Found Guilty of Fraud." 4 August 2004. http://pidp
.eastwestcenter.org/pireport/2004/August/08–04–01.htm.

"FSM Court Rejects Measure to Disqualify Judge." 19 August 2004. http://
pidp.esatwestcenter.org/pireport/2004/August/08–19–08.htm.

"FSM Speaker Fritz Resigns, Gets Lighter Sentence." 31 August 2004. http://
pidp.eastwestcenter.org/pireport/2004/August/08–31–01.htm.

"Tosiwo Nakayama, 1st FSM President, Laid to Rest." 18 April 2007. http://
pidp/eastwestcenter.org/pireport/2007/April/04–18–10.htm.

"Former Japan Leader Gets Warm Welcome in Chuuk." FSM Information News Release. 19 October 2008. http://pidp.eastwestcenter.org/
pireport/2008/October/10–27-re.

*Pacific Magazine*

"Interview: President Tosiwo Nakayama, Federated States of Micronesia."
7:3 (1982): 63–67, 70–73.

"'War' in the Micronesian Courts." 8:3 (1983): 16–17.

"People." 10:5 (1985): 50.

John Haglelgam, "Sovereignty Undermined: The Devil Is in the Fine Print."
29:4 (2004): 6.

Jessica Chapman, "FSM: Congressman Court Case Suffers Blows." 24 April

2006. http://www.pacificmagazine.net/pina/pinadefault2.php?urlpinaid= 21590.

Pacific Magazine and Islands Business. "FSM: Chuuk Delegation Wants AGs Out." 8 July 2004. http://www.pacificislands.cc/pina/pinadefault.php?urlpinaid= 2168.

Peattie, Mark R. *Nan'yō: The Rise and Fall of the Japanese in Micronesia, 1885–1945.* Pacific Islands Series Monograph no. 4. Honolulu: University of Hawai'i Press, 1988.

Petersen, Glenn. "Book Review Forum." *Pacific Studies* 10:3 (1987): 107–124.

———. "The Federated States of Micronesia's 1990 Constitutional Convention: Calm Before the Storm." *The Contemporary Pacific* 6:2 (1994): 337–369.

———. "A Micronesian Chamber of Chiefs? The 1990 Federated States of Micronesia Constitutional Convention." In *Chiefs Today: Traditional Pacific Leadership and the Postcolonial State,* edited by Geoffrey M. White and Lamont Lindstrom, 183–196. Stanford, CA: Stanford University Press, 1997.

———. "Politics in Postwar Micronesia." In *American Anthropology in Micronesia,* edited by Robert C. Kiste and Mac Marshall, 145–195. Honolulu: University of Hawai'i Press, 1999.

———. "Lessons Learned: The Micronesian Quest for Independence in the Context of American Imperial History." *Micronesian Journal of the Humanities and Social Sciences* 3 (2004): 45–63.

———. *Traditional Micronesian Societies: Adaptation, Integration, and Political Organization.* Honolulu: University of Hawai'i Press, 2009.

Pomeroy, Earl. "American Policy Respecting the Marshalls, Carolines, and Marianas, 1898–1941." *Pacific Historical Review* 17:1 (1948): 43–53.

Poyer, Lin, Suzanne Falgout, and Laurence Marshall Carucci. *The Typhoon of War: Micronesian Experiences of the Pacific War.* Honolulu: University of Hawai'i Press, 2001.

Price, Willard. *Japan's Islands of Mystery.* New York: John Day, 1944.

Ranney, Austin, and Howard R. Penniman. *Democracy in the Islands: The Micronesian Plebiscites of 1983.* Washington, D.C.: American Enterprise Institute for Public Policy Research, 1985.

Rauchholz, Manuel. "Notes on Clan Histories and Migration in Micronesia." *Pacific-Asia Inquiry* 2:1 (2011): 53–68.

Richard, Dorothy E. *United States Naval Administration of the Trust Territory of the Pacific Islands.* 3 vols. Washington, D.C.: Office of the Chief of Naval Operations, 1957.

Rosario, Frank, and John M. Simpson. "U.S. Bribe Attempt in Truk Hotly Debated." *Micronesian Support Committee Bulletin* 5:3–4 (Fall/Winter 1980): 16.

Schencking, Charles. "Bureaucratic Politics, Military Budgets, and Japan's Southern Advance: The Imperial Navy's Seizure of German Micronesia in the First World War." *War in History* 5:3 (1998): 308–326.

Schwalbenberg, Henry M., S.J. *Memoranda on the Compact of Free Association.* Truk, Eastern Caroline Islands: Micronesian Seminar, 1981–1984. A copy of this compendium is housed in the Pacific Collection, Hamilton Library, University of Hawaiʻi at Mānoa, Honolulu.

Scurlock, James D. *King Larry: The Life and Ruins of a Billionaire Genius.* New York: Scribner, 2012.

Thomas, John Byron. "Adoption, Filiation, and Matrilineal Descent on Namonuito Atoll." PhD dissertation, University of Hawaiʻi at Mānoa, 1978.

*Truk Chronicle*
  "Faichuk Citizens Meet with President." 1:11 (24 August 1979): 6.
  "In Memoriam: Masami Nakayama." 1:11 (24 August 1979): 7.

Truk District Congress. *Proceedings.* Truk District, Trust Territory of the Pacific Islands, 1957–1958, 1963. Copies housed in the Pacific Collection, Hamilton Library, University of Hawaiʻi at Mānoa, Honolulu.

Truk District Council of Magistrates. *Proceedings.* Truk District, Trust Territory of the Pacific Islands, 1954, 1956–1958. Copies housed in the Pacific Collection, Hamilton Library, University of Hawaiʻi at Mānoa, Honolulu.

*Truk Review*
  "Book of Parliamentary Procedures by Education Department." II:1 (1959): 11.
  "Truk Congress Holds Third Session." II:5 (1959): 3.
  "The Fourth Truk Dist. Congress." II:12 (1960): 1.
  "Napoleon DeFang Dies in a Jeep Accident." II:20 (1962): 1–2.

Trumbull, Robert. *Paradise in Trust: A Report on Americans in Micronesia.* New York: William Sloane, 1959.

Trust Territory of the Pacific Islands. Trust Territory of the Pacific Islands Archives. Microfilmed Records of the Trust Territory Government, 1952–1986. Honolulu, University of Hawaiʻi, Hamilton Library.

———. *General Elections to the Congress of Micronesia.* 19 January 1965. Saipan, Mariana Islands. A copy of this document can be found in the Pacific Collection, Hamilton Library, University of Hawaiʻi at Mānoa, Honolulu.

———. *Micronesian Biographies.* Office of Assistant Commissioner for Public Affairs. Saipan, Mariana Islands: Literature Production Center, 1965.

———. "General Elections to the Congress of Micronesia, 8 November, 1966." *Headquarters Highlights.* 1966.

———. "Interview with Tosiwo Nakayama." 30 August. Task Force on Education for Self-Government. *Dialogue for Micronesia: July 1974...December 1975.* Program No. 8. Saipan, Mariana Islands: Department of Public Affairs, 1974.

———. "Interview with Tosiwo Nakayama, Carl Heine, Leo Falcam, and Chutomo Nimwes." 22 August. *Dialogue for Micronesia: July 1974...December 1975.* Program No. 45. Saipan, Mariana Islands: Department of Public Affairs, 1975.

———. "Summary of an Interview with Senator Tosiwo Nakayama," 29 January. Task Force for Self-Government. *Dialogue for Micronesia.* Program No. 58. Saipan, Mariana Islands: Department of Public Affairs, 1976.

United States Congress. "Statement of the Honorable Tosiwo Nakayama, President of the Federated States of Micronesia to the Committee on Energy and Natural Resources of the United States Senate, May 24, 1984." In *Statements Before the Committee on Energy and Natural Resources, May 24, 1984, Regarding the Compact of Free Association.* Pacific Collection, Hamilton Library, University of Hawai'i at Mānoa, Honolulu.

United States Department of State. *Annual Report to the United Nations on the Administration of the Trust Territory of the Pacific Islands.* Washington, D.C.: U.S. Government Printing Office, 1948–1980.

United States Federal Bureau of Investigation. "Subject: Nakayama, Tosiwo," FOIPA No. 1136835–000. 2010. A copy of the material released by the Federal Bureau of Investigation under the provisions of the Freedom of Information Act is in the possession of the author.

University of Hawai'i at Mānoa. Micronesian Student Files of the International Student Office. 1950–1960. Pacific Collection, Hamilton Library, Honolulu.

———. "100 Contributions." The *100th Annual Commencement Exercises Program.* 2011.

Willens, Howard, and Deanne C. Siemer. *An Honorable Accord: The Covenant between the Northern Mariana Islands and the United States.* Pacific Islands Monograph Series no. 18. Honolulu: University of Hawai'i Press, 2002.

Woodward, Bob. "CIA Bugging Micronesian Negotiations." *Washington Post,* 12 December 1976, A1.

———. "Kissinger Tied to CIA Surveillance." *Washington Post,* 4 May 1977, A1.

Yanaihara, Tadao. *Pacific Islands Under Japanese Mandate.* London: Oxford University Press, 1938.

# Index

Bold page numbers refer to figures and maps.

# About the Author

David Hanlon is a past director of the Center for Pacific Islands Studies at the University of Hawaiʻi, Mānoa. A former editor of *The Contemporary Pacific: A Journal of Island Affairs* and the Pacific Islands Monograph Series, he currently teaches in the university's Department of History. Hanlon is the author of two previous works on the Micronesian geographical area: *Upon a Stone Altar: A History of the Island of Pohnpei to 1890*, and *Remaking Micronesia: Discourses over Development in a Pacific Territory, 1944–1982*. With Geoffrey M. White, he also co-edited *Voyaging through the Contemporary Pacific*. Hanlon's research interests include culture contact, missionization, development, cultural heritage, and ethnographic approaches to the study of history.